DATE			

FEDERICO FELLINI

FEDERICO FELLINI

HIS LIFE AND WORK

TULLIO KEZICH

Translated from the Italian by Minna Proctor
with Viviana Mazza

FABER AND FABER, INC.
An affiliate of Farrar, Straus and Giroux / New York

Faber and Faber, Inc.
An affiliate of Farrar, Straus and Giroux
19 Union Square West, New York 10003

Distributed in Canada by Douglas & McIntyre Ltd.
Printed in the United States of America
Originally published in 2002 by Giangiacomo Feltrinelli Editore, Italy, as *Federico*
Published in the United States by Faber and Faber, Inc.
First American edition, 2006

Library of Congress Cataloging-in-Publication Data
Kezich, Tullio.
    [Federico. English]
    Federico Fellini : his life and work— 1st American ed.
        p.   cm.
    Translation of: Federico. 2002.
    Includes index.
    ISBN-13: 978-0-571-21168-5 (alk. paper)
    ISBN-10: 0-571-21168-2 (alk. paper)
    1. Fellini, Federico   2. Motion picture producers and directors—
Italy—Biography.   I. Title.

PN1998.3.F45K49 2006
791.4302'33'092—dc22
[B]   2005051868

Designed by Jonathan D. Lippincott

www.fsgbooks.com

10   9   8   7   6   5   4   3   2   1

Frontispiece: Tullio Kezich, Federico Fellini, and the movie critic Pietro Bianchi, Milan, 1960.

Contents

Dear Tullio,
How many years of talking, and bullshitting . . .
But years of true friendship!

With Love [signature]*

---

*Fellini's inscription to the author in his 1980 book, *Fare un film* (Making a Film).

Introduction: September 1952, on the Terrace of the Hotel des Bains

There was some trepidation on my part at my first encounter with Federico Fellini. I knew his name and I'd liked *Luci del varietà* (*Variety Lights*, 1950)—but I had assumed that it had been conceived of and written by codirector Alberto Lattuada, and that newcomer Fellini's name had only been added to the credit out of friendship, or for contractual reasons. The truth is that I was a little perplexed by the boundless ambition of this screenwriter who wanted to become a director. I thought the qualifications for the job of film director (an undertaking later characterized by Fellini himself as "Christopher Columbus trying to command a crew that just wants to turn back") included the indispensable but loathsome ability to "assume authority"—as it would have been described under fascism. I couldn't see how such an attitude was consonant with a writer's temperament.

The meeting had been arranged by the actor Leopoldo Trieste, a mutual friend, during the 1952 Venice Film Festival on the terrace of the Hotel des Bains (immortalized by Thomas Mann in *Death in Venice*). Federico had probably preferred this hotel to the more sumptuous Excelsior because it looks like the Grand Hotel in his hometown of Rimini, a reminder of his childhood. Or maybe his troupe hadn't been considered VIP enough for the grander hotel. We met on September 7, the day after the screening of *Lo sceicco bianco* (*The White Sheik*), which didn't do badly with the public, though the critical mood seemed to suggest that nothing particularly favorable was forthcoming.

Gathered around the thirty-two-year-old director that day on the terrace was a little group of people in wicker armchairs. There was constant coming and going and I don't remember exactly what anyone was talking about, but once I'd insinuated myself, I felt as if I were a new member of a merry fraternity. I suddenly felt lighthearted and relaxed, like (to use another typical Fellini expression) Pinocchio among the puppets—or like Jim Hawkins in *Treasure Island*: among the pirates who tell "sailor tales in sailor tunes."

Federico was still skinny back then and wore his hair long over his neck. I remember thinking something was *off* at our first encounter. Maybe he was trying to make me feel that way, with those mannerisms I later came to recognize as the director's own quirks—sideways glances, pauses, that almost imperceptible smirk. We discussed the Italian films in competition that year and I was somewhat embarrassed to be talking about these particular films with the person who'd written them all—from Pietro Germi's *Il brigante di Tacca del Lupo* (*The Bandit of Tacca del Lupo*) to Roberto Rossellini's *Europa '51*. The brashness of youth led me to admit that both pictures had left me cold. And Federico replied that the major defect of film critics was how abstract we were. Then he expressed the utmost solidarity for Germi: "Where the *bersaglieri* slither up the mountainside like worms—wasn't that a wonderful scene? But more important, you can tell it comes from a true story. Amedeo Nazzari's character is based on one of Tullio Pinelli's relatives . . ." When the conversation turned to Rossellini, Fellini's tone changed from respect to devotion: "I like everything he does. I always like him." By declaring himself to be unreservedly of the Rossellini camp, Fellini was revealing himself as a believer among the skeptics.

Even though I agreed with his positions at the time (it's true that *Tacca del Lupo* isn't a run-of-the-mill film, and that Rossellini's shift out of neorealism was something many of us were slow to grasp), I was most struck by his delivery. Under the sun and in the wind off the Adriatic, the names of Germi and Rossellini had a different ring than they did in the debates at the cineclub, or in the petty quibbles among the churlish scribes. I started to realize that my arid and labored vision of cinema had yet to grow—it was a branch that might one day put out leaves. While sitting with these new companions, overflowing with energy and openness, I felt as if I were embarking on a brighter path.

The insidious and ominous cold war atmosphere tested our frazzled nerves in those days; the specter of the Salazar Project seemed to weigh heavily on Italy—and we were unconvinced (at least some of us were) that Stalin would provide any salvation. The Rosenbergs were being marched toward the electric chair in the United States, and General Eisenhower would shortly be elected president. We were all fomenting the discord that would ultimately bring Italy to the battle over Majority Law (aka the trickster law) that the Christian Democrats would eventually use to consolidate power.* We were oppressed by the fear that the country was sliding to the right, back toward the old order—and we were looking to cinema to take a political position, launch real accusations, and aggressively choose sides. We were disillusioned by the political inwardness that followed liberation, and we wanted cinema to take on our social issues diagnostically—we even expected it to be prescriptive. In the cineclub we were constantly evaluating films based on how big or small their influence might be on current events or the future. "Does this film explain the real causes of evil in the world?" we'd ask, and "Does it offer any contribution for change?" We rejected classic antimilitarism, like *All Quiet on the Western Front*—because by condemning the First World War, such films hadn't managed to stop the Second. It was considered an embarrassment that documentary filmmaker Robert Flaherty's *Man of Aran* was a mere recounting of the changing of the seasons and that he hadn't been able to champion a revolutionary conscience. There was a hunger for the "positive hero," for a messiah of political cinema.

I realized right away that such concerns held little sway in Fellini's circle. There was no talk of political duty—either that day in Venice or at any of the many encounters that followed. They spoke of other matters; they were even frivolous. Federico operated on his own frequency, and he was in it for the long haul. Watching him interact with people was like watching one of his future films, the way he moved so easily from the serious to the silly, from the grotesque to the pathetic. He used irony to diminish drama and celebrated oddities entirely on a different plane from the ideas that held such currency at the time. It must seem strange to use so many words in order to explain a very simple thing—but it is this quality that is so fundamental to understanding the problems inherent to Federico Fellini's biography. Why did his films meet with such incompre-

---

*Majority Law was a proposed amendment to the Italian Constitution giving the prime minister's party an automatic majority in the parliament, superseding the system of direct representation.

hension in Italy during his first and most passionate decade of production, for example? Why was the political left so slow to recognize whose side the director was on?

When he first came to the world of cinema, Fellini irritated people by openly rejecting ideology. He was in fact almost apolitical—at least in terms of how the notion of being political was presented, or rather imposed, at the time. Politics and soccer, effectively the most traditional topics of Italian society (both high and low), left Fellini feeling like a bored little boy listening to adult conversation. When I was with Fellini (and I'm thinking of the young Fellini, before he became a guru and was assaulted on a daily basis by the media, and forced into commenting on serious issues), we talked about school days, about what Rome was like when he first lived there after escaping from Rimini, about people in common, about psychological typologies and fables, about books that barely anyone had heard of, astrology, curious stories that appeared in the back of newspapers, of dreams, parents, women. Only in moments of intense spontaneity might we find ourselves talking like Marcello and his disturbing friend Steiner in *La dolce vita*, about a "clear, useful art that will have meaning tomorrow."

At our first meeting on that terrace on the Lido of Venice, Fellini launched spontaneously into the story of *La strada*. For me it was a moment caught between magic and embarrassment. I was worried by the idea that he was working on a film/fable—even one with neorealist influences. So genuinely worried, in fact, that I promised myself I'd actively discourage him if I ever had the chance—a promise I later had the opportunity to fulfill. And yet at the same time I could see the new vistas this narrator was beginning to unfurl, his new perspective on ancient realities: impoverished Italy; the cold muddy fields that the traveling entertainers (the subproletariat of theater) trod upon; the primitive, even brutal, relations between men and women; the peasant world at the margins of reconstruction; lost languages; magic; childhood; and ancestral memories. Naturally and unconsciously this new cineast was preparing to knock down the walls of the petit bourgeois culture that had burgeoned alongside a united Italy (especially in Romagna, central Italy, where Fellini was from—a region marked by temporal power), to challenge a middle class that had erased all traces of the culture that had come before it. Fellini was considered a crepuscular sketch artist in his early films and he was appreciated as such, or merely tolerated. But the sad odyssey of Gelsomina—that elusive, and, for many, crypto-Catholic figure—became a rallying cry. For years in essays, public debates, in the cafés along via Veneto, Fellini, with his defiantly anti-intellectual spirit, was accused of being "outside culture." Not until the 1970s did the intellectual left begin to rediscover the legitimacy of the fable form, recognizing its mythic, symbolic, even subversive potential. Horizons wouldn't broaden until after Stalin, Benedetto Croce, and Pope Pius XII had all disappeared. When intellectuals eventually did strike out into that foreign terrain, "the science of man," many were surprised to find that the director of *La strada* had already cut the path.

In the more than forty years since our friendship began on the terrace of the Hotel des Bains and until he passed away, I watched clashes brew and solidarities form within the ranks of Fellini's most loyal followers: "Fellini is always true to himself" versus "Federico has changed"—a perfect contradiction. Thinking back, I would say that both are true. The creator of 8½ knew how to pull off the impossible task of being faithful to himself and never refusing to let things change. How? It's a difficult story to tell, almost impossible to explain. The religious faith he'd been indoctrinated into as a child, then lost along the way—the faith he periodically referred to with the confused anxiety of trying to recover something—left our hero with a firm belief in destiny, chance, and circumstance. It carried him through unexpected choices, from one phase to the next of his career, which he started and continued without any specific goal until he discovered his cinematic mission. He believed in chance meetings, in love affairs, and in friendships—all of which came to him with incredible speed, and were like constant revelations that tended to endure. He lived inside of things with indomitable curiosity and unflappable openness. He abandoned himself to what Dostoevsky called "the river of life." He was serenely aware that the river always carried you somewhere. The book you are holding, written by a companion on that journey, aspires to be the ship's log for this mysterious and glorious existential itinerary.

FEDERICO FELLINI

Was He Born on a Moving Train?

"The most remarkable event in Federico Fellini's life occurred on a train. He was, in fact, born in the first-class compartment of a train that ran between Viserba and Riccione; to be precise, the place was Rimini." This is how Fellini's birth is portrayed in an undated newspaper clipping from some time after the First World War, found in a scrapbook that Giulietta Masina's father kept. It seems that Fellini was born in extraordinary circumstances and, despite the use of the word "precise," the entire story is as hazy as any of the many myths surrounding our hero—he was always in motion, driven perpetually by the pathology of wanting to be somewhere other than where he was.

Hard luck for the biographer, who after consulting the newspapers of the period must now take on the burden of dismantling the first of many Fellini legends. The improbable achievement of being born on a moving train was indeed an impossible achievement on January 20, 1920. For at six o'clock on that very morning, the trains going through Rimini, a little city on the Adriatic Riviera in Romagna, were stopped for a rail strike that continued for ten days. Two local papers exchanged insults over the matter of the strike. The Catholic paper, *L'Ausa* (named for a river of the region) raged against the "mania for striking" and offered an "Elegy to the Lazybones." As if that weren't enough, the paper went on to expose the scandal of "more than 281 bottles of champagne corked on the eve of the event—a Red Vigil." *Germinal* retaliated with disparaging references to "clerical rabble-rousers," and commended the organizers of the meeting in Teatro Vittorio Emanuele where the vote for the strike had been held.

The two newspapers reveal a curious coincidence. The same Tuesday evening that Federico was being born, Annibale Ninchi of the neighboring town Pesaro—"a young, likeable actor, who more than once made the room tremble with intense emotion"—appeared in Ercole Luigi Morselli's play *Glauco*. Forty years later, the same actor will bring Federico's father, Urbano Fellini, back to life in the film *La dolce vita*. In the end, even if building a biography necessitates dismantling some mythologies, it can also yield new ones. Accordingly, one might posit that alongside the crib of the future Poet of Cinema, there stood two fathers: Urbano and Annibale, the real-life father and the fantasy father.

Which is to say that on that historical evening, Signora Ida Fellini (née Barbiani) was not traveling on any train. She was in her apartment in viale Dardanelli, 10, behind the Grand Hotel, enduring the pain of labor under the ministrations of the doctor her husband had run through the pouring rain to fetch. The baby was positioned badly, and complications mounted. With the assistance of forceps, the infant saw first light, thunder and lightning, at 9:30 p.m. There are at least two contradictory reports of the time of birth: Fellini's own ("I was born at 12:15 in the morning on the last day of Capricorn"), and the birth certificate, which registered Fellini's entrance into the world at 11:30 a.m. (It's worth noting that this unreliable document also distorts Federico's surname, giving it as "Fillini.") Generally considered a Capricorn with Virgo rising, our protagonist has a complex star chart, brimming with contradictions that the most eminent astrologists have labored over.

Born in Rome in 1896, Ida was the daughter of Riccardo Barbiani and Maddalena Leali. Her father's family came from Rimini. They were Socialists and wholesale egg merchants. Her mother's family was seventh-generation Roman.

Ida and Urbano's marriage is that kind of romantic tale passed down through the family, recounted with smiles and characteristic vagueness—as when you leaf through a photo album and can't quite remember the names of all the people in the pictures. Their story goes something like this: Just before the First World War, in a boardinghouse near the Termini train station, not far from the Barbiani household, a refugee from the province of Romagna takes up residence. Affable and good-looking, the youth hails from a farm outside Gambettola—a village known in local dialect as *e Bôsch*, which means *il Bosco* (the forest)—off the via Emilia which runs from Cesena to Rimini, not far from San Mauro, the birthplace of the poet Giovanni Pascoli.

Urbano was born in 1894, the fourth of five children, to Luigi Fellini and Francesca Lombardini, small landholders and managers of a dairy and a general market. Uncle Federico, our hero's namesake, died at twenty-two years old, after jumping on a land mine in 1918 in the last days of the war. Urbano, not exactly a lover of country life (in later years he typically claimed he was born in Cesena, not Gambettola), went to Rome in pursuit of fortune and took a job as an assistant in a pasta shop. It could be said that he felt stifled in Gambettola, the same way that a quarter of a century later his son Federico would suffer the limited horizons of his provincial hometown.

Urbano fell in love with his neighbor on via Manin, and his love was returned. Ida was a comely girl; Urbano was lively and charming. But from the very beginning, they didn't have much in common. He was a country boy, she a city girl. He had to earn his keep, she was provided for. They had contrasting personalities and would maintain those differences for the rest of their lives. Urbano was extroverted, spirited, sociable. Ida was private, her habits austere. The Barbiani family disapproved of Ida's suitor from the start; they thought she could do better than Urbano. And yet Ida held her ground. The couple eloped and Ida let herself be swept off to Urbano's family house in Gambettola. Relations between Ida and her family were inalterably compromised—perhaps also because her mother died suddenly from puerperal fever during the same period. Ida's mother had given birth to seven children and was only thirty-nine when she died, and Ida found it difficult to forgive herself for splintering the family so acrimoniously. For their part, the Barbianis would never attempt to reconcile once they'd condemned and disinherited Ida—she was considered a degenerate. Ida, who tended toward melancholy anyway, ended up retreating into silence and piety.

Near the end of 1919, the newlyweds moved from Gambettola to Rimini, where Urbano started a wholesale business that dealt primarily in coffee and cheese, which he would maintain for the rest of his life. When their firstborn arrived, the couple was still officially resident in Gambettola, and that's why Federico's residency status in Rimini is listed as "tem-

porary" on his birth certificate. His younger brother, Riccardo, born thirteen months later, would also be registered "temporary."

According to the custom of the time, Federico was swaddled like
salami for the first five months of life to ensure he'd grow straight. At
seven months, repeating after his father, he could imitate animal sounds.
At one year, he could walk. He was a robust and ruddy baby and it wasn't
until later that he would start losing weight at such an alarming rate that
he earned the nickname "Gandhi."

In a little book entitled *Federico Fellini, mio cugino* (Federico Fellini,
My Cousin), Fernanda Bellagamba collected memories of the director,
among which is this lost recollection of Ezio Lorenzini's:

> A few months after Federico's birth, the family moved for a short
> period, unofficially, to Rome—a city that Ida was perpetually
> drawn to . . . Urbano continued to work as a wholesale food mer-
> chant in the city . . . but the move was called off a few months
> later after Ida failed to reconcile with her father—and because Ur-
> bano, made anxious by the situation with Ida's family, was unable
> to build a new clientele . . . They decided to leave again defini-
> tively when Ida learned she was pregnant with Riccardo, her sec-
> ond child. They went back to Rimini.

(Other subsequent attempts to return to Rome would follow—on the eve
of World War II, and during the immediate postwar period.) Urbano's
business began to flourish after their return. He started traveling constantly, visiting clients in the provinces and abroad, going as far as France
and Belgium. Urbano had a pleasant way about him and he inspired confidence—someone even nicknamed him the "Prince of Salesmen." Politically he was a Republican, and would butt heads with the local Fascist
Party—though he was never made to drink castor oil, as portrayed in a
scene in *Amarcord*.

A travel guide from the early 1920s reads:

> The city of Rimini is handsomely situated on the Adriatic shore at
> the intersection of the Bologna, Ancona, and Ravenna railway
> lines. It is officially in the province of Forlì and is part of the Ro-

magna region. Its political borders notwithstanding, the spoken dialect of Rimini has more in common with the music of the Marches region, with which it also shares a regional character. The people are industrious and principally engaged in maritime and fishing businesses.

The guide goes on to explain that the municipality was home to approximately sixty thousand people. (Presently, the population is more than twice that.) It describes the famous villages and hamlets that constitute the greater metropolitan area. The town of Riccione will become Benito Mussolini's favorite beach destination, though the dictator proclaims an overt antipathy for Rimini itself, which he inexplicably characterized as "rejected by the Marches and rejected by Romagna."

The journalist Sergio Zavoli, one of Federico's oldest friends, wondered what Mussolini's problem with Rimini was:

Did he object to the fact that it had no genuine civic history, or any authentic passions of its own—because it was marginal, even from a geographical point of view, unclaimed politically, and culturally spurious? Mussolini might have been entirely right to draw such conclusions, because Rimini was never a force to be reckoned with, as Ferrara, Forlì, or Ravenna were. Rimini absorbed fascism with a kind of resignation or assent or endurance—whatever it was, it happened without fanfare.*

These socio-anthropological notes are useful for explaining how Fellini's ironic "a-fascism" was typical of Rimini.

Federico proved to be a solitary and reflective child. He was in every sense more sedate than Riccardino, who drove everyone to despair and had a penchant for destroying things. Federico's personal vision of his childhood is revealed in his cartoon strip *Richettino, bambino qualunque* (Little Rico, Regular Boy) that ran in late 1941 in the weekly newspaper *Marc'Aurelio*, which brought into focus the mutual incomprehension between children and adults. That dynamic shifts nicely, however, as portrayed

*Yet Rimini was never what could be described as a hotbed of antifascism, either.

in the boy's friendship with an adult from outside the family unit—
Teresina, the maid. Constantly perplexed by his parents' conversations
and rules, Richettino hatches a series of revenge fantasies and escape
plans: rebellion born alongside blossoming consciousness.

Fascism evolved from dictatorship in 1925, the same year Federico
entered into elementary school with the Sisters of Vincenzo. After that,
he moved on to the public school, Carlo Tonini on via Gambalunga. He
was an average schoolboy, which seems entirely unrepresentative of the
fierce intelligence and intemperance that characterized his later years. In
this light, Fellini's subsequent determination to portray himself as a reluctant, uninterested student seems a slight exaggeration. He was, rather,
a typical child with a knack for drawing, living in a typical provincial Italian city, stuck between fascism and the church. The magical adventurous
period of Fellini's childhood came during the summer vacations he spent
in Gambettola at his paternal grandmother's country house—revisited
later in *La strada* and *Amarcord*. This was Fellini's immersion in a rural
way of life, in a place still connected to the customs and mannerism of
the previous century. This was a world apart, lush nature, colors, and
mystery, where antique dialects blended into often incomprehensible
phonetic patterns, where people practiced old-fashioned crafts, where
vagabonds and Gypsies wandered—a world that simmered in Federico's
citified imagination.

One precocious incident foreshadowed Federico's later fascination
with the connection between film and dream. The boy baptizes the four
corners of the bed in his grandmother's house with the names of Rimini's
four main movie theaters: the beloved Fulgor, the Savoia, the Sultano,
and the Opera Nazionale Dopolavoro. Lying on that bed, turning from
one corner to the other, Federico has his first experience of things envisioned, the collecting of images in luminous perception. Between dream
state and wakefulness he has paranormal experiences, imagines he's flying like an eagle or is transported into an alternate universe—like Little
Nemo in the Winsor McCay cartoons.

The summer of 1927 is the date standardly put to a "major historical
event" (which was in reality only a bit of pseudo history): the first escape.
There would follow a second and third escape—the last being the definitive one. Apparently excited by a show put on by the clown Pierino (later

evoked in the film *I clowns*), it seems that as the curtain fell, the boy ran away to join the circus. Both the alleged fugitive's mother and his entire family have always denied it ever happened. Yet decades later Fellini was still insisting that there was a nugget of truth in it. Perhaps that nugget was the simple desire to belong forever to the circus after the joyful and shocking experience of seeing it. For that reason, one might almost be justified in saying that, in one form or another, the first escape really did occur . . . although it didn't last a couple of days; it lasted a lifetime. As for the story itself (core material for Fellini fans), it's up to you whether to believe it or not.

Another not even remotely factual event—according to the evidence provided in school records—is Fellini's notorious tenure at the religious institution of the Padri Carissimi in Fano, his third and fourth year of elementary school. There is no proof whatsoever that Federico even set foot in the institution. Riccardo, however, was sent there—and perhaps Federico experienced the ruthless discipline and consequent trauma vicariously through his little brother. Nothing is diminished, however, by the fact that the real protagonist was Riccardo and not Federico—especially not the verisimilitude of the corresponding episode in 8½. Ennio Flaiano, who cowrote the screenplay, was also a former religious-school boarder and in fact considered himself to be the subject of that scene—so much so that over the course of a long-lasting dispute with Fellini, he would complain: "He stole everything from me, even my life story."

Despite the fact that he preferred to be remembered as a hellion, all evidence points to the fact that Fellini was quite a well-behaved little boy. He played with a toy theater and claimed he wanted to be a puppeteer when he grew up. He'd spend hours messing around with crayons and paint. When he was old enough, he became a devoted reader of *Corriere dei Piccoli* (a newspaper for children), which he collected and had bound. From the late 1920s, and into the early 1930s, the lively stories about unforgettable characters with their spectacular illustrations made the little newspaper very popular. There was Pat Sullivan's *Mio Mao* (also known as *Felix the Cat*), and *Bibì and Bibò* (*The Katzenjammer Kids*) by H. H. Knerr, George McManus's *Jiggs and Maggie*, and *Fortunello* (*Happy Hooligan*) by Frederick Burr Opper. There were numerous Italian contributors alongside these Americans: *Bonaventura* by Sto (Sergio Tofano) and

Pier Cloruro de' Lambicchi by Giovanni Manca—who made the drawings alive with his magic paints (as Fellini did with the portrait of Anita Ekberg for the poster for *Le tentazioni del dottor Antonio* (*The Temptations of Doctor Antonio,* 1962). But the wonderful characters in the cartoon by Ligurian illustrator Antonio Augusto Rubino were what really captured Federico's imagination. Rubino's colorful drawings profoundly influenced the world vision of the director-to-be, as well as his style and sense of humor. Iconography expert Paola Pallottino has brilliantly documented the surprising relationship between Fellini's *La strada* and Rubino's cartoons from 1919 and 1920, which featured a boy name Girellino and a Gypsy named Zarappa—likely ancestors of Gelsomina and Zampanò.

During this same period, or soon after, Federico was a voracious reader of Emilio Salgari's adventure stories. He mastered the jargon of the pirates in these tales and put it to use in his childhood games—making everything end with some kind of galloping fantasy, which notably never involved any kind of physical effort or athletic activity whatsoever. When it came to soccer, Fellini swore that he never touched a ball in his life and that he had no interest at all in the national championships—a genuinely rare character trait in Italy. Though he was born on the Adriatic, Fellini boasted other equally strange achievements: he never once donned a swimsuit, and he never learned to swim.

As for other books, Federico didn't become an avid reader until old age, when he began to suffer insomnia in the 1970s. We know very little about his ancient literary predilections, save a few titles. There was *Robinson Crusoe,* read in an abridged version at ten years old (he was both a little bored and a little intrigued by the main character). He never got to the end of *Gulliver's Travels;* but at fourteen, he fell in love with *Oliver Twist, Treasure Island,* and the novelist Joseph Conrad. Fellini remembered reading Homer and Edgar Allan Poe's "The Black Cat" for school. The Poe story reemerges when Fellini begins work on his episode for *Histoires extraordinaires* (*Spirits of the Dead,* 1968).

It might seem strange, but Fellini rarely went to the movies as a child. When asked to identify films that influenced him, he would claim to remember watching *Maciste all'inferno* (*Maciste in the Underworld,* 1925), which starred Bartolomeo Pagano. The recollection appears in the television special *Fellini: A Director's Notebook* (1969): there he is one Sunday afternoon, dressed like a sailor and sitting on his daddy's knee in a crowded and noisy movie theater. For Federico, the movie theater was where you went with friends to make a ruckus, or for a romantic encounter (imaginary or otherwise)—like Titta's adventure in *Amarcord* when he approaches the pretty lady named Gradisca. Or like Fausto's more aggressive maneuverings in *I vitelloni* (*The Young and the Passionate*, 1953). But the director always seemed reluctant to admit he'd seen other people's movies, as if even in that distant childhood, he wanted to extricate himself from the notion of influence.

During the first ten years of their marriage, the Fellinis moved several times. The family started out on viale Dardanelli, near the water (which in Rimini meant "on the other side of the tracks"). After returning from Rome, they moved into the center of town: first to the Palazzo Ripa, corso d'Augusto 115; then to the Palazzo Ceschina on via Gambalunga 48, near the Politeama Theater—that was on the first of April 1926. February 1929, when they moved to the Palazzina Dolci at via Clementini 9, was a bitter-cold winter. Ida was pregnant with Maddalena, who was born on October 7, 1929. Federico and Riccardo welcomed their sister with some curiosity, and immediately nicknamed her "Bàgolo" (for "little trouble-maker"). On April 21, 1931, the family moved yet again—just one door down to the house at via Dante 9 (now via Dante 23).

Federico got through elementary school without ever having to move from his school on via Gambalunga. In 1930, he was enrolled in the Ginnasio-Liceo Giulio Cesare on corso d'Augusto. His desk partner for the next eight years would be Luigi Benzi, better known as Titta—or "Il Grosso" (for "big"). The son of a building contractor, Titta is a constant presence in the memoiristic articles that Fellini wrote for the newspaper *Marc'Aurelio*. He reappears in the script for *Viaggio con Anita* (*A Trip with Anita*) and can been seen again in aspects of the protagonist of *Amarcord*.

When they had their fill of fisticuffs between the Trojans and the Achaeans—a daily reenactment held on via Ugo Bassi—Federico and Titta would organize their friends and make trouble, sometimes letting little Riccardo tag along too. The gang's aim was to torment housewives and shopkeepers by stealing their sheets off the laundry lines and nicking salt cod from the soaking bins in storefronts. Once, after the daily divvying up of the plunder in Titta's garage, Riccardo got the idea of burying his take in a neighbor's garden and was surprised in the act by a supervisor from his father's warehouse, who then turned the boy over to his mother. She dragged Riccardo to church and made him get down on his knees and beg forgiveness from the Madonna.

Ida was as unflappable and severe a disciplinarian as Urbano was absent and permissive. Federico's warm memories of his father were more than anything the consequence of how Urbano watched over his children's lives without ever trying to run them. There were of course some exceptions, passing furies, a handful of spankings, and broken plates—but for the most part the paterfamilias left discipline to his wife. The burden of passing moral judgment on Federico's and Riccardo's repeated escapades fell to her. Urbano was almost always on the road, and Ida would beg her children to behave. When they didn't, she grew anxious and dramatically beleaguered, thus becoming an ongoing source of guilt to her boys. When they were little, she put them to bed at 8:30, making sure they said their prayers every night. When they got older, she expected them home by 7:30.

In June 1935, Federico and Titta sat a second-year exam at the Liceo Monti of Cesena. They were sent in full-dress uniform to Forlì, where they joined in King Vittorio Emanuele III's escort when he came to inaugurate the Melozzo show. Federico thought the sovereign looked like a rabbit, and he made the other boys laugh by doing impressions of him. In August 1936, Federico went to camp in the mountains of Verucchio, twenty kilometers outside of Rimini. While there, he executed a series of caricatures of the musketeers of the *balilla*.* The caricatures were reprinted under the title "Scouts, 1936" in the single edition of *La Diana* published in February 1937 by the Balilla Troop of Rimini. The pictures bear the signature "Av. Fellini, Federico" ("Av." stands for avant-garde). This is probably Fellini's first published work. In the young man's talented hands, caricature was a tool for making friends and earning his first wages. At school, he won the hearts of his teachers by drawing colorful portraits of them.

The young illustrator's fame spread, and the manager of the Cinema

---

*During fascism, boys between eight and fourteen years old were made to participate in the *balilla*, a kind of Boy Scouts with a military emphasis.

Fulgor commissioned him to draw a number of portraits of celebrated actors for the marquee window displays. But Fellini's first major undertaking as an artist was in the summer of 1937: seventeen-year-old Federico teamed up with a friend, the older painter Demos Bonini, and they set up a portrait shop hoping to attract vacationers. Their shop—which foreshadowed a later Roman enterprise, the Funny-Face Shop—was on via IV Novembre, practically across the street from the cathedral. It was a spacious storefront with a back room. Under the signature "Febo" (the combined initials of Fellini and Bonini), the partners executed caricatures and silhouettes cut out of black paper and pasted onto a white background.

The academic year 1936–37 was the most important of Fellini's Rimini years, later to be memorialized in the popular cartoon entitled *Secondo liceo*.* Federico refers to himself in the third person here as well, using only his surname, and throughout the story depicts himself as a more disruptive student with a far more catastrophic tenure than was in fact true. Out of a highest grade of eight, Federico's average was seven. He earned a couple of eights and only three sixes, in math, physics, and military culture.

In Fellini's stories about his school days, which ran in *Marc'Aurelio* in 1940 and 1941, and was reprised for several months in 1946 and 1947 in *Travaso delle Idee*, Federico draws a picture of himself as a smart aleck, a disrespectful student. On December 7, 1940, *Marc'Aurelio* runs a cartoon entitled "Compito in classe" (Class Work):

> Looking off into the distance, the professor says, "Agesilaus's forced march reaches the city of Corinth before sunset . . ." The professor slowly climbs up to the podium. "Corinth. Did you all get that?" Benzi repeats the last phrase and writes it down slowly . . . Fellini checks his fingernails and decides the time has come to do what he's been thinking about since the day before . . . It must be nice outside . . . it's raining and the café must be full of people. Fellini closes his dictionary and textbook. He stands and,

---

*"Secondo liceo" is a "curious" grammatical formulation that suggests Fellini is writing about a second high school attended rather than the second year of high school, which the piece is more evidently about. The author too is at a loss to explain this turn of phrase.

wearing a drawn, miserable face, approaches the podium. "Professor," he says, "I don't feel well . . ." "Would you like to leave?" And he's sprung! Here comes Fellini bounding down the corridor . . . He feels very, very good, and in order to be nice to the school janitor he asks him to tell him that war story one more time. "Tell me again, Luigi . . . You were out on the Piave front one night . . ."

In the *Travaso delle Idee* six years later, Federico depicts his first day of his second year at Giulio Cesare like this:

At one end of the piazza a thin, rumpled boy with a dirty kerchief on his head emerges from the rain. He's cool and collected. He turns into the school's main entrance. He stops in the foyer to smoke a butt and wait . . . But to wait for what? It's already 8:45! Dear readers, even if it is the first day of school, Fellini must maintain his reputation and it is imperative that he arrive late . . . He smokes, inhaling through his nose because he's still nursing a cold. At nine o'clock on the dot, he will head in . . .

This is the same rebellion as Richettino's, the young student's alter ego goaded by his uneasiness in the impenetrable "grown-up world"—family on one side, school on the other. The school register shows that in that one single school year, the student Fellini was marked with sixty-seven absences, almost a record.

First love bloomed in the house on via Dante, Federico's last address in Rimini. The year was 1936, the object of his affection, Bianca Soriani, a sweet girl from across the way. Born in Pescara in 1922, Bianca moved a lot, trailing after her restless father who ran a typography business. Little Bianca attended the vocational institute. She had two sisters and one brother—all of them lying in wait to intercept communications from the boy across the street, and to spy. Federico liked Bianca, he compared her to dynamic actresses like Kay Francis and Barbara Stanwyck. But these heady fantasies led only to bad tempers all around. Ida told Bianca's mother to keep a better watch over her daughter, resulting in a rash of beatings for the little girl—and she was actually confined to her room for several days. The story unfolded in the atmosphere of heightened emotions and ignorance typical of the day. But the adolescent blush of Federico's ardor didn't keep him from living it very intensely—so intensely, in fact, that he actually fainted when faced with the umpteenth parental obstacle to seeing his "Bianchina." The episode reveals quite a lot of sensitivity and vulnerability in an otherwise apparently serene young man. The fainting itself is representative of Federico's most ardent desire—to escape, which started when he got a sense of who he was. The loss of the senses is simply another way of extricating himself from the tyranny of the adult world. Fainting is in a way just like the sudden departure from class. Herein lies the link to the legend of the second escape, which is even less credible than the first. Federico and little Bianca—who in truth never ventured together farther than the city outskirts by bicycle a couple of times—sneak onto a train headed for Bologna. After several hours of flight, the rail police capture them.

In October 1938, a couple of years later, Bianchina and her family moved again, leaving Rimini for Milan. Bianca's father had bought a printing shop there. Her departure is perhaps one of the principal motives driving Fellini's eventual decision to leave Rimini. The couple exchange letters and Titta remembers a trip he and Federico made to Milan in March 1939 so that Federico could visit his beloved. The tale of this love affair would later become confused with his marriage in the young man's fantastical memory. Bianca's character was sometimes named "Pallino" or "Pallina" ("little ball" for her button nose) in the stories later published in *Marc'Aurelio*. This was also the name of Cico's wife ("Cico" is short for Federico), who would be played by Giulietta Masina on the radio.

In a letter dated February 19, 1986, Bianca wrote: "Maybe Federico did want me to leave my parents and join him in Rome, but a girl would never dream of doing something so dramatic back then. Even though I was constantly fighting with my parents, I was brought up in such a way that I would never have dared something like that." Instead, the distance sent Bianca along a different path. She fell in love with Roberto Mercatali, whom she worked with at Montecatini,* and they were married. In the same letter she recounts:

---

*Montecatini is a large chemical producer that merged with Edison in 1966.

That's how it ended between me and Federico. For him 1940 couldn't have been a very prosperous year, but every now and then he'd round up enough money to come visit me. On one of those visits, while he was waiting for me outside of Montecatini, my sister came and took him by the arm and led him away, explaining that I felt for him but that I had a new boyfriend, and Federico should be told . . . At a certain point that day, I was walking with my future husband just a few meters in front of my sister and Federico. He looked like he'd been crying and I don't remember too much more. I don't remember what we said, how the four of us all stopped and stared at one another, how we broke up. Maybe I tried to wipe the memory out of my mind so I wouldn't suffer . . . After that, Federico must have gotten in touch with my fiancé. He asked him if he could ever make me as happy as Federico promised he would. The answer was that it wasn't any of his business anymore and he should stop worrying about it . . .

Mercatali was gifted and had artistic talents. He wrote and painted, but seemed constantly dissatisfied with both himself and the world around him. The moment he completed a painting he'd turn it to the wall. "For several years we had no news of Federico," writes Bianca.

He looked us up suddenly when he came to Milan to screen his first film. After that he always wanted us to come to every one of his screenings . . . He became very involved in my husband's illness, and during the worst period he called often. He even tried to set us up with doctors he knew in Milan and Rome. For me, the sole fact that he existed always gave me a sense of comfort, of faith . . .

Unfortunately Bianca's marriage ended with Roberto's suicide, something that had been foreshadowed more than once over the years. Left alone, she told her story in the novel *Una vita in più* (One More Life), published initially in serial form for a weekly paper, running under the title *Paura del vuoto* (Fear of Emptiness). In the character named Pierluigi, we recognize Federico.

2

Dreaming of Journalism

His family was boring and school was exasperating—it seemed he'd already experienced everything that Rimini could offer. The year was 1938; Federico was eighteen and impatient. The time had come to start making a living. There wasn't a lot of money around at home and children were kept on a short leash anyway—as was the moral code of the day. But not being too indulgent was generally considered part of a healthy upbringing. So literally and figuratively money was scarce. Federico was beginning to suffer the first pangs of a bad rapport with finances, which he'd endure for the rest of his life. It was never hard for him to earn money, but once he had it, he'd never know how to manage it sensibly: no sooner in his fist than gone—dispersed in every improbable direction. Financial matters aside, Federico is brewing the perhaps more important desire to *do* something. The urgency of expression is welling up in this idle, recalcitrant young man. Before long he will begin submitting stories and drawings to newspapers. The first paper to accept something for publication is the popular *Domenica del Corriere* in the section called "Cartoline del pubblico" (Postcards from Our Readers) on the second-to-last page: "We pay twenty lire for every postcard selected for publication." Federico's postcard ran in the February 6, 1938, edition. It's entitled "Gelosone" and is a drawing of an animal trainer talking to his acrobat wife. The caption for the husband runs, "You don't have to hold so tightly to Giorgio's hand when you perform the leap of death. Okay?" There's a similar kind of schoolboy humor running through all of Federico's postcards—a dozen or so of which were published in *Domenica del Corriere* over the course of the year, all signed "Dis. di Fellini" (Drawing by Fellini). The postcards were to some extent the work of a beginner. But Federico got a real break when his partner Demos Bonini took the initiative of sending several of the young artist's drawings to the weekly *420*. We can reconstruct the order of events through letters exchanged with the editor of the section "Telegrafoo."

Named after a deadly long-range German cannon, *420* was a weekly broadsheet of political satire founded in Florence in 1914 by Giuseppe Nerbini and published through 1943. Federico would remain critically distant from the more aggressive political side of *420*, known for a certain fascistic gang mentality (*squadrismo*) peculiar to the city of Florence. There was always a big drawing on the front page by Buriko (Antonio Burattini), whose work seems to encapsulate an irreconcilable contradiction between elegance and coarse propaganda. The paper took potshots at Negus,* the Jews, Radio Valencia—the Voice of Republican Spain, the Soviet Bear, the Red Dean of Canterbury,† France and its ongoing labor strikes, shrinking family size,‡ and English journalism—as encapsulated by the figure of Walter Closet (whose head the paper routinely portrays in the shape of a toilet bowl). The first response to "Fellas, Rimini" reads: "Don't send articles anymore, or any writings in general—we're up to our ears in it already" (January 9, 1938). But the aspiring journalist doubles his efforts and the next month receives a more encouraging response: "Fellini, Federico, Rimini. It seems impossible not to like you. You have the future in you—at least the future of the next generation of *420*—if you have as much of a gift for perseverance as you have for humor. Keep on sending your material. You know how it works—once you've gotten in a couple more good ones, things we really like, then we'll have to move forward." That month *420* reformatted and got bigger, expanding to fifty drawings in each issue. With more space to fill they likely had a need for more material. It is nonetheless difficult to pick out Federico's pieces, though they must be there, because at a certain point in the letters we

---

*"Negus" is the Ethiopian word for king: the reference is to the war between the Italians and the Ethiopians.

†Lord Cecil: Nobel Peace Prize laureate and Archbishop of Canterbury, the "Red Dean," a Socialist, and a peace activist.

‡Under Mussolini, large families were prized, and even rewarded financially.

read: "Fellini, Federico, Rimini. You will have no doubt noticed and been pleased to find that a number of your pieces have been lucky enough to find a home in the pages of *420*. We are also pleased with this development . . ." Fellini was probably writing captions for cartoons—at that time the practice was to use both a gag writer and an artist. On September 18: "In response to your inquiry, our publication is perfectly receptive to all that is spirited and original." The tone suggests that Fellini finally made it, and is confirmed by a drawing appearing in that same issue, signed "Fellas." It shows a husband and wife on a beach that looks just like Rimini: the woman is chiding her husband for staying in the water too long and getting numb. Off in the horizon is the silhouette of the ocean liner from *Amarcord*.

Fellini never lived "several years in Florence" as is sometimes claimed. His own version of the story is in fact more plausible: "I stayed for fifteen days the first time I went to Florence, and a couple of months the second time." Conceivably, during the second half of 1938, after graduating from Liceo Monti and before starting work at *Marc'Aurelio*, he commuted between Rimini and Florence, and then between Rome and Florence, in order to continue working with Nerbini at *420*. He certainly never wrote comic books—though he was fond of saying he did—and he didn't illustrate the Italian version of *Flash Gordon*. In the fall of 1938, Alex Raymond's* name disappeared from the pages of *L'Avventuroso*, the weekly where it had run on the front page since the paper's launch on October 15, 1934. Under pressure from ultra-Fascist parents and educators, the minister of popular culture had been insisting for months that the quality of publications for young people be improved, and condemned the prevalence of American comics, which were seen as vessels of antinationalist ideology. All of the made-in-the-USA features were cut from the paper and sales began to plummet—just as Fellini was feathering his nest with Nerbini. The editors mobilized their forces, and pleaded with contributors to generate more material to replace the missing features. So Fellini would lend a hand during this period. The apprenticeship under Nerbini was important because it gave young Federico the opportunity to learn from within the workings of a publishing house with several titles and na-

*Alex Raymond authored *Flash Gordon*.

tional distribution. What's more, those early publications in 420 built his confidence as a writer and cartoonist, which will serve him well in the more sophisticated climate of *Marc'Aurelio*.

Federico and Titta were inseparable during these years. They earned their diplomas together in the summer of 1938. A strange twist of logistics in the scheduling of their final exams took them to far-flung places: the written portion was given in Cesena, and the oral portion at the Morgagni *liceo* in Forlì. The summer is also critically marked by the suicide of a classmate who plunged into depression after failing his finals. This event would introduce another excuse to resent the useless and oppressive school—a motif that insinuated itself in Fellini's heart and led to the harsh condemnation we see in *Amarcord*. As the year drew to a close, Fellini's time in Rimini also seemed to end. There were no dramatics, but the departure pained him nonetheless. The moment of the third escape had arrived—and this one was definitive.

3

Rome

"We'd always talked of leaving, but then one morning, without a word to anyone, one of us really did leave . . ." says the voice over the final scene of *I vitelloni*. Without saying goodbye, Moraldo leaves his hometown, his family, his friends at the pool hall. "But weren't you happy here?" asks Piccolo* from the sidewalk as the train begins to move away. The bright, handsome face of Moraldo, played by Franco Interlenghi, reveals that he doesn't know how to answer. Yes, he was happy. But . . . And through the window of the moving train, he imagines he can see his friends all asleep in their beds—Alberto, Leopoldo, Fausto, Riccardo. A lump forms in his throat as the train speeds up. A new chapter has opened, and the young railway worker smiles at Moraldo the way Paola will smile at Marcello at the end of *La dolce vita*. Because that's all part of what's so hard about growing up—the unavoidable, wrenching farewells, as you take your first confident steps into the vast world. If you listen closely, you'll note that the voice that says "*Addio*, Guido" doesn't belong to the actor Interlenghi but to Fellini himself, taking over the microphone in the dubbing studio, as if he wanted personally to seal his farewell to youth.

Fellini's actual departure from Rimini wasn't nearly as poetic, according to the friends he left behind. They insult him affectionately using local slang, call him a *patàca*,† and explain that he didn't even leave alone

---

*The young railway worker (here called Piccolo, for "small") whom Moraldo befriends sees him off at the train station.
†A jerk, or asshole, in Romagnolo dialect.

but with a group. Titta Benzi swears he remembers the very day they all left together to go to Bologna, January 4, 1939—a date that more or less coincides with the dates the Rimini registrar has recorded for Fellini's official move to Rome on March 14, 1939. Whether or not it counted as a sad departure, and whether or not goodbyes were said, Fellini's arrival in Rome is portrayed in a celebrated scene in *Roma*. A dark, slender young man wearing a white linen suit arrives at the Termini station. He gets off the train, hands his suitcase over to a redcap who looks like an old clown, and then makes his way through the chaos of the city. Right before his bulging Alice-in-Wonderland eyes, there pass priests, soldiers, nuns, hawkers, police, sailors, beautiful women, members of the secret service, and other assorted rabble. The billboards in the station include one enormous movie poster with the faces of Vittorio De Sica and Assia Noris from *Grandi magazzini* (which was actually released in October 1939, a few months after Fellini's historic arrival). The young man is both shocked and thrilled as he dives into the frenzy of Italy's capital, allowing himself to be swallowed up as if by a starving, protective, and dangerous giant mother. We shouldn't forget that Federico had been in Rome as a newborn and then again when he was thirteen or fourteen. He retained a vivid memory from the second trip when he'd gone on a tour of the city monuments with his maternal uncle Alfredo and gotten lost—a traumatic episode—separated from the group while they were visiting the catacombs.

According to Fellini, this is the story of the third escape: a young, ambitious man, seduced by vague promises of work from a journalist he has met, leaves his hometown to embark on an adventure in the big city. It is the perfect premise, except reality is actually more complex. The real hero of the story is a girl from Rome who escaped twenty years earlier, leaving her family behind in order to marry a penniless man from the provinces. Now a mother of three, Ida has grown painfully nostalgic and would like to make amends with her older brother. She wants her husband to transfer his business to Rome—but Urbano has worked hard to get where he is in Rimini and can't just up and leave it all. But since her firstborn has just completed high school and is ready for university, Ida determines to exploit the situation and declares that she should go be with him, at least until he gets settled.

Hoping the move would become permanent, Ida closed up her house, loaded the furniture onto two trucks, and left Rimini, Maddalena in tow. Their new address in Rome is via Albalonga 13 near the Piazza Re di Roma. Federico moved in with his mother and sister, while Riccardo and his father took a furnished room back in Rimini. Having lost all hope of ever having a priest in the family, Ida decided that a lawyer (like Federico's friend Benzi) would be a good alternative. Federico was thus obligated to enroll in the university program (where according to Maddalena he finished only one or two examinations), though all he can really think about is becoming a journalist. Back in Rimini, Urbano would attempt to interest Riccardo (a future accountant) in his work, bringing him along to the warehouse, getting him third-class rail tickets to see clients in the Marches. But Riccardino discovers that he has a voice and dreams of becoming a lyric tenor or an actor.

Urbano visits Rome a couple of times a month, but Riccardo's Roman incursions grow more and more frequent, until one sunny day, he moves into the house on via Albalonga too. While Federico makes the rounds of newspaper offices, his brother takes up voice lessons and hangs around film productions hoping to win a bit part. (Riccardo's teacher, Giulio Moreschi, appears in *Lo sceicco bianco* as the hotel doorman.) The boys are out all day long, never come home for dinner, and often return very late at night. Sometimes Federico doesn't come home at all. Left alone with Maddalena, Ida starts missing Rimini and within the year packs all her furniture back onto the truck, loads up Maddalena, and sets off for home— with a dangerous journey over the snow-covered mountain range, Passo del Furlo, ahead of her.

Ida's final attempt to interfere in her children's lives consists in securing a furnished room for her youngest son in a widow's boardinghouse near Piazza Tuscolo. She is devastated to learn that after only a few days, Riccardo is seduced by the landlady. Though he continues to study voice, at twenty-two he'll marry his teacher's seventeen-year-old daughter, claiming that it was because he'd sung *Prendi l'anel ti dono* from Bellini's *La sonnambula* one too many times, and resign himself to a reviled career in sales in order to pay the rent. In the meantime, he does briefly attend the Centro Sperimentale di Cinematografia, winning a small part in the film *I tre aquilotti* (The Three Pilots, 1942), directed by Mario Mattoli.

On July 16, 1942, Fellini dedicates an epistolary article to Riccardo in *CineTeatro RadioMagazzino* under the title "Lettera al fratellino" (Letter to My Little Brother), complete with blessings, advice, and photographs of Riccardo taken by Elio Luxardo, photographer to the stars.

Once they've closed down the apartment on via Albalonga, Federico and Riccardo live separate lives. They look alike and this could be one reason they don't seek out each other's company—it's a pattern that will continue in the years to come. When their paths do cross during the most difficult months of the Roman apprenticeship, Federico always reminds his brother that the most important thing is to tell their parents that everything is working out fine in order to keep them from interfering. Ida's return to Rimini is a definitive cutting of the umbilical cord for the two brothers—the conquest of freedom, a new life flush with things to do and no obligations.

During this period Federico has a dream that will mark him. The dream is a weaving together of relief and cynicism, love and regret. In the dream, he's returned to Rimini and landed at the Grand Hotel. The doorman says to him, "Strange, there's a couple staying here who have your same last name . . . those people over there." He gestures to a man and woman sitting on the terrace looking out over the sea. Even though their backs are to him, Federico recognizes his mother and father—and yet in some sense, they don't really look like them. He shrugs, as if to say, "What of it?" Stumbling upon his parents in their intimate space—rather than as archetypal mother and father figures—is an indelible image. They exist here as man and woman, nothing more. This scene will be re-created in the screenplay *Il viaggio di G. Mastorna*.

Rome is Ida's city and Federico's nostalgia for it is womblike; the move from Rimini felt more like a return than a departure. Changing cities was like letting go of his real mother's apron strings in order to grab those of his Great Mediterranean Mother—a figure he will later come to identify through his forays into Jungian psychology. It is a consuming relationship, laced with freedom, fear, relief, and solitude—all the unknown factors that the vast, longed-for larger world can pile on perilously, almost threateningly. He won't turn back in life, although he's continuously turning back in his creative work. And yet the solitary traveler will soon feel the need of a feminine presence to stand in for his mother, someone who will provide definitive shelter.

Federico seemed to prefer for his Roman friends to think he lived alone—that way, he could participate in the riotous mishaps of boarding-house life. He didn't even tell Rinaldo Geleng, his best friend at the time, what his real living situation was. Federico had met Rinaldo by chance when they were both standing in front of a delicatessen window hungrily contemplating the unattainable treats within. Rinaldo, who is Fellini's age, is a relative of Ottone Geleng, the Prussian painter responsible for making Taormina a tourist destination. In the screenplay *Moraldo in città* (Moraldo in the City), Geleng is named Lange, and the two young protagonists embark on a business project together, trying to earn money from their art (as in real life). This would be Fellini's bohemian period: they decorate store windows and circulate among the cafés, drawing caricatures. Fellini had already dabbled in this kind of enterprise in Rimini, but Geleng is the more successful of the two because he is quite an accomplished portraitist. He panders to his clients' vanity with handsome and accurate renderings. Fellini, meanwhile, gets distracted by the zoological peculiarities he tends to perceive in people's faces—he ends up producing something closer to a bestiary than a portrait gallery, drawing giraffes, elephants, rhinoceroses, and other animals. Often his clients refuse to pay for the final product. Geleng and Fellini root about for other jobs, trying to piece together a living—dressed as ancient Egyptians they find work in the summer stock production of *Aida* at the Terme di Caracalla.

It's not entirely clear whether Federico embarked on these ventures for fun or money. Friends from the period remember he was always broke—even after he started drawing quite a good salary from *Marc'Aurelio*. In an interview, the actor Alberto Sordi remembers that when they were friends they'd entertain themselves by taking pictures of Federico wrapped in a bedsheet striking "monumental" poses. The title under one of Sordi's pictures runs: "To Federico Fellini, Rome and Her People, 1940." In the picture Federico seems undernourished. But Geleng has the impression that Fellini endured hardship only in order to keep company with his friends. In those days he'd go so far as to spend the occasional night on a park bench despite the fact that there was a comfortable bed waiting for him back at via Albalonga. But Fellini was a thin man anyway and that certainly encouraged the impression that he didn't get enough to eat.

All of that aside, Italy was on the threshold of war in those months.

Appetite will turn into hunger before long. Food starts growing scarce, and rations are instituted on February 1, 1940. Federico never turns to his family for help and they don't offer any. Whether real or fabricated, this bohemian period with Rinaldo and cohorts doesn't last long—it's a time of raucous tomfoolery, or *vitellonate*—to use the expression that Fellini himself coined for *I vitelloni*.* Fellini and friends rent a carriage to take them home one night; they tell the driver to stop when they are around the corner from home, claiming they want to get out for a minute and "stretch their legs"—and they never reappear. They frequent cafés that hand out free leftovers to "artists" after the dinner shift. They run up a tab with Bruno at Ristorante Donatello on via Milano near the Forum, where the regular clientele includes Luigi A. Garrone. A middle-aged "seditious journalist" from Piemonte who's been blacklisted for his anti-Fascist sentiments, Garrone is fat, ruddy, and an extraordinary raconteur of journeys he never made. He eats for free and lingers after dinner, drinking wine. He speaks with a soft *r* and enchants his listeners. He even picks up occasional acting work—he plays the vagabond on the beach who frightens the little protagonist of De Sica's *I bambini ci guardano* (*The Children Are Watching Us*, 1944). Under the name Gattone (big cat), the journalist appears in the treatment of *Moraldo in città*, where he narrates his own sad end. That same figure is recycled for the 1958 film *Fortunella*, where the character of the dying man in the hospital is named Professor Golfiero Paganica (played by the American actor Paul Douglas).

Fellini was bewitched by Garrone, but he also recognized his self-destructiveness. Garrulous Garrone was frightening—he was the point of no return, the symbol of an unhinged life, sliding toward catastrophe. In his person he was an object lesson in creativity and rigor, inspiration and craft, dream and work. It's even better if the work feels like a game, which is what it's like for Federico during the early months of his new Roman life, after making his first foray into the editorial offices of *Marc'Aurelio*.

*See Chapter 16 for a more extensive discussion of the term *vitelloni*.

4

A Thousand Newspaper Articles

I'm writing you from the San Silvestro post office, the same room I'd come to twenty-five years ago, before I had anywhere to take refuge or a typewriter of my own. I'd come here to churn out my little sketches for *Marc'Aurelio*—this very room, crackling with life like a fire in a hearth, the big window looking over the square, the rumbling and screeching of buses outside as they come into and leave the end of the line . . .

Fellini wrote this never-before-published letter to his friend Anna Giovannini from the central post office in Rome. The great director clung to his bizarre habits. He continued:

In the dead of winter I wore white canvas shoes, and tried to get into Caffè Aragno to drum up some business with my drawings to buy dinner and a pack of Macedonias to smoke at the movies, maybe even go clean up at Cobianchi* . . .

When he was still in Rimini and imagining himself in Rome, young Fellini's vision didn't include Cinecittà at all. He dreamed of *Marc'Aurelio*. In those years, the Roman newspaper with the stoic emperor's bust on its masthead had a massive distribution. And this was despite the fact

---

*Cobianchi, precursor to the health/beauty spa, was an international chain of public baths, "daytime hotels" for cleaning, steaming, grooming. It was very successful in the period between the wars.

that priests from their pulpits railed against its wicked influence on young people. Fellini was a loyal reader of the twice-weekly publication and longed to become a contributor. He overcame his shyness one day on the beach and approached one of the founders, Ferrante Alvaro De Torres, who he recognized from a portrait that had appeared in the paper. A songwriter (of ultranationalist songs like "La sagra di Giarabub") and a bit of a free spirit, De Torres is gracious when Fellini approaches his beach umbrella carrying a sheaf of drawings and writings. The journalist thumbs through the pages, reading here and there, and decides the boy has talent. Of course knowing how to write or draw doesn't get you far in Rimini—but if one were able to come to Rome . . .

So one of the first places Federico heads when he arrives in the city is *Marc'Aurelio* with its seat on the second floor of a large building on via Regina Elena, where Angelo Rizzoli's offices are. But the receptionist, Gigione, redirects Federico to the daily paper *Il Piccolo*, where De Torres is an editor. And so there, in Palazzo Sciarra, the impressive benefactor welcomes Federico into a real newspaper. With its emphatically "Red" masthead, *Il Piccolo—Giornale d'Italia* is an articulate and lively paper. Compared with other dailies of the time, it is somewhat more open-minded and often puts entertainment items—like opera or theater openings, even film reviews—on the front page. Fellini's entrance onto the masthead in 1939 coincides with the death of Pope Pius XI (February 10); the election of Eugenio Pacelli to replace him—the first Roman in 218 years to hold the papal seat—under the name Pius XII (March 3); the conquest and incorporation of Albania into the Italian principality (February 17); and the fall of the Spanish Republic. The March 24 headline, MADRID, COMMUNISM'S GRAVEYARD, is splashed across the entire front page. Tension builds and the war draws ever nearer: the urban centers start to empty out, the supply of meat and fish is limited and then rationed, eventually the driving of private automobiles in the city is suspended.

It would have been difficult for the aspiring journalist to feel secure in his work at *Il Piccolo* under the circumstances, and so he'll also venture over to the grayer, statelier newspaper *Il Popolo di Roma* with its offices on via del Tritone. When scanning his memories from this period, Fellini loved to remember himself as the kind of reporter you'd find in a Georges Simenon novel, chasing robbers and solving crimes, and he claimed his career as a reporter was aborted by the passing of a law that prohibited *cronaca nera*—or crime reporting. It is more likely, however, that Fellini's ephemeral tenure at the daily newspapers had something to do with the way his imaginative temperament was at odds with the simple obligation to report facts.

On a return visit to *Marc'Aurelio* one afternoon, Federico meets another aspiring journalist, Ruggero Maccari. The two men are almost the same age and quickly form a friendship—which is encouraged by Stefano Vanzina, alias Steno, who is working as the secretary at the newspaper. (This is a remarkable early encounter between three future cineastes.) The two collaborate on gags for cartoons, working at a bar or at Maccari's house at via degli Scipioni 12—or even at Fellini's house, where Ida sometimes convinces Ruggero to stay for lunch.

Fellini ends up telling the best version of the story of how he worked his way into *Marc'Aurelio* in a March 7, 1939, article entitled "E' permesso?" (May I Come In?). Riffing on the idea of what it's like to be a beginner, Federico wrote: "Is this young Fellas a man of quality? Does he show promise?"—underscoring the feeling of being discouraged by editors and future colleagues for his attempts to write jokes. But this experience never dampens his faith, and in fact just a few months later, Fellini can be counted among the most regular contributors to the paper. He often signs his work "Federico," sometimes only with the initial "F.," and more rarely even as "Fellini." Born into a new life in the big city, our hero comes to be known simply as Federico.

In his first months on the job, the rookie will only ever see Vito De Bellis from a distance. The former sports bureau chief for *Il Popolo di Roma*, De Bellis was just over thirty years old when he became deputy editor of *Marc'Aurelio* after the paper launched on March 14, 1931. Published by Rizzoli from Milan (who will later produce *La dolce vita*), the "biweekly that all Italy reads" has a print run of more than 300,000 copies, comes out every Wednesday and Saturday, costs forty centesime, and offers six pages of cartoons, doggerel, and stories—some of which even bear the byline of Anton Chekhov. The political satire runs only on the first page, where, fortunately, Federico seldom appears. Regular attacks emasculated France, Roosevelt, and the Jews, and the dark, super-patriotic drawings can be chalked up to a frat-boy sense of humor and a vaguely surrealist aesthetic. But the paper's general attitude is one of ironic detachment. The vehement political satire of *420* appears in *Marc'Aurelio*'s pages as well, but more as if it were an obligation, without conviction—their own polemics seem to run more emphatically toward anti-intellectualism. They regularly take potshots at literary salons and writers—and the personal attacks are hardly subtle. Indeed, sometimes the responses of the injured parties turn violent. At the time of Fellini's arrival, everyone is still talking about how the comic Ettore Petrolini had been so enraged by a pan that he trashed the editorial offices.

When he is at long last admitted into the editor in chief's sancta sanctorum, Federico finds himself sitting across the desk from a man who reminds him of Victor McLaglen—John Ford's traitor in *The Informer*. De Bellis greets him with hearty laughter and cries of "I'm so pleased with your work . . . They like you! They like you!" He's referring to the regular column that Fellini has started writing, over which De Bellis will go on to exert a polite but implacable criticism. A gregarious man—a professional with a strong sense of his public—he is something of a foil to Federico's own unadulterated ease. De Bellis takes the youth under his wing, calls him "little man," and increasingly involves him in the life of the newspaper. Their relationship is serene despite De Bellis's impatience with Federico's careless habits and frequent lateness. An editor in chief of the old school, De Bellis is sensitive to his privilege, and Fellini continues to address him formally until his death on June 19, 1986.

Early on, Federico and Ruggero are invited to attend the Wednesday and Friday editorial meetings. This is where De Bellis communicates new governmental orders and the editors toss around ideas for feature stories, the political cartoon for the front page, and the headlines and slug lines for current events. The meetings start at five and run past midnight. Where politics are concerned, Federico doesn't usually pay attention. He's like a distracted schoolboy—which doesn't come out of antifascism so much as an overwhelming disinterest. After Fellini wrote a piece about the blackouts during the air raids, De Bellis told Fellini that he was "not well liked above." Far from damaging him, that bland censorship seemed to confer a vague, emerging prestige on the young man. Aware of his contributor's political disinterest, De Bellis typically covered for him, fudging about his vices, and joking about his long hair when Fascist Party secretary Ettore Muti visited the newspaper and was being introduced to the staff of editors and writers. As each editor stood up and offered their name and column title, it became clear that this would be a bad start for Fellini. At his turn, Federico gave a Roman-style salute, clicked his heels, and cried out: "Fellini. Will you listen to what I have to say?" Muti, who'd never seen Fellini's column or its brash title, was startled and replied brusquely, "Certainly, I will hear you out, Comrade Fellini."

Destined for quick notoriety, Fellini's column "Will You Listen to What I Have to Say?" debuted July 26, 1939. It always opened with the same formula, "I'm talking to you, my round little mistress," and it closed with the same sentence followed by "but will you listen to what I have to say?" Over the year and a half that the column ran, the interlocutor changed regularly. Sometimes it was a waiter in a white shirt, or a kid from the city outskirts, a diva from a variety show, a tobacconist wearing a black apron, a handyman with an American-style mustache, and so on. Even this early column seemed to cultivate the strange fauna that would eventually populate Fellini's cinema.

Federico is quickly imitated. On December 13 a reader writes in to the letters section, "I'm speaking to you, Mr. Editor. Will you listen to what I have to say?" On another occasion the "Evil Editor" responsible for answering readers' letters in the section called "Rispondiamo a tutti" (We Have an Answer for Everyone) tells two readers from Tripoli, "Our publication is now overflowing with pleas to 'listen to what I have to say . . .' and Federico is getting a swelled head over it. He comes to the office on horseback, talks with his eyes half shut, and he's requested that his column be printed on silver paper. If you don't want to get him fired, you'll stop quoting him and send us instead some pictures of naked black women." The character of Pallina, plump mistress and archetype of Fellini's theater, appears for the first time in the column. She will go on to be renamed Bianca, after the lost love of Rimini.

As Federico moves beyond the mannered comedy of his early work, he tends to want more and more space in the paper, until he is allotted as many as three or four articles per issue—building something resembling a real diary of life in the provinces: an early *Amarcord*. In the same way that he will find common appeal through cinema, Fellini's prose drew in young readers with its confident we're-among-friends tone. From the set pieces about schoolboy pranks to the implacable self-ironizing that will characterize the psychoanalytic meanderings of 8½, themes emerge in these early writings that will be absorbed into his future work, starting with his uneasy relationship to his hometown, and his resentment toward the complacency of those he left behind. One installment of "Will You Listen . . . ?" is written for an old friend. He invents (or quotes from) an unpleasant exchange with a former schoolmate who teases him:

> So what about women? With a career like yours, who can tell? What's happening with your classes at university? You haven't abandoned them entirely, have you? After all, a degree always comes in handy . . . You're so different now. Don't you remember your old friends? When are you going to buy an automobile? How many starlets have you kissed?

The subject of friendship inspires Flaubertian pessimism in an article published on November 23, 1940, entitled "Due amici si incontrano" (Two Friends Meet). Set at the bottom of the front page with a byline, like a human-interest feature, it shows two friends who meet at the train station after two years of not seeing each other and start off reminiscing "about the good old days" and end up exchanging insults and then punches.

Meanwhile, Aldo Fabrizi has been introducing Federico to the world of variety shows and that results in an installment of "Will You Listen to What I Have to Say?" dedicated to the celebrities of variety: "There are no mothers here, just boys with their cracking voices, the technical apprentices—young men who take care of everything—and drooling old men. When the star appears on the stage, the crowd erupts, howling like beasts . . ." Another "Will You Listen . . . ?" focuses on the variety-show acrobat, the opening singer, the dancers. On November 13, 1940, Federico initiates a new column, "Il riflettore è acceso" (The Spotlight Is On), which begins with the line: "Shall we speak of the sidekicks of variety, the straight men . . ." One description that ran on January 25, 1941, depicts a scene that Federico had likely stumbled onto while visiting Fabrizi after the show in his dressing room. A friend from the market of

Campo de' Fiori, where Fabrizi once worked, comes by, and instead of being enthusiastic tries to spoil Fabrizi's success by insinuating that people in the audience are speaking poorly of him. "I even defended you," claims the friend. "I said: Shut up! Even a ruffian like him has the right to earn his bread!" Federico's vision of the theater world is already formed and very similar to what we'll see later in *Luci del varietà* and *Roma*.

August 17, 1940, marks the debut of the column with the Chaplinesque title "Luci della città" (City Lights), a series of sketches from around the city. The first piece is "At the Restaurant," followed by "Furnished Rooms," "Hotel by Day," "On a Bench," "In the Public Garden," and "Diner," to name a few. Another long-running column is entitled "Come si comporta" (How to Behave), which opens with a proposition such as "How a man behaves when going with a maid . . ." One of the last remnants of Fellini's regular print work, this column runs through 1942, and consists of observations about the behavior of men when surprised randomly in their daily life (the author himself is often the focus). Here we see the birth of a Fellini device, writing an article about an article—the way 8½ is a film about a film. The March 15, 1941, piece is a perfect example—"How to behave when you have to write this column . . ."—as is another inevitable proposition, "How to behave when you know the actors in the variety show personally . . ." or the article of January 21, 1942, "How to behave with a loan shark . . . ," yet another vice Fellini will never relinquish.

The uninhibited autobiographical nature of such public confessions is brought home by the January 24, 1942, piece in which he describes a melancholy birthday spent alone and without festivities. The article runs four days late, for the writer has in fact spent his twenty-second birthday in the big city on January 20, and discovered that solitude is ultimately the price paid for freedom.

"Secondo liceo" (Second Year, High School) was also very popular with young people. Another early version of the school days of *Amarcord,* this column began December 7, 1940, and ran in more than forty installments. The main character is Fellini and his friend Titta Benzi—the two are inseparable—along with the beloved Bianchina, and other characters from the recent past. The romance between Federico and Bianchina is even more exalted in the column "Primo amore" (First Love), where

Fellini writes about himself in the third person, referring to Federico, the character, who eventually becomes Cico. Prophetically, the title of the column changes to "Oggi sposi" (Married Now) on February 28, 1942. Through the wedding of Cico and Bianchina, Fellini foreshadows his marriage to Giulietta—whom he hasn't even met yet. In the March 28 installment, Titta arrives sheepishly in order to pay a visit to the newly-weds—his arrival closes the circle of continuity that links all of Fellini's articles into a single long ironic self-portrait.

Because of his youth, he's known around the newspaper as the *mozzo* (the kid, or gofer) and is "one of the most valued members of the weekly—the editor in chief's pet and his colleagues' favorite because he is just a pipsqueak." The young humorist's overnight success is heralded one night by the audience of a slapstick revue called *Baffi '41* which ran from February 17 to 23 at the Cinemateatro Quattro Fontane* in 1941. Each evening, the spotlight would fall onto the audience and pick out a celebrity. One evening Federico is astonished to hear his own name announced over the loudspeaker followed by thunderous applause. It was Fellini's baptism into popularity.

Marc'Aurelio pays well, but Fellini is certainly earning his keep. He has a constant supply of articles: "Raccontino in fasce" (Little Story in Bandages); "L'altro giorno" (The Other Day); "Al caffè" (At the Caffè); "La fiaba che più ti piace" (Your Favorite Fairy Tale)—a series of fairy tales in which various characters are offered a wish come true—"Notturno" (Nocturne); "Richettino bambino qualunque" (Little Rico, Regular Boy); "Scagli la prima pietra" (Toss the First Stone); "Nuvole" (Clouds); "Diciamo e pensiamo così . . . ascoltando i misteriosi rumori notturni" (We Think and Speak Like This . . . Listening to Mysterious Noises at Night), which evolves into "Di notte le cose parlano" (At Night, Things Speak); and on it goes for a number of issues. This column will become a radio series, as so much of his early journalistic activity will feed later projects.

This period at *Marc'Aurelio* is reflected in a little undated book entitled *Il mio amico Pasqualino* (My Friend, Pasqualino), signed by Federico—

---

*Le Quattro Fontane are four fountains that stand opposite each other at a crossroads in Rome's historical district. There was a theater in the area at the time, where Federico would have seen the show.

more of a seventy-four-page notebook than a book. The design on the cover has a drawing of a little man tipping his hat. There are ten chapters with a prologue and epilogue, in which Federico sketches out a portrait of Pasqualino, a character who seems unmistakably an alter ego. This project is a sort of para-literary expression of the psychoanalytic culture Fellini had already unconsciously become immersed in, with inflections of Gogol and Kafka. (Marcello Marchesi was making all his colleagues at the newspaper read *The Metamorphosis*, which had been translated into Italian a few years earlier.) Fellini's little book can be compared to that masterpiece of American humor *The Secret Life of Walter Mitty*, by James Thurber, which Danny Kaye brought to the screen.

As he begins writing more and more for the radio, and his notoriety as a screenwriter is spreading, Federico's biweekly newspaper contributions begin to diminish. Fellini's last columns—save some sporadic exceptions—run toward the end of 1942. When readers write in to the letters section to complain, the Evil Editor in the column "We Have an Answer for Everyone" replies, "No, Federico is not off on any amazing adventures. He does continue to make brief appearances at our offices—but the instant he appears the tailor who tirelessly stalks him for monies due emerges from one of his thousand hiding places, forcing Federico to make a speedy exit, disappearing like an arrow through the doors of *Marc'Aurelio* . . ." The jocular tone and the introduction of a tailor to whom Fellini owes a debt are ludicrously dated. But there's some pathetic reality in it. The "amazing adventure" is an allusion to the military draft, and the Evil Editor is actually making a veiled reference to the regular column from the Russian front written by a young humorist, Tommaso Benedetto, who is De Bellis's nephew. Benedetto's war correspondence has been running for months on the front page under the title "La più bella avventura" (The Most Amazing Adventure). On August 7, the paper runs the following note: "We have had no news of Benedetto, our brave soldier on the Russian front, since last December. Our hearts are with him, as we anxiously and faithfully await his return." The return never comes, but, in the meantime, the letters section continues to riff lightheartedly about Federico's absence. March 3, 1943: "No, Federico has not married Bianchina. She did get married, but not to him. Though the difference is slight, we feel its import nonetheless . . ."

In truth, Federico is not being pursued by creditor tailors but by draft cards. He's been of conscription age since 1939 and has mounted every ploy available to avoid serving. Where the draft is concerned, Federico's creative talents reach the apex of virtuosity—and he actually profits from the ensuing confusion around the war's acceleration and the stepped-up bombings. He engineers a series of postponements, all ruses—heart palpitations and a hyperthyroid condition (evidenced by his bulging eyes); then he floats from one military hospital to another, starting in Celio and moving to Bologna, taking advantage of dual residencies in Rome and Rimini. And just as the ruses begin to wear thin, a bomb demolishes the Bologna military record archives, leaving Fellini without documentation or ID of any sort (not even for food stamps). Taking advantage of the tumult, he disappears. Before long, things would be rectified, and the Fascist regime would fall on July 25, 1943, not far in the future.

The *Marc'Aurelio* period was happy, though the happiness masked a phase of shameless political apathy. Anyone living under the Mussolini dictatorship during its last years experienced the schizophrenic tug between official loyalty to the regime and the intrinsic freedom of humor. But the uncertain prospect of liberty makes people distressed and frightened about the future. While Federico is working regularly and in hiding, his colleague Marchesi responds to the events of the summer of 1943 by proposing the formation of a new political party: PUM (*Partito Umoristico Mondiale* or Party for a Comic World). If history unloads all of its contradictions on you, you might as well laugh about it.

5

A Dramaturge Is Born

The weeks leading up to 1941 saw a change in the programming at EIAR (Italian Radio Broadcast Corporation), which until then had been monopolized by venerable comics writing in the old-fashioned style. The new strategy envisions bringing small shows with a modern slant to the microphone, and using the talent of popular newspaper humorists for the scripts. On December 12, under the direction of Nunzio Filogamo, the variety show *Caleidoscopio* (Kaleidoscope) airs with an interlude, "Il cerino" (The Match), which is cowritten by Fellini and Ruggero Maccari. The sketch starts with one guy asking another for a match, and ends with the first guy walking off with the second guy's cigarette, as well as his holder, jacket, pants, and girlfriend. Over half a century later, speaking from a nursing home, Filogamo remembers Federico as "extroverted, always cheerful, and lively—someone who got along with people."

Soon after "Il cerino," Fellini and Maccari team up again to write a whole show, *Mancava il finale* (There Was No Ending), which is followed up almost immediately with *Il viaggio ideale* (The Perfect Journey)—a "railway drama"—on January 4, 1941.

The archives contain an interesting script entitled *Città del mondo* (City of the World) signed by Federico and Maccari. The permission slip from the censorship board is dated July 29, 1940.* The script opens at

*The author is using communications from the censorship office to date the scripts in the archive.

the Termini station in Rome with an arrival scene that prefigures a parallel scene in Fellini's *Roma* thirty years later. There is a guided bus tour of the city that goes down the prophetic via Veneto,* where our Correspondent interviews a *gagà* (trendy slang for a dandy or snob). Other stops on the route are the Terrazza del Pincio with a view of the city, the Forum, and the Colosseum. There's a sketch where Tigellinus† introduces a little number to be performed by the emperor Nero. For the grand finale "Twenty-four Lions *Twenty-four!*"‡ descend into the audience and a massacre ensues. This sophomoric script is obviously the work of twenty-year-olds, but in it we find situations and themes that will remain close to Fellini's heart and emerge in later work, such as *La dolce vita*, *Satyricon*, and *Roma*.

The *Radiocorriere* called the show, *Vuoi sognar con me?* (Do You Want to Dream with Me?), an "affirmation that dreams are the cinematographers of indigents." Populist sentiment aside, this equation—dreams equal cinema—seems to anticipate a cornerstone of Fellini's philosophy.

Filogamo also directed *Una notte cadde una stellina* (One Night a Little Star Fell), which was broadcast on May 22. A variation on the theme of falling stars and wishes, the show declares that "Dreams that become reality never make anyone happy," so it's better to be content with daily life's little pleasures. It's a moral tale worthy of Cesare Zavattini§—but also recalls Thornton Wilder's *Our Town*, the American play that touched the hearts of Italian audiences in 1940 when it ran with Elsa Merlini in the lead.

On the evening of December 25, Fellini and Maccari broadcast *La rivista sotto il tavagliolo* (The Show from Under the Napkin), a twist on the traditional hiding place for the Christmas letters children write. Fellini and Maccari were also responsible for a similarly unique show called *Intervista con una panchina del parco* (Interview with a Park

---

*Prophetic because in years to come via Veneto will be the destination of choice for Rome's artistic society and the centerpiece of *La dolce vita*.

†Gaius Ophonius Tigellinus was the praetorian prefect under Emperor Nero.

‡The syntactical form is an old-style emphasis in Italian radio broadcasting, where an impressive number was repeated before and after its object.

§A screenwriter and central figure in Italian neorealism, and the author of *Ladri di biciclette* (*The Bicycle Thief*)—the quintessential moral tale of the type that the author refers to.

Bench) about a journalist who climbs over a park gate at midnight to interview a bench. This script passed the censor on April 24, 1942.

Over the summer of 1942, Fellini's radio work takes on a personal note. This is the period generally thought of as when Fellini met Giulietta Masina—and the transposition of the Cico and Pallina characters to the airwaves. The fact is that, with the creation of the radio series *Terziglio*, Fellini begins to write alone. The brainchild of Cesare Cavallotti, a functionary from Piedmont, the innovative programming of the series features mini-plays structured as "a game for three players," whereby each week three different authors write separate but contiguous scenes on the same topic to create an hour-long show. Fellini contributes to the September 3, 1942, broadcast of *Terziglio*, built around the theme of "Una lettera d'amore" (A Love Letter). Notable here is that the script didn't pass the censors until June 10, while on June 6, Fellini published a short story in *Marc'Aurelio* practically identical to the radio script. In both, the Author (here we have the narrator as a character—so typical of Fellini's work) tells the story of a Sad Little Man: Five years earlier, the man, Roberto, was living happily in a little village and engaged to Adrianella (a transparent reference to Federico and Bianchina's love story). Roberto goes off in search of his fortune with the idea of earning money for their wedding. Since neither of the two lovers know how to read or write, every day Roberto sends Adrianella a blank sheet of paper. As time passes, he learns to write, but realizes that he's no longer in love with his old girlfriend. As time passes, he marries and has two children, but continues to send Adrianella blank sheets of paper. On her birthday, he sends two.

Fellini signs his radio plays with his full name (as opposed to the newspaper articles, which he will continue to sign "Federico"), and pours his entire poetic sensibility into the scripts, along with the vast repertory of themes and the cast of characters he has accumulated over two years of writing for newspapers. His nascent talent for dramaturgy blossoms in the radio work. The young writer has no difficulty spinning out a play a week for Cavallotti. And though Cavallotti's program provides for contributions from a variety of rotating comic writers, Federico becomes one of the most regular contributors.

The routine is always the same. Cavallotti telephones on Wednesday afternoon to give the theme for the following Monday. Because he is habitually lazy, or perhaps distracted by other commitments—to newspapers and cinema—Fellini always waits until Sunday night to put anything down on paper. Fellini is living at the time in a boardinghouse at via Nicotera 26, room 9. He frequently ends up asking Riccardo Aragno, another contributor to *Terziglio* who lives in room 5, to lend him Simpamina—an amphetamine popular among students studying for exams. Simpamina is such a vogue that in 1942 *Marc'Aurelio*—always attuned to current trends—publishes an exposé about the drug with interviews of illustrious doctors and the headline: HOW DAMAGING IS THE REGULAR USE OF PSYCHIC STIMULANTS? A bit out of sorts, Federico will stumble into the station on Monday, his script in hand, ready to withstand Cavallotti's inevitable criticism: "Nobody is going to get this." But judging by reviews in newspapers, *Terziglio* continues to be a success.

Fellini contributes to the show's second broadcast, on September 8, 1942, with a sketch called "Moglie e marito" (Wife and Husband). Pretending not to know his own contributor, Cavallotti describes the show in *Radiocorriere*: "Fellini, who must be very young, [presents] a lyrical account of two newlyweds at long last in a position to hire a cleaning lady. Cico and Pallina* are the young husband and wife that all of us dream of becoming or have once dreamed of becoming." The characters are the Author, Cico, Pallina, and Rosetta. The Author introduces the newlyweds and then remembers that we already know all about their marriage, their dismal honeymoon, and other escapades. "Maybe they got married too soon," he wonders, "maybe they are still too young to be husband and wife." There follows the scene where they meet Rosetta, their first maid. Pallina and Rosetta, who is only fifteen, joke and get to know each other, and start playing catch. Cico comes home and is stunned at first to see them on such friendly terms, but then he joins in. The short scene is slightly impertinent, in an anti-classist sense, throwing out an endorsement of spontaneity. It is an obvious criticism of how the bourgeoisie treat their domestic help. The experience of Cico and Pallina posits a new approach to an old dynamic, something less serious and more honest—without hypocrisy or authoritarianism. This is perhaps an indication

---

*These are names that will sound familiar from their adventures in the newspaper; this episode with the maid, Rosetta, is also lifted from the April 22, 1942, column "Oggi sposi."

that the social mobility initiated during the war has begun to have a permanent effect on Italian society.

Cavallotti is a little perplexed by Fellini's work, yet he admires it. After commissioning "Di notte le cose parlano" (At Night, Things Talk), Cavallotti characterizes the play in *Radiocorriere* as "fabulistic": "Really there is no proper plot, rather a series of sensations, expressed and born all in the same moment." He goes on, "In this short but serious project, Fellini most definitely channels a literary sensibility, and yet he hasn't seemed to totally liberate himself from his childlike interest in noises and onomatopoetic sounds." In truth, this fantastical radio play is a testament to Fellini's discovery of the magic in everyday life—it's the same magic that will later fill Giulietta's world of spirits. Though he is still a young man, Federico is already nostalgic for the perfect visionary enchantment of childhood.

Fellini's poetics evolved along with his mastery of new tools, and new dramatic possibilities, as evidenced by the subsequent broadcast (passed by the censors on August 27 and aired on September 24), "Camere ammobiliate" (Furnished Rooms). The story sets up not one but two rooms, the first being what parents dream about for their faraway son: the doorbell has the same ring as the one at home; the landlady who answers the door looks a lot like Mama. The similarities grow alarming when we learn that the landlady's husband has the same name as Fellini's father, Urbano, and her daughter is called Maddalena, like his own little sister. The Author finds himself standing before a perfect replica of his father, who is explaining that "A college degree is worth everything in life," while the landlady forces him to recite the Our Father with Maddalena. Young men like Federico dream of another kind of furnished room, however—something like the harem in 8½. It is located in a modern building on a central street, the doorman has seven lovely daughters, and it's the tenant's chore to keep them all happy. The friendly landlady introduces him to his fellow borders on the fifth floor, explaining: "There were men here too, but when I found out you'd be coming three days ago, all these girls suddenly wanted to move in . . . dressmakers and designers from the shops on this street, the ballet corps of the Teatro Reale, eight actresses, six singers, two artists who want to paint your portrait, three university coeds, and a Russian princess." Practically assaulted by the attentions of the gentler sex, and in a foreshadowing of *La città delle donne* (*City of Women*, 1980), the Author declares, "Full steam ahead with furnished rooms!"

"Viaggio di nozze" (Honeymoon) is aired on October 5, having passed the censor the same day. The head of the censorship board, Leopoldo Zurlo, made various cuts to the script. The little Fellini-esque skit is as usual introduced by an Author: "This is the story of the honeymoon of two newlyweds you've already met, Federico and Bianchina, also known as Cico and Pallina. These are young newlyweds—too young, perhaps— for after a year of marriage they still aren't definitively married." The unconsummated marriage sets up an unreal atmosphere, a suspended, dreamlike feeling. After a "long, long, interminable trip, standing in the aisle of a chilly train, the tired, cranky, disappointed newlyweds arrive in a strange, unfriendly city." They wander for a long time, and get to a "door in a dark, damp stairwell." A small, skinny woman answers the doorbell and agrees to rent them her son's room because he's out of town. Author: "And so the newlyweds find themselves alone in an old room with one window overlooking an unlit alley." There are sighs, tears, kissing—and the little idyll goes on until they are interrupted by the son, who suddenly arrives and throws the couple out onto the street, where a stupendous moonlit landscape rises over the pathetic gray scene. The timid, lethargic sensuality of the newlyweds juxtaposed with the coarse rented room, and the sudden violence of the angry son could even be labeled proto-Fellini. Disturbed by the unsettling proximity of these delicate fictions, Zurlo marks the script up with his thick purple pen.

Cico and Pallina star in another *Terziglio* episode, "Primo amore" (First Love), which passes the censor on October 3, 1941, and is aired on October 20. This sketch takes place before they're married—happiness is a dream of the future. Pallina wants lots of children, but Cico doesn't. They are on the brink of arguing about it one day in the park when a small child emerges from the hedges. Cico is reluctant and Pallina enthusiastic as they attempt to take care of the baby. They talk to it, she cuddles it, and Cico spends his last pennies to buy the child candy. Suddenly the nanny who lost the baby in the first place shows up, whacks the baby on the back of his head, and drags him away. Cavallotti comments: "This sketch shows Fellini in his crepuscular mode—it's so delicate and is structured more around intentions than words, told more with emotion than passion." At this point we can see the critic/producer Cavallotti joining the ranks of so many Fellini producers to come who find themselves prisoners of the author's subtle seductions.

The script for "Giochi di società" (Society Games), which passed the censor October 18 and was broadcast on November 10, tells of a party that Businessman Tagli is throwing for his 110 employees. The Author arrives bearing a "mysterious little machine that repeats your words, comments, and conversations from the distant past." Commenting on this scene Cavallotti says, "This device can be considered crepuscular, meditative—an effective way of delving into every man's intimacy, of discovering the honesty of earlier days, the hopes, dreams, and aspirations that life ruthlessly erases, little by little."

EIAR celebrates a second Christmas with Fellini on the December 25, 1942, broadcast of *Terziglio*. Cico and Pallina are set up in their "too-new house" and plan to celebrate Christmas playing a rousing board game. But Pallina invites a mendicant over, and she and her husband end up watching the stranger sleep.

The series continues in 1943, but because of paper rationing *Radio-corriere* downsizes, which affects the theater reviews. The February 20 broadcast, "Primo impiego" (First Job), is described like this: "As it opens, the Author peeks in the auditorium door. Instead of coming in he motions us to follow him out into the street. Should we obey this strange request? Of course! This is Federico Fellini, after all, we trust him not to disappoint us." And so we "drive" with Fellini out to the sublet on the periphery of Rome where Cico and Pallina live.

"Rifugio di montagna" (Mountain Retreat) ends on a magic note—and for the first time *Radiocorriere* lists the actors' names. Giulia Masina is among them. Giulietta also appears on June 19 in "Invenzioni" (Inventions). Set in the third-class waiting room of a little train station, a troupe of vagabond comedians try to get some sleep on the benches. A guardian angel appears and gives one of the dancers a most beautiful dream (you can't be more Fellini than this). In "Centenari" (Centenaries), broadcast on July 3, we can perceive traces of the ongoing polemic between writer and commentator. Cavallotti writes: "Fellini finds irritation in simple things." The last *Terziglio* that Fellini writes is "La casa nuova" (The New

House), passed by the censor on July 12 and performed on July 17. After repeatedly warning her driver and the Neapolitan handyman to be careful moving their stuff into a new apartment, it's Pallina who ends up breaking a precious mirror.

It isn't until after the war that there appears a proper radio drama entitled *Le avventure di Cicco e Pallina* (The Adventures of Cicco and Pallina)—*Cicco* gets two c's now. The drama is written by Fellini and performed by Giulietta. It's a fifteen-minute Sunday broadcast produced by a perfume company and running a number of episodes after November 1946. During this same period, while leafing through radio program guides, we find a number of Fellini productions. He is perhaps keeping busy with old ideas, reviving dead sketches while waiting for the world of cinema to completely absorb him.

6

Miss Giulia

There's something new in Moraldo's life—the something new is Andreina. He saw her almost every night. Almost without him realizing it, the evening stroll with her had become a habit. Andreina is refreshing, lively, poised. She's from a wealthy family and that shows in everything she does; she has a certain innate self-confidence, common sense, and a ready optimism. She has everything Moraldo lacks.

The hero falls in love, as recounted in the 1954 screenplay for *Moraldo in città*—a film based on a true story that never got made. It's the summer of 1943: the Allies land in Sicily on July 10 and the bombing over Rome steps up. The San Lorenzo section of the city is hit on July 19, leaving 166 dead. Mussolini is deposed on July 25, and the Badoglio government* declares Rome an "open city" (a demilitarized zone) on August 13—an ironic prelude to the brewing tragedy. Things suddenly heat up on via Nicotera when Riccardo Aragno, a frequent dinner companion and movie buddy, is arrested, taken to the Regina Coeli prison, and then to the Castelfranco Emilia penitentiary. Ever indifferent to politics, it's like Fellini fell from outer space when he learns that Aragno has been arrested and accused of collaborating with the underground group Partito d'Azione.† Aragno escapes from prison and after an adventurous journey, reappears, a wreck, at via Nicotera. He sits down at the table and passes

*The interim government under the war commander Pietro Badoglio that took over after Mussolini and negotiated the armistice with Allied forces and opened hostilities with Germany.
†Partito d'Azione (Party of Action), an anti-Fascist political party in the 1940s, was based on ideas of progressive socialism.

out. Federico has to carry his friend to bed. The bond between them will remain strong long after the war, and long after Aragno has moved to London. Later, he will be the link between Fellini and a new friend, Stanley Kubrick. Reflecting on their time together as housemates and colleagues at the radio station, Aragno observed: "Federico wanted to be a cartoonist. He was very talented. He didn't care that much about writing and he never thought about the movies at all."

The brief courtship of Federico and Giulietta plays out against this gloomy backdrop. They meet for the first time at the radio station in the autumn of 1942 and dated for nine months. Giulia Anna Masina was born in San Giorgio di Piano on February 22, 1921. Her father's family is from the Emilia region and her mother's family from the Veneto. Until the age of thirty, her father, Gaetano, worked as a professional violinist with the Ghione Orchestra, playing operas in Italy and abroad. He's a big, handsome man and even performs onstage as a Gypsy in *L'amico Fritz*. But he abandons his career in music to marry Angela Flavia Pasqualin, a teacher from San Donà del Piave who works in San Venzano di Galliera in the Bologna countryside, near San Giorgio di Piano—where the Masina family is originally from. After getting married, Gaetano goes to work at Montecatini, a local pesticide manufacturer. Giulietta is the first of four children. Her younger sister Eugenia—named after her mother's brother Eugenio Pasqualin, who married into a wealthy family from Lombardy—is born in 1922. Giulietta's uncle and his wife, Giulia Sardi, live in a lovely apartment in Rome, on the parlor floor of via Lutezia, at the intersection of viale Liegi near Piazza Ungheria. The couple love art, music, and the theater. They circulate in an intellectual crowd, going to openings at La Scala, and traveling to Milan, London, and Paris. Giulietta stays with them for a few months in 1925. Although she's only four years old at the time, her aunt and uncle take her to the theater, and during the intermission Eugenio takes her backstage to meet a very famous man, Luigi Pirandello. Uncle Eugenio dies just a few years later, at the age of forty-six, leaving his wife desolate. Because she dearly loves her young niece, the widow proposes that Giulietta come live with her to keep her company, and the family agrees.

Aunt Giulia is an extraordinary figure in Giulietta's life—she's attractive, slender, and exuberant, and with her Lombardy accent, strongly resembles the popular comic actress Dina Galli. An independent thinker, Aunt Giulia decides not to send her niece to elementary school, and Giulietta keeps up her education by studying at home with her mother during the summer, and in so doing manages to pass all of her state exams. When the time comes for middle school, Giulia sends her to the private school Orsoline. It's a progressive institution that, aside from its name, has little in common with the grim religious school depicted in *Giulietta degli spiriti* (*Juliet of the Spirits*, 1965). Giulietta remains at the school for the next eight years and discovers her interest in theater there while participating in school productions.

As a young woman, Giulietta studies singing in the contralto range, but she doesn't have a robust enough voice to be a professional singer. Her stature is an obstacle on the piano as well; her fingers are too small for the keyboard. She runs into similar challenges in classical dance. Her artistic education thus leads naturally to acting. Her last performance at Orsoline in Carlo Goldoni's *La famiglia dell'antiquario* (*The Antiquarian's Family*) is a huge success. Once at university, where she's studying modern literature, Giulietta is attracted by an announcement for the Teatro GUF (Gruppo Universario Fascista, the Fascist theater troupe, which, despite the name, has no political affiliations) and she goes for an audition. Some of the top people in youth theater of the time are involved: Enrico Fulchignoni, Gerardo Guerrieri, Ruggero Jacobbi, and Turi Vasile. At the audition, the young actress performs a scene from *La famiglia dell'antiquario* and a single last line from Luigi Pirandello's *Vestire gli ignudi* (*To Clothe the Naked*), and is immediately invited to join the Studium Urbis, the university theater, which after the war is renamed Teatro Ateneo.

It's an amateur group, entirely unpaid and fueled by enthusiasm. They rehearse for two or three months at a time for a three-day run. Giulietta debuts in a program of three one-acts: Thornton Wilder's *Happy Journey*, Rabindranath Tagore's *L'ufficio postale* (*The Post Office*), and Pirandello's *All'uscita* (*The Way Out*). Giulietta plays a middle-aged mother in *Happy Journey*; she's a fourteen-year-old boy in the second play, and a prostitute in the third. Masina was a boyish girl at the time; she only weighed about ninety-three pounds, and enjoyed these metamorphoses. Her eccentric triptych debut is a hit with the audience. During the 1941 theater season, her name appears on posters for plays by Plautus and

Ludwig Tieck. Among other roles in 1942, Giulia performs in *Le trombe d'Eustachio* (*Eustachio's Trumpets*) by Vitaliano Brancati, an emerging writer from Catania. After a nervous breakdown, Brancati returns to Sicily for treatment and offers the young actress his position teaching literature at the Liceo Margherita di Savoia. She stays there for three months but, quickly realizing that teaching isn't for her, continues acting, going from the university group to the Teatro delle Arti, and then to the Argentina and on to the Quirino.

When Silvio d'Amico, one of the most important critics of the day, is amazed to learn that Masina doesn't have a theater background, he encourages her to enroll at the Accademia d'Arte Drammatica, where he is president. The playwright Gherardo Gherardi, then counselor at the Teatro Eliseo, has also offered the up-and-coming actress an attractive contract. But Aunt Giulia digs in her heels—Giulietta is free to have as much fun as she likes playing in the theater, but she must get a university degree (which Giulietta will eventually do, after much delay, in 1945 with a thesis on Christian archaeology). In the meantime, frustrated at not being able to take advantage of the many opportunities being presented her, Giulietta forges on in her somewhat unstructured acting career. For a time, she performs in live musical-comedy radio broadcasts with EIAR, acting and singing in a number of variety shows and operettas. She occasionally works with the dramatic company of the EIAR, but enjoys the variety shows more—and she particularly loves working on the show *Terziglio*, where she performs in the adventures of Cico and Pallina, written by Federico. Giulietta is practical, and likes the fact that she earns a handsome fee for her radio work, whereas theater never pays well. And of course the fame counts for something too. Radio is a booming business and comedy reviews have a broad and devoted public.

When Fellini appears in Cesare Cavallotti's office one fall day in 1942 he doesn't make much of an impression on the young actress who's there meeting with the boss. She shakes hands with the tall, thin, quiet young man, and that's the end of that. Later on, Federico phones her to ask for a head shot—or maybe that's just an excuse. He's working with the ACI (Alleanza Cinematografica Italiana)—Vittorio Mussolini's (son of Il Duce) film company—on the movie *Ogni giorno è domenica* (*Every Day Is Sunday*), and there may be a role for her as a young newlywed. He calls her "the Duse of the University Theater"—after the celebrated stage actress Eleanora Duse. This is the beginning of a very short courtship and a very long marriage. It's a classic movie meeting; there's an offhand request for a photo for a role in a film that will eventually be shot (without either Giulietta or Federico's name attached to it) two years later in the halls of the Venice Biennale, which were used as a movie studio during the Mussolini republic.

They agree to meet at 1:30 p.m. on via delle Botteghe Oscure outside EIAR. Though she's accepted the invitation to lunch with "the movie guy," Giulietta certainly can't let her aunt know—so she eats at home, then rushes to the date, and eats again with Federico at a restaurant in Piazza Poli, next to the statue of Triton. It's a very luxurious restaurant, and Giulietta worries that her date has made a mistake, brought her to the wrong restaurant, and won't have enough money to pay. But when the check comes, Federico casually pulls a hefty wad of cash from his pocket. Later, Giulietta will tease him and claim that she never again saw Federico with that much money in his pocket. At the time, in Rome only a year, Fellini is already earning a lot of money writing for papers, radio, and the movies. His wife-to-be described him as a lanky (even emaciated) young man with long hair and sparkly eyes, charming and funny. Friends from that period remember the new couple as steady and forthright. They didn't engage in any games—on again, off again—or inhibitions. They saw each other and chose each other, once and forever.

Vasile, a manager of the Teatro GUF, recalls Federico "sitting all alone in the audience watching the rehearsals. It was sweet; we could all feel that Giulietta was acting for him, she was flattered by his attentions, which he was sly about. Giulietta thought she was ugly—she was very upset one day and told me that. But she cut a lovely figure. She never would have imagined that she could be the focus of such devoted attention."

From the beginning it seemed like the differences between the two were greater than the similarities. They came from such different places, had different educations and different approaches to life. Next to Federico, who has no idea where he's headed and is totally unconcerned about it, Giulietta is a phenomenon of determination. In a way, she has exactly the same middle-class values that young Fellini worked so hard to reject through his trail of (real or imaginary) escapes. But he's strangely attracted to these qualities in a potential partner for life. Worn out by the carousel of furnished rooms and boardinghouses, the young man finds a safe harbor at Aunt Giulia's tidy home on via Lutezia. And though he is somewhat put off when Giulietta lectures him about getting a life strategy, Federico feels sheltered by her. He doesn't give up flirting with other women, but he does it with a sense of security that Giulietta is beside him. Fellini's bohemian friends are initially surprised that he's fallen for a woman so physically different from the flashy, voluptuous girls he'd always been attracted to—the kind of girl known in Roman argot as *bona*, later to be known as the "Fellini type." But Federico says that Giulietta's elfin aura cheers him up. On the one hand, he's critically aware of the fact that he's found a strong woman who will support him; on the other hand, the romance could be seen as a surreal relationship that he fabricated with a character sprung to life from the pages of a fairy tale. In fact, they bring out in each other a whole series of childlike aspects; and whether consciously or not, throughout their life together, both will continue to feel as if he or she is the son or daughter of the other. Later on, they'll also discover a great bond with regard to work: they're both tireless perfectionists, ready to sacrifice in order to deliver their very best. The union on the artistic level will be indissoluble. More than forty years will pass between *Terziglio* and *Ginger e Fred*.

Returning to their first encounter, we must keep in mind what an uncertain period of history this was. In 1943, young people may have felt an urgent need to build a relationship, form bonds with the world around them. Many people in their twenties decided to marry during that period, sometimes before heading off to war. Rinaldo Geleng marries on June 6, 1943, in the church of San Sebastianello to a fellow student from the academy. The Fellini brothers are among the guests. Federico draws the invitations. Riccardo sings Schubert's *Ave Maria* and everything more or less proceeds like the wedding scene in *I vitelloni*. To cap it off, an emotional Federico seals the ritual with the sly remark "Rinaldo, this is the end . . ." In fact, many things are to end that fateful summer of the armistice. But other things begin. The first son born from that marriage, Giuliano Geleng, will be a painter like his father and thirty years later will create the famous *Amarcord* poster with all the characters lined up in a row. The second son, Antonello, will be a set designer and a frequent collaborator with his father's friend.

7

Za's Little Slave

It's not just Fellini; all screenwriters' stories are difficult to tell. But between reticence and contradictions, Fellini always managed to obfuscate any clear identification to himself in his films. He often denied that he was involved in projects that we now know he definitely participated in, while in other instances he'd invent autobiographical tales he was unlikely to have ever lived. Of course, throughout history and into the present (and not just in Italy), the attribution of a screenplay is a complicated matter. The number of people's hands through which a single script may pass is not an insignificant consideration. Some writers work alone, others with a partner; some (a scant few) write, and others only talk; there are writers who get their name in the credits and others who don't—not that they necessarily work any less.

Cesare Zavattini wrote: "Cinema is a collaboration where everyone tries to erase everyone else's work." As for Fellini the screenwriter (at least during the war years), the opposite is true. He tended to erase his own work, or at least minimize its importance. The only reason he wrote for movies was because it paid more than writing for the newspapers or the radio. But his contributions began and ended on the page: he never visualized scenes and when working with others he'd put a lot of ideas out onto the table—and was never terribly concerned about whether they ever made it into the movie. Yet Fellini worked almost exclusively as a screenwriter in the decade after 1942, over time allowing himself to become involved in production as an assistant director in addition to collaborating on art direction on occasion. As the journalism and radio writing gradually fell away—eventually tapering off altogether in 1947—he steadily gained a real profile in the movie industry. Filmographies attribute twenty titles to him, half of them before the Liberation. Undoubtedly he also worked on a number of screenplays that were either never produced or became movies much later. It was in fact in his capacity as screenwriter that he won his first Oscar nomination for *Roma, città aperta* (*Open City*) in 1946, and then again in 1949 for *Paisà* (*Paisan*).

The traditional story of how Fellini first came to the cinema starts when humor writers from the staff of *Marc'Aurelio* were recruited to work on movies for the Piedmont comedian Erminio Macario under the direction of Mario Mattoli, a master of the *spettacolo leggero* (or farce). Federico is *not* one of the ten writers who worked on the script of *Imputato alzatevi* (*Accused, Please Stand*), which was released in October 1939. A full-page interview with these functionaries of hilarity ran on May 27 in the weekly *CineMagazzino,* which Fellini briefly wrote for, contributing short stories and articles often signed "Fellas." In the interview Marcello Marchesi explains why so many writers were called in for just one screenplay: the goal was to come up with gags that "may not specifically drive the plot of the movie, but that make it more fun to watch, and funny— and have the attitude of a cartoon." This is the environment in which Fellini's emerging talent began to develop, and a partial explanation of his continuing predilection for the short form, not to mention the signature layout of his films, which often seems to reference a journalistic structure.

Some filmographies list young Fellini as a gag writer on two movies starring Macario and directed by Mattoli, *Lo vedi come sei?* (*You See What You're Like?*, 1939) and *Non me lo dire* (*Don't Tell Me*, 1940). This is how Fellini used to tell it: "One day, I was working at *Marc'Aurelio*, and the director Mattoli came in. Everyone said that he earned mountains of money. He had a script that had been written for Macario, and maybe he'd read somewhere that they did this in Hollywood, but he wanted us writers to read the screenplay and spice it up, and that's how I started writing for the movies. I wasn't working in film yet; I basically did the same thing for Mattoli that I did for the paper—found jokes, made up scenes, developed ideas . . ." (Perhaps the movie *Il pirata sono io* [*I'm the Pirate*, 1940], for which he was paid 1,000 lire, represents Fellini's real start as a gag writer. Ennio Flaiano, the critic for *Cineillustrato*, described the movie as "a fantastic adventure set in Emilio Salgari's landscape." Salgari* was Federico's favorite writer as a teenager.) Macario liked to recall how pleased he was with the kid from Rimini's input; he wanted the producers to pay him more, and when anyone protested, he would answer, "Fellini is twice as good, even three times as good, as the others."

Talking about his early work in the movies, Fellini would explain that he'd started out as a "little slave"—a behind-the-scenes collaborator—to Cesare Zavattini, aka "Za," who had enough work to fuel a bustling screenplay factory, one that would continue to attract the best young minds for the next thirty years. At the time when Fellini made his first forays into the world of cinema, Zavattini was a critical figure. A longtime newspaper and magazine contributor with two books, *Parliamo tanto di me* (We Talk a Lot About Me) and *I poveri sono matti* (Poor People Are Crazy), Zavattini had invented a new brand of humor: uninhibited, open-minded, surrealist journeys, with a marked sensitivity to place of origin and local social phenomena (he came from a farming community in Emilia-Romagna himself). Starting around 1940, Zavattini brought a thrilling new approach to a national cinema that had paled in the shadow of the American film industry. We don't know much about young Fellini's relationship with Za. Certainly, the eighteen-year difference in age and Za's considerable fame would have put Zavattini in the role of master, employer, even father figure. And perhaps that's why Federico didn't linger in Zavattini's nest for long—but rather experienced him as a sort of education, a film school with no schedules or lesson plans, no exams, and no diplomas. While in Zavattini's circle, Fellini met Piero Tellini, son of the famous opera singer Ines Alfani Tellini, whom Fellini admired. Three years older than Fellini and a former student of the Centro Sperimentale, Tellini had already gained a reputation as a screenwriter. He worked on the script for *Quattro passi fra le nuvole* (*Four Steps in the Clouds*, 1942), into which he'd incorporated a number of Fellini's suggestions. The two work together occasionally, although they are not always both credited. But the real story of Fellini as a screenwriter doesn't actually begin in the world of cinema; it all starts with variety shows and his encounter with one of the most popular comedians of his day, Aldo Fabrizi.

*Emilio Salgari (1862–1911) was the most popular adventure writer in Italy.

8

A Modern Comedian

What was an Aldo Fabrizi show like? Back when Fellini first met him, the press was hailing Fabrizi as "the modern comedian." Ennio Flaiano describes a typical show:

> It would start with music, mostly wind instruments. Fabrizi would come onstage, wearing tails and a fedora, and he'd launch right into a routine. His connection with people in the audience was almost instantaneous; they got his language, recognized it from the funny pages, and sympathized with his easygoing morality. After the show the public would cry out for encores—favorite jokes and biting witticisms. When it got late, Fabrizi would have the orchestra play galloping music, to signal the end.

Flaiano's article ran on June 3, 1939. During this same period Fellini officially came into the world of variety by paying a formal visit to Fabrizi backstage between shows at the Corso Cinema. Fellini and Ruggero Maccari were working on an article to be published in *CineMagazzino* (June 18, 1939) under the title *"Che cos'è l'avanspettacolo?"** (What Is

*The term *avanspettacolo*, literally "preshow," is quite specific to Fascist Italy of the late 1920s and early 1930s. In the broadest sense, it is a kind of variety show, or low-rent musical-comedy review; and the term is more or less interchangeable with *variety* for the purposes of imagining what the show itself would be like. But formally speaking, it is an even poorer form of variety—as, desperate for both venues and gigs, small variety troupes would mount their forty-five- to sixty-minute reviews in third-run movie theaters, playing between screenings; the propaganda films were a little portion of the general showing, mostly reserved to Hollywood movies. As the title of Fellini's 1939 article suggests, the meaning of the term is not exactly fixed in stone.

Avanspettacolo?). There's no byline on the feature article, which includes eleven half-invented interviews, but Fellini's style is unmistakable—and that's not even taking into account the fact that, among the accompanying illustrations, there's a wonderful drawing of Totò* signed by Fellas.

> We bribed the ushers, paid off the doormen, flattered the coat-check attendants, seduced the dancers and chorus with promises of a splashy article—and that's how we've worked our way onto the stage of every theater in Rome. There in the wings, between a comedy routine and a dance number, while the audience is clapping and the stage manager is hollering for us to get out of the way, we ask eleven men and women to tell us how they would describe *avanspettacolo*.

The answers, written, or at least edited, by the interviewers (though signed by the interviewees) offer opinions that seem highly defensive and reveal a great deal of regret over the lack of attention from critics for their art form. Fabrizi in particular complains that the press ignores him and proposes that the best newspapers should run variety-show reviews on the front page.

With his comic characters, Fabrizi was a big favorite among Roman audiences. He'd already worked in radio and even recorded discs. He was born in Rome at the turn of the century. His father died when he was young and Fabrizi dropped out of elementary school in order to earn money to support his mother and five sisters. He had the fierce temper of an autodidact and a lively approach to writing. He came onto the variety scene with a host of silly characters and songs. His debut at Corso Cinema in Piazza San Lorenzo in Lucina was almost accidental, but he went on to develop a whole cast for himself of typical Roman characters—truck driver, street vendor, guard, and so forth—for whom he would create reflective monologues about life. Fabrizi toured this one-man pageant throughout Italy and even brought the show to Broadway, though after a certain point he would come onstage for guest appearances only at the end of a show, in order to perform one of his incomparable monologues on the state of the world.

---

*Totò (1898–1967) was Italy's most popular comic actor ever, and a vanguard of *avanspettacolo*.

Proud of his two young journalist friends, Fabrizi would spend long evenings after the show in their company at Caffè Castellino in Piazza Venezia, where all the artists gathered. From there, Aldo and Federico would walk home together under the barely lit Roman sky (streetlamps were darkened to blue for the air raids) toward their neighborhood, which lay just beyond the San Giovanni wall. The comedian lived at via Sannio 37—an address that had him convinced he would die at thirty-seven. They'd chat as they walked, and often just strolled aimlessly. In the preface to Flaiano's book, *Lettere a Lilli e altri segni* (Letters to Lilli and Other Signs), Giuliano Briganti wrote:

> Perhaps in order to possess Rome in a literary sense, one needed to walk through it at night, cross the empty streets, see the last people hurrying home, past the darkened windows, the noises from the bars and nightclubs as they shut down. This is the heart of the ritual—wandering for hours at night, trying to "capture" the city, to discover its secret places and become a part of its atmosphere, to feel Roman at last, to possess the eternal sensation that lingered long after the last bar closed.

Sometimes Fellini and Maccari were invited by the actor to eat with his family; and Fabrizi would in turn go to the Fellini household on via Albalonga. A photo of Federico dating from this period is signed: *"To a father, companion, brother, and friend, Aldo Fabrizi, with great admiration and friendship."* When the actor's son, Massimo, celebrates his first communion and confirmation, young Fellini is named his godfather, and when Fabrizi goes for a cure at the Fiuggi springs, Ruggero and Federico visit. A group picture from that trip that Fabrizi sends to Maccari reads: *"If water were wine, you would have never left."*

A less probable tale from this period has Fellini traveling the provinces as "company poet" with a show called *Faville d'amor* (Sparks of Love)—also the title of Checco Dal Monte's show in *Luci del varietà*. There's no evidence that Fellini ever appeared on a rural stage as the second to the principal comedian (or *capocomico*), although Maccari did have this adventure, under the alias Rino Riccama, when he happened to be in the south of Italy toward the end of the war—an experience he recounted in the screenplay for Alberto Sordi's 1973 movie *Polvere di stelle* (*Stardust*). In a letter dated February 1, 1962, from Fabrizi to Fellini's first biographer, Angelo Solmi, the comedian explains,

> I never heard of this *Faville d'amor*, which according to Fellini played for peasant audiences and performed shows full of slapstick and put-ons—where Fellini was the poet, set designer, actor, and backdrop painter, and where six out of eight of the dancing girls would engage in boisterous arguments over his affections . . . It's just a coarse, random invention. As were the jerry-building, the shoddy accommodations, the midnight arrivals and dawn departures. As far as I know, Fellini became famous without ever leaving Rome.

It is true, however, that Fabrizi used material that Fellini and Maccari gave him in the routines that begin with the line "Have you ever noticed . . . ?"

During the same period, working off material they were writing for the newspapers, Federico and Ruggero sold material to other comics as well—Fanfulla and Erminio Macario among them. The two writers either negotiated directly with Rome-based troupes or, for others, worked through an agency in Milan run by the Neapolitan lawyer Giulio Trevisani (who will later redeem himself as a theater critic for the daily newspaper *l'Unità*). The procedure was standard: the actor would pay cash for material and then register the rights to the sketch under his own name, taking the copyright. This was a typical arrangement in the world of variety, giving head comics and agents a way to bump up their income at a writer's expense. It was a small-time racket that writers put up with because theater supposedly paid better than print. The fee was always agreed upon ahead of time, but it wasn't always something that the writers could bank on. The painter Rinaldo Geleng remembers accompanying Federico to Milan—by train, without tickets, so they had to hide in the restroom the whole trip—in order to try and collect on money that Trevisani owed him.

The war years took a toll on stage shows, however. A feature article in *Marc'Aurelio*, January 29, 1941, ran with the title "Why is the sun setting on variety?," a much more pessimistic piece than a similar one from *CineMagazzino* two years earlier. Macario, who was interviewed for the former article, actually located the origin of the crisis ten years earlier: "Variety lost its footing after cinema got sound." Cinema was growing by leaps and bounds, and there was no one standing on the bedraggled front lines of variety who could cross over.

"Full steam ahead on *Avanti c'è posto . . .* [*Go Ahead, There Are Free Seats*]" ran an article in *CineMagazzino* on June 18, 1942. The film starred Aldo Fabrizi, who, according to the article, "made a name for himself bringing everyday characters to the stage." Fabrizi wanted Fellini—who insisted that he and Cesare Zavattini came up with the story idea together—on his project, and before long, the young man would be known in the press as "Fabrizi's renowned screenwriter." Fellini signed a contract with Giuseppe Amato, the producer, whom he would meet again twenty years later on *La dolce vita*. He's listed in the credits as Federico, coming right after Fabrizi and before Zavattini and Piero Tellini. *CineMagazzino* confirms that "the plot is based on an idea of Fabrizi's, who then wrote the treatment and screenplay in collaboration with two popular humor writers, Federico and Zavattini, and the director Mario Bonnard."

It's a scrap of a movie, only eighty-five minutes long, and the somber winds of war ripple throughout. The story: Cesare (Fabrizi) is a ticket collector on a bus who is competing with the driver, Bruno (Andrea Checchi), for the love of Rosella (Adriana Benetti), a naïve waitress who's been mugged on the bus. In the end, Bruno, who's managed to win Rosella's heart, enlists in the army, leaving the loser in the contest for her affections, Cesare, to take Rosella on a mad dash to the train station where the troops are embarking for Africa. Part father and part lover—often seen as a Don Juan in his role as protector—Fabrizi has a ribald brashness, which he will later come to temper. The melodrama of variety in the film occasionally emerges as sarcasm, revealing more than anything the schizophrenia of an Italy trying to find itself somewhere between romantic comedy and the impending disaster of war.

Avanti c'è posto . . . is a huge success when it's released in September 1942 and the critical response is nothing less than explosive—in a September 25 review in *Cinema* an anonymous editor writes that the movie is "an insult to the truth," adding that "Fabrizi is offensive, revealing his miserably limited, lower-middle-class vision . . . His appearance is unpleasant . . . His talent is negligible, as is his acting experience. In the most dire sense he's unrivaled in his negative virtues . . . His philosophizing is stomach turning . . ." This harsh criticism will show up in the October 25 edition, where another contributor, Mestolo (aka Massimo Mida Puccini), takes issue with Volpone, who had written in the newspaper *Bertoldo* (October 2):

> This small film's merit lies in the fact that it's a true story, not *true* in the objective sense, which doesn't exist, but rather true to psychology and the punctilious observation of little things, the truths that surround us, which are really quite essential to these tales about nothing . . . It's interesting that Bonnard, working closely with two intellectual writers and a veteran of variety, has made the best movie of his career . . . When you think about it, *this* should be our new approach to cinema.

Mestolo counterattacks by saying that Volpone's words "offended us in the most violent of ways," repeating, "He really demonstrates not only a lack of understanding about filmmaking but also a total lack of critical sensibility and taste." It was Mestolo, however, who got it wrong, because Volpone, whose real name was Pietro Bianchi, was a master of criticism and also perfectly captured the essence and novelty of the movie.

The reception of Fabrizi's second movie, *Campo de' Fiori* (*Peddler and the Lady*, which came out in the fateful July of 1943) in *Cinema*, by the magazine's principal critic Giuseppe De Santis, is equally harsh. De Santis, soon-to-be director of *Riso amaro* (*Bitter Rice*, 1949), criticizes Fabrizi, "who had gained success and made an exorbitant amount of money from *Avanti c'è posto* . . . , but still purportedly wanted to be paid more than a million lire for *Campo de' Fiori*," despite the fact that he "doesn't deserve to be called an actor." Roiling with the outsizedness of the overpaid actor, the movie is "an offense to common sense," and plunders the "streets of lies," propagating a "black market atmosphere."

Such disparate criticisms reveal the variety of positions that will lead to a deep division in Italian cinema, even after the Liberation. *Cinema*, with its crypto-Communist intellectualism, favors films such as Luchino

Visconti's 1943 debut, *Ossessione* (*Obsession*), while disparaging the traces of variety and popular journalism that are being transposed into cinema. Even at the time of the release of *Avanti c'è posto . . .* , there is an embryonic split among the ranks, pitting Fellini and Visconti against each other, a rivalry that will continue into the 1950s. These respective aesthetic ideas are beginning to gain ground according to a perfectly coherent logic of choices and omissions, and, against this background, Fellini's anti-intellectual approach is clearly delineated: he is an accomplice to the reviled Aldo Fabrizi. Further, as a humorist, Fellini distinguishes himself from many of his peers who are already either writing for cinema or about to do so. Though he contributes to many magazines and newspapers, Fellini never publishes reviews or essays or opinion pieces à la Volpone or Mestolo. Even his rare interviews seem to be impressionistic digressions about encounters with various characters more than they are "intellectual" journalism—as a journalist he is practically a creative writer. His pieces could best be described as "memory tales," free-form accounts of things seen, or philosophical tirades.

Fellini's collaboration with Fabrizi constitutes the core of his work in film until the Liberation and, to a certain extent, beyond that. When Roberto Rossellini seeks Fellini out to work on *Roma, città aperta*, it is because he's trying to find a way to get to the popular comedian Fabrizi. For *Campo de' Fiori*, which was produced by Amato, Fellini appears in the credits as a screenwriter alongside Fabrizi and Tellini.

In the film, Fabrizi plays a fishmonger. Anna Magnani is a fruit vendor who has the adjacent stall in the market at Campo de' Fiori, and she is in love with him. But Fabrizi falls instead for Elsa, played by Caterina Boratto, an elegant lady who is leading a double life. Betrayed in the end by his own lofty dreams, Fabrizi's character casts himself in fantastic adventure stories, which he recounts to the barber, played by Peppino De Filippo, and then stumbles into a real misadventure of his own. This film is a rich artifact because of what it portends. On one hand, it introduces Magnani and Fabrizi as a couple; they will appear opposite each other again in *Roma, città aperta*. On the other hand, the film debuts the irresistible double act of Fabrizi and De Filippo, destined as a team to become a pillar of Italian comedy. Traces of Fellini are evident in their witty repartee and there is also something Fellini-esque in the portrait of the underworld of cardplayers and grifters who will reappear in *Il bidone* (*The Swindle*). It is certainly worth recognizing that Boratto will return in all of her splendid maturity as the epitome of feminine beauty in 8½. But for the moment, *Campo de' Fiori* is an occasion for the future director to make important contacts. He meets Magnani, who he will come to know better working under Rossellini, and De Filippo, who is one of his favorite comics and the future protagonist of *Luci del varietà* and *Le tentazioni del dottor Antonio*. In this group of character actors animating Fabrizi's movies, we find a sort of incubator for Fellini's cinema.

The third movie of the trilogy, *L'ultima carrozzella* (*The Last Wagon*), will be directed by Mario Mattoli. (Fellini and Mattoli had already met while working with Macario on *Avanti c'è posto . . .*) During this film the relationship between the charismatic Fabrizi and his literary sidekick Fellini grows more intimate and increasingly exclusive. In fact, Fabrizi alone is credited for the story idea as well as for the screenplay along with Fellini.

Fabrizi, who actually got a driver's license in 1925, is fully plausible as one of the last horse-drawn gurney drivers who refuses to be ruined by the invasion of taxis. The story, set among sporadic war references, goes like this: The hero meets Anna Magnani's character, a café singer, when he drives her to the train station. But she forgets her suitcase with a diamond in it (a present from an admirer) on his carriage. When Aldo returns the suitcase to her, hoping to receive the 500-lire reward he's read about in a newspaper ad, Anna accuses him of substituting a paste diamond for the real one. There is friction between the two characters onscreen and between the two actors off screen (their relationship was fated to degenerate even further during *Roma, città aperta*—where the personal conflict could be felt on the set). After a burlesque trial Fabrizi's character is acquitted of fraud and set free. As the movie ends, Fabrizi sits high on his carriage—now a man of means—and orders the horse to take him home. This is the point in the movie where Fellini had suggested that they have the horse talk—it's an episode that Aldo Fabrizi will frequently recall as proof positive that Fellini was a madman.

The movie came out in December 1943 and Italian audiences were divided. Despite the critical praise for a "slick screenplay," the movie doesn't really do anything for Fellini's career, although while on the set

Fellini does meet assistant editor Leo Catozzo, who would go on to edit many of his films. Catozzo was also the inventor of the ingenious Catozzo presser, which transformed the editing process in the early 1960s, eliminating acetone and introducing the use of Scotch tape.

The harmony between Fellini and Fabrizi would last for another three or four years. They announced a number of new collaborations. Fellini was offered the opportunity to codirect a new film in Argentina, *Emigrantes (Immigrants)*, with Fabrizi. But he turned it down because he'd already made other commitments and wasn't entirely convinced about the project and because he was beginning to cultivate a reluctance to leave Rome (an attitude that over time became second nature). In the summer of 1948, Fabrizi set off alone for South America.

The best work to come out of the Fellini-Fabrizi collaboration during the postwar period is *Il delitto di Giovanni Episcopo (Flesh Will Surrender)*, directed by Alberto Lattuada. In order to pin down the exact date of the production, winter 1946–47, we need only to look at the scene in which Fabrizi is seen shoveling snow in a completely blanketed San Peter's Square in Rome—an extraordinary event of nature that the production didn't hesitate to take advantage of. The story is a screen adaptation of Gabriele d'Annunzio's novella *Giovanni Episcopo*, which Fabrizi loved, bought the film rights for, and brought to producer Carlo Ponti at Lux Film. At this time Fabrizi was one of the biggest celebrities in Italian cinema—he even had international recognition—but he wanted an ally in his dealings with the director, and so he told Alberto Lattuada that he would be sending over "a special person" to help, adding, "He has two heads."

The two-headed writer doesn't have far to walk. From via Lutezia, he just crosses viale Liegi in order to get to the ground-floor apartment at via Paganini 7, where Lattuada lives with his wife, Carla Del Poggio.

By June of 1946, Lattuada, a native of Lombardy, was already a successful director. His movie *Il bandito (The Bandit)*—stylistically somewhere between neorealism and melodrama—had been hugely successful, whereas his first movie, *Giacomo l'idealista (Giacomo the Idealist)*, based on Emilio De Marchi's novel of the same name, instead had been more *calligrafico*—formal, observant. After graduating with a degree in architecture from the polytechnic in Milan, Lattuada had gone on to participate in the founding of the Cineteca Italiana.* He'd worked for Mario Soldati on *Piccolo mondo antico* (*Old-Fashioned World*, 1941), who reported that, "Alberto is an unreconstructed fussbudget." But really he was just a young man, born in 1914, who'd quickly mastered the art of leadership on the movie set.

There was nothing to suggest that Fellini and Lattuada would ever get along. Alberto came from a culturally refined background, and had a formal education. He came to cinema through photography, a passion that was wholly alien to Fellini, who'd never taken a picture of anything his entire life. Lattuada was also a cinephile. While meditating on the *Giovanni Episcopo* project, he'd been consumed by the emotional experience of watching Orson Welles's *The Magnificent Ambersons*, which of course Fellini hadn't seen.

Surprisingly the two men quickly open up to each other. Out of the sixty-page d'Annunzio story—a clever Dostoevsky imitation published in 1891—Fellini and Lattuada fashion a liberal and inventive twenty-page treatment. The problem is that Fabrizi, who commissioned the project, doesn't like it, and doesn't pass up the opportunity to expound on the value of the concrete to his collaborators. As far as Fabrizi is concerned, their treatment might as well include a talking horse. So he gets Suso Cecchi d'Amico and Piero Tellini on board to help with the screenplay. Tellini tries to avoid the project because Lattuada has a reputation as a slave driver, keeping long hours and scheduling all-nighters in front of the typewriter. Fellini, on the other hand, is oddly inspired by this strict discipline. He seems to think of it as if it were a new kind of game. He enjoys working all night, and he also takes delight, as dawn hits, in extricating the extraordinary admission from Lattuada: "I'm really tired."

Perhaps the hallucinatory atmosphere of d'Annunzio's *Il delitto di Giovanni Episcopo* resonated with those sleepless nights on via Paganini. The novella is a first-person account of a humble office worker who is locked in a duel with a rough, ignorant character named Wanzer. Lack of judgment led Episcopo to marry a beautiful waitress who worked at a cheap hotel, and he is outraged when Wanzer returns from Argentina (whence he'd fled) to steal his wife. This is the outrage that breaks the camel's back and Episcopo takes revenge by murdering his rival. Federico

*Cineteca Italiana is the Milan film archive.

is less than reverential to the original and makes the story his own. Epi-scopo is a little man who spends his life going back and forth between the office and his furnished room. He is "struck down" by a sexpot—the representation of the eternal feminine. Elements in the film that in retro-spect herald Fellini's poetics are a noisy and debauched New Year's cele-bration, the Trevi Fountain, and Alberto Sordi with a pool stick in hand as he will appear again in *I vitelloni*. Fellini's collaboration with Fabrizi has given him a taste for characters on the edge of things. Lattuada has a unique talent for shooting Roman nights and fog and for depicting the archive office where Episcopo works (a real office in San Michele's hos-pice), as well as for portraying the clerk's attraction to the world of *café-chantant*—mimicking the morbid atmosphere of Josef von Sternberg's *Blue Angel*. As for Fabrizi's highly restrained performance, critics will in fact remark upon his similarity to Emil Jannings in the role of Professor Rath—Lola Lola's (Marlene Dietrich) lover in *Blue Angel*.

And yet there are always battles on the set. As coproducer, Fabrizi challenges the director's artistic needs. Lattuada, unruffled, sends the ac-tor rowing to lose weight and simply ignores his opposition to the casting of Greek actress Yvonne Sanson—a woman who the director describes as a "monument to flesh." Alberto Sordi plays a shady part in the movie and, assisted by his friend Fellini's screenplay, begins developing what will be-come his signature role: the insolent troublemaker. Fabrizi had harbored reservations about Sordi ever since he'd seen him impersonating a Ro-man soldier in a variety show, and Fellini recalls how irritated Fabrizi was at his co-actor's brash efforts to get noticed. During the shooting of *Epi-scopo*, he complains that Sordi is trying to steal his scenes. The result, however, is a success. The film wins critical praise and a prize in the technical category at the 1947 Venice Film Festival, and is later hailed by critics as the best film of the year alongside De Santis's *Caccia tragica* (*Tragic Hunt*). Although he is proud of the film, Fabrizi will never again be able to stomach artistic screenwriters and despotic directors and his tastes will gradually bring him back to a coarser mainstream cinema.

The names Fabrizi and Fellini will appear again together on a few more titles in the 1950s. Fellini persuades Rossellini to use Fabrizi as the lone professional actor among the real-life characters in *Francesco giullare di Dio* (*Francis, God's Jester*, 1950), for which he plays the part of the tyrant Nicolaio who invades a city with armies of barbarian warriors and military machines like the ones seen in Alessandro Blasetti's historical epics. Fabrizi's growling performance is delivered almost entirely from inside a suit of armor hanging from a pulley. When the naïve priest, Ginepro, is brought before Nicolaio, the actor rolls his eyes and roars like an ogre, certainly the most Fellini-esque routine of Fabrizi's career. The grotesque makeup and convulsive speechifying is really quite like a cartoon of Fellini's invention.

The other part Fabrizi takes on during this period is more conventional. *Cameriera bella presenza offresi* (*Position Wanted*, 1951) was a film made with the futile aim of relaunching the career of Elsa Merlini, a star of the frivolous prewar comedies, by surrounding her with big names. For Fabrizi, Fellini created a foolish traveling salesman who is just trying to have a peaceful summer holiday. Lattuada and Fellini's announcement of *Luci del varietà*, however, leads to some real tension between Aldo and Federico. Fabrizi thinks of himself as Fellini's mentor in the world of *avanspettacolo*, and he takes offense at having been excluded. His revenge is to accept a role in Carlo Ponti's movie, *Vita da cani* (*A Dog's Life*, 1950), an overt competitor with *Luci del varietà*. Fabrizi collaborates on the screenplay alongside several writers, among them Maccari, who has returned to the movies and will go on to be Fabrizi's dedicated screenwriter for another twenty films.

The friendship between the actor and Fellini falls into disrepair after Fellini's frequent public accounts of his real (or imagined) experiences with Fabrizi in the world of variety. Federico embellishes the anecdotes, creating an ongoing comic romance where he plays the marginal role of the clumsy intern, while repeating (and probably partly inventing) scenes and incidents that Aldo ardently denies ever took place. Fabrizi isn't happy about Fellini's constant harping on the dreadful conditions the old theater companies operated under, which the actor insists are a misrepresentation. He will never understand the affection in Fellini's irony and thus continues to contest both the real and fictional stories. They part ways and will meet again after that only at the occasional event. Fabrizi is left with the bitter taste of what he considers a friendship betrayed—a rather common impression among Fellini's former companions.

Federico would go on to say that he personally had nothing to do with the success of movies like *Avanti c'è posto* and others. He would say that he didn't invent either the plots or the characters and it was Fabrizi who brought real innovation to the scripts. Fellini characterizes these movie projects as having both the lively spark and the limitations of *avanspetta-colo*, but he never forgets the populist spirit that Fabrizi brought to them and the solidarity of their partnership—in particular the obsession with realism that the comedian was always trying to convey to his collabora-tors, insisting, "We're doing real life here!"

More than once, in the years to follow, the director is inspired to re-sume his collaboration with the great actor. But Fabrizi has become a walking stereotype—both too recognizable and too dominating. In 1968, while working on *Fellini Satyricon*, Federico carelessly lets people know that he's thinking of casting Aldo as Trimalcione, but then at the last minute he selects Mario Romagnoli (known as *Il Moro* or the moor)—a popular Roman gadfly. For Fabrizi this slight is a dramatic and unforgiv-able offense, which ultimately kills the flagging friendship. But we can see in the intense and tormented relationship between Federico and Aldo the repetition of a father-son dynamic, complete with misunderstanding, resentment, and regret, as well as admiration and even affection, inter-twined. The final sublime scene from Shakespeare's *Henry IV*, when Henry V, newly crowned, pushes his old friend Falstaff away forever, might be the most apt illustration of this minor chapter in Italian cinema. In the letter Fabrizi wrote to Angelo Solmi, he scripted a harsh conclu-sion to his relationship with Fellini: "In the end, I gave more than I got."

9

One Movie After Another

The war rages on, the situation in Italy is growing worse, and Fellini is on the brink of being recognized as one of the top screenwriters in the business. The cult of the director may be growing, but producers have by now realized that the writers are both practically and artistically critical to their projects. Good writers are winning acclaim and top salaries, and are even being fought over. Fellini rides this tide into the industry, his lively ideas, imagination, and innovation on grand display at *Marc'Aurelio* and on the radio. A robust sense of curiosity was the force that made him a good screenwriter, and curiosity, more than an engagement with society, is what will be the driving factor in the rebirth of Italian cinema.

At this point, Federico thinks of cinema as just one of the many newspapers that he contributes to—except that it has better distribution and pays handsomely. He isn't particularly attached to his creations. He sells what he can, and what he can't sell easily, he sells cheap. He tosses ideas onto the table and forgets about them, the same way he's always done with journalism. Many writers of the day are flirting with Cinecittà, playing the field with journalism, radio, theater, and variety, and, although he's now been attached to several very successful movies, Fellini makes no assumptions about his contribution to their popularity, either at this time or later. He never becomes a part of the core operation, but generates ideas without following them through to the end of the process. He never envisions a finished movie and has no interest whatsoever in actually making one. Rather, he's quite seduced by the intense, itinerant teamwork—the pressure, the vulnerability to circumstance, and the unpredictable—not the least of which is the weather. On top of that, he takes pleasure in observing the fauna of moviedom, the vast and varied human typologies. In 1942, Fellini is a little like Carlo Goldoni when he traveled on a ship of comedians from Rimini to Chioggia. It makes sense that Valentina Cortese noticed and remembers Fellini hanging around the edges of the set of *Quarta pagina* (*Page Four*) in Turin: "On the avenues along the park of Valentino . . . there was this young man standing there, his hat pushed back from his open, easygoing face, likable, full of intelligence—brilliant. He'd stand there and jot down dialogues in that way of his, so typical, nonplussed and yet totally vibrant . . ."

Although he was pleased to have made a good impression on a pretty actress, he always denied he'd been in Turin during the filming of *Quarta pagina*. But the comedy writer Nicola Manzari, who'd worked with him on the radio, contradicted the denial. According to Manzari, Fellini had been asked to go to Turin in order to "write witty filler for the weak spots in the movie." Manzari said that the mobilization of eleven screenwriters—the largest team yet—was the innovation of the first-time producer, an over-the-top industrialist from Piedmont. This gentleman loved the ritual of cinema and gathered all of Turin's high society to play in the reception scene. It's the same stunt that Fellini will stage during the filming of *La dolce vita*—inviting Roman aristocracy out to the Palazzo di Bassano di Sutri.

Along with Piero Tellini, who was responsible for the idea of *Quarta pagina*, Federico contributed to this first of the Italian serial movies based on the model of *If I Had a Million* and *Un carnet de bal* (*Dance Program*). The premise of the film is the mysterious disappearance, perhaps murder, of a courier who is carrying a large sum of money. The insurance company hires a young lawyer (Claudio Gora) and his secretary (Valentina Cortese) to investigate. *Quarta pagina* is released in December 1942, and it's the only movie of those written by Fellini that actually comes out on schedule and before the armistice. At this point Fellini and Tellini have come to be considered "specialists in the field," according to *Cine-Magazzino*, "and quite well-proven judging by the recent successes of films they worked on."

Chi l'ha visto? (*Who's Seen Him?*) wraps in the summer of 1943 but doesn't come out until 1945. It's a curious movie inspired by the popular missing-persons section in *Domenica del Corriere*. The story and screen-play are by Piero Tellini and Federico Fellini. The director is Goffredo Alessandrini. The opening scene drops us into a quintessentially Fellini-esque situation: actor Virgilio Riento is attempting to recite a monologue from *Hamlet* to a restless audience in a small provincial theater in Vel-letri. Exasperated by the constant interruptions, the small-time actor throws the skull out into the audience and flees the stage. The master of ceremonies quickly replaces him with four tacky dancers. Riento is blocked on his way out of the hotel by a hysterical woman who is con-vinced that he is her brother-in-law who ran off on his wife five years ear-lier. The movie then turns into a variation of Allesandro Blasetti's *Quattro passi fra le nuvole,* in which the hero is trying to live a modest provincial life and forces his alleged daughter into a marriage she doesn't want. The variety-show background is pure Fellini, as is, perhaps, the taste for de-picting the petite bourgeoisie ironically.

We can be almost certain that Federico worked on the screenplay for *Apparizione (Apparition)* by the French director Jean de Limur and pro-duced by Giuseppe Amato. Shot in the summer of 1943, it's released early in the dark year 1944—when practically no one is going to the movies because of the bomb scares. A typical romantic comedy, *Ap-parizione,* which was officially written by Amato, Tellini, and Lucio De Caro, rides the mood of a smug society anticipating crisis—early signs of a new reality. Fellini's participation in the film is strongly suggested by the casting of Amedeo Nazzari, who plays himself, as he'll do a decade later for Fellini in *Le notti di Cabiria (The Nights of Cabiria)*. The story: A tor-rential downpour surprises the celebrity in the middle of a car trip and he is forced to stop over in a rural town. This same night Alida Valli is show-ing off the white dress she's planning to wear for her marriage to Mas-simo Girotti, a local mechanic. The movie star's sudden appearance shakes everything up: the bride-to-be is at first surprised, then intrigued; while her fiancé is startled, then jealous. What's striking is the regal grace with which the star handles the short encounter; we can appreciate the disquiet that descends on him in the end, back in his luxurious Gatsby house, his next screenplay in his hand, standing under a marble statue of himself. (It's an opulence we'll see again through Cabiria's starry eyes.)

Among the minor films that Fellini works on during this period—both credited and uncredited—one is unfinished. In the book *Cinecittà anni trenta* (Cinecittà in the Thirties), actor Guido Celano tells Francesco Savio how he "happened to be in Africa when the Americans arrived" and was forced to interrupt work on *I cavalieri del deserto* (*Knights of the Desert*, 1942) from a screenplay by Fellini. "I played the chief of the Tuaregs, the hero. [Luisa] Ferida was my daughter, and [Osvaldo] Valenti played a soldier. Then the director, [Gino] Talamo, got sick . . . actually, he was in a car accident. So Valenti and I were trying to convince Fellini to step in and direct. Fellini came down to shoot the first scenes. We did fantasy stuff with horses and Arabs and me." But the American landing at Bona called the production to a halt: "All of us—Fellini, me, everyone—had to make this treacherous flight home. The Spitfires were shooting machine guns at us, so we had to fly low, close to the water. Thank God, we all got back to Rome safely."

This account is consistent with others from 1942 and 1943 that place Fellini in the development office of ACI—Vittorio Mussolini's production company based on via Francesco Crispi. (This is where Federico first meets Roberto Rossellini, who collaborated with Mussolini on *Luciano Serra, pilota* [*Luciano Serra, Pilot*, 1938].) Fellini flew to Tripoli not only because of the emergency on the set but because he wanted to secure another extension on his draft order as well. If he was to be conscripted he'd have to join the Italian troops on the Greek front, and he opted for the not necessarily less disturbing itinerary of flying to Africa from the Salario airport.

At the airport in Tripoli, called Castle Benito (after Benito Mussolini), Federico is warmly greeted by Luigi "Gigetto" Giacosi, who will remain a close friend in the years to come. The situation in Tripoli is crazy: the city is under siege; there are bombs coming in from air, land, and sea. The crew is supposed to be shooting in the desert about twenty kilometers outside the city but spend most of their time in the underground shelters of the Grand Hotel. Ferida is pregnant and subject to emotional breakdowns. Valenti finds solace in cocaine, and Celano practices screaming like a jackal. The raids grow more menacing by the day, there's no film stock to shoot with, and the Ghibli winds are whipping. Coming out of the hotel one day, Fellini sees palm trees overturned on the roof and asks who put them up there and why. He's told that the trees were swept onto the roof in the force gales caused by the bombing. When English troops are only "twenty centimeters from the city" (as Federico would tell the story), the production manager Franco Riganti decides to send everyone home. There are only twenty-six seats on the last plane out of Libya, which falls into English hands in January 1943. Federico, Celano, and Gigetto stay behind in Tripoli, refusing to participate in the lottery for seats that the production company sets up. They manage to board a German military plane going to Castelvetrano in Sicily; they fly low, skimming the water in order to avoid being spotted by Allied forces. Struck dumb by being plunged into an adventure story, Fellini doesn't even have time to be scared. In the moment, all he seems to be able to focus on is the bundle of leather slippers, bracelets, and carpets that he'd wanted (but wasn't able) to bring back to sell in Rome.

The trip home to Rome from Sicily is a real odyssey—one of the few large-scale nonimaginary adventures of Federico's life, which may be why he never talked much about it. They traveled by train, car, bicycle, and foot, dodging machine-gun fire, and surviving nothing short of an adventure novel. This is when Fellini discovers the lovely piazza in Sciacca, blazing white in the sun, that he will later suggest to Pietro Germi as a location for *In nome della legge* (*In the Name of the Law*, 1949). The Messina channel crossing is yet another adventure inside an adventure. And it will be ten days after that before they reach Rome from Reggio Calabria—the train moves at a snail's pace with long unplanned stops for air raids, where the passengers have to race down the banks from the train and hide in the trees. Fellini recounts the story of the journey as "Il primo volo" (The First Flight), which runs in *Marc'Aurelio* on November 14, 1942, along with some cartoons in which he depicts himself on a camel in the desert. This episode is Fellini's first run-in with a movie that never got made, almost twenty-five years before he would face his own never-to-be-completed project *Il viaggio di G. Mastorna* (*G. Mastorna's Journey*), and it clearly marks the emergence of a new Fellini, no longer just a screenwriter, working and sketching at his desk, but a filmmaker out in the field. A man who from now on will not only write movies but live them as well.

10

Wartime Wedding

Saturday, October 30, 1943, Rome: Federico and Giulietta's wedding day, and a typical day during the final tragic act of the Second World War. There's a blackout and a curfew from seven in the evening until 5:30 the next morning. The newspaper, *Il Messaggero*—now reduced to a single page—reports that day that the Consiglio dei Ministri (the ruling council) approved expanded conscription for all men seventeen to thirty-seven years old. The news distresses Fellini, who is twenty-three at the time. In the same edition, new rules are outlined for workers heading to Germany, new rations are announced for salt and cigarettes, and a warning is issued about "alarmist leaflets appearing in people's mailboxes that attempt to cast the German authorities in a negative light." The inattentive doormen who permitted the circulation of such propaganda are threatened with internment in concentration camps. Local venues have reopened for business and Totò, Fanfulla, Rascel, and other comedians are performing again. In a sense, the atmosphere could be described as Fellini-esque. In the city section, there's a local bit about a grifter who sold a counterfeit coin depicting Julius Caesar to a farmer in Piazza del Cinquecento.

The mood is gloomy. The fall of fascism on July 25 had given people a sense of hope, which dried up by September 8. *Marc'Aurelio* stopped printing. Radio had become a bastion of propaganda. Cinema was practically nonexistent. Some people were contemplating escaping to the south of Italy—Mario Soldati and Dino De Laurentiis left right away. But at the same time, the movie industry was also moving in the opposite direction, north to Venice. The *gerarca** Luigi Freddi was pressuring cineasts to bring their art north under the black banner of a Fascist renaissance. When he calls Fellini at via Nicotera, Fellini pretends he's not home. Another big celebrity of the day, Osvaldo Valenti, calls with the same motives; he is gunned down by partisans on a Milan sidewalk in April 1945. A fellow screenwriter is plaguing Fellini with appeals for the cause, and it's his insistence that finally drives Fellini into full retreat until after the tempest has blown over. The Wehrmacht parade down the streets of Rome on October 3, effectively ending any illusion that it is an "open city," and people begin to realize that the road to freedom will be long and the toll will be high.

Like many other young men, Fellini is dodging the draft. Concerned about the possibility of a raid at via Nicotera, Federico takes shelter at via Lutezia. It is under these circumstances, and with Aunt Giulia's blessing, that Federico and Giulietta decide to rush their marriage. For safety's sake the ceremony is held in the apartment. A prelate from the church of Santa Maria Maggiore lives on the same floor, and has dispensation to preside over rituals at home using a corner bureau piece that opens up into an altar. There are only a few guests. The war keeps both sets of parents away. Aunt Giulia and her maid are there, along with Rinaldo Geleng (Federico's witness) and his wife, the actor Vittorio Caprioli (Giulietta's witness), Riccardo and his fiancée, and future in-laws. Riccardo repeats his performance of *Ave Maria* on the harmonium—and will repeat it again in *I vitelloni*. In the afternoon, the newlyweds will head to the Galleria theater in Piazza Colonna for a variety show and a movie and are surprised when Alberto Sordi takes the stage and leads the audience in a round of congratulatory applause.

The invitation that Federico designed for the event is just a series of drawings. On the front there are angels playing with a ball and a kite on a cloud—one angel stands apart looking down through a telescope. On the inside there are cartoon versions of Giulietta, dressed in white, and Federico in a tux with a top hat. They are kneeling in the middle of a heart, which is at the intersection of two country roads. Road signs over their

---

*The designation *gerarca* is for a person of authority at the highest level in the Fascist Party. Luigi Freddi was an adviser for Mussolini's father and an enemy of Vittorio, and played a large role in the founding of Cinecittà.

heads bear their names. Under the picture, two little birds hold placards with the two addresses: via Lutezia 11 and via Nicotera 26. The fourth page is a wish: a little angel in the corner jumps down toward a small house while his companions wave him off with handkerchiefs and the sun emerges from behind a cloud. An empty road sign stands waiting for a baby's name. This dream will be cruelly shattered.

A few months after the marriage, Giulietta falls down the stairs and has a miscarriage. She gets pregnant again and on March 22, 1945, they baptize their baby Pierfederico. He has encephalitis and dies on April 24, just over a month later. This will remain a painful chapter in the couple's life. Years later Federico would still refuse to discuss it, though Giulietta occasionally spoke of it in order to explain the puerperal fever that she suffered for quite a while afterward. Among the couple's most intimate friends, many speculated that the tragedy strengthened their spiritual union but prematurely ended their physical relationship.

The state of the postal and telephone service made it impossible to send news of the marriage to Fellini's parents, who learn of it only later on through the Red Cross, after practically all hell has broken loose in Rimini. Within forty-eight hours after the wedding, on Monday, November 1, 1943, at 11:50 a.m., American bombers come up from Tunisia to strike the small seaside town. In the book *Rimini bombardata* (Rimini, After the Bombs), Paolo Zanghini writes: "The population is caught completely unprepared. When the sirens go off they don't race to the shelters and . . . more than one hundred people die in the first raid." During the period of German retreat from the Gustav Line (passing through Cassino) to the Gothic Line* (which ran from Pesaro to Viareggio), "Rimini became a strategic target that Allied forces were determined to neutralize. The railroad, streets, and harbor suffer continual air and sea bombardment. The city's importance as a communication hub between north and south determined its destruction." The numbers are terrifying. Between November 1943 and September 1944, Rimini is bombed 396 times, and 607 civilians die. Out of a population of 70,000, only about 3,000 remain in the city in February. About 7,000 seek refuge elsewhere;

La linea gotica was German field marshal Albert Kesserling's last line of defense in the retreat over the Appenines.

among those are Urbano and Ida Fellini and their daughter, Maddalena. They go from Coriano to San Marino and then return to Coriano. Not even the Cinema Fulgor is spared. Zanghini concludes that "Rimini is a dead city." When the British enter on September 22, they tread on rubble.

Back in Rome, Federico is living his new marriage as a hideaway—he's legally nonexistent and so he has no coupons for rations. He leaves the house as little as possible, watching for Nazi or police inspections. They move a credenza in front of the window to use as a sort of jerry-rigged lookout point. But on October 29, while out in the Piazza di Spagna on a furtive walk, Federico is swept up in a mass roundup and forced onto a German truck. A bold and ingenious, almost Fellini-esque gag saves his life. Pretending he recognizes a Wehrmacht officer standing on the sidewalk on via del Babuino, he jumps out of the slow-moving truck, waving madly and shouting, "Fritz! Fritz!" He embraces the confused German soldier and then ends the little performance with a hand gesture of apology. In the meantime, the truck has moved on. The officer doesn't realize what has happened and Federico runs off to hide on via Margutta, a side street. He collapses breathlessly on the curb. Ironically, he is sitting very near the house where he'll live out the last period of his life.

Though this adventure should have taught prudence, Federico keeps taking risks during those difficult months, playing everything by ear and developing projects with whatever friends he has left in the city for a cinema that no longer exists. On February 18, 1944, a new law passes concerning draft dodgers. Offenders are given a window of amnesty to turn themselves in; after that dodging is punishable by execution. Federico doesn't even consider turning himself in. He prefers to lurch dangerously forward, coasting on his brashness and good luck until the Liberation of Rome on June 4.

The whole story of the first years of Federico and Giulietta's marriage is quite strange. They're separated from their families and surviving in a provisional and dangerous world. If Fellini wanted to escape his parents by leaving home, reality exceeded his every expectation. It's not until the summer of 1945 that the young man will return to Rimini to visit his parents and sister, who'd themselves just returned after the displacement of the bombings. The city is unrecognizable: "It looks like the moon." It's a marsh pocked with holes, a jungle of broken walls, and a desert of rubble.

The bright blue sea glimmers in the background, adding a surreal quality to this gruesome landscape. In the main square, renamed Tre Martiri (three martyrs), the Allied forces mount a model of their reconstruction plan for the city. Federico and Titta stop and look dubiously at the proposal for a Rimini that could be Las Vegas, but they don't have the heart to joke about it. When Fellini is preparing to leave, he presents his friend with a drawing of the two of them, small figures walking through the ruins. Moved, Titta has it framed, but later the drawing is stolen from the lobby outside his office and disappears forever.

11

Discovering Italy

One late summer day in 1944, in a Rome recently liberated by General Mark Clark of the Fifth Army of the Allied Forces, Roberto Rossellini stops to look in the window of a store on via Nazionale called the Funny-Face Shop. Inside, Fellini is drawing a portrait of an American soldier. This enterprise, with its eccentric name, is a rebirth of the store Fellini had in Rimini, Febo—and an attempt to survive the recession in postwar Rome. Newspapers have stopped paying for articles; there is no cinema, and no way to make ends meet. Other portraitists have followed Fellini's initiative, and the first copycat store opens on via Santa Maria delle Fratte, then on via della Vite, on via Tomacelli, in Piazza San Silvestro, Piazza Barberini, and the largest one on via Nazionale. At the Funny-Face Shop, you can have your portrait "executed in ten minutes" for three dollars. The take is divvied up at the end of the day: one part goes to the backer, who was the producer Domenico Forges Davanzati; another part to the bookkeeper; and the rest goes to the artists. Soldiers could also record their voice on a record to send home—though there was never any guarantee the record would work. All of the stores adopted the same signage, done in quintessential Fellini style: THE MOST FEROCIOUS AND AMUSING CARICATURISTS ARE EYEING YOU! SIT DOWN AND TREMBLE!

Some consider Rossellini's visit to the Funny-Face Shop to be the primary scene in neorealism. Rossellini has come looking for Fellini because he wants to work with him on *Roma, città aperta*. The meeting awakens Fellini's latent cinematographic vocation and brings him, finally and totally, into the world that will consume him for the rest of his life.

Rossellini proposes a collaboration on a screenplay at that point entitled *Storie di ieri* (Stories of Yesterday, later *Roma, città aperta*), an idea that grew out of a documentary about don Giuseppe Morosini's martyrdom. Morosini was the parish priest from the Roman neighborhood of Santa Melania who was executed by the SS on April 4, 1944, for having collaborated against the regime.

Rossellini was fourteen years Fellini's senior. He came from an upper-middle-class Roman family. His father was the renowned architect Angelo Giuseppe, who designed, among other things, the airport in Guidonia and several movie theaters. His younger brother, Renzo, was a popular musician. In the 1930s, Roberto lived a privileged life, enjoying the company of celebrities like Assia Noris and other beautiful women, and the exclusive clique who gathered around Edda Ciano, Mussolini's daughter. After becoming friendly with her brother Vittorio, Rossellini started working in film. His first collaboration with Vittorio was *Luciano Serra, pilota* (1938). After that he made a couple of documentaries about fishing. He first gained recognition as a director for his work on three war movies: *La nave bianca* (*The White Ship*, 1941), *Un pilota ritorna* (*A Pilot Returns*, 1942), and *L'uomo della croce* (*The Man with the Cross*, 1943). His attempt at a fourth project, *Scalo merci* (*The Loading Dock*), was cut short on September 8, however, despite the company's best efforts to keep it going by moving production to Tagliacozzo. (Marcello Pagliero finally completes the movie in 1945 and it is released under the title *Desiderio*.)

What made Rossellini think of Fellini? The principal reason was Fellini's friendship with Aldo Fabrizi—he was considered Fabrizi's creative muse, and it was essential to have a celebrity attached in order to start. (Rossellini's project also depended on the small amount of money provided by the countess Chiara Politi.) Fabrizi is perfect for the film, but needs convincing in order to accept half his usual fee of one million lire. Negotiations finally close, settling on 400,000 lire—hefty considering the wretched economy. Accounts of the contract signing itself vary, depending on who's telling the story. Sergio Amidei recalls that once Fabrizi heard about Rossellini's film, his eyes welled up with tears and he signed without hesitation. But according to Fellini, his friend stood still, the pen poised in the air for some time, and said, "But what if they [the Nazis] come back?"—a monumental question. One way or another the contract was signed, and then Fabrizi would go on to claim that he was the one who brought Fellini on to write just a few scenes for a screenplay that Amidei had already largely written.

What is clear is that the initial meetings between Fellini and Rossellini were held clandestinely, so as not to alarm the jealous and temperamental Amidei. Later on, Federico and Sergio will work together in the kitchen at via Lutezia, the only heated room in the house. But as writers the two don't get along. There is always some degree of competitiveness between them. The priest's lines are almost exclusively written by Fellini and we can imagine that there was some real collaboration with Fabrizi for the scene where don Pietro whacks a man on the head with a frying pan in order to make a more convincing tableau of the last rites for the German patrol. This is a rather incongruous scene, and the juxtaposition of comedy and tragedy is considered by some to be the seed of *commedia all'italiana*. Fellini's participation is formalized with a contract dated October 21, 1944. He is to have 25,000 lire to "collaborate on the first half of the screenplay" and to oversee "the screenplay and dialogue of the first half and review the screenplay and dialogue for the second half" [*sic*]. Unfortunately, the film industry lacks not only good grammar but also money. Most of the shooting of *Roma, città aperta* is necessarily improvised; the money comes and goes in a flash; equipment is hard to secure and the cameraman, Ubaldo Arata, is forced to use expired film stock. There are no studios for the interior scenes—Cinecittà is occupied by war refugees and so the company shoots wherever they find space.

Production moves forward despite the fact that no one really believes in the film. Happy to be working at all after so many fallow months, the actors and crew don't ask for much—and the same can be said of Federico. It's certainly evident that the movie's premise, which grew out of Amidei's experiences collaborating with the Resistance during the nine-month occupation, isn't the most interesting topic for a man who spent the same period without the slightest interest in politics. Yet during his sporadic visits to the set while they are shooting exterior scenes and in the basement of via degli Avignonesi 30 (next door to a brothel), Fellini remains impressed with Rossellini's instinct and technique.

Rossellini's directorial style isn't the least bit tyrannical. He doesn't yell or issue commands. He keeps a totally calm set and goes to great lengths to explain what he wants in the simplest of terms. He is sensitive when making references to recent history and the painful events that belong to the public collective, to Romans. The production is focused on just staying afloat, and yet there is a genuineness to the project—to the aim of recording "the stories of yesterday." There is neither the space for nor the capacity to "do cinema" in the fictive and melodramatic sense of the word. The director has the actors wearing their own clothes and hardly ever reshoots scenes because they need to save film and because he doesn't subscribe to the myth of the beautiful image. He treats the two tigers, Aldo Fabrizi and Anna Magnani, the same way he treats the many amateur actors on the set—not wanting to, or not able to, give in to the celebrity mystique, the *importance* they bring to bear on a project, or the demands they feel they can make. That goes even for the typically humble, cultish celebrity of variety-show veterans; and it goes for publicity too. Though he concedes Magnani and Fabrizi star positions in the opening credits, he lists them alphabetically along with all the others in the closing credits. He's irritated by Magnani's and Fabrizi's caprices, personality conflicts, and professional rivalry. Certainly, in the early months of 1945, Fellini learns a lesson from Rossellini about leveling the playing field when it comes to actors, how not to give them too much credit for their real or supposed charisma and how to value them simply and immediately for their specific work on the project at hand.

But Fellini tends to keep his distance from the set, not wanting to deal with Fabrizi's complaints about being involved in such a low-budget, shoestring production. Despite his gripes and reservations—which he's keeping up to some extent as a matter of reputation—Fabrizi loves the movie and makes invaluable contributions. He's able to offer suggestions that come out of his real knowledge of working-class culture. On March 2, 1944, Fabrizi had witnessed the murder of a pregnant woman, already a mother of five, at the hands of the Germans: Teresa Gullace was killed during a protest in front of the barracks that had been converted into a prison on viale Giulio Cesare. Set in the Casilino neighborhood, the scene of Anna Magnani's murder is more or a less a rendering of this real event.

Roma, città aperta is released on Monday, September 24, 1945, during the second week of the Festival del Teatro Quirino in Rome. There are twenty-two new films screened at the festival. Among them are *Henry V* with Laurence Olivier, Sergei Eisenstein's *Ivan Grozni* (*Ivan the Terrible [Part I]*), and *Les enfants du paradis* (*Children of Paradise*) by Marcel Carné. The Italian film receives a lukewarm reception. The press is divided; some praise the first part of the movie and criticize the second, while others claim that the torture scenes are too harsh. The most sophisticated critics find the directing to be conventional overall and the directing of the actors particularly sloppy. Almost all are in some way reluctant to hail Rossellini as an important filmmaker. Even the favorable criticism is tempered and tends to emphasize the movie's patriotic values. As for the political message—with the parallel martyrdom of the Communist activist and the priest—Amidei foreshadowed the idea of the *compromesso storico* (the "historical compromise" between the Catholic Church and the Italian left wing), which will blossom a few decades later when Enrico Berlinguer takes over PCI, the Italian Communist Party.

Despite the critical ambivalence, the audiences literally overflow the Cinema Capranica and Cinema Imperiale. *Roma, città aperta* makes more money than any other single film that year. In February 1946, the movie is released in New York at the Cinema World in Italian with English subtitles. It's a huge success. The press goes wild and Amidei and Fellini's screenplay is nominated for an Academy Award. This is Fellini's first run in the Oscar contest—he'll go on to greater recognition with the Academy later. The European market moves more slowly. At the Cannes Film Festival in September and October of that year, Rossellini reports that the official Italian delegation "deeply despises the movie," and in fact it only wins a consolation prize. (The Grand Prix International goes to *La bataille du rail* [*The Battle of the Rails*] by René Clement.) Yet only two months later *Roma, città aperta* will be a giant at the Paris box offices.

Reflecting later about that first experience with Rossellini, Fellini is often contradictory. On the one hand, he'll claim that he learned everything from Rossellini, and on the other, he'll say that Rossellini didn't teach him anything. Paradoxically, the two statements don't exactly cancel each other out. Rossellini is a key figure in Fellini's evolution: "He was like the traffic cop who helped me across the street." But certainly Rossellini's method—based on improvisation, subject to mood swings, often running late, not to mention that he sometimes takes off to make a telephone call in the middle of an important shot—is the opposite of Fellini's own total dedication, which could be seen in both his life and work once he became a director himself. Rossellini was a controversial character, a living legend, beloved and totally immoderate. He provides Fellini with an example of a lifestyle that the young man from Rimini will never attempt to imitate. There is nothing that Rossellini was known for—transcontinental adventures, numerous wives, trips to India and to the futurology center in Houston, a hunger for scientific knowledge, and the constant claim that cinema was already dead—that can be traced in Fellini. Even the penchant for lying, which both men were known for, manifests itself differently. Rossellini's lies are functional, strategic, motivated by the complexities of his adventurous life. Fellini's lies are abstract, childish, and often made for no practical reason.

Giulietta agrees with Federico that Rossellini is a fascinating personality, but she's suspicious of him and will never stop being so. Giulietta has developed a rationalist's vision of reality and won't accept the premise that creativity means disorder—she is quite convinced that artists need an orderly life. She worries that Federico's friendship with Rossellini is dangerous, and not just because of Rossellini's poor handling of money. But Roberto likes Giulietta. He calls her Patatinia (little potato) and wants to find a leading role for her. In the meantime, he offers her a debut in *Paisà*, in a short scene set in Florence. When Renzo Avanzo and Harriet White come down the stairs of a house in their feverish hunt for the head of the partisans, they aren't in Florence but rather on via Lutezia, a permission practically "stolen" from Aunt Giulia, who has also fallen under the spell of Roberto Rossellini's charms.

Paisà represents the most intense moment in Fellini and Rossellini's friendship, transcending even artistic collaboration. The situation here is reversed compared to *Roma, città aperta*. It is Fellini, not Amidei, who is the prime mover on the screenplay. The relationship between Rossellini and Amidei begins to degenerate at this point, as the writer from Trieste helplessly watches his original idea morph by the day.

The original concept was to make a series of seven episodes (which became six) about the experiences of American soldiers during the Italian campaign. In the credits, many different names appear as "contributors" to Sergio Amidei's screenplay: Klaus Mann, Fellini, V. Hayes (the American Alfred Hayes, who wrote the novel *The Girl on the Via Flaminia*, 1950), Marcello Pagliero, and Rossellini. Later, in the autumn of 1945, Klaus, tormented son of Thomas Mann, is hired to write the entire screenplay, *Seven from the U.S.*, none of which will actually be used—a common occurrence in the dog-eat-dog world of cinema—and the episode he cared the most about, *The Chaplain*, the death of a young Fascist, is cut wholesale without explanation.

Vasco Pratolini also contributes to the screenplay of *Paisà*. Rossellini and Fellini had met him in Naples, where he'd just moved from Milan in order to work at his wife's family house on two book projects, *Cronaca familiare* (*Family Chronicle*) and *Cronache di poveri amanti* (*A Tale of Poor Lovers*). He takes on the job of fixing the dialogue for the Sicilian episode, a story of a peasant girl (Carmela Sazio) who goes to her death while sympathizing with the American guards who can't understand her. Pratolini also works on the section set in Florence, about a single day, August 4, 1944, when German soldiers blew up all of the bridges along the Arno River except the Ponte Vecchio. Pratolini's name didn't appear in the credits for *Paisà*, because of a scandal that exploded during that same time over his alleged collaboration with Fascist police.

A slightly apprehensive film crew stands on the Beverello pier in Naples to welcome the ship bringing the American actors. The self-appointed producer, Rod E. Geiger, has billed the troupe as the rising stars of Hollywood. Geiger is really an advertising copywriter, though he is the son of a Broadway acting coach. He's a peculiar character who happened to be on via degli Avignonesi one night while *Roma, città aperta* was being shot. Like many soldiers on leave for the night, he thought the basement door of the set led to the brothel next door. That fateful night at the brothel was the key to Rossellini's success in the United States. Geiger sold *Roma, città aperta*, and wants to produce another Rossellini movie about the war in Italy—thus the conception of *Paisà*. But the American celebrities aren't worth the producer's enthusiasm. Harriet White is among them. She'll go on to marry the architect Gastone Medin and appear again in *La dolce vita* as Anita Ekberg's secretary. Some of the arriving Americans are not even actors, but Rossellini is unconcerned and finds a way to use them anyway. Characteristically, he prefers authentic faces to those of professionals.

Fellini ends up spending a night in jail during the filming of the movie, after getting lost in the belly of Naples with a female American journalist who was shocked by the poverty of the people living in the grottoes of Mergellina. Although the screenplay called for a series of locations from Sicily to the Alps, the bulk of the movie is actually shot on the Amalfi coast, near Maiori, a town Rossellini loved—and where he sets *Il miracolo* (*The Miracle*, part two of *L'amore*) a few years later.

The protestant chaplain, Newer Jones, and Sergeant Elmer Feldman, assistant to the rabbi in the U.S. Army's Seventh Division at Shunting Camp, appear in a scene set in a real monastery that figures on the Gothic Line. Soldiers from the same regiment appear in another scene that, according to the script, was meant to have been shot in Sicily. Rossellini recruits fourteen-year-old Carmela Sazio from the street to play the part of the sullen girl. Commenting on the use of real clergy in the film, a newspaper writes: "Their own ideas about how a chaplain thinks, acts, and talks have been totally incorporated into the sequence. Screenwriter Fellini won't have to make anything up." This intense and subtle episode foreshadows Roberto and Federico's 1950 interpretation of Saint Francis of Assisi's *Fioretti*, entitled *Francesco, giullare di Dio*.

Working on a movie that is characterized by a continually shifting perspective and new dilemmas with each passing day, Fellini discovers the heart of cinema, and is so challenged by it that he puts his best work into it. The same newspaper writes, "The star of the crew after Rossellini is without a doubt the young screenwriter, cartoonist, painter, and journalist, Federico Fellini. In the town of Maiori a joke has been circulating: *While you're sleeping, Federico is working*. Though some more malicious folk have responded with another saying: *While you're working, Federico is sleeping*."

When the production moves to Florence, Fellini becomes temporary director for the first time. During shooting, Rossellini falls ill, and in order to avoid losing a day of work, he has Federico oversee some shots. In the first one, a demijohn of water is being transported through the streets on a small cart under fire from Fascist sharpshooters. Federico immediately gets into an argument with Otello Martelli, the cinematographer. Martelli insists that the shot should be a high angle, while Fellini wants it to be low, at ground level. He's thinking about Giorgio De Chirico and his metaphysical urban landscapes. Martelli is entirely opposed to what he calls "the point of view of a rodent," so Fellini threatens to dig a hole in the ground for the camera, making the angle even lower. The flask rolls from side to side and bounces along the road. Two days later in the projection room, Fellini has his first experience of watching a scene he shot, confessing later that when the famous flask appeared on the screen, his stomach turned, "and in the dark room, I could feel Roberto's hand on me, patting my hair."

Although he's revealed entirely unexpected determination in his argument with the cameraman, Federico considers himself on the set just to help out, the way he might have been there, on the ready, to rewrite a scene for Mario Mattoli or Mario Bonnard. He has no sense that the movie belongs to him, and all of the technical considerations are alien to him. When he sees Martelli, surrounded by electricians, taking apart the camera in order to check it, the young assistant director doesn't have a spark of curiosity about the camera's innards. He doesn't understand and is, rather, indifferent to such aspects of filmmaking. He likes Otello, though, and watches with amusement his sudden outbursts and ongoing complaints about Rossellini's expeditious techniques. The more he's around the set, the more Fellini realizes that the person most responsible for a film's success isn't the director but the cinematographer. This was certainly the case for a number of years in old-school Italian cinema, where Federico was able to observe the work of master directors of photography, like Carlo Montuori, Ubaldo Arata, Massimo Terzano, Arturo Gallea, and Anchise Brizzi. Martelli is a disciple of Brizzi, meaning he follows American models, uses diffused light, and is fabulous at soft-focus close-ups of women's faces. When Fellini is ready to direct his first movie, Luci del varietà, he has Alberto Lattuada hire Martelli, and thus begins a strong partnership that will continue for more than a decade.

The time comes to shoot the last episode of the partisan sequence and the crew decides not to go to Val D'Aosta. It's August and the snow is all melted. Rossellini elects instead to go to the mouth of the Po River, between Porto Tolle and the Sacca di Scardovari, which necessitates a rewrite. Fellini redraws the whole episode so radically that when the screenplay is later published, only Fellini's and Rossellini's names appear on it. This is the decisive episode of the film, and is the only time that

Rossellini gets angry, after his assistants, Federico and Massimo Mida Puccini, fail to correctly cue a group of women to see the body of the dead partisan floating by.

Roberto is unusually tense and busy these days. He runs one shot after another without a break, fueled by intense inspiration. Federico and the others, attentive and bright, follow suit. It's the most important part of the movie and one of the moments that will go down in the annals of modern cinema—though it will be some time before everyone understands it. Initially Amidei is totally opposed: "The partisans come off as chicken thieves!" Once they return to Rome to shoot the episode of the soldier and Maria Michi, the third and last part of the movie, Rossellini starts acting like himself again. Amidei reappears on the set on via degli Avignonesi looking for reconciliation—in some part also because he's struck up a relationship with Michi, an attractive former movie-theater usher. But Roberto is already distracted and when the time comes to shoot the opening shot in Livorno—when the girl first meets the liberators—he delegates the job to Massimo.

Traveling through Italy while working on *Paisà* will remain one of Federico's most precious memories. Up to that point, he'd seen little of his country besides Rimini and Rome, and the discovery of new landscapes, towns, and local dialects stimulates his imagination to no end, and convinces him to make his life in cinema. That decision was also about Rossellini's unique ability—passed down to his apprentice—for making a day on the set feel like a picnic in the country with friends.

Paisà gets a tepid reception at the revived Venice Film Festival,* where it played closing night on September 17, 1946. When he arrives in Venice, Rossellini is still in shock about the death of his son, Romano, in Spain a few weeks earlier. Mida would report that he was crying in his room at the Luna Hotel after the press screening. The reviews are more confused than they are hostile. The modern style, the varying tone of the different episodes, Rossellini's disregard for convention, all cost him in their opinion. Fellini—who isn't in Venice, maybe because he has another job—runs into Amidei on the street and remembers only his pre-

---

*The oldest film festival in the world, the Mostra Internazionale d'Arte Cinematografica, founded in 1932, had suspended operations during the war, and reopened in 1946.

posterous attack on Rossellini for having decided to release the film in Venice. *Paisà* barely wins jury mention along with Olivier's *Henry V* and Carné's *Les enfants du paradis* from the committee of critics who are substituting for a formal jury that year. The prize for best film goes to *The Southerner* by Jean Renoir. Later on *Paisà* wins three Silver Ribbons (the "Italian Oscar") for best movie, best director, and to Renzo Rossellini for best musical score.

In December, after *Paisà* is released in theaters with a new cut, the reviews improve. But in an Italy overrun by American films, success is hard-won. Metro-Goldwyn-Mayer distributes the film halfheartedly—they have their commercial aspirations invested in other films for the 1946–47 season. The film finishes the year as the ninth most popular in Italy, which isn't bad, considering how poorly later Rossellini movies do. Encouraged by the Oscar nomination for *Roma, città aperta*, *Paisà* soon gains a wide following abroad, so much so that in 1949, it wins another Oscar nomination for best screenplay. In the meantime, the film receives the New York Film Critics Circle Award in 1948 for best foreign film.

Despite the fact that *The Hollywood Reporter* proclaimed him a "giant of the screen," Rossellini has a difficult time working in a cinema where inspiration—which some call "improvisation"—has already been displaced by the laws of the open market. To please Anna Magnani, with whom the director is having a stormy love affair in mid-1947, Rossellini shoots a cinematic interpretation of *La voix humaine*, a monologue by Jean Cocteau, a showpiece script for stage actresses. But right after that, he moves to Berlin to work on *Germania anno zero* (*Germany Year Zero*), the third installment in his war trilogy. This time around Fellini has other commitments and is feeling reluctant about traveling, so he doesn't join the project. Fellini comes back into Rossellini's fold upon his return from Germany, when the director asks Fellini to help him with *Una voce umana* (A Human Voice), which is too short at forty minutes for theatrical release. They need another episode and, tempted again by the Venice Film Festival, Rossellini wants to work on it immediately.

It's almost summer and the 1948 festival is scheduled for August. So Rossellini asks Federico to write a simple, inexpensive idea that will work for Magnani. After talking it over with Tullio Pinelli, Federico comes up with an idea that he'll reuse for Amedeo Nazzari's scene in *Le notti di*

Cabiria: the encounter between a suburban prostitute and the movie star who picks her up. Magnani doesn't like the idea and they have to think of something else. Fellini and Pinelli come up with the story of a shepherdess who's impregnated by a vagabond—she becomes convinced that she's going to mother Saint Joseph's child. In order to sell the idea to Anna, Federico tells her that it's based on a Russian legend. (Later he'll be unjustly accused of plagiarizing the idea from the Spanish novel *Flor de Santitad* [1904] by Ramón María del Valle-Inclán.) Rossellini is happy with the idea because it means going back to Maiori to shoot it. At the last minute, he wants Federico to act in it as well, to play the part of the fake Saint Joseph. Rossellini uses all his arts of temptation to convince him to do it, even puts a check for one million lire in his hand (though he asks for it back half an hour later). In exchange, Federico will have to be satisfied with a gift, a dark red Fiat Topolino, valued at 650,000 lire—the first of many fancy cars.

Federico's discomfort about acting is compounded by the fact that he has to bleach his hair blond for the part, a look that provokes much teasing from his friends. A meeting that Fellini and Pinelli attend with the conservative industrialist Guido Gatti at Lux Film takes an embarrassing turn as a result. Gatti is well known to be repulsed by anything at all smacking of homosexuality, and is icy to Fellini when he sees him done up as a blond. On the set, however, Magnani is pleased about working opposite an actor who has no chance of overshadowing her. When *L'amore* (the title for the composite *Una voce umana* and *Il miracolo*) is presented at the Venice festival, it is a personal triumph for Magnani. Only later will there be polemics over the "blasphemy" of the Fellini story—despite the fact that according to a French newspaper, the highest authorities in the Vatican approved the movie. *France Dimanche* reports that "the Pope thought that this modern interpretation of the Virgin birth as directed by a Communist was marvelous!" Unfortunately, Rossellini never was a Communist and there is no evidence that Pope Pius XII ever saw *L'amore*. We might speculate, however, that he would have found it inferior to the cinematographic model of the "ideal movie" that he'd previously outlined in a speech.

While the Catholic opposition to the movie is moderate in Europe, the American clergy will strongly oppose it. The dynamic Joseph Burstyn, who also launched *Roma, città aperta* in the United States, releases it as part of an omnibus picture, under the title *Ways of Love*, which also includes two short movies, *Une partie de campagne* (*A Day in the Country*) by Jean Renoir and *Jofroi* (*Ways of Love*) by Marcel Pagnol. In *The New York Times*, Bosley Crowther can't figure out whether the movie is an albeit heterodox glorification of faith or an atrocious insult to it. Cardinal Francis Spellman, who never saw the movie, denounced its purported "atheist communism," and pushes the chair of the licensing committee to veto any further showings of the film. But Burstyn takes the case to the Supreme Court and wins the suit with a decision that says it's illegal to impose ideological censorship.

After *L'amore*, Fellini and Pinelli rush to write another screenplay for Rossellini and Magnani, *La contessa di Monte Cristo* (The Countess of Monte Cristo), an amusing story about a vagabond musician who inherits the property of a peculiar man who has just killed himself. But the movie never gets made. Rossellini is feeling burdened by his relationship with Magnani and starts plotting his escape. On May 8, 1948, he is passed a letter: legend has it that the letter was saved from a 1947 fire at Minerva film offices. It's a short note from Ingrid Bergman in Hollywood, who says she's a fan of his work and would like to shoot a movie with him. Thus starts a flurry of telegrams back and forth between Italy and California. While Roberto is on the Amalfi coast shooting *La macchina ammazzacattivi* (*The Machine That Kills Bad People*, 1952), Magnani explodes with anger and famously empties a bowl of spaghetti over his head. Soon afterward, the director flies to Los Angeles and signs Bergman for *Stromboli*. On March 20, 1949, she arrives in Rome. That evening Rossellini introduces her to friends in his house on via Buozzi, which Fellini has festooned with cartoons inspired by the forthcoming work.

During the weeks and months that follow, the scandal of the passion between the Italian director and the Swedish actress takes on outlandish proportions—with the exaggerations, morbid curiosity, gossip-crazed paparazzi, and moral crusading. Exasperated, Magnani agrees to be in an American movie that will run in direct competition with *Stromboli*, and she goes to Vulcano, a nearby island, to shoot under the director William Dieterle. The world of Roman cinema is split; half with Anna and half with Roberto. Although Rossellini's half is markedly smaller, Fellini is

among them. He doesn't collaborate on *Stromboli* but is in regular telephone contact with the director and remains a loyal friend. Giulietta and
Ingrid get along too, and once the crew returns from the Eolie Islands
they see each other willingly, in Rome in the winter and at the Rossellini's
house in Santa Marinella during the summer. Federico and Roberto's collaboration starts up again with renewed enthusiasm for the project
Francesco giullare di Dio, one of the eleven *Fioretti* by Saint Francis of
Assisi, which Fellini and Rossellini adapt for the screen. Fellini used to
claim that he never went on the actual set, but simply chose the episodes
and drafted the screenplay.

The Catholics try to exploit the circumstances of Rossellini's amorous
misadventures in order to gain control of the Saint Francis project, but,
typically, Rossellini takes advantage of their interest without letting them
assume any control. His passion for the project is genuine. The idea of
adapting Saint Francis's *Fioretti* for the screen first came to him while
shooting *Paisà* in the convent in Maiori, and, as in that film, the actors on
this project are real priests as well. Shot in early 1950 in the mountains
near Rome, *Francesco, giullare di Dio* is the natural creative intersection
between the world of *Il miracolo* and the social fairy tale *La strada*. And
it stands to reason that four years later some of the same people who
worked on *Francesco*, such as Martelli and stage manager Gigetto Giacosi, will be on Fellini's *La strada* set.

The muddy, rain-beaten landscape where the Franciscans first appear
(walking back from a meeting with the pope) is similar to the wilderness
that Zampanò crosses. And the comic brother Ginepro, part half-wit and
part visionary, is an early incarnation of Gelsomina. The writers give that
role even more dramatic weight than they give Saint Francis, and he
is the protagonist of half the scenes. An old-style comedy frames and
contrasts the inspired lyricism of the other scenes, like the ones between Francesco and Chiara (Francis and Claire), or the famous scene
where Francesco kisses a leper. In this movie, the saint and his followers
are marginalized, out in the cold, and reveal no mystical truths. The project attempts to portray the poor of Italy and in the process also reflects
the contemporaneous growth in Italian academia of anthropology and
folklore studies.

These are new cultural perspectives that aren't really understood in

Italy during the postwar years, dominated by a crumbling right wing on one side and Stalinism on the other. The conflicted and reticent criticism of *Francesco* in the press recalls the ambivalence with which the scene in the convent in *Paisà* was received. The pseudo-left's incomprehension of Rossellini will be even more pronounced over *Europa '51*, and flare up against Fellini later for *La strada*. We can see the first strains of it when both *Francesco* and *Stromboli* are screened at the 11th Venice Film Festival in September 1950. The films aren't received badly, but both the church and the religious among the audience are perplexed. While the left is alarmed by Rossellini's increasing interest in religious subjects, the Catholics aren't accustomed to such worldly depictions of the lives of the saints.

The idea for *Europa '51* is born out of the comment that Fabrizi makes from the edge of the set one day to Rossellini and Fellini: Francis of Assisi was most certainly a madman. Irene, the protagonist of *Europa '51*, is a "typical" woman of the upper class, caught up in her mundane life. But then tragedy strikes—her son throws himself down the stairs in the middle of a dinner party. While little Edmund, who kills himself at the end of *Germania anno zero*, is a martyred victim of the war, little Michele is the victim of a "fragile peace." He kills himself while the dinner guests are academically discussing peace. The tragedy reveals to Irene that she has to change her ways and attempt to look beyond herself. But everyone around her—relatives, doctors, lawyers, politicians, and her priest—agree instead that she is behaving dangerously and that she must be committed to an asylum.

Fellini and Pinelli work together on *Europa '51*, which will be produced by Carlo Ponti and Dino De Laurentiis, developing the central themes of the story, particularly the suicide (not unlike the murder of the Steiner children in *La dolce vita*). Federico admires Roberto's courage in confronting the issues raised in the movie with a radically Christian approach, destined to pit everyone against him. *Europa '51* is an important turning point for neorealism and a brave attempt to make cinema that is about human beings. But while Fellini is intrigued by the enterprise, he also feels unprepared for, even frightened of, the social and political implications that Rossellini is infusing into the story, and he backs out of the project. Fellini is also scared off by the involvement of consultants from a variety of ideologies with contradictory suggestions, whom Rossellini, with his insatiable curiosity, brings to the project.

In the summer of 1951, the two screenwriters meet with Rossellini in Paris. It's Fellini's first trip to the city, and Roberto meets his friends at the station and then overwhelms them with a twenty-four-hour non-touristy tour of the Ville Lumière. Once they start working through the movie, however, the enthusiasm dwindles. In the meetings at Hotel Raphael with a group of French intellectuals, whom Enrico Fulchignoni has on call in order to help define the movie's philosophy, Fellini feels out of his element, and marginalized. For Roberto, Paris is just like Rome, while Fellini feels like an Italian abroad—he always will be. He doesn't speak French; he'll learn it later but never master it. He speaks a little English, but reluctantly, and keeps slipping back into Italian. One could say that Fellini will become an international figure without ever having gone international. The experience in Paris, the long disputes around the table that Roberto finds so amusing, leave Federico dazed. After talking to Pinelli, who basically agrees with him, and realizing that the French producer doesn't seem to want to pay anyone, Federico abandons the project as soon as he can and escapes back to Rome. Running recourse to any number of excuses he manages to get away with merely providing some friendly input. Neither Fellini nor Pinelli appear among the list of screenwriters. Yet Fellini still feels strongly sympathetic to Irene's tormented character and hasn't lost any enthusiasm for Roberto's work. *Europa '51* is shown at the 13th Venice Film Festival, in competition against Pietro Germi's *Il brigante di Tacca del Lupo*, which Fellini contributed to, and Fellini's own solo directorial debut *Lo sceicco bianco*. The resistance at Venice to Rossellini's new trend is a source of sadness for Federico.

After a number of announcements that Ingrid Bergman has retired from acting, Rossellini changes his tune and says that she's stopped acting only for other directors. This is one of the few typically Italian attitudes of Roberto's that Bergman openly resents in her autobiography. In fact, Roberto's stubborn jealousy kept her from acting for Fellini and others. And in the meantime, the friendship between the two men starts to fall apart after *Lo sceicco bianco*. Perhaps the older director has difficulty watching his student grow up. As to Rossellini's opinion about the movie itself, which he saw in a private screening long before it was shown at the

Venice festival, there are contradictory accounts. Some say he was affectionately enthusiastic; others say that he outright rejected it. The truth is probably somewhere in the middle. Roberto recognizes the value of the work, but dislikes a number of things about it. In particular, he would have wanted to reshoot the scene with Alberto Sordi and Brunella Bovo in the boat in the middle of the water, because it's too obvious that they are floating right off the shore. Fellini is annoyed that Rossellini pretends not to understand the difficulties of timing and money that are involved. And Roberto feels that as a new director, Fellini is resistant to criticism. "If a Raffaello painting has dust on it, you have to blow it off," he concludes impatiently.

After this little dark cloud passes, their relationship regains solid ground. And the following year, when Roberto is ill or just hibernating (it's hard to know the difference with him), Fellini stands in for him on the set to direct the trial scene in *Dov'è la libertà . . . ?* (*Where Is Freedom?*, 1954). This is Fellini's only chance, albeit as a substitute, to direct Totò, an actor he adores. He's so excited about meeting the great comedian that he calls him "Prince," just as the old crew did. Benevolently Totò answers, "You can call me Antonio."

Fellini follows Rossellini's changing fortunes with open solidarity—including his travels to India and a new amorous scandal. It seems that the two grow closer whenever things are difficult for one of them, but they do have a hard time getting along when things are going well. When *La dolce vita* comes out, Rossellini publicly criticizes it, saying that Fellini is going down the wrong path and that someone should stop him. The usual suspects run to report this to Fellini and when the two meet again there is quite a lot of embarrassment. "He looked at me as Socrates would have looked at his student Crito, if Crito had suddenly lost his mind," says Federico.

In the years that follow, the paths of the two friends diverge. Rossellini's statements about the death of cinema irritate Fellini. His theories about the educational use of television bore him. He's completely uninterested in Rossellini's historical films. And, as far as Rossellini is concerned, Fellini's films are nothing more than frivolous fantasies. They will continue to get along like brothers whenever they meet (often accidentally) or see the other's work flash by on the television—sharing that unique affinity that enables them no matter what the circumstance to locate the mutual affection, sense of humor, and admiration they always shared. Beyond the critical differences in their personalities and lives, the two men will always have recognition and surges of love for each other that come out of their indelible common history. When Roberto dies on June 3, 1977, Federico feels more alone in the world. In the years that follow, he will begin to recognize some extraordinary similarities between Rossellini and Casanova—the pleasure of acting in life as if onstage, fabricating your own self-image, the constant courtship of other people (especially women), the tenuous pleasure of living each day as if it were the last, short-lived cultural infatuations, and an infallible sense of the practical combined with moments of extreme generosity.

12

Writing Is Easier When There Are Two of You

After the war, the lights of the sign over Lux Film, at via Po 36 (a modern building stands in its place today), blaze throughout the night. Riccardo Gualino, an influential businessman from Biella who started investing in movies after a successful run in big industry during the 1920s, heads up the production company from a distant, hard-to-reach office on the third floor. The musicologist, Guido Maggiorino Gatti, also from Piedmont and a friend of Gualino, is artistic manager of the society. His office is located on the second floor. Independent producers work out of the first floor, under the general manager Valentino Brosio. Carlo Ponti from Milan is among this group, along with the Neapolitan Dino De Laurentiis—both quickly rise to prominence.

When reminiscing about Lux Film, where he was practically a permanent guest—waiting for his writing fees to be cashed—Fellini would describe the flurry of actors, directors, writers, and film crews going in and out. *"Lucchessefilme,"* as it was known in the insider jargon of the Roman movie world, is where Fellini first meets a sharp-nosed, slight man named Tullio Pinelli. Pinelli is a lawyer from Turin who abandoned his career and dragged his wife and four children to Rome to work in the movies. One day, near the end of 1946, Fellini and Pinelli run into each other in Piazza Barberini, where they are both reading the same paper posted at a newsstand. Pinelli remembers,

> I realized that the young guy named Fellini was reading the opposite side of the same paper. We said hello and started chatting and

immediately got along. Meeting each other was a creative lightning bolt. We spoke the same language from the start. We took a
walk and ended up at his house on via Lutezia, where he lived
with Giulietta and her aunt. We were fantasizing about a screenplay that would be the exact opposite of what was fashionable
then: the story of a very shy and modest office worker, who discovers he can fly, so he flaps his arms and escapes out the window.
It certainly wasn't neorealism. But the idea never went anywhere
either.

It was yet another episode replaying Fabrizi's brusque rejection of
Fellini's talking-horse proposal.

Pinelli was older than Fellini, but had come to Rome later. He was a
civil lawyer back home, and before that had worked for Manlio Brosio, an
anti-Fascist, future government minister and cousin of Valentino Brosio,
the partner of Lux. He came from a long line of patriots. (His great-uncle
General Ferdinando Pinelli held back the uprising of the bandits in Calabria following the unification. Amedeo Nazzari plays the character
based on him later in *Il brigante di Tacca del Lupo*.) For the decade that
he practiced law, Tullio Pinelli was an unusual lawyer; for one thing, he
worked mainly in the theater. In 1932, Erminio Macario puts on stage
Pinelli's first play, which is written in regional dialect. This is one of the
few direct links between Pinelli and Fellini—Fellini had written gags for
one of Macario's movies. Pinelli continues writing plays, among them *La
pulce d'oro* (The Golden Flea), *I Porta* (The Porta Family), *I padri etruschi*
(The Etruscan Fathers), and the critics eventually start taking an interest
in his work. In a 1943 review of *Lotta con l'angelo* (Battle with an Angel),
Silvio d'Amico writes, "The level of this writing far surpasses the base,
humiliating work that we've been too long accustomed to." In the wake of
the success of *I padri etruschi* at the Teatro Quirino, Valentino Brosio got
Gatti, the president of Lux Film, to invite Pinelli to via Po. A lover of literature who is convinced that cinema never attains artistic status, Gatti
is always trying to recruit eggheads into the industry—ideally eggheads
from the north. He asks the lawyer from Turin to work on the screen
adaptation of Pushkin's *The Captain's Daughter*, and is so pleased with
the results that the movie actually gets made, with Mario Camerini di-

recting, in 1947. The playwright is offered an exclusive contract to write three screenplays a year and scout novels for adaptation. Mario Soldati made *Le miserie del Signor Travet* (*His Young Wife*, 1945) from a screenplay cowritten by Pinelli. After a number of years swinging between Turin and Rome, Pinelli moves to the capital.

Of theatrical genres, Fellini only ever loved variety. He would never watch repertoire theater and rarely accepted invitations to openings unless a friend was involved. He disliked the mannerisms of some stage actors in particular but was principally annoyed by the lack of control that a theater director could exercise over effects, gestures, and tone. He couldn't stand the way a show would change from one night to the next, and hated the idea that the fruit of extensive research and preparation would be subject to such variation, not to mention the whims and varying interpretations of actors. It would probably be safe to assume that Fellini's interest in Pinelli did not rely on his theatrical work. Quite the opposite. Fellini was likely surprised to meet an intellectual who shared his blossoming interest in the fantastical and marginal, and who had cultivated a lively impatience with the then-popular interest in magic realism.

After the war, Fellini would never work with Piero Tellini again. But his experience, over five or six years, at this point led him to believe that it was better to team up for screenplay writing. Ideally, even, to find a partner you get along with, who doesn't cry about the dog eating his homework every time he's feeling lazy. Pinelli, a colorful character hiding behind a veneer of respectability, had been suffering the heaviness of all of those years spent in courtrooms and tiny theaters. He instantly accepted the offer from Lux Film—not just for the money but also because he was attracted to the vitality of the movie world. Some people have speculated that the writer sensed an irreversible decline in Italian theater, and jumped shipped like a rat. Regardless, Federico and Tullio met at the perfect time—they were both riding an interesting yet uniquely mercurial moment, typical of those surprising, innovative years. They both longed to laugh and wanted to work together. The ex-lawyer, almost forty then, let his exuberant new twenty-seven-year-old friend drag him into brand-new situations. What connected them was their "complementary diversity," as Pinelli so astutely defined it. Many ideas came out of their conversations, but, as one also needs money to live on, Tullio got his friend involved in writing the screenplay for Duilio Coletti's *Il passatore* (*A Bullet for Stefano*, 1947), about the adventures of Roman bandit Stefano Pelloni, as played by Rossano Brazzi. It's a mediocre movie that you'd watch today only in order to see Alberto Sordi in a secondary role as a bandit, restless and anxious to do anything that might capture the attention of other directors.

Fellini and Pinelli quickly refined their working technique. They would sit across from each other at their typewriters and divvy up the scenes. Sometimes they'd stop to chat—the best ideas burst out of nowhere—and then they'd continue working individually at home. Federico recalled, "Pinelli and I used to split the day in two parts, because we were frequently working on more than one screenplay at a time. In the morning, we'd tackle the trickier screenplays—for Lattuada, Germi, Rossellini. And we'd dedicate the afternoon to not necessarily less important directors but the more mainstream ones, like Gennaro Righelli, Raffaello Matarazzo, and other glorious directors who never expected anyone to take a movie too seriously."

When Fellini involved Pinelli in a new Alberto Lattuada project, their urge to wander, to follow their curiosity (typical of Italian cinema at the time), was able to be fully realized. Fellini had become good friends with Lattuada and one project was to collaborate on the script for *Senza pietà* (*Without Pity*, 1948) based on a treatment by Ettore Maria Margadonna that had been circulating with the title *Arrivederci, Othello*. It was the story of an impossible love between a black man and an Italian prostitute that ends tragically. The story was set in the pine forest of Tombolo near Livorno, which had become an inferno, overrun with soldiers, black marketeers, military deserters, and prostitutes who'd migrated there from all over Italy in order to earn money. You can't write a movie like that sitting around a table, so with the approval of Clemente Fracassi, the production manager (and later executive producer of *La dolce vita*), the two writers set out to visit the scene of the crime. The expedition was risky and uncomfortable, "an audacious investigation of the criminal world that controls the region between Tombolo and the port of Livorno," according to one newspaper.

Fellini and Pinelli, however, enjoyed themselves and repeated the experience whenever they could. When they were offered a chance to work on a screenplay about the Camorra in New York, the team took a room at the Excelsior Hotel in Naples and went out to interrogate the workers, until they were found out and run out of the city. They stayed in Trieste and its outskirts for three weeks, venturing beyond Zone B of the Free Territory posing as Swiss journalists, in order to write *La ragazza di Trieste* (The Girl from Trieste), which was to be produced by David O. Selznick, star Alida Valli, and be directed by Mario Soldati. Their trip was full of adventure and the treatment wasn't bad, but the movie never got made. Other U.S.-backed star vehicles for Valli never got made either, such as a Camerini movie titled *Felice paese* (*Happy Country*), for which Cary Grant was slotted to play the lead—an American mining engineer who discovers that Italy is too beautiful a land to be sullied by oil mining and the short-term exploitation of natural resources.

Over the course of these trips—most enjoyable when useless—the two writers made invaluable connections. They met Riccardo Bacchelli, for example, when working on the screenplay for *Il mulino del Po* (*The Mill on the Po*, 1948). This Lux Film project also came out of Gatti's ambitious plan to make Italian cinema more refined. Fellini and Pinelli were given Bacchelli's three-volume tome to start with. Fellini read the first volume, Pinelli read the second, and neither of them read the third. With Lattuada they found a section in the second volume to develop—a tragic love story between Berta (Carla Del Poggio), the miller, and the peasant Orbino (Jacques Sernas), who dies tragically. The story is set in Polesine at the end of the nineteenth century, a period of revolutionary ideas and bloody repression. Through interminable conversations with Bacchelli, who'd come to Rome for the purpose, Fellini and Pinelli had a chance to rediscover the characters and atmosphere. The three often ended up in a trattoria where Bacchelli assumed the role of food guru. Their meals were endless. Bacchelli had ritualistic ideas about feasting and recommended to his friends that they chew more slowly. There was less agreement about the screenplay than about dining. When Fellini read the minimal, dramatic dialogue aloud to the novelist, Bacchelli would retort, quoting sections from the original text—sections that said the same thing, but with more words. Upon hearing the protests that audiences would surely laugh at such verbosity, Bacchelli replied, "Can't you tell them *not* to laugh?"

Bacchelli was fabulously friendly, though, quite the opposite of the embarrassingly laconic Genoese director for the project, Pietro Germi. But the collaboration, starting with the country retreat in Pitigliano at Pinelli's family house, where they wrote *In nome della legge*, was an enduring one. The two "screenwriting aces"—as they were referred to in the papers—worked on another script for Germi, *La famiglia* (which was never made). And their explorations continued. They went to Naples to research *Il re di Poggioreale* (*Black City*, 1961), which ended up in other writers' hands. They went to Germany to accept an award for *Il cammino della speranza* (*Path of Hope*, 1950), where Pinelli practically forced Fellini to go see the cathedral of Köln that many years later would appear, black and menacing, in the set design for *Il viaggio di G. Mastorna*. Other explorations took them to brothels in Genoa and Turin, where they worked on *Persiane chiuse* (*Behind Closed Shutters*, 1950), though their names didn't appear in the credits.

These were years of initiative and fervid labor, intellectual exchanges and new experiences. The team of Fellini and Pinelli was almost immediately successful, as can be gleaned from a 1947 article in the weekly paper *Bis*, claiming that the most important writers in Italian cinema were Zavattini, Tellini, Amidei, and Fellini. They earned about half a million lire for a treatment, half a million for an adaptation, half a million for a screenplay—though Zavattini actually earned a million per project. According to the article, these screenwriters, mostly from the provinces, "used to go and live in the places they wrote about." They liked to meet up at the trattoria Cesaretto on via della Croce or at one of the Rosati caffès, in either Piazza del Popolo or via Veneto, or on one of the terraces of via Margutta. Each writer had a specialty. Fellini was good "at putting a story together." Tellini "structured each scene." Pinelli wrote "color and set up situations that create atmosphere during the planning stages." And then "Fellini often writes the final dialogues, sitting at the assistant director's side, and might even change an ending or a situation after surveying opinions of the typists in the copy shop." When Fellini and Pinelli signed on to write *Odyssey* for Georg W. Pabst (a job they didn't finish), the newspapers announced a forthcoming "*Odyssey* by Fellini, Homer, and Pinelli."

Over time, Federico and Tullio came to increasingly enjoy the game.

Tullio remembered an endless "cattle call" at the Lux office when they were casting *Terroni*, which ended up being renamed *Il cammino della speranza*, so as not to offend their southern audience.* For days on end, men and women of all ages were paraded before Germi, who just sat, smoked Tuscan cigars, and was inscrutable. It's likely that Fellini's own method for "looking at people" grew out of such experiences. A marked distinction started evolving at this point between Fellini and Pinelli, as they cultivated different attitudes toward the "movie factory." Pinelli never went on the set. He would grow exasperated at the slowness of filming, with all its stops and retakes. He never even considered becoming a director. You need a certain kind of personality to direct a movie: boundless patience, unshakable decisiveness, and incredible stamina. The writer from Turin didn't feel that he had any of those qualities. The two partners sometimes discussed it, though—as they were emerging from one meeting or another with an impossible, egomaniacal director. But Federico didn't always entirely agree with Tullio, who saw things through the lens of theater. Federico saw things as a journalist; he was accustomed to rewriting and cutting as needed. But he agreed that to be a director one has to be a maniac, a humorless dictator. He had always been determined not to follow the rules, and had no intention of learning how to suddenly lay them down. Discussions and aspirations aside, one must take into account how busy they were during that period. There wasn't much time to think. One didn't think, one took action, moved forward, week after week, one contract after another.

But Federico, almost unconsciously, started spending more and more time going around and less time sitting at a table. He'd jot down scenes at the last minute, sometimes during the night—as he used to do for the radio—and he gave in to a growing urge to leave the house early in the morning and not come back until quite late. He went to production meetings and script meetings, business breakfasts, auditions and casting calls, was on call for any emergency that a director required immediate help with. Fellini was a master of emergencies. At script readings, Federico often fell into a trance as he watched the director run the lines he'd just written with the actors. And even if he didn't admit it aloud or to

Terroni, meaning "people of the soil," is a slur on southern Italians.

himself, he started feeling that the movie set was home—where he'd come in order to put an end to all the anxious running away.

This was Fellini's life before *Lo sceicco bianco*; he was a lifeguard, a problem solver, a handler of emergencies. It's raining, so they need to change the screenplay to accommodate the weather. The actress shows up and she's ten years older than expected, so the character has to be revised. The costar broke his leg and can work only sitting down. The production has the budget for only twenty-five extras instead of the one hundred the script called for—some kind of solution has to be found, but a good one, an invisible patch. After all this changing, cutting, racing around, and discussing, night falls and you still need to go back to the projection room with the director and cameraman to see what's been shot over the last two days. And when doubt struck, he'd call Pinelli, who would be eating dinner at home with his family.

Recalling Fellini's astounding energy, Clemente Fracassi said, "He had no personal agenda. He chattered happily, enjoyed his life as it was. He liked the world of the cinema, the women, the crazy hours. He seemed happy. When he entered the room it was like spring had blown in." The cheerfulness was fated to fade over time, though it never completely disappeared. After 8½, "People started saying that he was washed up, a sellout, and that he used people." But Fracassi thought the truth was otherwise. "He was Machiavellian in the best sense of the word. He understood the pragmatism of cinema. He was an incomparable follower of the rule of results, that the movie itself is more important than anything else. Fellini taught that cinema called for clear ideas, hard work, and the ability not to care about anybody else."

As to the relationship between Fellini and Pinelli, the two friends had, after all this time, begun to unconsciously influence each other. They even began taking on each other's character traits. Fellini appreciated the solid education in traditional dramatic writing that Pinelli gave him—even though he would never be dogmatic about it—and also came to recognize how important it was to have a thoughtful script and to write and rewrite dialogue. On the flip side, rigorous Pinelli grew more open to possibilities and coming in contact with Federico's sensibility helped him develop an appreciation for the fairy tale and fabulism that he'd already dabbled in with his play *La pulce d'oro*. For the playwright, *La strada* would be the ideal point of convergence between his interior poetic world and Fellini's world. But the most important thing that Pinelli learned from his traveling companion was how to love the cinema as a reflection of life, even though, as a writer, he couldn't get the name recognition he might have won elsewhere. Pinelli wasn't afflicted by the syndrome of the unhappy screenwriter, seeing himself as plundered and then betrayed by the producers and directors. He acted like F. Scott Fitzgerald, who was always just barely acknowledged in Hollywood but remained fascinated with it and involved. He was the opposite of Ennio Flaiano, who was perpetually embittered, convinced that his work was undervalued. Tullio was that rare case of a satisfied screenwriter: "The job of screenwriting must be accepted for what it is. Fellini tended to want to control it, but the advantage of collaborating with a genius had many rewards, as well as many compromises and many disappointments."

Over the course of the long collaboration, what was complementary about Fellini and Pinelli seemed to be communicated through osmosis. Pinelli worked on the screenplay for every movie Fellini made—up to *Giulietta degli spiriti*, which Pinelli backed out of because he differed with Fellini over the direction of the movie. But he withdrew without melodrama, and without explanation. He still worked as Giulietta Masina's consulting writer and scripted two big television successes for her in the 1970s, *Eleonora* and *Camilla*. It wasn't a matter of chance, of course, that Pinelli's name appeared again alongside Fellini's in the credits for *Ginger e Fred*—Giulietta's first Fellini film after *Giulietta degli spiriti*. At that point, when the two writers came back together, they had eighteen years of collaboration behind them, which was more important than the twenty years of working apart. The old playwright remembers, "One morning I heard the doorbell and it was Federico. He'd come to ask me to read the story for *Ginger e Fred*—as if we'd just seen each other the night before! And we got along famously."

13

A Moveable Feast

In ten years working as a screenwriter, Fellini neither saw himself as the type to direct nor ever anticipated that he would make the big leap. At least nobody ever remembered him saying anything of that sort. Tullio Pinelli always thought that his writing partner stepped behind the camera "because they offered," which might be true. But on a deeper level it was also true that *Paisà* was a revelation. Fellini enjoyed that intense, chaotic, nomadic experience, and there was a change in him. It would be some time before the future director would recognize the signs of his mysterious vocation in the bramble of ambitions and mixed desires, but the process is already under way and unstoppable by the end of the 1940s. Cinema resolves one of the contradictions in Fellini's character, reconciling his constant need to escape—anywhere—with his ethical imperative to do something he can call his own. Fundamentally cinema was a way to avoid familial and social obligations while expressing himself, like cutting school in order to recognize what was important. To escape everything and run after an ambition of his own invention, or his own intuition, meant the world to him.

Unlike his constant companion Tullio, who is bored on movie sets, Federico is enamored of the traveling party that is putting together a movie. Alberto Lattuada realizes very early on that Fellini is in the throes of refining his relationship to cinema. Their collaboration would continue for five years after *Il delitto di Giovanni Episcopo*, and over that period, Federico worked on the screenplays of *Senza pietà*, *Il mulino del Po*, and *Luci del varietà*. He was also Lattuada's assistant director on *Senza pietà*, and codirector on *Luci del varietà*.

His experience on *Senza pietà* was almost as important as *Paisà*. After the adventurous research expedition with Pinelli, Fellini takes Clemente Fracassi, the executive producer, around Livorno to scout locations. Once the shooting starts, in late summer 1947, the assistant director also assumes the job of preparing scenes for the next day. He manages to go thirty-six days and nights with no sleep, working with Fracassi, choosing locations, scheduling actors, handling emergencies. He's good at rounding up prostitutes (who find him irresistible), and he makes friends with Allied officers by talking in a crude, entirely invented "blue-collar" English. Federico is gradually turning into a real movie animal, capable of the most Machiavellian behavior. On the set, you need to be prepared for anything. One day there's a fight and the director ends up actually caught by the tie in a stranglehold by a petty criminal. Lattuada most likely would have been throttled—if the actor Folco Lulli, a former officer with the Resistance, hadn't shouted and threatened to throw a chair.

Such a constantly tense atmosphere feeds unpredictable situations. When the director complains because the gunshots hitting the ground near the protagonist, played by John Kitzmiller, don't look realistic enough, the general manager, Bruno Todini, a famed sharpshooter, offers to shoot with a real gun. So Kitzmiller jumps up and down while Todini shoots a full round of ammunition at his feet. The black actor—a former chemical engineer who'd slipped accidentally into movie acting with *Vivere in pace* (*To Live in Peace*, 1947)—has a rush of euphoric adrenaline more thrilling than anything he would ever experience again for the remainder of his career.

Working on *Senza pietà*, Fellini learns to deal with the unpredictable. He likes shadowing Lattuada, he likes the way the director will just plunge the camera into the crowd, as in the nightclub scenes, telling the actors and extras to relax and go with the moment. Working in and around the city of Livorno, Federico also learns a lot with respect to technique as style. He would often say that Lattuada, "with his whistle and megaphone," would forever be the symbol for him of a director's authority—much more so than Rossellini, who always managed to look like a bystander on the set.

But the critics slam *Senza pietà*, labeling it a black market of tired melodramatic literary stereotypes. *Senza pietà* improves from a postmodern perspective and in comparison to the work of directors such as

Rainer Werner Fassbinder. Along with an obvious capacity for blending facts into American-style nostalgia, Lattuada has a knack for sort of punching the audience in the face. Carla Del Poggio, a popular romantic-comedy actress, plays the lead. She appears in the opening scene, enshrouded in rags, a wayward (read: wanton) girl who made her way to Livorno hitching rides on freight trains. The first image of her: sitting with her legs wide apart on the edge of a freight car, dangling her feet over the side, she yawns, scratches her head, spits, and takes off her shoes. The movie is a love story between her and Kitzmiller's black soldier. The evil Mafia boss (played by Pierre Claudé, the manager of Hotel Majestic in Rome), who's said to "own Livorno," objects to their affair. His "godfather" character is dressed in white; he's impotent and sadistic—based on Popeye in Faulkner's novel *Sanctuary*. The literary and cinematic citations (most certainly not Federico's contributions) are the movie's way of winking at the audience, an attempt to be mainstream and sophisticated, with rich naturalistic details and bookish touches, brimming with inspiration and cleverness.

But also important is Lattuada's decision to cast Giulietta, who he had seen onstage, to play Marcella, a short, awkward prostitute who befriends the heroine. She is a secondary character whose plotline parallels the main one. In writing Masina's first major cinematic role, Fellini seems already to be exploring the key moment of *Le notti di Cabiria*, when Cabiria gets ready for her wedding. Marcella bustles around, preparing her bags, ready to run off with her black boyfriend, a deserter. She packs some things for herself and grandiosely hands the rest off to friends. The only part of this scene that's not echoed in *Le notti di Cabiria* is when she offers her embroidered shirt cuffs to a clearly less fortunate girl. At dawn, Marcella heads down to the beach. A boat arrives and the girl runs toward the sea, then turns back to hug her friend. The shot is beautifully framed by Aldo Tonti: the actresses' faces bright against the somber background, the foam glistening on the surf, and the steely horizon. Nino Rota's sentimental music swells. The episode flips the meaning of the title (*Without Pity*), transposing onto Marcella, who foreshadows the heroine's own fate, an irresistible and pathetic tenderness.

At the 1948 Venice Film Festival the audience erupts in a spontaneous burst of applause when the two women hug. It's the instantaneous and triumphant materialization of a career for Giulietta, who had been unable to come to Venice—she was still confined to bed after her miscarriage—and can't believe what she's hearing when Federico, nervous and emotional, calls to tell her what had happened. Giulietta won a Silver Ribbon for best supporting actress for *Senza pietà*, and accepted the award in August 1949 at an event in Rome held at the dance club La Lucciola. Audiences like her, critics respect her, but the producers just want her to play prostitutes.

You have only to look at the roster of who worked on *Senza pietà* to appreciate its importance in Fellini's formation. There are certainly a number of big names—not the least of which is Lattuada, who will offer, practically force, Fellini into his first directing job on *Luci del varietá*. The executive producer, Fracassi, would go on to be an exceptional collaborator with Fellini during his most creatively intense period: from *La dolce vita* to *8½* to *Giulietta degli spiriti*. Aldo Tonti, the cinematographer, shot most of *Le notti di Cabiria*. And, perhaps most significant, Fellini met Nino Rota, whose soundtrack for *Senza pietà* was inspired by American spirituals. The set and costume design were by Piero Gherardi, who would also go on to work with Fellini (some of the very same rags made a fantastic encore appearance in *Le notti di Cabiria*).

Fellini returns to Venice a year later on August 22, 1949, as the screenwriter for the new Lattuada movie, *Il mulino del Po*. The film wasn't in competition because it had already screened a few weeks earlier at the Locarno Festival. It received a mostly positive reception in Venice, but also drew some perplexed criticism, typical of the time. It was a period of political tilt (on the heels of the April 18, 1948, elections[*]), and Lattuada had endeavored to maintain a balanced position about the class struggle through his astringent realism and sophisticated style. Neither the right nor the left approved. Maybe Fellini's apoliticism, or rather, his nonpartisanship, had played a part in this egregious neutrality, but in the end, the film was well received and would go on to be considered one of the pioneer movies about the peasant class, which paved the way for

---

[*]The 1948 elections were particularly fraught. Fearing a large win by the Communist Party, America got heavily involved, tensions were high, partisanship between left and right was exacerbated, and in the end the Christian Democrats took the majority.

such luminous successors as Bernardo Bertolucci's *1900* (1976) and Ermanno Olmi's *L'albero degli zoccoli* (*The Tree of Wooden Clogs*, 1978).

Il mulino del Po incorporates the use of nonprofessional actors (as did *Senza pietà*), most notably Giacomo Giuradei. He plays the burly well-meaning Princivalle, a character who seems to have stepped out of American literature, and recalls in particular Lennie in John Steinbeck's *Of Mice and Men*. The fight scene between the women and the soldiers hired to replace the striking mill workers inspired clamorous applause and immediately went down in history. Fellini was replaced as Lattuada's assistant director on this film (as he'd been substituted on *Germania anno zero*) by Carlo Lizzani. Federico hadn't wanted to do it. The success of the film, however, was very good for Fellini's reputation and strengthened his bond with Lattuada.

After the war, Federico continues working as a screenwriter, and also takes on the occasional job as assistant director. In 1948 he works with his old friend Mario Bonnard on *Città dolente* (*Grieving City*), the only movie ever made about the Italian exodus from Pola after the Yugoslavian occupation. Between 1945 and 1950, Fellini also works (uncredited) with Gennaro Righelli and Raffaello Matarazzo. Fellini remembers a movie he wrote with Matarazzo "just for fun" about "why Italians always cut in line." But the directors who ultimately really figure in Fellini's path to becoming a director are Rossellini, Lattuada, and Germi.

The collaboration with Pietro Germi is paramount. In five years they worked together on four major films of late neorealism. The executive producer on those projects, Luigi Rovere, would go on to produce Fellini's first solo effort. In 1948, Rovere has just turned forty, and has a lot of experience behind him. He was a former furniture salesman who had broadened his interests to cinema during the war years. He worked as a stage manager, fitter, and manager on films produced by FERT.* Around 1941, he befriended a very smart production secretary from Torre Annunziata who had studied acting at the Centro Sperimentale. His name was Agostino De Laurentiis (aka Dino); and this was how RDL (Rovere–De Laurentiis) came into being just after the war. They would produce

---

*FERT (idest Ferri Enrico Roma Torino), a Turin-based production company formed in 1919, produced more than 180 movies.

Lattuada's *Il bandito*, and other Lux movies: Mario Camerini's *La figlia del capitano* (*The Captain's Daughter*), Carlo Borghesio's *Come persi la guerra* (*How I Lost the War*), and Duilio Coletti's *Il passatore*. Those movies have already come up in relation to Pinelli's early writing career, but Fellini and Rovere would meet for the first time over a revision of *Il passatore*. After that, Luigi and Dino split, and Luigi is looking for good ideas to develop independently.

Rovere had made a rule for himself: every night he would read something by an unknown writer. And that's how he happened across a novel titled *Piccola pretura* (Little Court). The next morning he runs to meet the author at his home. Giuseppe Guido Lo Schiavo was a judge who'd written a book about his experiences in the court of Barrafranca, Sicily. He was asking 300,000 lire for the movie rights, but Rovere is so confident that he pays 500,000 instead. They are less enthusiastic about the project at Lux Film. Gatti asks Luigi Zampa and others if they're interested in directing the film and everyone refuses. Just when Rovere is about to give up, he stops by the projection room where Renato Storaro (father of the brilliant future cinematographer Vittorio Storaro) is showing *Gioventù perduta* (*Lost Youth*). The movie was Germi's 1947 directorial debut and thirty-five filmmakers (including Fellini) had signed a letter supporting the film when it was ludicrously threatened with censorship. Giulio Andreotti, the government undersecretary for entertainment at the time, replied to the letter in a way that reveals the politicians' rush to put an end to neorealism: "Perhaps railing against nonexistent phantoms represents a convenient preformulated plot for some people— and perhaps that's the reason behind the fact that there hasn't been a well-made movie to equal the great three, *Roma, città aperta*; *Sciuscià* [*Shoe-Shine*]; and *Vivere in pace*, in a long time, and nothing at all which has brought us success abroad." Rovere's vision is less clouded, however, and in just a few scenes of *Gioventù perduta* he recognizes the work of a legitimate director. He gives Germi *Piccola pretura* to read and the director agrees to take it on. Then Fellini and Pinelli sign up as well. The film, *In nome della legge*, shot on the outskirts of Sciacca, and starring Massimo Girotti, is the story of a courageous judge's solitary battle against the Mafia in a small town in the middle of Sicily. His nemesis is a gentlemanly Mafia boss, played by Charles Vanel. Tragic conflict arises when a young man, a friend of the judge, is killed by the Mafia. But in the end, the mafioso saves the judge's life in a move that is as noble as it is improbable. When the movie was released in the summer of 1949, the bandit Salvatore Giuliano was still on the run in Palermo, and just two years earlier (on May 1, 1947) had led a massacre against unarmed farmers in Portella della Ginestra. But audiences and critics saw *In nome della legge* as a kind of Sicilian Western. They liked its formal qualities and beefy narrative. The film's success consolidated the team of Germi, Rovere, Fellini, and Pinelli.

After *In nome della legge*, Fellini starts spending every morning in Rovere's office and becomes the producer's closest collaborator. He spends many hours in that room, chatting, talking through projects, and sketching. Sometimes Germi would come by too, even though he isn't a good talker. He's a grumpy man from Genoa, six years Fellini's senior. He'd studied at the Nautical Institute before enrolling in acting classes at the Centro Sperimentale. Later he worked as Alessandro Blasetti's assistant director and was considered quite a little tyrant—feared for the silences that could erupt into rage. Germi isn't easy to get along with, but Rovere values the partnership and has more projects for him. The team works on an idea about southern Italians who illegally cross the French border looking for work. The movie starts in Sicily and ends in the Alps on the French border, moving through Naples, Rome, and the countryside of Emilia. This episodic structure imitates *Paisà*, and the original title, *Terroni*, recalls Rossellini. But the real model for the story is *The Grapes of Wrath*, which was made into a movie in 1940 by John Ford, the director that Fellini most admires.

Germi is silent and elusive. He tends to solve problems by appealing to people's goodwill. He has all the characteristics that Fellini dislikes, including a clear preference for well-constructed stories with a beginning and an end. Fellini and Pinelli would joke about him—the way children at school do about a teacher—but sometimes Fellini is unable to contain his impatience. That said, he's also very interested in Germi's work style, and respects both his integrity and his professional determination. He likes collaborating with Germi and gives him his best—even though the films often head in directions he doesn't approve of. There is, for example, an argument about the ending of *Il cammino della speranza*, the renamed *Terroni*. Near the end of their odyssey, the southern refugees are stopped by the border police. Will they make it to France? Fellini wants them to be sent back. Germi wants them to cross over. And even though the movie has a happy ending, the ministry doesn't go for it and denies the project state funding—until the press intervenes on its behalf. The movie ends up being more successful abroad than in Italy, where it doesn't garner much activity at the box office, winning prizes at the Karlovy Vary Festival, the Golden Laurel from Selznick, and first prize at the Heidelberger Fimkunst-Tage (Germi was awarded an abstract painting that he never put on display).

The next movie that Fellini and Pinelli work on with Germi is produced by Cines Company after Rovere rejects the project, and this time around, things go differently. Heretofore Germi had always prevailed in debates, but Fellini wins this argument. What really stands in the way of telling a story about the adventures of four misbegotten criminals—who after a Sunday robbery at the stadium are undone by their own ineptitude—isn't Germi, but Fellini. Curiously, no one comments on the embryonic Fellinisms—and early reference to *Il bidone*—evident in *La città si difende* (*Four Ways Out*), which is soundly booed in Venice on September 10, 1951. The title promises a cops-and-robbers movie, but misleads. What is seen on the screen are criminals who self-destruct—as opposed to criminals who are vanquished by the forces of order.

Germi likes order and harmony, and is uneasy with this film. He doesn't like the actors and may have been struggling with how to direct them. The story is sort of a criminal version of *Moraldo in città*—a screenplay that wouldn't be written until much later, but the seed of which is already in Fellini's mind. The movie's setting visits both the famous and the hidden parts of Rome: the fry shop, luxury restaurants, boardinghouses, the apartment of a kept woman, the dog races, a sculptor's studio, the Termini train station, a couple on a tram renewing their vows by exchanging rings (this same scene appeared in *Marc'Aurelio* as a short story). There are many early formulations of Fellini's mythology here. Renato Baldini goes into a fountain at night to retrieve the suitcase with the loot—as Anita Ekberg will go into the Trevi Fountain in *La dolce vita*. Painter Paul Müller draws people's pictures in restaurants, just like Federico used to during his bohemian phase. Then the painter, suffering a mortal wound, struggles up a slope by the side of the road, as Broderick Crawford will do after being beaten by criminals in a similar situation in *Il bidone*. It's easy to understand why Germi is ill at ease. He has a good collaborator in Fellini, but he doesn't have one who is going to follow his distinctly more conventional vision.

The next film, and Fellini's last screenplay, is *Il brigante di Tacca del Lupo*, back under Rovere's protective wing. Here Fellini returns to more traditional formulas. Taken from an original text by Riccardo Bacchelli, Pinelli infuses new life into the story by drawing on his own family's history. One of Pinelli's ancestors was a soldier who held back the bandits after the king "conquered the south" of Italy. Fellini, on the other hand, is interested only in the mundane and historical aspects of a "guerrilla war," but doesn't have much affinity with the final result—a staunchly nationalist-populist film done up as an action movie. He had squelched Germi's personality in *La città si difende*, but on this project, he makes a concerted effort to stand back and play the somewhat perplexed collaborator.

The private screening at Cinecittà is greeted with resounding success. Everyone except Rovere is convinced they've made a good movie. Rovere doesn't like the female lead, Cosetta Greco, who at that time is the director's muse. When Rovere admits as much to Germi after the screening, the director just shrugs. The critics and public in Venice, however, tend to share Rovere's opinion and a harmonious relationship goes south. *Il brigante di Tacca del Lupo* marks the split between Germi and his producer, as well as the disintegration of the team that had made *In nome della legge*.

Fellini is growing increasingly less interested in screenwriting, and doesn't even want his name listed in the credits of *Persiane chiuse*, another Rovere production, shot in Turin. The producer, still convinced that he needs to be introducing new talent to his roster of directors, wants Gianni Puccini to direct. Puccini was one of the critics who coined the concept of neorealism in the journal *Cinema*. But after the first three or four days on the set crisis sets in. Rovere claims that the day laborers aren't up to snuff, but it's Puccini who gets fired, and the movie is left without a director. Federico doesn't want to get involved, even though he's in Turin with Giulietta, who once again is playing a sweet, pathetic prostitute (she even has a death scene in a hospital this time). Rovere does, in fact, ask Fellini to step in and direct, but Fellini refuses and suggests Luigi Comencini instead, calling him personally. In order to keep production moving while Comencini is en route, Fellini agrees to shoot the scene in which the police discover a corpse in the river. This is when he meets Arturo Gallea, a veteran cinematographer with every trick in the world up his sleeve, and who will later work with Fellini on *Lo sceicco bianco*. The small task of filming one scene is accomplished with a professionalism that impresses Rovere, and, as soon as he sees the rushes, he determines to commission Fellini to direct a movie.

After all, since 1948 the movie magazines have been announcing the (alas, perpetually postponed) directorial debut of Federico Fellini. He was to have directed, among other films, *L'elefante e il ragioniere* (The Elephant and the Accountant), based on an idea by Zavattini, which would eventually become *Buongiorno, elefante!* (*Hello, Elephant*) in 1952. He was to have directed *Cristo si è fermato a Eboli* (*Christ Stopped at Eboli*), about which Federico himself had been in discussions with the author, Carlo Levi. (Francesco Rosi eventually made the film in 1979.) But Fellini never seemed really interested in becoming a director, neither immediately nor eventually. And in the meantime he'd been undergoing a significant physical change. One newspaper (from about 1949) ran an article entitled "Quanto pesa il cinema?" (How *big* is cinema?) in which it's reported that "Fellini has gained twenty kilograms in three years and now weighs ninety kilograms" (about 200 pounds). His weight balloons while he's busy codirecting *Luci del varietà* with his friend Lattuada.

14

Stardust

Luci del varietà / Variety Lights

Fellini's first directing project, *Luci del varietà*, is launched under the optimistic banner "a movie that will be famous"—and that will be a box-office travesty. The idea for the undertaking was codirector Alberto Lattuada's. He'd been involved in a series of failed projects after *Il mulino del Po*, is fed up with producers, and wants to make a spectacular (and rigorously apolitical, so as not to make a stir at the ministry) movie on his own.

Fellini would never, not even later in his career, manage to produce his own movies. It seemed as if such an entrepreneurial enterprise was at odds with his idle nature, his incorrigible habits, and his psychological need to have a father figure around to battle with. So it wasn't easy for Lattuada to convince Fellini to embark on a production together—even though the "cooperative" aspects per se were murky. In early 1950, the papers remarked with curiosity on this "co-op of husbands and wives" (the two directors and their wives, Carla Del Poggio and Giulietta). Lattuada's sister, Bianca, a first-rate production manager, came in on the project, while his father, Felice, composed the music. Film Capitolium* provided 65 percent of the funding, including technical expenses and lead actor Peppino De Filippo's fee. The cooperative kicked in another 35 percent and the members worked for free.

Figuring out what the movie would be about didn't take long. Just a few conversations between Fellini, Lattuada, and Tullio Pinelli, and everyone agrees the movie will be about *avanspettacolo*. The first titles

---

*The independent production company was formed exclusively for *Luci del varietà*.

they come up with are *Figli d'arte* (Children of Art) and *Piccole stelle* (Little Stars). They finally settle on *Luci del varietà*, or *Variety Lights*. The movie tried to capture the phenomenon of variety shows, a subject so close to Fellini's heart in his days as a journalist, but these were fading lights; the world of *avanspettacolo* was already disappearing, and within a few years, with the introduction of Cinemascope and fixed big screens, it would become a mere memory.

The plot centers on a scrappy small-time actor who becomes Pygmalion to a young girl, falls in love with her, and then loses her. It wasn't a new story: in *Sidewalks of London* (1938) Vivien Leigh abandons Charles Laughton to pursue the success and love of Rex Harrison. The same plot reappears in Charlie Chaplin's *Limelight* (1952). In *Luci del varietà*, a small-time comedian, played by De Filippo, falls in love with the young Del Poggio, an ambitious loafer who joins his show and wins wild applause when her skirt falls off. The comic is so attracted to the girl that he forgets all about his devoted partner, played by Giulietta, and gives up everything to mount a revue to showcase her. But the girl leaves him when she's offered a bit part in a big variety show, and he returns to his regular life and Giulietta.

The decision to do *Luci del varietà* the way they did constituted a rather mild critique of the industry—it was a move that went out of its way not to offend. But the producers guild, obsessed with the idea it might be displaced, was unhappy with the precedent of a director going directly, with no intermediaries, to the Banca del Lavoro for funding. Maybe that was why Carlo Ponti financed a competing project, *Vita da cani*—a star vehicle for Aldo Fabrizi—despite having passed on a similar project put forth by Fabrizi and Fellini just a year earlier. Ponti recruited a group of screenwriters for the project, all of whom were and will be important figures in Federico's life: Steno, Sergio Amidei, and Ruggero Maccari. The film was directed by Steno and Mario Monicelli. Nino Rota wrote the music, and a young Marcello Mastroianni played one of the leads. Clemente Fracassi, who would go on to work closely with Fellini, was the producer. There's even a cheerful, smiling picture of Fabrizi visiting the *Luci del varietà* set while Lattuada and Fellini were working.

Vita da cani was the more accessible and more realistic of the two films. It also had a similar plotline: a besotted comedian tries to help out an aspiring starlet (Gina Lollobrigida) and is abandoned by her just when things are all coming together. The first part of *Vita da cani* was set in a small town and the second part in the city. Critics said that the best scenes were the opening nights out in the provinces. Ponti's movie worked within the established industry infrastructure and was finished by early October, before *Luci del varietà*, which caused the smaller picture some harm. The Comitato Tecnico per la Cinematografia (cinematographers guild), perhaps at the urging of the producers guild, didn't award *Luci del varietà* any of the additional funding reserved for film projects of exceptional artistic value. And even though the critics liked it, *Luci del varietà* was a commercial failure. In the box-office season 1950–51, it came in sixty-fifth among Italian films. *Vita da cani* came in thirty-fourth and made twice the money. The bad returns were a heavy blow for Lattuada and Fellini, who would be paying back the loans for years.

When things don't pan out, it can create a testy atmosphere between friends. The relationship between the collaborators started to sour after this project. Fellini was also on the brink of debuting as a director himself, and would be leaving screenwriting—leaving no opportunities for further projects together. When Fellini started getting famous, there would be some messy arguments over who was the real author behind *Luci del varietà*. Fellini's new fans tended to attribute it entirely to him, and some interviews with the directors—possibly edited for effect— seemed to reveal a genuine grudge between the two. But there is no actual mystery behind the movie. The credits list Lattuada and Fellini as the authors. The only reason the names weren't listed in alphabetical order is that at the time, Lattuada was one of the biggest directors around, while Fellini had just started. People who participated in the film—shot in the summer of 1950 in Rome, the Scalera studios, and Capranica for the exterior scenes—remember a pleasant, relaxed atmosphere. It was all friendly and cheerful, there were no fights, and everyone believed in the movie's chances for success. Lattuada was the principal in charge but Fellini was always there and it's clear from the themes, characters, locations, and approach that it is all part of a distinct aesthetic trajectory, and that the seed of the project was the *Marc'Aurelio* column "Il riflettore è acceso" (The Lights Are On). It was a collaboration between equals, an unusual event in the movie industry, which is perhaps why the project was so difficult to understand and gave way to much debate in later years.

Bianca Lattuada would say that her brother directed every scene, except for a few, which Fellini shot, such as the scene where the troupe walks through the countryside, early in the morning after the party at the rich man's house that ended badly; the scene at the poorhouse; and that in which John Kitzmiller walks through the city at night with his trumpet. Looking back at the movie now, however, it does reveal aspects of Fellini's poetics, even though this was only the dawn of his career: the vision, the startling dialogue, and the grotesque or pathetic touch—all set in a traditional story line. Compared to *Vita da cani*, Lattuada and Fellini's movie had perhaps a more bizarre take on things, but there isn't ultimately that big a qualitative difference between the two films. They both belong to the cinema of the twilight years of neorealism, when people were looking for an interesting way to be entertaining, a genre that would eventually come to be called *commedia all'italiana*. The artists were at last tired of endlessly defending neorealism against the government's constant lament that the genre waved Italy's dirty laundry for the world to see.

After the failure of *Luci del varietà*, Lattuada and Fellini reacted in directly opposite ways. Lattuada went back to Ponti and De Laurentiis, to reap his revenge with the movie *Anna*—which took in one billion lire at the box office. It was a melodrama starring Silvana Mangano as a nun who is also a mambo dancer, and was the biggest Italian success abroad since *Riso amaro*. This was proof for Lattuada that he could make a blockbuster if he wanted. In the same way, Fellini could have gone back to being the prince of screenwriters. But instead he felt that this experience had irrevocably changed everything.

15

It All Happened in Five Minutes
Lo sceicco bianco / The White Sheik

There's a good story that Federico liked to tell—with theme and variations—about the five minutes during which Fellini became Fellini. It was
September 1951. The first-time director arrives late on the set at the
beach of Fregene. The cast and crew and a camel, borrowed from the zoo
in Rome, of *Lo sceicco bianco* are all set up for their first shot. There are
actually two film crews on the beach, a crew within a crew, because this
is a scene about a picture-story being shot on the beach. In this part of
the movie, Wanda Cavalli (Brunella Bovo), a starry-eyed young newlywed
dressed in veils like an exotic dancer, is introduced to Fernando Rivoli
(Alberto Sordi), a rake disguised as a comic-book hero sheik. The way
Fellini tells the story, it was as if he had a tape loop going in his ear expressing ambivalence about what had led him to try to direct, dismay
over having this commitment he'd made, sudden amnesia, a total inability to concentrate, embarrassment over bossing around Leonida Barboni
(Pietro Germi's cinematographer), who was standing in for a few days for
the veteran cinematographer Arturo Gallea, who was really more fatherly
and reassuring.

   According to Fellini's version—of the truth—in his book *Fare un film*
(Making a Film), he spent all of the first day shooting the scene of Alberto and Brunella in a little boat that was supposed to be out in the open
sea. Fellini's first directions on the set are a battle, almost a bad dream,
but he gains confidence and loosens up and it becomes almost like a
game: Camera ready! Actors in position! Take one, lights, camera, action!
And cut. Good. Let's get that again. Take two, camera, action . . . The

whirlwind that consumes Fellini spins out at almost at the same rate as the march that Nino Rota will write later for 8½—and this is only the beginning. This is Fellini's birth as a director.

And then there are other versions of the story. In his autobiography, *Fellini e Rossi, il sesto vitellone* (The Sixth *Vitellone*), Moraldo Rossi, assistant and brother of actress Cosetta Greco, remembers that they spent the first day filming at Fiumicino on the mouth of the Tiber and then had to toss all the film, because of bad weather and Fellini's inexperience. The next day, they moved the whole operation to Fregene, a beach that belonged to Ignazio Mastino—a Sardinian (he later opens a restaurant on the location that is popular with movie people). This was where Sordi finally managed to show off, reciting the surreal monologue he'd written for his sheik character. On this second day Federico seemed more confident, but he knew that when one worked for Luigi Rovere, the risk of getting fired was always looming—it had happened to Gianni Puccini.

Other versions of those first days of production often neglect to note the fact that Fellini wasn't a total novice. He'd stood by the camera and handed down orders before: in Libya on the set of *Il cavalieri del deserto*; on the set of *Paisà* in Florence and *Persiane chiuse* in Turin; not to mention the number of auditions he'd directed and his work on *Luci del varietà*. In any event, the path that landed Fellini on the beach in Fregene followed a traditional course. In the 1950s, before the French New Wave, aspiring directors could start either in documentaries, like Michelangelo Antonioni, Luigi Comencini, Dino Risi, and Luciano Emmer, or as screenwriters or assistant directors. Some, like Carlo Lizzani, followed both paths simultaneously. You needed to find a producer who would trust you with his money—there was no public funding for cinema at the time—and it was typical for projects to make the rounds of producers before finding a backer.

Such was the case with *Caro Ivan* (Dear Ivan), a twenty-page typewritten treatment signed by Antonioni, viale di Villa Massimo 24. It's not dated but we can guess that the director wrote it in 1949, just after finishing the documentary *L'amorosa menzogna* (Loving Lie) about *fotoromanzi*—graphic photo-comics, stories narrated in a succession of stills, such as *Bolero Film* and *Grand Hotel* that were the preferred reading in provincial and small-town Italy. According to Antonioni's documentary, graphic novels sold two million copies each week and reached five million readers. They served as a "portable cinema," and offered a forum where readers wrote in (under assumed names) with their own fantasies—often fantastic enough to rival the heroes themselves. *Caro Ivan* was inspired by the idea of a letter sent in to a *fotoromanzo* entitled "Come tu mi vuoi" (As You Like Me). It's the story of a young man, new to Rome, who'd just left his girlfriend back home in Imola and begins an affair with an actress. He gets involved in acting and starts posing with the actress for the magazine. But the girlfriend, seduced and abandoned, suddenly appears to break the idyll. The comic mood is disrupted with a suicide—a reminder that playing with emotions is a dangerous game.

When Antonioni was still waiting for news about *Cronaca di un amore* (Chronicle of a Love), he spent a few weeks considering doing *Caro Ivan* as his first feature film. Carlo Ponti, who had signed on as the producer, called in Fellini and Tullio Pinelli to write the screenplay. It was Pinelli who suggested: "Let's tell the story of a young bride who runs away from home to meet her favorite actor." Fellini added: "So, let's have her run away during her honeymoon." Ivan morphed into a young groom from Altavilla Marittima who comes to Rome on his honeymoon (another scene in the Termini rail station!). His bride, Wanda, disappears from the hotel. Wanda has sneaked away to the editorial offices of the weekly graphic magazine *Incanto blu* (Blue Enchantment) wanting to meet the hero of her dreams, Fernando Rivoli, aka The White Sheik, whom she'd written many letters to, signing them "The Passionate Doll."

An extraordinary scene unfolds in front of Wanda in the courtyard of the old building at via Maggio 24. This pageant is the debut of Fellini's ragtag cinema world. A procession of costumed characters descends the stairs of the building. There's a march playing in the background—the first of many march variations that Nino Rota will compose for Fellini, inspired by Julius Fucik's *Einzug der Gladiatoren* (*Entrance of the Gladiators*). There is Felga, the mysterious Greek woman; Omar, the bedouin; and a clutch of black men. People scurry around waiting trucks; orders are shouted—this is the underbelly of filmmaking. In a trancelike state, Wanda boards a truck and follows the crew to Fregene, where they are going to shoot an adventure sequence. The young bride is captivated by this new world, which is fabulous to her eyes, but actually revealed here in all its grotesque squalor. Meanwhile, Ivan is scouring Rome for her. The newlyweds are reunited in the end, after narrowly averting tragedy, and wind up in Saint Peter's Square, waiting to be received by the pope along with 200 other couples.

In *Fare un film*, Federico recalls that, "Antonioni didn't really care for our version of the story. He'd shake his head silently and look perplexed." But then, while he was working on his documentary, *La villa dei mostri* (*The Villa of Monsters*) in Bomarzo, Michelangelo fell ill and the *Caro Ivan* project was handed over to Alberto Lattuada. After Lattuada abandons it too, Federico realizes that he has a soft spot for the little tale and proposes himself as director. Rovere, who is producing it, encourages him. He understands the young writer and the way he puts a comedic screen between himself and reality; he thinks Fellini has the bearing of a leader. But when questioned by a reporter, the novice director denied that there was a holy fire burning inside him. "I don't have any messages for anyone," Fellini claimed. "I just would like to get deeper into cinema through storytelling, the way I would do with friends at a bar." He'd have been happy going on as a screenwriter, but directors tend to corrupt the idea of the screenplay—and there's no point in that. Not to mention the fact that for someone like Federico, who is always drawing pictures of things anyway, the visualization of characters and situations is a perfectly appropriate move forward.

As preparations for the movie proceed, Fellini considers a number of different candidates for the role of the groom, whose neurotic search for his dearly beloved constitutes the dramatic weight of the story. Alberto Sordi is out, because he'd already flubbed an audition with Lattuada for the part. Totò is too expensive. Carlo Croccolo, Erminio Macario, and Renato Rascel are other possibilities. Rascel will actually end up taking a role in another movie about comics—because in Italian cinema, everyone copies everyone else—called *L'eroe sono io!* (I'm the Hero!), a Lux Film production which is released in May 1952, several months before *Lo sceicco bianco* opens. The overlapping schedule of similar projects echoes what happened with *Vita da cani* and *Luci del varietà*. Even though Fellini is still at a point in the project where he's not sure that he entirely believes in it, he offers the role to Peppino De Filippo, whom he'd always admired and had befriended while working with Lattuada. At the last minute, however, Peppino isn't available and Fellini replaces him with the nonactor Leopoldo Trieste. Thirty-four-year-old Trieste is a working playwright from Calabria, who has authored the plays *Frontiera* (Frontier) and *Cronaca* (Chronicle) about current events. He's attracted to cinema because he hopes to earn some money and meet women. After completing the script for *Sulla via di Guadalupe* (On the Road to Guadalupe), he's offered the leading role by Nino Bazzani, producer and director of the film. The hero is a priest who is executed by a firing squad during the Mexican revolution—like Henry Fonda in John Ford's *The Fugitive*. *Sulla via di Guadalupe* was shot in the countryside near Rome, and is almost an early spaghetti Western. But the project stops midstream when it runs out of money. Bazzani organizes a screening of the material he's shot, in a vain attempt to court new backers for the project. Fellini, who happens to be in the building, peers in on the screening, and is blown away when he sees Trieste's face on the big screen.

Even though *Sulla via di Guadalupe* is a tragic movie, Federico feels unapologetically cheerful. He asks about the strange Mexican priest and immediately calls him—and with that call he accomplished two tasks for the price of one: he gets a groom for his movie and wins a friend for life. "Poldino" (Fellini was trying to convince Trieste to assume a stage name like the old-time comedians) charmed everyone with his sparkling personality, his deep southern cultural roots, his laconic sense of humor, and his adventure stories about roaming the city at night in search of the perfect girl. Fellini discovers his new protégé is also a sensitive reader and an invaluable confidant. Trieste will go on to be Fellini's most constant and secret counselor among a number of secret consultants he calls on when working on a project.

Of course this account of how the two friends met over a stolen shot from *Sulla via di Guadalupe* is Fellini's. Trieste tells another story. According to the playwright, the two met at Galleria Colonna, where variety actors typically convened and milled about, trying to make contacts (a typical scene at the Galleria is portrayed in *Luci del varietà*). They meet there through a mutual friend, Giulio Calì, who played an Indian magician for Fellini and Lattuada in *Luci del varietà*. Fellini observes Trieste's lustful stares at the passing dancers and says, "Well, three-act plays are totally the wrong approach. You shouldn't have gone into culture if you wanted women." A few days later, Fellini calls Leopoldo, saying he's reflected on it, remarking, "You're so funny and you don't have the slightest idea that you are"—and he invites him to audition for *Lo sceicco bianco*. Leopoldo is intrigued and accepts. He's deemed convincing in the role and when he learns how much money they're offering accepts immediately. Theater loses a promising playwright, but cinema gains one of its most original character actors. Leopoldo will go on to appear in more than a hundred movies over the course of the next fifty years. Referring to Leopoldo's vocation as a playwright, Federico liked to think of himself as the young man's "fatal corruptor." Trieste's brilliant debut is clouded only by the fact that Fellini decides to have Carlo Romano dub his voice.

Faithful to the example set by Rossellini, Fellini casts his film as if he were recruiting for the Foreign Legion. He doesn't care about what the actors have done before and he's unmoved by the idea of their market value. For the role of the sheik, Federico calls on his friend Alberto Sordi, who's just had a colossal failure with his first leading role in *Mamma mia, che impressione!* (Mamma mia, What a Shock!, 1951), produced by Vittorio De Sica. Alberto is moved by Federico's faith in him. They're old friends—there's even a photo taken by Sordi of Fellini on a park bench from the bohemian days—but he's worried about failing again and thinks he can smell catastrophe brewing. There's apprehension on the home front too. Giulietta is confident that her husband will offer her the role of Wanda, but after a diplomatic intervention by Ennio Flaiano, she wins instead the role of Cabiria, a prostitute whom Ivan meets in piazza Campitelli the night he's wandering the strange city. Disappointed as an actress and offended as a wife, Giulietta considers refusing the part. But Federico explains that Wanda needs to be able to project a simpleminded candor—a provincial innocence totally foreign to Giulietta's personality. For that, he calls on Brunella Bovo, who's just acted in *Miracolo a Milano* (Miracle in Milan) directed by De Sica, which didn't do well at the box office. Fellini will have Rina Morelli dub her voice. The rest of the cast is made up of caricature-esque actors, like the old theater veteran Ernesto Almirante, who plays the director; Fanny Marchiò as the magazine editor; and Gina Mascetti, the sheik's wife. There are a number of performers from the world of variety too, like Jole Silvani from Trieste, the statuesque prostitute who appears with Giulietta. We'll see her again as a crazed biker in *La città delle*

donne—proof that Fellini never forgets a friend. Among the many nonactors, there is Ugo Attanasio, Carla Del Poggio's real-life father, playing the
authoritative uncle and Vatican bureaucrat.

The cast is a peculiar bunch, but the crew of technicians and creative
collaborators is very carefully chosen and Fellini will continue working
with them over the long term. During the last stage of preparations,
Flaiano comes on to work with the faithful Pinelli on the screenplay.
Fellini knows Flaiano—a writer, rationalist, and extreme secularist—
from his time at *Marc'Aurelio*. Flaiano worked at *Omnibus* and the two
newsrooms were very close. Fellini probably feels that Flaiano's aphoris-
tic humor is a good counterbalance to Pinelli's poetic tendencies. A single Flaiano sentence reestablishes the grotesque mood of a screenplay
written to go against the grain. This "license to mock" is the principal
contribution of the third screenwriter.

Bringing on Flaiano—who'd written the novel *Tempo di uccidere*
(Time to Kill)—also unpredictably links Fellini to the intellectuals who
converge at Rosati and others at the via Veneto caffè. In that social set,
Flaiano is considered the lightning rod. With some sporadic exceptions,
Fellini and the literary world will share a long history of mutual diffidence
and perhaps tacitly decide not to merge. Fellini, creator of *Lo scrittor
Pompelmo* (Grapefruit, the Writer), never aimed to become a novelist,
while the via Veneto clique is too consumed with its own elite vocation to
pay tribute to a filmmaker—or, as Fellini likes to define himself, "a petty
cartoon journalist." Nonetheless, Flaiano will bring some new contacts
and admirers to Fellini, which won't alter the fact that the way Fellini
sees scribblers and eggheads is how he depicted them with the tragic
character of Steiner in *La dolce vita*—he is respectful, but wary.

In September 1951, just after shooting on *Lo sceicco bianco* has started,
the first-time director argues with the production manager, Enzo Provenzale, an intellectual and nervous redhead from Messina. Though Provenzale laid out a strict plan of production, Fellini has already begun to
express himself leisurely (as will be his custom), and he strays from the
script, changes scenes in the moment. He's not improvising—because he
always knows what he wants and how to get it—but he also doesn't
ignore ideas or developments that come to him as he's working. His
method is defined within the first week of shooting and that's more or

less how he will always be. He works very well with flexible, laid-back managers, like Gigetto Giacosi, Clemente Fracassi, and Pietro Notarianni. But Provenzale tries to be a tough guy and is crushed. Being sensitive, he takes offense and determines to never set foot on the set again, watching over the production from whatever small bar there is nearby and using a secretary as a go-between. He never appears again at Hotel Ginevra on via della Vite, where they shoot some scenes in the hallway, on the stairs, and in the rooms. As the movie progresses, life in the small hotel continues. It's often exhilarating and unpredictable; the crew feels as if they're on a holiday—an impression typical on Fellini's sets. In the midst of all this euphoria, no one complains about the shooting going longer than planned—until Christmas, in fact. Rovere seems unconcerned as well. He knows that it's useless to contradict such a director, even as the cost of the project balloons from the projected 120 million lire to 160 million.

When the time comes to think about music for *Lo sceicco bianco*, another life-meets-art relationship is born between Fellini and his composer. Nino Rota was born in Milan on December 3, 1911. He's nine years older than the director. His maternal grandfather was Giovanni Rinaldi, a pianist from Genoa known as "the Italian Chopin." His mother, Ernesta, is also a pianist, and Nino's paternal grandfather, Pirro Rota, was a set designer from Forlì. Nino Rota was a child prodigy, with Mozartean talent. At only ten years old he could count among his admirers Gabriele d'Annunzio and Arturo Toscanini. He went on to be the favorite student of Ildebrando Pizzetti and Alfredo Casella. He won a scholarship to the United States, where he started becoming interested in composing for the movies. Just after his twentieth birthday, he writes the soundtrack for *Treno popolare* (Working-Class Train), directed by Raffaello Matarazzo. By 1943 he's working steadily, mainly at Lux Film, where Guido Gatti is a big fan. After that, the musician begins working as a teacher and director at the conservatory in Bari, and continues composing for theater and film. Over the course of his career, he will write scores for 140 movies.

Fellini and Rota meet directly after the war. Fellini is coming out of the offices of Lux Film on via Po and sees the maestro Rota standing at the bus stop. He asks which bus he's waiting for, and Rota names a bus that doesn't pass there. But as Fellini is trying to explain that Rota is standing in the wrong place, the bus, incredibly, arrives. The scene, like something Fellini himself would have invented, typifies the relationship between director and composer, which will go on for twenty-five years— a phenomenon of empathy, irrationality, and magic.

The perfect understanding between the two men is immediate. They don't need to test it and will never need to exchange many words, or engage in discussions or arguments. The composer Carlo Savina, who was often the third element in the group, doing arrangements and orchestra direction, can't recall a single disagreement between Federico and Nino. That was primarily due to Rota's angelic disposition, illuminated by inspiration. From the beginning, Rota understands Fellini's twofold aesthetic of cheer and melancholy. The opening music of Lo sceicco bianco already reflects this—a carnival fanfare that moves into sentimentalism. The formula will become a characteristic and archetypal component of Fellini's cinema through Prova d'orchestra (Orchestra Rehearsal, 1978) and, some say, even after. Rota seems able to read his friend's soul and translate his capricious mood swings into music. He doesn't need any instruction and avoids the debates over ownership that compromise so many artistic collaborations.

Rota is endlessly available and has exceptionally broad taste. Though deeply influenced by Casella's Stravinsky background, he is an eclectic who loves all music regardless of whether it's highbrow, popular, his own, other people's. Sometimes he sees no difference between any of them. He imitates and paraphrases, cheerfully stealing from himself and from the entire history of music. But the booty of his thefts is always colored by his individual expression. This characterizes him as it did Rossini and other great manipulators—the ability to transfer entire sections from a movie to an opera or vice versa, or from one movie to another, such as the song "Vola nella notte" ("Fly Through the Night") from Roma, città libera to I vitelloni; as well as the theme to Il bidone that also ends up in Fortunella; while a tune from Fortunella became the now-iconic theme song for The Godfather.

The fact that Fellini is untouched by the intense musicality typical of people from Romagna, and has no particular love for music and a limited knowledge of the field, is not a problem. Nino is happy to adapt himself to the slight motives, heavy rhythms, and signals that Federico likes. The musician works with the director's ideas and often recommends prerecorded music. Sometimes they're unable to use it because of copyright issues, but in the meantime they rise to the challenge and have a ball doing it, sitting together at the piano, watching new musical ideas blossom under Nino's fingers, and riffing on the music they played while shooting a scene. All of it done in "shamefully little time," as Rota used to say.

Perhaps Fellini is unaware of the great strides he made between *Luci del varietà* and *Lo sceicco bianco*, which is released on the heels of the 1950 jubilee—an event that marked the nation.* The movie prefigures the themes of small and large mythologies that Italians seem to feed on. The tone is mocking but also transcends the descriptive sentimentality and cartoonishness of *Luci del varietà*. It's already a shift, a foreshadowing of Fellini's declaration of impatience, revealed in *La dolce vita*: "Can't we be a little bit braver? Are we capable of stopping these lies, these false illusions, this fascism, this blandness, these sterile passions? Everything is broken. We don't believe in anything anymore. And so?"

But this revolutionary message isn't even clear to Fellini yet—and certainly not to the others. The movie world and the critics—the public even less—are unable to discern that under this light tale, there is the political and social resentment of someone who has evidently forbidden himself from making any serious statements. From the moment that the movie is ready to be seen, the people who made it don't know how to define it, much less sell it. And a period of confusion sets in, which will last for eight months. In January 1952, while Fellini is editing, Rovere is convinced that he has a hit on his hands. But rumors in the industry threaten to crack his confidence. One Sunday afternoon, while heading over with Flaiano to a private screening of the movie in a screenroom near via Veneto, the producer runs into Angelo Rizzoli and the director Mario Camerini, who invite themselves along. Their comments at the end are *sympathetic*, though tinged with sarcasm. When they suggest cuts and changes, Flaiano angrily replies, "There's nothing to cut; if anything, we might add," which ruins forever his relationship with Rizzoli. The comment was repeated in print and speculation ensued that the powerful Milanese mogul disliked *Lo sceicco bianco* out of self-interest. Rizzoli is one of the biggest editors of graphic novels, and perhaps he worries that such an open satire might create confusion in his readers.

---

*The story is set during the 1950 jubilee year.

A battle explodes during the selection for the Cannes Film Festival. Angelo Solmi, critic for the weekly *Oggi* (and later Fellini's first biographer), supports the film and wants it to be the fourth Italian film in competition along with *Due soldi di speranza* (*Two Cents Worth of Hope*) by Renato Castellani (which will share the Palme d'Or with Orson Welles's *Othello*), Lattuada's *Il cappotto* (*The Overcoat*), and *Umberto D.* by De Sica. At the last minute, however, the selection, which had been considered official, is retracted and *Guardie e ladri* (*Cops and Robbers*) by Steno and Mario Monicelli takes the fourth slot. (Piero Tellini will win the Prix du Scénario for the screenplay.) The movie season has already launched and it would be unproductive to attempt a summer release. The only thing to do is wait for the Venice Film Festival, where *Lo sceicco bianco* opens on Sunday, September 6, 1952.

The Venice screening doesn't go badly and earns laughter and spontaneous applause. Fellini remembered it as "the atmosphere of a soccer match" and admitted that perhaps the movie "had won some sympathy." The bad news came when the reviews were published. They ranged from tepid to hostile. There were a few enthusiastic fans—Callisto Cosulich, one of the few critics who immediately understood the movie's quirkiness, found a fitting description: "the first anarchic Italian movie." Among the negative reviews, the magazine *Bianco e Nero* claimed "such a cheap movie, vulgar taste, narrative potholes combined with conventionalism—one should legitimately doubt whether Fellini's entry onto the scene as a director should interest us, furthermore that it should be permanent."

When it hits the theaters, *Lo sceicco bianco* earns almost nothing. Rovere is staunch, however, and says, "We've made a beautiful movie, five years ahead of its time." Some thought that one of the reasons the movie failed was its title; audiences thought they were in for an adventure movie. Unfortunately, the failure of *Lo sciecco bianco* is not the producer's only failure of the time. His distribution company goes belly-up too, which affects the movie and costs him hundreds of millions of lire. Later on, Rovere said that if he hadn't been struck with financial disaster he would have gone on producing Fellini's films, starting with *La strada*, which he'd wanted to do from the moment he'd seen the treatment. Later on he noted that even with Rizzoli's recut of *Lo sceicco bianco* in 1961, after *La dolce vita* had such a big success, the movie didn't earn a dime. Rovere's fatalistic conclusion? "Some things are just born that way."

16

Farewell, Youth
I vitelloni / The Young and the Passionate

Fellini's work in the 1950s, from *Luci del varietà* to *Le notti di Cabiria*, is full of goodbyes. This is the decade of change in Italy, from agricultural to industrial, and mythologies, like fascism, that had loomed strong until recently are now fading. The Fascists are growing old, the church won't acknowledge changing times, and young people restlessly look abroad for examples of a more robust democracy. On the one hand, everything seems static because of the continuing influence of obsolete traditions and moral codes—especially in the south, where illiteracy and unemployment are persistent problems. But on the other hand, something new has erupted in daily life, a rampant business culture and growing wealth, the decline of the patriarchal family model, motorized transportation bringing outlying areas into communication with commercial centers, and television to rouse the sleeping provincial regions.

In just a few years, three monumental figures—each somehow representative of the status quo—disappear from the scene: Benedetto Croce (1952), Stalin (1953), and Pope Pius XII (1958). In academia, the death of the Neapolitan philosopher is the twilight of the hegemony of idealism and an end to the outlawing of the "pseudo sciences" that until that point had been barred from scientific legitimacy. The human sciences make new advances, psychology and psychoanalysis gain recognition, and new methodologies are introduced in critical analysis. De-Stalinization in the wake of the 1956 Hungarian crisis muddies what was the polarization between the left and the right in the immediate postwar years. New spaces open up in politics, and will lead to new forms of government and positions not inspired by rigid doctrine or ideological elitism. There are even changes in the church: Pope Pius XII's successor, Pope John XXIII, brings an end to the intransigent exclusion of the laity and the cult of the Madonna, initiating reflection on how to better respond to the ecumenical aspirations of a newly democratic world.

Characteristically, Federico has an instinctive rather than concrete sense of the vitality of this complex intellectual and sociological transformation. Unlike most Italians, he may not have been good at or passionate about holding forth on political issues in open forums. Rather he has the fervor of a not particularly cultured man who had little interest in school, but who attentively reads a lot of newspapers every day. And even though he came of age in the anti-intellectual environment of *Marc'Aurelio*, he has begun to devote his evenings to reading. Fellini is often accused of being apolitical in a hyper-politicized, left-wing creative environment. He is even accused of being reactionary. But he is really an artist who lives modernity as a natural absolute, and so his work often mirrors, even predates, big societal changes. The six and a half movies that the director makes during this decade are a farewell to small-town Italy, provincial patriotism, variety shows, comic strips, Gypsies, grifters, and prostitutes. And in this context, *I vitelloni* (1953) has distinct autobiographical elements and plays a critical role in Fellini's artistic evolution. The film was conceived of as a charismatic comedy, but becomes a generational phenomenon.

Even though the experience of *Lo sceicco bianco* was turbulent, people close to Federico say he seems unconcerned about the bad reviews and nonresponsive public. He is unmoved by the blow to his reputation of a second failure right on the heels of *Luci del varietà*. It might have taken a lot less to compromise another man's career, but Fellini has developed an uncanny self-confidence and simply acts as if his movies were a hit. His collaboration with Tullio Pinelli has stepped up. Fellini has been thinking for some time about a modern fairy tale to be called *La strada*, and in early 1952, he wanders around Lazio scouting locations. It's like he's swimming upstream, ignoring everyone else's opinions—particularly those of potential producers intimidated by the unrecognizable genre. Adding to their wariness, the fantastical *Miracolo a Milano*, a bold and inventive film from the super team of Vittorio De Sica and Cesare Zavattini, is a flop at the box office. But the screenplay is written. Luigi Rovere might have been brazen enough to come on board, but business is going so badly that he almost immediately passes it on to Lorenzo Pegoraro, a former calligraphy professor who had ambitiously turned to the world of cinema.

In the meantime, offers are coming in to Fellini, trying to lure him toward mainstream cinema and away from film as personal expression. One temptation is to work on the adaptation of the play *Il seduttore* (The Seducer) by Diego Fabbri, for which he could cast Leopoldo Trieste and Giulietta. There is another movie to shoot in Indochina about missionaries that both Pietro Germi and Roberto Rossellini have turned down already. One producer proposes a movie with the former Miss Italy Fulvia Franco and her husband, boxer Tiberio Mitri. And Carlo Ponti, resurrecting an old treatment of Fellini's, wants him to direct a detective movie for Lux Film. The wide range of choices is proof that there is still respect for Fellini in the movie world, despite the failures. But Fellini is determined to use his prestige to mount a movie that's entirely his own. The man from Rimini has learned that he must believe in himself, or at least exhaust every avenue before giving up. Fellini is like Michelangelo Antonioni in this respect, a man whose artistic trajectory is evolving along something of a parallel track, and with whom Fellini shares a mutual respect. But Fellini does things his own way, figures out for himself how to play the game and where and when—and he won't take any practical advice. His answer is always the same: It's *La strada* or nothing. Pegoraro thinks a movie about a traveling show is too risky. He's not prepared to do anything riskier than making a comedy, so after an afternoon-long consultation with Ennio Flaiano, Fellini emerges with the idea for *I vitelloni*.

The movie develops in a rush; the title, utterly essential, is welded fast to it from the start. *Vitelloni* comes from *vidlòn*, a term in Rimini dialect that working people use to refer to the students, the bourgeois young men living in towns along the Adriatic coast and those who, generally speaking, have nothing to do, frittering their way through steamy summers and the days of winter. The word, a dialectical neologism fallen into common usage, is a source of long debate. According to some, the expression originates in the Marche region and not in Romagna. It's also commonly heard in the dialect of Flaiano's hometown, Pesaro. The writer offers this explanation of the word's origin in a 1971 letter:

The term *vitellone* was used in my day to define a young man from a modest family, perhaps a student—but one who had either already gone beyond the programmed schedule for his coursework, or one who did nothing all the time . . . I believe the term is a corruption of the word *vudellone*, the big intestine, or a person who eats a lot. It was a way of describing the family son who only ate but never "produced"—like an intestine, waiting to be filled.

In Rimini, young men of this ilk are still called *birri*. It's a mistake to assume that Fellini was making a movie about his own life, which he *will* do with *Amarcord*. Fellini was never a *vitellone*; he left home long before he hit the *vitellone* age. The characters evoked in the movie—Fellini's friend the painter Demos Bonini, for example—were all eight to ten years older than Fellini and Titta. They sported big coats, grown-up hats, long scarves, and small mustaches, and they all had well-groomed hair. Such a pack never would have paid attention to two adolescent high school students.

All that aside, the title makes the project a riskier venture. Distributors are ready to sign on, but the title must change. Someone proposes *Vagabondi* (Vagabonds), to which Fellini's laconic response was: "Then you'd have to add an exclamation mark: *Vagabonds!*" The title also creates translation problems abroad. In the United States, it will be distributed as *The Young and the Passionate*. In the United Kingdom, it's *The Drones*; in Germany *Die Müssigänger*; in Spain, *Los inutiles*. Only in France will they keep the title, *Les vitelloni*.

The development of the movie is a cheerful period. Federico rises to the challenge and can't wait to start. Even though working on the screenplay brings back memories of Rimini, of his family and gang of friends, he doesn't want to test the sensitivity of his hometown by setting the movie there. So he decides to invent an imaginary town built from bits and pieces taken from here and there—just as twenty years later, he'll reconstruct Rimini in the studios of Cinecittà for *Amarcord*. (It's interesting to note that in his whole career, Fellini never shot a single image of his hometown.) Apart from that, the funding for *I vitelloni* comes up scant and it's necessary to somehow "steal" a set. The scene in which the protagonists stand in the harbor and look out over the winter sea—now one of the classic images of the Adriatic—was shot on the beach of Ostia, like all the seascapes in the movie.

Intrepid Gigetto Giacosi, who had been with Fellini on the hair-raising flight from Tripoli, is the man to produce a film on shoestrings and promises. Gigetto keeps the situation under control and rallies the actors like a field officer. "You are the *vitelloni*," he tells them. "He wanted you. But remember I'm the one who *needs* you, I need your faces." Against the advice of everyone, Fellini wants Alberto Sordi, who is very unavailable. He's on tour with Wanda Osiris in the variety show *Gran Baraonda* (Big Ruckus), and the crew has to chase him from one stop to the next, following him to places like Viterbo and Florence, in order to film him. And that's why the movie starts at the Teatro Goldoni in Florence, which had long been condemned after a rat infestation. The all-night party is shot there, using props from the Viareggio Carnevale. Production hiccups forward, partly because of logistical problems but mainly because of lack of funds. Federico is perfectly calm in the middle of this calamitous atmosphere. He'll actually go on to try and re-create these same circumstances whenever he's able. Sometimes, however, the schedule is really too tight and he frets that Otello Martelli, the cinematographer, is working too lengthily on the lighting for the interiors. Conflict between "Signor Otello" and Fellini is inevitable and certainly doesn't prevent the two from continuing their collaboration until *La dolce vita*. But between all the stops and starts, Martelli ends up being only one of several cinematographers who work on the film.

Smuggled into the cast by Fellini against the producer's most ardent wishes, Sordi is now considered box-office poison in the movie world. So much so that the distributors demand a clause in the contract that his name won't appear on posters. But it will actually be *I vitelloni* that launches Sordi's career, and after this appearance he'll be like parsley instead of poison on the Italian screen. In 1954 alone, for example, he'll appear in fourteen films. His success stems mainly from a single scene—inspired by something that really happened to Fellini and Titta. The *vitelloni* are driving back from a day in the country and pass by some workers repairing the road. Sordi's character, Alberto, can't resist the temptation to taunt them. Leering out the car window he cries, *"Lavoratori!"* (Workers!), and then flips them the bird and gives them a raspberry. "Hard labor!" he persists and then their car breaks down—right there. Terrified, the coward runs off, the workers in hot pursuit, and the *vitelloni* are all caught and soundly beaten.

It seems that Fellini is particularly attracted to actors whose professional situation is in tatters. For the lead, Fausto (he's named after the actor Fausto Tozzi, who was originally supposed to play the part but then backed out), Fellini isn't interested in Raf Vallone or Walter Chiari, both of whom the distributors are pushing. He ignores pressure from Sordi to cast *him* as the lead—only later does Sordi accept the part of Alberto. Fellini instead chooses the unknown actor Franco Fabrizi, a former dancer of Wanda Osiris, for the lead and has Nino Manfredi dub him. He's not related to Aldo Fabrizi, and he's just come off a disastrous movie, *Cristo è passato sull'aia* (*Christ Passed by the Barn*)—the title says it all. And Eleanora (Leonora) Ruffo, who plays his wife, just starred in *La regina di Saba* (*The Queen of Sheba*). The kid from *Sciuscià*, Franco Interlenghi, also adds his lot to this motley crew. His character is named Moraldo, after Moraldo Rossi, the assistant director. And then there are some old-school stage actors, like Enrico Viarisio, Paola Borboni, and Carlo Romano. Fellini's brother, Riccardo, appears in the role of, more or less, himself. In addition, there are three second-tier French actors (Jean Brochard, Claude Farell, and Arlette Sauvage) sent over by the skeptical coproducer Cité Films. There's even an appearance by a celebrity of the Third Reich, the Czech actress Lída Baarová, famous for her stormy love affair with Joseph Goebbels, Hitler's minister of propaganda. At thirty-eight she's lived through every kind of adventure and misadventure—from being persecuted by Hitler, who wanted to protect his propagandist's family, to the Communist jail in Prague, a subsequent escape to Argentina, and a hiatus in Spain. This beautiful, mysterious woman could conceivably be heading into her sunset years, but life still has movies and adventures in store for her.

They try to convince De Sica to take the role of the homosexual actor. The great director is busy working on *Stazione Termini* (*Indiscretion of an American Wife*), but he takes a meeting with Federico in the restaurant car of a train parked on an unused track. He is very kind but doesn't accept the part. He realizes that there is very little money in it for him, and, given the role and the period, he also doesn't hide the fact that he's concerned about being marked as actually gay. So he bids Fellini farewell and tentative luck for the film. Some people suggest that Fellini not reveal the character's homosexuality when talking to Achille Majeroni, the glorious stage actor who ultimately does accept the part. His scene is one of the funniest in the movie. The *vitellone* Leopoldo, an aspiring playwright (a saucy self-satire by Leopoldo Trieste), is trying to get his first play produced, and so he tries to trick an old stage actor who's reinvented himself in variety into reading one of his plays. But during a late-night walk on the beach, he discovers, to his horror, that the artist's intentions toward him are entirely sinister. Majeroni reads the screenplay without really fully understanding it. He's hesitant and keeps protesting, "There's something dodgy about it, something that might make people think . . ." The director keeps answering that there's nothing at all, not to worry, and so forth—and then makes fun of the actor behind his back.

Shooting on *I vitelloni* began in December 1952, stopped for Christmas, and resumed again on January 15. It's an itinerant production, with many different locations: Florence, Viterbo, Rome, the Kursaal Hotel in Fiumicino. What remains unvaried are the good spirits of the crew. They enjoy being together, eating together every evening. There's no money, but, in the tradition of movie people, they dine in the best restaurants in every city they visit. This is a great social moment in Fellini's life—he immerses himself in the breaks and the tomfoolery in order to counterbalance his mood swings. There are battles with Pegoraro, who, good professor that he was, looks at the rushes and warns, "You, sir, are a sadist and you like ugliness." To offset the impending disaster that he's sure *I vitelloni* will be, the producer quickly invests in a parallel project, one he considers a guaranteed success. But *Scampolo '53* (Midget '53), with the starlet Maria Fiore in the lead, is a bust, while Fellini's movie, to everyone's astonishment, is one of the biggest hits of the season. Unfortunately, Pegoraro in a moment of uncertainty had sold the movie to Angelo Rizzoli—cheap.

That it would be a success was evident from the start. At the Venice Film Festival, on August 26, 1953, the audience and critics at last unanimously declare that a new director has been born. Even the jury, presided over by the poet Eugenio Montale, who'd declared that he despised cinema and considered the form "an inevitable font of prostitution and delinquency," recognizes the movie's merits and awards it the Silver Lion. This year no one takes home the grand prize. There are six Silver Lions and Fellini's film places second, after *Ugetsu Monogatari* (*Tales of Ugetsu*) by the Japanese master Kenji Mizoguchi. The entire cast of *I vitelloni* goes to Venice with Fellini and stays at the Hotel des Bains. They drink a lot and sleep little, all feeling like they're living out the final chapter of the movie. Federico will be back at the Venice festival, but he'll never again relive the joyfulness of that period. Even the few, moderate, and respectful detractors among the Italian critics don't manage to cast a shadow over the festive mood.

The signature of a director who experiments with storytelling techniques is already in place in the 104 minutes of *I vitelloni*. Instead of narrative, the author moves from the description of a situation into an articulation of significant episodes over a year, from the end of one summer to the beginning of the next. The movie is divided into four main parts, which are then split into a number of secondary sequences. There is an epilogue, in which the youngest protagonist leaves home, bidding farewell to adolescence. The first chapter is an account of the shotgun wedding between Fausto and pregnant Sandra, Moraldo's sister. The second chapter, while Fausto and Sandra are away on their honeymoon, plunges us into the everyday life of the *vitelloni*. In the third chapter, we watch Fausto fail in a halfhearted attempt to keep a secure job in a religious-artifacts store: he tries to seduce the owner's wife. And in the fourth chapter, a variety show called Faville d'amore (the invented name that Fellini so loves reappears) comes through town. And again Fausto betrays his wife with a lovely Neapolitan soubrette (Maja Nipora), who plays Italy in the show, wearing towers on her head. Like in *Luci del varietà*, we are immersed in this innocent and sensual vision of variety. The women are but attractive caricatures. They'll start becoming monstrous only in Fellini's later work. Fausto's philandering leads to the worst marriage crisis yet, which with difficulty is nonetheless resolved. After the couple reconciles and heads home, the narrator explains, "Fausto and Sandra's story ends here for now. The story of Leopoldo, Alberto, Riccardo, and the rest of us . . . well, you can imagine how it goes." The only one who escapes his fate is Moraldo, who leaves for the big city.

We already mentioned the reservations that some critics, mainly Italians, had about *I vitelloni*. Young leftist reviewers in the early 1950s believed that cinema had to represent social problems in a politicized way, and even offer remedies. It was common in the Italian cinema of the day to surround any "engaged" movie with an investigation of the themes it presented—even if the lesson wasn't used in the movie itself, or the movie contradicted it. Those who were instinctively more in tune with Fellini for his pragmatic, light approach felt a little guilty when social problems weren't clearly stated, or when reality hadn't been honored in a scientific way. Of all the criticisms, the only one that perhaps holds up concerns Fellini's total absolution of the older generation. Not even Fellini really approved of a world where a conservative generation had given their lives up for their more or less degenerate children. And he always claimed, "We spent the second half of our lives making up for the mistakes that we made in the first part of our lives as a result of our upbringing." Perhaps the director had let himself get carried away with the dynamics of circumstances in this movie, because in the end, someone really needed to beat some sense into Fausto—he deserved it.

I vitelloni is Fellini's first film with international distribution. It was huge in Argentina and had a good run in France, as well as in the United States, where it was released in November 1956 (the title of the *Newsweek* review is "Marty—Italian Style"). In 1957, it is a hit at Everyman Cinema in Hampstead, London. The movie wins many awards, among them three Silver Ribbons for best film, best director, and best supporting actor (Sordi). Filmmakers all over the world look to it as a model—there are so many imitators, it's impossible to list them all. In Spain in 1956, Juan Antonio Bardem shoots *Calle mayor* (*The Lovemaker*). In 1959, the Italian exile Marco Ferreri makes *Los chicos*. Both films pay tribute to *I vitelloni*. In 1960, Francesco Maselli shoots *I delfini* (*The Dauphins*) in Ascoli Piceno. In 1963 Lina Wertmüller, a debut director (and Fellini disciple) who had developed in an entirely original way under the shadow of her famous teacher, adopts Fellini's structure to tell an intimate family story in *I basilischi* (*The Lizards*). *I vitelloni* also has an influence on later films, like Martin Scorsese's *Mean Streets* (1973), George Lucas's *American Graffiti* (1974), and Joel Schumacher's *St. Elmo's Fire* (1985), as well as many others.

This time Fellini's success is so great that he is flooded with offers for a sequel. One producer offers him a blank check to make *Le vitelline* (the female version). The director is unmoved by all these temptations and rejects the offers. Only later, during a break in the shooting of *La strada* in January 1954, does Moraldo come to mind, and Fellini starts entertaining some new ideas. Along with Pinelli and Flaiano, Federico bangs out a screenplay, *Moraldo in città*, which some say is one of the projects that he was most attached to but ultimately will never make. Regardless, we will see that *Moraldo in città* plants the seed of an idea for *La dolce vita*.

Setting *Moraldo in città*, like *I vitelloni*, in the fifties is more a choice of necessity than anything else because of how scarce funding is. *I vitelloni*, set in 1953 in an unnamed beach town on the Adriatic, recalls an atmosphere and some events of Rimini, 1938. *Moraldo in città* traces, with almost the fidelity of a diary, Federico's first experience of Rome in 1939: making the rounds of the newspapers looking for work, his friendship with a painter named Lange (obviously Rinaldo Geleng), the death of the bohemian journalist Gattone, a stormy relationship with a sophisticated lady, and true love found with Andreina. Moraldo goes through a serious crisis, but in the end he rediscovers hope in the spectacle of the world— as will Cabiria. The project never makes it beyond a treatment. It doesn't even get developed into a screenplay. Producers are, as usual, unconvinced. It's too melancholic, too fragmentary; the love story is weak; there's no real happy ending. But the theme is important because it's a kind of bridge between old and new Fellini, between the lighthearted journalist he was at *Marc'Aurelio* and the mature storyteller he becomes in *La dolce vita*, which is in the end a kind of elaboration of *Moraldo in città*, with many similar themes and characters. (Starting with the protagonist's name: originally Moraldo, it becomes Marcello Rubini once Marcello Mastroianni is cast.) After having processed his teenage years in *I vitelloni*, and resolved his relationship once and for all with Rimini (at least that's what he thinks at the time), Federico attempts fifteen years later to define the contradictions of those years when he was almost but not yet a citizen of Rome. This theme will return, not only in *La dolce vita* but also in *Roma* and *Intervista*, though with less attention to the facts and a greater focus on setting, environment, and emotions.

17

A Little Bit Kafka
L'amore in città, Un'agenzia matrimoniale

There's an intermission between *I vitelloni* and *La strada,* during which Fellini makes *Un'agenzia matrimoniale* (A Marriage Agency), a segment of the omnibus movie *L'amore in città* (*Love in the City*). This is Fellini's first opportunity to put his short-form abilities on display. The format will continue to attract him throughout his career; his love for the anecdote and short story may have come out of his work at *Marc'Aurelio.* Taking on Riccardo Ghione and Marco Ferreri's project, however, reveals a certain lackadaisical bemusement. *L'amore in città* is conceived of as the first installment of an ambitious new cinematic journal to be called *Lo spettatore,* the first theme of which is love in the city. Ghione and Ferreri are impoverished but plucky producers working out of Faro Film. Ferreri is the future great director of *La grande bouffe* (1973), an unusual character from Milan who abandoned veterinary studies and then a job in marketing for a liquor company before coming to film. Between 1950 and 1951, he and Ghione produce three issues of a cultural-cinema news publication called *Documento mensile*, an enterprise too good to last in the fearsome world of cinema. Now the team wants to set up a yearly movie almanac. It was the indefatigable Cesare Zavattini who originally came up with the idea and is coordinating the project, which never evolves beyond the prototype, *L'amore in città.*

The goal is "to minimize the space between life and spectacle," a formulation that grows out of Zavattini's proclaimed ideal journalism: an attentive account of small facts and everyday characters. *L'amore in città* comes out of neorealism's twilight, when the movement is already "tired"—yet this project will assume a notable position within the genre. The product isn't as good as its theories, though. The idea of putting together a group of directors to develop movies around a single theme proves utopian. In fact, each director ends up shooting his own segment as if it were an episode in a collective, but without the slightest interest in what his colleagues are doing. This is what will happen in the other group projects that Fellini contributes to: *Boccaccio '70* and *Histoires extraordinaires*.

In his essay "Diario cinematografico," Zavattini acknowledges that he failed to create a unity of intention among his contributors: "We only had sporadic contact with one another," he writes. So there is no central idea or perspective on the theme that unifies the movie. *L'amore in città* is a perfect example of the risk of "total realism," which is to say the reduction of an investigation to simple and dispersed facts and phenomena, with no links between them, and ultimately no guiding concept. Carlo Lizzani's investigation of prostitution and Michelangelo Antonioni's suicide of passion both emanate from interesting ideas, but their products don't achieve the same level that the themes themselves do in the abstract. Dino Risi makes a brilliant piece about a dance club; and Alberto Lattuada comes up with some heavy-handed mockery about the way Italian men turn to look at every woman who passes by on the street. In Zavattini's episode *Storia di Caterina* (Caterina's Story), the drama of an adolescent mother is reenacted by the girl herself. His fussy, anxious precision has him trying to reconstruct events truthfully in minutiae, which is a strong contrast to the stylistic energy of his codirector, Francesco Maselli, an Antonioni disciple. While Zavattini and Maselli attempt the impossible, the replication of reality, the other directors opt for more documentary-style interpretations. Fellini slyly decides to represent a "false truth." He never did agree with Zavattini's theories, because he always believed that on the screen, everything has to be invented.

Some people maintain that Fellini went undercover himself to actually investigate the real marriage agency, Omega, that the story is based upon. According to others, however, this is just a "neorealist alibi" that Fellini offered to Zavattini, a façade of theoretical solidarity. The one sure thing is that nothing in *Un'agenzia matrimoniale*, written with Tullio Pinelli, was "taken from life," starting with the two professional actors.

Antonio Cifariello, dubbed by Enrico Maria Salerno, uses his own name for the role, visibly perpetrating this volatile dynamic of fiction and truth. Cifariello had already appeared in several movies and will go on to become one of the most popular faces of "sentimental neorealism." Later, having become an acclaimed TV documentary director, he will die in an airplane crash in Africa in 1968. The girl, Rossana, is played by Livia Venturini, an actress and voice-over artist who will later appear as the little nun in *La strada* and in several other movies. Gianni Di Venanzo's camera work is interesting here. He will work again with Fellini as a consultant on the last black-and-white picture, 8½, and on the first color one, *Giulietta degli spiriti*. During this, their first encounter, they didn't have time to get to know each other, according to Federico.

The story follows the fearless journalist Cifariello into the bowels of a huge building in Rome as he looks for the marriage agency Cibele. The location is really the San Michele hospice on Lungotevere Ripa, the same place where *Il delitto di Giovanni Episcopo* was shot. The journalist tells the agency owner that he has a childhood friend who lives in the country with his wealthy parents, and that he suffers from epilepsy. Cifariello tells the woman that doctors think marriage may be his friend's only hope. A few days later the woman procures a candidate for him, Rossana, whom she delivers to the journalist, sending the girl off with the admonition "Do you understand—you're going to go be a lady?" Cifariello tells her that her date is a very rich man who suffers from lycanthropy—the moon has a terrible effect on him. The girl is entirely sympathetic, exclaiming "Poor man!" before asking, "But is he a nice person?" Her parents are farmers and she's in a temporary living situation in the city but she can't stay there. She doesn't know how she's going to survive, and marrying a wolf-man seems like a feasible solution. "If he's nice, I know myself, I can grow attached." The journalist isn't prepared for such an answer and doesn't have the courage to continue with his ploy. "It would be better to forget about this," he warns her. "Sorry." She shrugs, downcast, as if she's just gotten confirmation of her own inadequacy. "I knew it wasn't for me."

When *L'amore in città* is released in November 1953, it doesn't really capture the imagination of the public. Critics, however, are interested in it—Fellini's segment in particular. They read into its meta-realism, and there's not a review of the film that doesn't make reference to Kafka and the dark rooms the journalist passes through at the beginning of the episode. The movie is released abroad much later in a cut version, as Lizzani's segment about prostitution is deemed dishonorable to the national image and is censored out. In Paris (February 1957), André Bazin declares *Un'agenzia matrimoniale* to be "good, though not purely Fellini-esque," and he praises the director's "characteristic blending of landscape and character."

During this brief collaboration, Fellini and Ferreri build a cordial, genial rapport, but it won't develop into friendship—in part because Ferreri moves to Spain soon after. Many years later, after Ferreri becomes more famous, they will find themselves in competition, especially over Marcello Mastroianni, who becomes everyone's favorite actor, and frequently "betrays" Fellini with Ferreri. Once, when the two met by accident at Cinecittà, it is reported (by an amused bystander) that Federico teased Marco, asking, "Who's more famous? Me, or you?" To which Ferreri responded, "I don't know about that sort of thing. But I could tell you who's better." This would be one of the few situations in which Fellini lost a battle of wit.

18

Reality Is a Fairy Tale
La strada

Vocation is a kind of interior command you can't ignore. Sometimes it hits you early in life and sometimes later. You know it's there when it possesses you like an inescapable existential criterion. When it's real, there's no room to argue about timing, convenience, common sense, the pursuit of an easier life. Vocation is flush with chromosomes, traumas, hopes, memory, intuition, frustration, accident, and history. It's impossible to discern the exact moment when vocation becomes a conscious factor; it's impossible to analyze it in all of its complexity.

Fellini's cinematic vocation hits its climax with *La strada*. It starts in early 1952, while the novice director is editing *Lo sceicco bianco*. At this point Federico has been working in the movies for about ten years, and he's done everything: written, consulted, made decisions, solved problems, offered opinions, and become increasingly responsible for the whole show. But he always thought that beyond everything, he really wanted to be a painter; if not that, then maybe a journalist. And he has also always wanted to keep the door open for other professional opportunities—at least any that involved a pen and paper. For Fellini is essentially at ease when writing; he's an intellectual against his own will, lost in the maze of cinema partly out of curiosity and partly out of greed. This was the scenario until he became a quasi-director and then a real director. In the dim light of the editing studio, as he compiles the sequences of his first film, he has a revelation and realizes for the first time that he's holding a means of expression in his hands. The awareness that he's somehow learned to control a language melds with his urgent need to communicate. At thirty-two, Fellini, with clarity and pride, finally knows what he wants to be when he grows up—and what he will be forever. It's not incidental that the various demands of production had forced him to make *I vitelloni* and *Un'agenzia matrimoniale* first, even though *La strada* was already perfectly formulated in his head, a fantastical theory that will incubate until it can emerge into the light. On a practical level, the movies in progress, especially *I vitelloni*, are not merely work but are deeply consuming. The day-to-day exigencies of these projects will all be part of a preparation for that ultimate difficult, decisive test: a movie that will be made when its time comes.

What's the story behind *La strada*'s long and laborious screenplay? Fellini and Tullio Pinelli start with the idea in abstract. These are the adventures of a wandering horseman in the Middle Ages. Then the worlds of Gypsies and circus life start to edge their way into the story. Pinelli tells it this way:

> Every year I used to drive from Rome to Turin to visit the area, my family, my parents. At the time, the Autostrada del Sole* had not yet been built and you had to go over the mountain roads to get there. I saw Zampanò and Gelsomina on one of those mountain roads: there was a big man pulling a rickety cart, draped with a banner with a picture of a mermaid painted on it. A small woman pushed the cart from behind. This tableau reminded me at once of every experience I'd ever had in my explorations of Piedmont—the markets, the fairs, the people moving from town to town, and the crimes that went unpunished along the road. So when I got back to Rome, I told Fellini that I had an idea for a movie. He said, "I have an idea too." Strangely, we both had very similar ideas. He'd thought of vagabonds too, but his idea mainly focused on the small circuses that were around then . . . We put the two ideas together and we had a movie.

They work out a system for writing the screenplay, which started in 1951 with the rough draft and was worked into a final version in 1953, after a

---

*Italy's principal north-south motorway, which until recently was the most direct route down the peninsula.

feverish revision with Ennio Flaiano—who never liked the movie idea at all. This ritual will hold for future Fellini films, especially the ones that will somehow mark a new direction in his writing. The next step of the ritual is "the dance of the producers," as the screenplay frenetically passes from hand to hand and enthusiasms wax and wane.

La strada is born under Luigi Rovere and then goes to Lorenzo Pegoraro, who shares Flaiano's doubts and doesn't want to cast Giulietta Masina. He's open to any other solution, and even asks Fellini to audition Maria Pia Casilio, the little servant girl from Vittorio De Sica's *Umberto D*. The director agrees to the audition, but the idea was conceived with Giulietta in mind and switching to another actress would be as radical as changing director. Masina's professional situation at the time that negotiations are dragging on is rather paradoxical. She is critically acclaimed and has won many awards, but to producers she is still the pathetic prostitute from *Senza pietà*. Envisioning her in the role of Gelsomina the vagabond requires too much of a leap of imagination for the mediocre minds of movie businessmen. Pegoraro abandons the project, and other producers continue to say: *La strada*? Maybe . . . but not with Masina.

Rather than telling Giulietta the whole story, Federico gives her a draft of the treatment. Tears come to the actress's eyes when she reads it and she can't wait to get onto the set. Immediately after, however, a tussle over Gelsomina starts brewing between the two. She thinks of the character as a sort of Cinderella, an ill-fated victim, a perfectly sweet creature. The author, on the other hand, has an entirely different image of her in his mind. To him, she's a strange brand of fighter—an idea that he starts projecting onto his mulish wife. The costume and makeup tests start immediately after *Lo sceicco bianco*, even though the hope of making *La strada* at this point is still close to nil. Photographers shoot hundreds of pictures and Federico studies them, and then draws and paints all over them. He has Giulietta cut her hair and bleach it yellow. He puts shaving cream and talcum powder in it to make it shaggy. He digs up a shredded T-shirt and tennis shoes and socks, a top hat and a short skirt with an elastic waistband, a military-issue coat and a soldier's cape from the First World War, bought off the back of a shepherd in the Abruzzi. The wool is so stiff against Giulietta's neck that it leaves a bruise. Giulietta, just thirty years old and still pretty, would prefer to look nice onscreen. But Federico seems determined to deprive her of any elegance—even in life. In fact, the many party dresses the actress buys are destined to languish uselessly in the closet because he doesn't like to see her "dressed up like a lady."

The story of *La strada* doesn't attract producers' interest. Young Gelsomina, dressed in rags, looking half like a priest, half like a clown, is sold to Zampanò, a Gypsy who puts on shows in small towns and at fairs. He has a strongman act—he breaks an iron chain with his chest muscles. Without fanfare, he teaches Gelsomina how to assist him in the show, how to be a maid in their traveling house, and how to be a sort of wife. When she tries to escape one night, the little slave sees Il Matto (the crazy man) walking a tightrope high above a crowded square. Her new friend tries to teach Gelsomina to have faith in life, but meanwhile is himself irresistibly drawn to provoking Zampanò, and ends up dying in a fight with the Gypsy. The woman descends into abject depression after this, and the story moves toward a tragic ending. Zampanò's regret comes, but too late.

Gigetto Giacosi, who'd discussed the project at great length with Fellini while they were engaged in the adventure of shooting *I vitelloni*, brings Fellini to via della Vasca Navale in the Ostiense district, where Carlo Ponti and Dino De Laurentiis have set up shop in the former warehouse of the Carro di Tespi (the itinerant opera company). The two producers have teamed up for now, but everyone knows it won't last. After sharing the executive role in all of their projects, Ponti and De Laurentiis will argue over the preproduction of King Vidor's *War and Peace*. Dino is ambitious and wants to concentrate their efforts on a few titles that have a good shot at international distribution. Carlo would rather reduce their risk by producing more movies at lower costs and going only with sure things—if Totò is in it, all the better. Another point of contention is that De Laurentiis tends to preach the religion of shooting in and providing studios—which will lead him to create Dinocittà on via Pontina in the early sixties—whereas Ponti sees the producer's role as a business coordinator, free from the burden of managing studios and services. When they split in 1956, De Laurentiis acquires the rights on all the films they produced together, including *La strada*, which had been seen all over the world at that point.

There isn't much discussion about budget, which Fellini, really wanting to make the movie, agrees to keep incredibly small. He thinks that he can pay his actors and crew with honoraria and favors. But the debate keeps coming back to casting. Federico liked to recall how Dino kept pushing his own wife, Silvana Mangano, to be cast as Gelsomina—although the producer has denied that. The strange thing is that Federico and Dino respect and love each other and also delight in each other's company. In their own way they've been friends since their first encounter and will continue that friendship.

Unfortunately their respective ideas about cinema are just too different for there not to be conflict. Dino doesn't even speak English, but he acts American, thinking of the Hollywood system as the only way to make good movies. Fellini instead believes in European cinema, and what the French will call *politique des auteurs*. But Dino has boundless admiration for Federico and Federico likes Dino's personality. They are almost the same age (De Laurentiis was born in Torre Annunziata in 1919), though Dino treats Federico the way a wise man would teach a boy genius who has no appreciation for practical matters. Dino's outbursts, his Neapolitan invocations and sentimental appeals to friendship are lost on Federico, while Federico's creative caprices never fail to elicit outright rejection from the producer. They will argue about *La strada*, and paradoxically about how to save two characters destined to die. Fellini is unhappy with Il Matto's death (Pinelli objects that the movie loses meaning without the death); and Dino wants Gelsomina to survive in the end. So he hires veteran screenwriter Ennio De Concini to consult. De Concini makes a number of suggestions before respectfully bowing to Federico's intransigence—he recommends Dino do the same.

Let's return to 1953: to the first round of a long boxing match. It begins with a director and a producer in their early thirties. Giacosi is in the middle, a servant to two masters—or, rather, a double agent—in the best tradition of production managers. He is exactly like Mario Conocchia, the Producer in 8½, a character portrayed with both love and disdain. De Laurentiis also wants to wield some influence over the casting of Il Matto and begs Fellini to audition Walter Chiari and Alberto Sordi—that same guy who only a few months earlier was construed as a sure commercial disaster. Doing his leaden, grim character, Sordi could perhaps play Zampanò (and in some way will do so in *Fortunella*), but he's the dead opposite of the airy, lyrical Matto. Federico knows that already, but in order to avoid saying no all the time, he makes the mistake of giving Sordi an audition. The outcome will remain a point of embarrassment for a long time between Sordi and Fellini. They will basically never work together again, and will lose track of each other, except for occasional friendly reunions. They meet again on a movie set many years later, when Federico agrees to play himself in a scene with Alberto for the movie *Il tassinaro* (*The Taxi Driver*, 1983). Assistant director Moraldo Rossi also auditions for the part of Il Matto, only because he has the acrobatic abilities the role requires.

By a strange coincidence, the director ends up finding the entire cast for *La strada* in a studio on the set of another movie, *Donne proibite* (*Angels of Darkness*), produced and directed by Giuseppe ("Peppino") Amato. The prostitutes are played by Linda Darnell, Lea Padovani, and Valentina Cortese. For this film, Giulietta has been promoted from prostitute to the role of the madame. Peppino, desperately besotted with Darnell, directs the movie, speaking an absurd combination of English and Neapolitan. Federico is overcome by sympathy for this picturesque character—who he'd already met when Peppino was producing a project that Fellini was working on with Aldo Fabrizi. (Amato will come to the rescue in the future when *La dolce vita* falls into crisis.) Anthony Quinn is also working on *Donne proibite*, while another American, Richard Basehart, stops by at times to pick up his wife, Valentina. After a few dinners together, Federico realizes he's found both his Zampanò and his Matto. He grows particularly friendly with Basehart, who he'd admired as an attempted suicide on the top of a skyscraper in *Fourteen Hours*, 1951. Basehart has a sweet disposition and a smile that reminds Fellini of "Charlot."*

Production on *La strada* begins in October 1953, and between upsets and interruptions will continue into the spring. In the meantime, a man named Savitri shows up. He's a chain-breaker and a fire-eater, and his wife Ambretta is always at his side. If Federico were looking for real-life models for his Gypsies, then he's found them here. Savitri will choreograph Quinn's strongman performances, help him prepare the chains, and teach him how to talk and act. Quinn, also working simultaneously

*Charlie Chaplin's French nickname, used also in Italy.

on *Attila* for Ponti and De Laurentiis, really notices the difference in how he is treated between one set and the other. For the historical blockbuster he has a heated trailer and a number of assistants—his future wife, Jolanda Addolori, among them. Under Fellini, though, he often has to do his own makeup sitting in a chair by a wall in a nondescript small town somewhere. It's difficult for someone from Hollywood to renounce some privileges, and the Mexican actor has a hard time getting into the spirit of the film. But, because he is an artistically sensitive performer, the problems vanish once he understands the quality of the project. Basehart's unfailing considerateness, the incredible dedication of the entire cast and crew, and Gigetto's prankster-like diplomacy all also contribute to helping Quinn relax. Working on *La strada* will be an indelible memory for loyal Zampanò, who will send a letter to Federico and Giulietta in 1990, noting, "The two of you are the highest point in my life.— Antonio."

A few weeks later Giulietta has an accident. While shooting the scene in the Bagnoregio convent, she trips over the cart and dislocates her ankle, which means they have to suspend shooting. De Laurentiis, who agreed to the lead actress under duress, hasn't yet given her a contract and there are rumors that he hopes to switch her out now. But when executives at Paramount screen the rushes, they reserve their highest praise for the actress, and De Laurentiis is ready with his reply: "She's on contract with me. I have her on an exclusive." He orders Giacosi to get Giulietta to sign the contract immediately. She receives a third of Quinn's fee.

In February 1954, production starts back up. Otello Martelli takes over from Carlo Carlini—who's departed over artistic differences—as cinematographer. This isn't uncommon among cinematographers, and will be repeated with Aldo Tonti on *Le notti di Cabiria* and Ennio Guarnieri on *Ginger e Fred*. The temperature often drops to minus five degrees centigrade and the small hotel in Roccaraso where the troupe is staying has no heat or hot water. Sometimes, on the way back from the set, the crew and cast are so cold that they climb into bed fully dressed with their hats on. Giacosi is heroic as he takes the troupe from Viterbo to the mountains of Ovindoli to Fiumicino, over no less than thirty different exterior sets. He has a gift for getting by on little money. For the circus scene, the director hires caravans, tents, and performers from Circus

Zamperla, and after this, the Zamperla family will provide Italian cinema with some of its best stunt work. The car that explodes after Il Matto dies is an old Balilla of Savitri's (Savitri manages to earn something back in this deal). Basehart's tightrope act over the piazza in Bagnoregio is performed by an acrobat so proud that he refuses to walk when firemen show up with a safety net. His dignity won't be compromised like that in front of the 4,000 (unpaid) extras that Giacosi managed to gather in the square by convincing the local priest to move up the April 8 celebration of the town's patron saint by a few days. On March 25 in Ovindoli, "Saint Gigetto" (Giacosi) even created snow—as there was no real snow—by collecting thirty bags of plaster and all the bed linens he could round up in the area, more than a hundred, which he laid out behind the actors.

Fellini admires the ingenuity of his organizer and sometimes teases him by requesting impossible things. One day he bursts out, "Where's the elephant?" Gigetto disappears and returns an hour later, totally cool, with an elephant. But as the days drag on, the work weighs everyone down and the cheerfulness dwindles. The cameraman is using arc lights to flatten the grays, which are hurting Giulietta's eyes, and she has to wear bandages over them for a few days. Although apparently immune to fatigue, Federico also starts to feel the pressure. His collapse, following a sudden listlessness and an uncontrollable foul mood, comes in the middle of shooting a scene in the harbor of Fiumicino, three weeks before the end of the movie. (But this is part of a backround story that we'll return to.)

Suffice it to say that the director's mysterious illness doesn't interfere with either the timing or the quality of the final product. Some people even claim that Fellini agrees to shoot some extra scenes with Quinn for *Attila*. De Laurentiis claims otherwise—he'd asked Fellini to do some work on *Attila* to get him familiar with the actor. In any event, the shooting wraps in May and the dubbing begins. The director isn't convinced by the actor hired to dub Quinn and suddenly remembers the splendid work of Arnoldo Foà dubbing for Toshiro Mifune in *Rashomon*. He makes an urgent request to get Foà, who ultimately arrives at the last minute, and does the entire part to perfection.

To get a picture of the opening night of *La strada* in Venice, September 6, 1954, we have the unbroadcast commentary of critic Tino Ranieri:

The night was strange and harsh. There was no warmth out there. The audience was distracted, restless, and irritable. When Fellini and Giulietta Masina entered the theater, they were greeted with only a few wan glances. This was how the movie started—in an inexplicably chilly atmosphere. We can only speculate that festival attendees were exhausted . . . But *La strada* is not a failure. It's a good, even beautiful at times, movie . . . The audience, who rather disliked it as the screening began, seemed to change opinion slightly toward the end, yet the movie didn't receive—in any sense of the word—the response that it deserved.

The chilliness persists into the following night and tensions erupt when the awards are announced by Ottavio Croze, a jeweler and the director of the festival. Since early August, rumors had been circulating that the government would boycott Luchino Visconti's *Senso* (*Livia*), a Lux Film production. According to some, it shouldn't even have made it into the competition. At the time, Visconti is considered the leader of the Communist opposition to the cinema of the Christian Democrats, and after he made *La terra trema* (*The Earth Trembles*, 1948), leftist critics had elected him the flag bearer of neorealism. The Milanese aristocrat had started feeling a little suffocated in this role: he doesn't renounce his decadent intellectual life and will go on to become a widely acclaimed opera director. On the flip side—a consequence of the same myopia, based on crude politicking and reductive opinions—Fellini has been named champion of spiritualist cinema, waging war against traditional materialism.

As everyone waits for the results, there are whispers that the international jury, presided over by the ambiguous and melancholic writer Ignazio Silone (there are five Italian members on the jury and each one is under every conceivable kind of pressure), had decided to ignore *Senso* and give the prize to *La strada*. But the jury is split. One contender is a sumptuous nineteenth-century literary movie, and the other a sociological fairy tale; a contest between Countess Serpieri and Gelsomina the vagabond. They make the solomonic decision to give the prize to a third contender, *Giulietta e Romeo*, despite the fact that Renato Castellani's genial Shakespeare adaptation has a distinctly embalmed quality. When the Golden Lion is announced the dissent is almost universal. Four Silver Lions are awarded: Elia Kazan's *On the Waterfront*, Akira Kurosawa's *Seven Samurai*, Kenji Mizoguchi's *Sanshô dayû*, and *La strada*—"for an interesting attempt by a young director and writer that confirms his sensitivity and independence." Even though the recognition is so generic (with words like *interesting, attempt,* and *young*), all hell breaks loose in the auditorium. Visconti sits stiff as marble, while his supporters start whistling and riotously contesting the decision. Half of the room applauds and thus the evening of September 7, 1954, goes down in history as the call to arms between observant neorealists and fans of a new kind of cinema. The climax of the evening comes when Moraldo Rossi attacks Franco Zeffirelli, a Visconti supporter. Punches follow and Rossi escapes the clutches of the carabinieri only thanks to the determined intervention of De Laurentiis. Shamefully, with two wonderful actresses to choose from in Alida Valli and Giulietta Masina, the jury decides not to award any prize for best actress. But the protagonist of *La strada* earns a standing ovation from the crowd outside of the Cinema Palace—oblivious to what's happened inside. The entire episode has to be taken in the context of its time, and the visceral indulgences of cold war ideology. We also have to take changing tastes into consideration, something that becomes clear when we remember that no one made a peep when *Rear Window* didn't win a mention, while today it's considered one of Alfred Hitchcock's masterpieces.

A sterile opposition grows up between Fellini and Visconti supporters in the almost ten years following the brawl over *Senso* and *La strada*. It's an artificial division, because Communist Visconti is not the political absolutist that many take him to be. He comes from nobility and has a link to those traditions; what's more, he's irretrievably attracted to decadence. On the other hand, Catholic Fellini is anything but a bigot—as polemics over *La dolce vita* will make evident. While the leftist read on *La strada* is that it's reactionary, the Centro Cattolico Cinematografico has its own reservations: "As it is very difficult for a young person to discern the exact meaning of the film, and as the male protagonist demonstrates a lack of moral constraints, we recommend the movie for adult audiences only." Visconti, for his part, after the boycott of *Senso*, goes on to disparage Fellini's movie as "neo-abstractionism." A few days later, Visconti sees

Fellini in the lobby of the Pincipe di Savoia hotel in Milan and avoids him. For years to come, the two directors go out of their way not to run into each other or to simply ignore each other. There are funny anecdotes about the situation. While parking his car in Piazza del Popolo, Fellini warns his passenger, "Close the window very tightly, because if Visconti were to walk by he'd spit inside." And when *La dolce vita* comes out, Visconti is reported to have said, "Those people are the kinds of aristocrats my waiter would find aristocratic." Giulietta is the only one who keeps receiving gracious recognition from the count, and she attempts to keep channels open between the two directors. Thanks to her, there will be a monumentous reconciliation at the 1963 Moscow Film Festival (where 8½ takes first prize): a hug between the maestros in the lobby of the Moskva Hotel that wipes out ten years of misunderstanding.

After that, the relationship between Federico and Luchino is cordial. Fellini even goes to the 1967 Venice Film Festival to see *Lo straniero* (*The Stranger*), produced by Marcello Mastroianni. At the end of the screening, he is among the first to congratulate Visconti. "It's your best movie," he tells him, though, as this adaptation of the Albert Camus novel is one of Visconti's worst productions, the compliment could be taken with an ironic vein. In 1969, the count returns the favor and comes to Venice for the opening of *Satyricon*. At the end of the screening he blows Fellini a kiss with a huge gesture from across the room. If some gentle ribbing continues to liven up the relationship, the two directors now think of each other as being on the same team. They share antipathy for the protests of the youth movement, as they reveal on television during the Spoleto Festival in 1970, where they exchange melancholic commentary, gloomy predictions, and compliments. Federico says, "I like shaking hands with my colleague Luchino, because he's proven to be coherent and sane, and I sympathize with that. I really admire the way he expresses himself, his commitment, and the humility with which he approaches his artistic endeavors." Then, glancing over at Visconti, he asks, "Are you happy?" This tribute is perhaps slightly hyperbolic . . . humility is not Visconti's most renowned trait. Visconti wryly answers, "Very happy. I'd just like to get those comments written up on a small tombstone." A few years later, when Visconti is paralyzed, Fellini visits him frequently and genuinely admires his stoic ability to work to his last breath.

Pietro Notarianni, Visconti's loyal production manager, joins Fellini's camp after Visconti's death, lending to the impression that although the two great directors had very different artistic visions, they were similar at least in their total dedication to work.

Returning to 1954: *La strada* is received very differently in Italy than abroad. Some people in Italy appreciate the film: Pier Paolo Pasolini, for example, names it a masterpiece. But the good reviews are coming primarily out of a culturally depressed environment. The power in Italy in the fifties belongs to the right, while the culture is all in the hands of the opposition, and it will continue like this until the center-left—the Socialists—takes control of the government. At this point, though, the ideological divisions are extreme and Fellini is demonized as a traitor to the neorealist mission. Critics make every effort to find faults with his movie after the opening in Venice. Some say that it starts out okay but then the story completely unravels. Others recognize the pathos in the end, but don't like the first half. The recurring descriptors are old, fake, insincere, literary, unrealistic, pathological, childish. The reviewers also contradict each other. Some criticize the movie's excessive naïveté and others claim it's too clever. Some say it lacks style and others say that it's too ornate.

The debate, which continues for some time in the pages of magazines, reveals the dominant culture's inability to embrace a fairy tale (despite the fact that the biggest leftist editor, Giulio Einaudi, had already published in 1946 the critical essay "Morphology of the Folk Tale," by Soviet scholar Vladimir Propp). Not only do leftist critics fail to read between the lines for the theme of marriage but they also trip over the character of Il Matto and argue against his spiritual intrusion into the materialism of Italian cinema. In point of fact, the left is not considering the "other" Italy—the marginalized subproletariat—and is demonstrating a remarkable ignorance of the culture of anthropology, which, riding on the success of Carlo Levi's book *Christ Stopped at Eboli*, is on the rise in Ernesto De Martino's studies of the south of Italy.

It's interesting to look at the articles from that period. On one side, there is hostility to the representation of the exceptional; and at the same time, on the other side, critics rail against anachronism, heavy subjectivism, inhumanity, confusion, arrogance, and invented conflicts. Not incidentally, Luis Buñuel's *Robinson Crusoe* was received with cursory, pity-filled notices in Italy. In France, where surrealism has gained significant ground, *La strada* has an entirely different reception. Reviewers cite painters like Marc Chagall, Brueghel the Elder, and Georges Rouault, and writers like Paul Claudel and Eugenio D'Ors (from his studies of baroque art), as well as the philosopher Emmanuel Mounier. There is a tentative comparison with Buñuel, and daring reflections about sacred values. George Sadoul, the most authoritative Communist critic of the time, who initially had agreed with the negative reviews of his Italian counterparts, changes his mind. In Paris, popular enthusiasm is growing, while in Italy, reviewers write ironically about the cultural backwardness of France.

La strada becomes the culminating event of a long and fertile reconsideration of Italian cinema by French critics. Roberto Rossellini's films with Ingrid Bergman come in for reevaluation, in particular *Viaggio in Italia* (*Journey to Italy*, 1953), along with those of the new director Fellini (even though the analysis of his work is more perplexing) and the *commedia all'italiana*. In the meantime, Robert Hawkins, a staunchly mainstream reviewer, writes in *Variety* (September 14, 1954), that *La strada* "is that quintessentially 'artistic' film that elite critics rave about and distributors don't like to handle. It was more common right after the war and is basically a rarity now. For this reason, it should be strongly supported and talked about. The film needs cutting before it can be prestigiously distributed in the United States."

Soon the movie is riding a tide of international success that goes far beyond the cautious provisions of the *Variety* review. Once it hits the mainstream movie theaters, it even does relatively well at Italian box offices, especially considering how inexpensive it was to make. *La strada* makes less money than *Senso* or *Giulietta e Romeo*, but it didn't cost as much as either film. As further proof that the Silver Lion it won at Venice wasn't a mistake, Fellini also earns two Silver Ribbons for best movie and best director. *La strada* rakes in more than fifty awards on the international circuit, from Austria, Germany, Poland, Holland. In Belgium it takes the critics' prize; in Japan a slew of different awards; it's Denmark's best movie of the year; in France it receives another critics' prize and three Victoires; and in the United Kingdom it takes home a prize from the Stratford Festival. Following a March 1955 gala in Paris at Salle Pleyel, thrown by De Laurentiis to celebrate the film's many recognitions, *La strada* embarks on a tour of every festival on the planet. Giulietta and Federico are invited everywhere. They accept trophies and statues in places they've never heard of. And, just after receiving the film critics award in New York, they hit the jackpot: an Oscar in 1957 for best foreign language film. It's the first prize ever given in this category (previously, there was only a "special award").

On March 27, 1957, Federico, Giulietta, Pinelli, Quinn, and De Laurentiis are all at the RKO Pantages Theater in Hollywood. Giulietta is compared by critics to Jean-Louis Barrault, to the mime Marcel Marceau, to Harry Langdon. She's called a "female Chaplin," "*Chaplin femme,*" "*weiblicher Chaplin,*" "*Chaplin mujer.*" Chaplin himself will only discuss her many years later in an interview with *The New York Times* (February 1, 1966): "She's the actress I admire most." But in Hollywood in 1957, critics are already swooning with appreciation. At a banquet, Gelsomina can't keep herself from asking Clark Gable for an autograph, to which "the King" regally replies, "Tonight, it's my turn to ask you for an autograph." Fellini, as always facing honors and duties with a sense of irony, is so happy in America that he accepts an invitation from Burt Lancaster's company Hecht-Hill-Lancaster to stay on for another month and a half to develop a secret project. *La strada*'s success solidifies over time, and though Fellini deflected with laughter Alexander Korda's proposal to make a sequel, "The Adventures of Gelsomina" doesn't seem like such a ludicrous idea looking back at it today. Nino Rota's score was a hit in the United States as well and was turned into a song, "Stars Shine in Your Eyes."

La strada is somehow the movie that tells the story of a personal psychic journey. It's a real dream, a story told against all odds, that describes the "clinical diagnosis" of its author. And for this reason, it's open to infinite interpretation, annotation, and theory. If it's true that each of us has a personal story, *La strada* is the most painful and also enigmatic fairy tale of Federico's life. Many critics have tried to apply any number of formulations to its analysis. But the author disliked the reading that posed the story of Gelsomina and Zampanò as a metaphor for marriage in a prefeminist age—the brutal male and the humiliated, submissive woman. Yet when the movie came out he happened to comment, "This is what most marriages are like." And so it is legitimate to see in the fairy tale an archetypal gender struggle, lived out and assimilated during Fellini's childhood. His father was extroverted and dominating (let's not forget that Urbano was a traveler by profession, like Zampanò), and his mother consoled herself through transcendence (not unlike Gelsomina). Giulietta argued with those who took *La strada* to be a reflection of their marriage. According to this interpretation, the author himself is Zampanò and this is his confession of obtuse and neglectful behavior toward his wife (and Giorgio, Giulietta's husband in *Giulietta degli spiriti*, is just a well-groomed Zampanò). Masina rejected any identification of herself with the little victim Gelsomina and, she has said, preferred to be identified with Cabiria's fiery optimism. She explained that it had been very hard to play Gelsomina and she succeeded only because she was such a disciplined actress.

But if Gelsomina isn't Giulietta, then who is she? Masina's answer was simple and surprising: Gelsomina is Federico. He's the one who left his house on the sea and climbed aboard a caravan. He learned the art of clowning and decided to use it to reveal "the reality of the soul" in the face of the vastness of existence. Giulietta would continue with this interpretation, claiming that in the psychological theater of this film, the author is like the trinity: Gelsomina, Zampanò, and Il Matto all at once. It was poetic tension superimposed on a mystical backdrop, brutal pragmatism and irony pushed to the point of self-destruction. The pantheistic revelations of Gelsomina when she immerses herself in nature or talks to children belong to a "child Federico," along with the references to Romagna, his landscape, and the poetry of Giovanni Pascoli, while Zampanò's insatiable wanderlust is also a Fellini trait. (He lived, reflected, and discussed everything from his car for years, always moving. And even when he stopped driving, his life continued in perpetual motion.) And Il Matto, transcendental clown-philosopher, is Fellini too when he says, "I'd like to always make people laugh." But it can be a dangerous game for an artist to put all of himself into a single work.

19

Lea, "la Paciocca," and the Others

Let's return to the harbor of Fiumicino; there are about twenty days left of shooting on *La strada*. What happened? "It's as if someone, without any warning, suddenly turned out the lights." Federico remembered that dreadful moment like a blast, a sudden psychic emptiness, a plunge into depression. Many years passed, and it would still provoke anxiety; he later described it as "a sort of psychic Chernobyl." A black cloud drops over you, drowns your mood and spirit in an opaque vertigo, that dreadful resurgence of all the anxieties you ever felt as a child. At the time Fellini doesn't want to tell anyone about it, not even Giulietta, who might be frightened by it, or Gigetto Giacosi, who might call Dino De Laurentiis on the spot, announcing disaster. He has to stick with it and forge ahead. The troupe is staying at a hotel in Latina. That night, Federico excuses himself from dinner, saying he's tired and has a headache. But he can't fall asleep. From this point forward, sleepless nights follow upon murderous days of work, and the director lives in fear of a total collapse.

Over the weekend, Giulietta, who has figured out there is a problem, calls a psychoanalyst. Emilio Servadio's appearance in Federico's home on via Lutezia in the spring of 1954 heralds the official entry of psychoanalysis into the world of Fellini. Up until that point, Federico barely knew anything about the "Jewish science." He'd read a few pages of Sigmund Freud, and nothing more. Psychoanalysis entered his life as first aid, not as an intriguing cultural phenomenon. Servadio ascertains the symptoms, and then, directing Federico to remain calm for the moment, promises a diagnosis once he's had a chance to explore the patient's mind. In the meantime, he recommends that Fellini concentrate on the task at hand, because finishing the movie is essential. They can address the problems, perhaps start real therapy sessions, after that. Somewhat soothed by this meeting, Federico manages to get through to the end of the movie and then immediately heads to Servadio's office on Piazzale della Province. But he goes to only a couple of sessions. He's ultimately embarrassed by the relationship between patient and analyst. The chiming of the clock that marks the end of each session is like a bureaucratic ordinance (talk now, stop talking now), and when he's on the couch he feels claustrophobic, like he's suffocating. One day Servadio sees his patient gasping for air and rushes to open a window. There's a big summer storm brewing outside, and Federico, who's loved storms his whole life, can't resist the urge to get outside and be in it. Inventing an excuse, he escapes. Umbrella-less in the downpour, he seeks shelter under a nearby tree, and, like magic, a new page turns in Fellini's life, a rather secret page, but one that seems to lead the way out of the tunnel of depression with the illumination of possibility.

Later on, when Servadio is well over ninety years old, he will challenge Fellini's entire version of the story in a confidence to his colleague Simona Argentieri. There weren't many sessions, but there were more than two, and, according to Servadio, they weren't useless. There was no storm the day Fellini ran out of his session, though something important really did happen—something Argentieri describes as a classical case of "escape into healing."

What did happen during that real or made-up summer storm? Fellini, cowering in the rain under a tree, sees a woman with an umbrella emerge, seemingly from nowhere. "Can I offer you shelter?" The invitation is attractive; the woman is majestically beautiful. When he'd recount the scene (to his most intimate friends), Fellini would improvise a clever repartee, the kind of verbal ping-pong typical of "sophisticated comedies." According to Fellini, she's all curves and looks like she's stepped out of a fashion magazine. The lawyer Titta Benzi met the woman and seconded Fellini's description. She has the figure that will ultimately come to be associated with the Fellini woman. Under the tiny umbrella, the couple make an instant, spirited connection, which will be continued out of the rain that same afternoon, and will go on—enduring distance and a number of hair-raising breakups and reunions—for a number of years.

You cannot write a biography of Federico without including a chapter about him and women. Although you must also be very careful about how you address the subject. First of all, it's essential to clarify that in a marriage that lasted half a century, Fellini was frequently unfaithful, but always entirely monogamous. He was fascinated by women, talked about them constantly, and just like his *vitelloni*, often joked about sex, drawing dirty pictures with dirty captions on restaurant napkins. In conversation, the topic of love would always emerge as a happy obsession—so much so that friends would tease him: "He who talks a lot does very little." And Federico would reply with a clownish scowl, and threaten to expose the "insatiable dragon" he kept hidden in his pants. Nobody really knows how things were, but one thing is certain: in a life flush with temptation and opportunity, there wasn't a single woman, no matter how attractive, who could disrupt even for a moment the solidity of the director's marriage—a marriage that saw its golden anniversary. Federico never changed his mind about the woman he'd chosen at twenty years old to be his family. Having Giulietta at his side was a necessary constant to his existence—despite the moments of impatience and the arguments and occasional misunderstandings typical of all marriages.

Federico was more cherub than Don Juan, and he liked to play with women of any age, and perhaps, when playing, gave them the impression that they meant something to him. There are so many memoirs written by women claiming they were his lovers that it's practically a literary genre unto itself—and certainly deserves some study. Through both good and bad, these sentimental and erotic entanglements would often give way to the fantasy—of whoever was the favorite of the moment—that their relationship had been the important one. It was the vanity of being able to think that they'd gotten close to the famous man, or even had the chance to reject him. But this fantasy was more about Fellini's interactions with people, men included. He always managed to convey the impression, even if it lasted only a moment, that you had a special, exclusive relationship with him. Bernardino Zapponi's memoir, *Il mio Fellini* (My Fellini), is illuminating on the subject:

> He always had a girl at his side (a different one on every movie), in the sound room or editing studio. She would be a sort of comfort figure, humble and devoted, who would hold his hand and share

his enthusiasm or rage. When the movie was finished, the little friend would disappear. It's certain that Federico, fascinated, practically obsessed, by femininity, would let his women embrace him, hold him, even cherish him—but he was always prepared to free himself, jump out of it like a frightened cat.

In one of his last interviews, Fellini himself commented, "A woman has a message, and life's pleasure comes from waiting for the message, not from the message itself." Women would often be driven to despair over him, but without justification, because despite all appearances to the contrary, there was only one woman for Federico. And Giulietta was just as loyal to him. The proof is the strength of their artistic collaboration—from the radio to the big screen, it was a legendary partnership that took them through movies like *Luci del varietà, Lo sceicco bianco, La strada, Il bidone, Le notti di Cabiria, Giulietta degli spiriti,* and *Ginger e Fred.*

There is, nonetheless, a hidden subplot involving Fellini and a couple of women who inspired him over the long term. And maybe this story doesn't really begin that rainy day under the umbrella. There were fleeting affairs before that—not even worth giving names and faces. But Lea Giacomini from San Marino was the first other woman who did come to mean something in the great director's life. Fellini said her irresistible sensuality was behind the endurance of their passion. We can infer, based on conversations and partial confessions, that the character of Yvonne Furneaux, Marcello Mastroianni's nagging girlfriend in *La dolce vita*, was inspired by Lea and her difficult personality. Some people have whispered that the night scene of the two arguing in the car, when he drives off leaving her alone on an isolated street in the city outskirts, was based on reality—the only difference being that, in real life, Lea responded much more violently. She threw stones at Federico's new Flaminia sports car and destroyed it. Another character, Marisa, "the sex train" in *La voce della luna* (*The Voice of the Moon*, 1990), also seems inspired by the same woman's exuberance, though, according to Fellini, by this point Lea had already died in a mental hospital in Emilia-Romagna. We have nothing more than a few drawings, done by her beleaguered lover, by which to remember her.

The ubiquitous Titta Benzi, who sometimes accompanied Federico on his romantic escapades to Mount Titano in San Marino, remembered a few anecdotes. Late one night, Federico asked Titta to drive him to San Marino and then wait in a bar while he went to surprise Lea. By the time the bar was ready to close, Fellini had still not returned. So Titta stood waiting, in the freezing cold, under a portico for hours on end. Federico finally reappeared when it was almost dawn. Numb with cold, Titta attacked him: "How dare you leave me out here in the cold all this time?" And Federico casually answered, "But what about our friendship?"

In another incident, many years later, Federico again asked Titta to drive him to San Marino. It had been a long time since he'd seen Lea, but he'd had the idea that he wanted to go say hello. They parked near her house and the director hesitated, and made no move to get out of the car. Titta asked, "Are you going or not?" Federico answered, "Listen, Lea is probably older now, right?" "Of course. We were born in 1920 and she was born in 1918, I think. Of course she's older." Federico quickly decided: "Forget about it. Let's go home."

People in San Marino and Rimini talked a lot about Federico's affair with Lea. But only a few people knew about another longer and more intense relationship with Anna Giovannini. (That is to say, not many people knew about the affair while Federico was still alive.) Even Marcello Mastroianni, Federico's doppelgänger and, he thought, main confidant, knew nothing about Anna. Marcello was actually upset when he read the details of the affair in the press after the director's death. "I used to tell him everything about my grisly affairs. He'd laugh a lot but never tell me anything about himself. Now I remember that he'd sometimes ask me to take him to Piazza Ungheria for an appointment. He'd get out of the car and then stand waiting for me to drive off before he headed in one direction or the other. Clearly he didn't want me to know which door he was running to."

In June 1995, two years after Federico's death, Giovannini emerged from almost forty years of silence. She gave interviews, shared photographs, drawings, and love letters. She got the satisfaction of being billed in a newspaper headline as "Fellini's real companion in life." But that was an exaggeration. It is certain, however, that this lady, with her grooming and voluptuous figure, was the model for the character that Sandra Milo played in 8½. Fellini called her "la Paciocca," which the dictionary defines as "a cheerful plump person with a good personality." Anna was five years older than Federico, born in 1915 in Kosice in what is now the Czech Republic. She'd lived in Trento and moved to Rome in 1952, where her daughter Patrizia was born. One newspaper dared to say that Patrizia was Fellini's daughter, but that would have taken a miracle even greater than he, the great magician, was capable of. The child was five years old when the two met, a fact confirmed by a cheerful drawing celebrating the couple's thirtieth anniversary.

On May 14, 1957, while driving his Chevrolet along the Lungotevere, Fellini caught a glimpse of a feminine shape and was fascinated. He followed her into the Ruschena bakery and struck up a conversation. She didn't recognize him, and in the nervousness of the encounter, misheard his name and called him Enrico—to which he replied, "Not Enrico, but Federico! I'm Federico Fellini!" At the time, Anna was working the register in a friend's pharmacy, but at her illustrious suitor's insistence, she left that job in order to be completely available to him. She was immortalized along with her daughter in a portrait by Rinaldo Geleng, which can easily be considered one of his most inspired paintings. Anna Giovannini never threatened Fellini's marriage, even though she knew that Giulietta—who'd been put on alert by the usual well-meaning souls—was jealous. There's even a reference to this in *Giulietta degli spiriti*, in the unpleasant scene where Mario Pisu, the unfaithful husband, is followed and filmed by a private detective.

In reality, Federico was only photographed, not filmed, but he reported feeling very upset ("totally alienated") when forced to look at himself, furtive and clumsy, walking to his lover's house. The series of pictures that were published in a women's weekly on November 7, 1971—the director and his girlfriend, caught off guard by paparazzi and a blaze of flashbulbs while coming out of a restaurant—was potentially more alarming in terms of the effect they could have had on his family. But the magazine published the photos under the headline THE REVENGE OF THE PAPARAZZI, giving the impression that the woman in the picture was one of the many actors in the movie *Roma* and that Fellini was just taking her home after a day spent shooting. We should actually give a nod to the Italian press for being consistently respectful and even a little complicit with the maestro—it would have been an easy matter to expose one of his affairs. There were only a few exceptions, such as the despicable picture (a "scoop") of Fellini on his deathbed at the Policlinico.

As Anna tells it, Federico was always a thoughtful and passionate companion. But he was also liable to erupt into jealous rages, like when he found flowers sent by an admirer in her house and threw them out the window, risking hitting someone on the head. "Basically," Anna says, "in the name of his love, he surrounded me with nothing." Their whole affair was a parallel life, a story that blossomed and thrived in the mood of another time. What's certain is that Fellini never neglected his lover, and was, according to some, desperately alarmed when she had health problems in 1989.

As for the rest of the director's secret life, it was all rather comical up through his last years—the never-ending phone calls, messages, and appointments in absurd places. It was a source of amusement and a subject of lighthearted gossip on the set. Fellini blithely courted famous and nonfamous actresses, enjoying playing the part of the great seducer that he really wasn't. When he was in production on *La dolce vita* and a friend kept haranguing him to reveal whether he'd had sex with Anita Ekberg, he'd reply, "You should certainly please tell everyone that I have." In this respect, it's also worth noting the anecdote that Indro Montanelli repeated to Tiziana Abate for his memoir *Soltanto un giornalista* (Just a Journalist):

> When Anita Ekberg got to Rome to start work on *La dolce vita*, the first thing she did was call Federico and invite him over to her hotel. She greeted him lying naked on her bed, ready to do the deed. But Federico wasn't one of those guys who walks around with a loaded gun, and he panicked. The only excuse he could come up with was to simulate appendicitis, which he did so effectively that he was actually operated on.

None of it is true. Anita, far from offering herself to the director, accepted the role under duress at the insistence of her agents, Hank Kaufman and Gene Lerner. Lerner was so exasperated by her reluctance that he finally told her, "If you don't sign this contract, I'll sign it for you!" It's not impossible that Fellini invented Montanelli's fable, where the only embarrassment was the doubt cast on his own sexual potency.

The sexual-inadequacy rumor was repeated throughout Rome's movie community, and it's as untrue as the legend of Federico as an incorrigible Casanova. In his book *Diario di un cronista* (A Reporter's Journal), Sergio Zavoli writes, based on firsthand accounts, that Federico was sixteen when he first went into a brothel along with some motley friends in Rimini, but that his sexual initiation actually happened in Florence in 1938. That experience, in a brothel behind the Baglioni Hotel (where the painter Giove Toppi brought him), was rather traumatic and left a bad memory. It actually left him with an intractable "anxiety about sex," explains Zavoli.

According to some reports (impossible to prove), Fellini paid for a nose job for one starlet, gave another an encyclopedia, surprised a third one with an airplane ticket to go abroad—maybe because he wanted to get rid of her. He used to tire quickly of these superficial relationships. They were amusing at first, but he disliked having to keep seeing women that he had only briefly desired. Sometimes he even banned them from appearing on the movie sets. He also frequently didn't get anything like what he deserved back from them. One of his lovers, less discreet than the others, revealed the story of their relationship (true or not) in a tell-all book and dared to leave it along with an affectionate dedication to Masina with the porter at via Margutta. In this embarrassing situation, the Fellinis behaved with class. They gave no comment, offered vague answers to the journalists who called ("Oh really? That woman wrote a book? When I have some spare time, I'll read it . . ."), and the story ended there.

Eventually Giulietta grew accustomed to Federico's peccadilloes and stopped taking offense. She was so sure about the terms of the deal (that bound her to her man) that she could even laugh off the affairs. Bernardino Zapponi, a longtime family friend, explains that Federico "would never have even considered leaving Giulietta . . . Not only because she was a pillar in his life—his affection for her aside—but also because she remained a perpetual enigma to him. Giulietta's strength was her mystery." Father Angelo Arpa, a priest who was close to Fellini, said something similar but more poetic: "Giulietta wasn't only his support; she was his breath."

20

Martyr for the Con
Il bidone / The Swindle

The current version of *Il bidone* runs ninety-two minutes, though a number of catalogues and film guides clock it at 105 minutes. When it was first released, at the 16th Venice Film Festival on September 9, 1955, it was more than two hours long. Any number of misadventures befell this unusually jinxed undertaking along the road to Venice—a story that would explain the half-hour difference between one cut and another. In early 1955, *La strada* is wildly successful and producers are tripping over each other to get Fellini's next film. But Dino De Laurentiis passes on *Il bidone* after reading a draft of the screenplay; other producers react similarly. The producer least opposed to the project is Goffredo Lombardo at Titanus, and after long reflection, he agrees to take the film on.

Unlike *I vitelloni*, Fellini didn't have an unknown word in this title. In Italy, the expression *bidone* (a "slang expression meaning scam, swindle, or slightly over-the-top deception or prank," according to the Zingarelli dictionary) has been in wide circulation for at least fifteen years. The expression was first used by students in Lombardy, but encompasses (or rather encompassed) a world living on the edge of a society, cheating and grifting, lying and committing crimes. It's a world that cannot be historically plotted, whose borders are impossible to draw, filled with protagonists who can't be unmasked. But Federico has always known some of the players, people he met during the poverty of war and right after, when, between the black market and other struggles, everyone more or less had resorted to the grand art of getting by (or *l'arte di arrangiarsi*). The movie's release in the mid-fifties, however, coincides with a calmer moment: Italian life is settling into reconstruction and on a path of economic growth, people have to rely less and less on tricks for their survival. *Il bidone* is a movie about the fading craft of deception, and thus about the decadence and death of the con. It's much more of a crepuscular film than it is the lighthearted picaresque one it might seem in the ads.

Inspiration came, as it often did for this director, from stories people told him: in this case, from conversations with an elderly con man he'd met at a trattoria in Ovindoli while shooting *La strada*, as well as from his friend Eugenio Ricci, aka Lupaccio (old wolf), who is said to have sent Fellini to Cinecittà in 1940 to sell a fake diamond to Assia Noris or Osvaldo Valenti. The movie is conceived during a particularly opaque existential moment in Fellini's own life, right after the big depression that followed *La strada*, and in some ways it helps to defuse that negative charge. From the moment that Federico begins developing the idea (with Tullio Pinelli and Ennio Flaiano), an intense, tragic face becomes lodged in his mind. He wants Humphrey Bogart to play the lead, Augusto, because he thinks he has "the typical face of a con man from Calabria." Bogart, unhappily, is already sick with the disease that will kill him only two years later, so Fellini has to find someone else. Frank Sinatra's name comes up, but Fellini is put off by the singer's reputation for arrogance. Someone proposes a French actor, Pierre Fresnay, or Jean Servais—who starred in *Du rififi chez les hommes* (*Rififi*, 1955). Meanwhile Federico, who never goes to the movies—he'd stopped going once he started making them—and hasn't seen *All the King's Men*, is stopped dead in his tracks when he sees Broderick Crawford's face on the film's poster. Crawford won an Oscar for *All the King's Men* in 1950. He's a heavy, melancholic actor with warm, slanted eyes. He's also perfect for the film, and, after a quick exchange of telegrams, Crawford signs on.

Brod is a delight from the first moment he steps off the airplane. He's thrilled to be in Rome, drinks mineral water for breakfast, and gets along with the director—they're fast friends by the dessert course of their first dinner. The American actor, whose parents were also actors (Broderick is his mother's surname and Crawford his father's), has been in the business since he was a baby. He's just coming through yet another failed marriage and speaks bitterly of it. Federico endeavors to cheer him up: he's in Italy now; it can be a sort of holiday and he'll get to do a good movie while he's at it. The director may not even be aware of the fact that the actor played in Steinbeck's *Of Mice and Men* on Broadway, but he instantly treats him as if he were Lenny, a big-hearted giant with slow reflexes and an unpredictable something lurking under the surface.

Production is set to begin in Marino in late April. Nobody had calculated that they would get there during the same period as the local wine festival, but when Brod arrives at the Castelli Romani, he runs smack into a procession of allegorical floats and people dancing in the streets waving branches and singing odes to Bacchus. At first the actor seems perplexed—but eventually, once he figures out what's going on, he is unable to resist. Fellini would later explain that his lead actor dove into the parade and disappeared, turning up again two days later, asleep in a trench.

Then they find out that Crawford's contract had stipulated a whole list of prohibited, and permitted, beverages. In fact, Brod had just come out of a major detoxification, and the effects of the treatment have been completely undone by the run-in with the wine festival. From that moment forth, it's pandemonium. The actor recites his part in "a cloud of alcohol," according to Fellini. Not only does he forget his lines, but he doesn't even know what he's doing or where he is. He frequently bursts out crying, or explodes in wild overconfident exuberance. One day he doesn't recognize Fellini, and another day, right in front of Giulietta, advises him never to get married.

Fellini is desperate and tries everything. He gets prompters to help with the lines, uses ropes and wooden poles to maneuver the actor through scenes. It doesn't look like he's even going to make it to the end, and every take seems like it's going to be the last one ever. The studio's doctors are worried, but Crawford comes through. In fact, he's a tough man and not only will he make it through this movie, but he'll go on to survive another thirty years of acting. He's a sort of biological-meets-artistic miracle: perfect on the screen in the part of Augusto. Though only forty-four at the time, his character is supposed to be forty-eight but look ten years older. Brod's interpretation is a combination of acting chops and deep human sensitivity. Through Augusto, Fellini offers glimpses of genuine suffering and hopeful naïveté—perhaps the same impulse that had driven Crawford as a young man temporarily out of theater to become a sailor. In his own crazy fashion, the actor brings to the film a sort of intimate pain, something that evokes respect and pity.

Apart from the difficulties with the lead, production proceeds in an atmosphere of feverish normalcy. Every one of Fellini's sets has a different quality, always determined by the director's mood. Federico doesn't feel deeply connected to this project. After the playfulness of *I vitelloni*, and the vertiginous total commitment of *La strada*, he feels oddly detached from *Il bidone*. (The same feeling occurs, far more radically, many years later on the set of *Il Casanova*.) This time around Fellini isn't enchanted with his characters, or guided by them; he's simply telling their story. The cast and crew, on the other hand, are rather enchanted by their director. There's the idea, later developed into a theory, that Fellini's sets are showpiece work environments, happenings in and of themselves, with value and significance entirely independent of the movie. On the set of *Il bidone* the cast and crew are captivated by Fellini—someone even starts calling him "Il Faro" (the beacon). Later he'll be called "the poet of cinema" and "maestro," always with a mix of irony and reverence.

The exterior scenes are shot in Marino and the surrounding area, while the interior scenes are all done in the Titanus studio. The entire week of June 10, the studio is set for a New Year's Eve party in the home of a big-time con man. (Dario Cecchi was the set designer.) Looking back at this scene later, critics will see a rehearsal for *La dolce vita*: each character, mostly drawn from the ranks of the underworld, carefully selected according to a hyper-realist, expressionist aesthetic, coupled with a daring appreciation for deception. Federico thinks of this scene as a movie within a movie. He shot it with the deepest engagement and referred to it as "hell." This will be the first of many hells he portrays—and a precursor to this scene can be seen as far back as the New Year's Eve party in *I vitelloni*. Another setting that will recur and become characteristic of Fellini's work is the nightclub—also a big part of Augusto's story. The nightclub scene, just like the nightclub scenes in *La dolce vita*, is shot in the Canova bar (a destination for people hanging out in Piazza del Popolo and a refuge for characters of all classes and kinds, where the director was a regular). The movie theater where Augusto takes his daughter to the movies and one of his victims recognizes him is shot on location in the Cinema Euclide in Piazza Euclide. The exterior scene is shot in front of the Cinema Flaminio. From July 5 to July 10 they shoot in a town near the aqueduct of Acqua Felice, outside of Porta Maggiore. The scenes of the final scam are all shot near Cerveteri. The closing sequence, Augusto's death scene, is done in the studio on July 16.

Things start moving at breakneck pace when there are only forty days left before *Il bidone* is set to open in Venice. The producer, Lombardo, finally believes in the project and heartily declares, "This time, nobody's going to keep the Golden Lion from us." The editing is done on two separate Moviolas by two different editors, Giuseppe Vari and Mario Serandrei, working simultaneously. Serandrei is a highly cultured intellectual with good taste, used to talking things over in depth with his directors. But there's no time for discussion here.

The first version of the movie is agonizingly long, 4,600 meters of film, and must be cut. As a result, some important scenes wind up in the trash and Fellini feels their absence like an amputated arm. But the fate of the movie takes precedence, and in this battle against lengthiness, all window dressing falls to the cutting-room floor. Secondary characters lose their stories—even the painter Picasso and his Iris (Basehart and Giulietta), and the vain Roberto (Franco Fabrizi)—simply disappearing from the screen at a certain point. Augusto remains, solitary, something of a monument still standing amid the rubble of demolished buildings. He's a well-dressed Zampanò, a circus strongman dumped among the bourgeoisie to repeat his survival performance.

Augusto is how Fellini might have ended up as an old man—or at least that's what some benevolent enemies used to predict for him in the days of his Roman bohemia. But now that Fellini is a success he pauses to look at this other self, this guy with no art and nowhere to go, a failure, broken and ready for the trash. Yet this other self is also a man, a brother, a mirror image. Evoking him serves to exorcise him, reject him, and bury him . . . all of which provokes the same fear you might feel when dreaming of your own funeral.

Nino Rota composed the score in record time: the soundtrack was laid on August 28. In the intervening period, doubts have cropped up over the ending. Serandrei wants to end on a close-up of Augusto, but Fellini selects the shot of the two women farmers and their children walking off, a less desperate image. Editing wraps on September 5, at the very last minute, considering the time still needed to develop and print the film and get the reels to the Lido before the end of the festival.

Il bidone opens in Venice on September 9, and the mood is tense. The left is pitted against Fellini after his battle with Luchino Visconti last year, and the mega-success of *La strada* has made people want to temper the phenomenon. To top it off, Giulietta, who is visiting her former maid, Anna Leonardelli (whom she has stayed close with), at the hotel she runs in Trentino, reads in a Milan newspaper that she's run off to London with Richard Basehart. The rumor that Masina has left Fellini to be with Dick, her husband on the set and Valentina Cortese's husband in real life, sails from one newspaper to the next, and from the moment the Fellinis land on the Lido with the Baseharts, they're assaulted by journalists. Fellini's brilliant solution—as usual, when dealing with the press—is to announce that, in the next film, Giulietta will play a country nun and Basehart will be a priest. You can't get more innocent than that! The truth, however, is that the seemingly amiable director bandying with the press is extremely nervous, not about his wife's alleged infidelity but because they rushed the editing process and he didn't have time to properly think it through. Fortunately, the picture of the Fellinis and the Baseharts together puts an end to the gossip.

At the screening Fellini sits next to a government minister who keeps asking stupid questions: "What kind of car is that? Isn't Basehart married to Cortese? Why isn't she in the movie?" There is a lot of coughing from the audience and after the first half they start leaving. Some people are unhappy because the movie isn't funny. What happened to the prankster who made *I vitelloni*? they wonder. A terrible storm kicks up outside and the trickling exits turn into a real exodus. The government minister persists: "Could you introduce me to Valentina Cortese?" In short, it's one of those nights that a person would prefer to forget entirely. The journalist Angelo Solmi reports that "there wasn't even a battle, just some weary clapping at the end, and then, heads lowered, the audience filed out, leaving Fellini and Masina with the sinking sensation that their film had been iced." On the night of September 10, the Golden Lion, which Lombardo thought was in the bag, goes to Carl Theodor Dreyer's *Ordet*, and the jury, presided over by film critic Mario Gromo, doesn't give *Il bidone* a single prize, not even an honorable mention. In that moment, Federico decides never to bring his movies to the Lido again. He will return to Venice, however, only fourteen years later in 1969 to present *Satyricon* out of competition.

If critics were divided over *La strada*, they are unanimously negative about *Il bidone*. After the chilly reception and criticism following the opening, the reviews are biting: Fellini pulled a fast one. This isn't a masterpiece. He's rehashing old themes. He doesn't like his characters. He's dwelling on pathological cases. He's making fun of poor people. And so on. Some critics predict, "We think Fellini will never get anywhere if he keeps on repeating his private creations ad infinitum." A "pope" of leftist criticism echoes that sentiment: "It's a total failure of a work and among the most unpleasant and inept in the entire history of cinema, not to mention that it's also shoddily executed and presumptuous." Although not all reviews adopt such apocalyptic condemnation, they all agree that the movie was a mistake. Fellini's supporters are, once again, the small group who'd liked *Lo sceicco bianco*—perhaps even fewer in number this time. The director eschewed facile solutions, predictable resolutions, and flashy devices, criticisms which cast a positive light on the more irritable judgments. The nonpandering character of Fellini's tragicomedy is, in fact, the film's most significant asset, alongside the manifest capacity of the director to transfer reality into a fantastical dimension.

Among the various offshoots of neorealism, this film will eventually be revealed as one of the most original and fertile. Fellini thrust his antihero, trapped in a Kafkaesque system of judgment and condemnation, into the objective world, where characters are alienated or indifferent. *Il bidone* defies definition and is an insult to dogmatic critics. It is also so outside the realm of the tastes of the time that some reviewers (including the priests at the Centro Cattolico, who write that "Augusto's final illegal act is done for the greater good") entirely misread the film, claiming that in his final scam the hero, disguised as a priest, actually returns the money to the handicapped girl and finds redemption through death. This is just what Crawford's character might have done were it a Hollywood production, but in Fellini's movie, the sight of the sick girl only reminds Augusto of his own daughter's problems. It is for her sake that he attempts the final scam and tries to cheat his accomplices, which is what kills him in the end.

This is Fellini's lowest moment. *La strada*'s vindication over the bad press in Italy had come from abroad, but this time there's to be no consolation whatsoever. Gloomy days will follow in the headquarters of Titanus on via Sommacampagna. Lombardo entirely lost faith in the movie and it's released in theaters along with an extraordinary pamphlet entitled, *Il bidone: film umano e polemico nei giudizi positivi e negativi della critica italiana* (*The Swindle*: A Human and Polemical Film According to Positive and Negative Judgments of Italian Critics)—an attempt to mitigate the anti-Fellini attacks in the press by positing the whole thing as a debate over ideas. The box-office numbers are disappointing, and even international distribution is slow. The film won't be released in the United States until 1964, earning another bad review by Bosley Crowther in *The New York Times*: "a bad move." Pauline Kael will be more diplomatic, stating "it doesn't work, but it's not insignificant." Later on, everyone—friends and enemies alike—will come to speak of *Il bidone* as an important movie, and some will even resurrect it as Fellini's most daring and rigorous endeavor.

21

A Kindly Soul of the Streets
Le notti di Cabiria / The Nights of Cabiria

Toward the end of 1955 Goffredo Lombardo calls a meeting with Fellini, who is under contract to do a second film with Titanus. Revenue statements showing miserable box-office earnings for *Il bidone* are strewn about the desk and the producer seems to be gearing himself up for a battle.

> He started telling me the whole story of Titanus, from the pioneer days under Gustavo and Leda Gys, his father and mother—she was a wonderful silent-film actress—and he started telling me how I was responsible for bringing financial ruin to this marvelous company, and so on and so forth. What could I do? I think I satisfied Goffredo beyond his wildest dreams by ripping up the next contract, making *Il bidone* the first and last film I did with him.

The game of chance seems to work only when Fellini produces a successful film. Abandoned by Dino De Laurentiis prior to *Il bidone* and by Lombardo after it, Fellini is fed up with producers and would really prefer to do it all himself. But the notion of soliciting funds directly from banks remains, as always, a pipe dream. Federico will never overcome his staunch resistance to the commitment and responsibility on the business end of things, and he can't find anyone else to do it for him.

He'd rather occupy himself with new projects, of which he has at least four in development at this point. The first one is about a man with fifteen wives and fifteen families, all of whom he's trying to please—a utopian scenario that will materialize a few years later in the harem scene of 8½. The second project is titled *La piccola suora* (The Little Nun) and it's the same idea he tossed into the jaws of the reporters on the Lido to sideline the Basehart–Masina scandal. The idea, a mystical fable, came to him while reading a manuscript he found in the library of the Bagnoregio convent during *La strada*. It's about a nineteenth-century nun who comes to be thought of as a saint because of the little miracles she performs, like making flowers blossom in vases or causing people to hear celestial chanting. The convent starts buzzing over these phenomena and an investigation by the highest ecclesiastical authorities is called. The nun has to go to the Holy Offices in Rome to sit for rigorous interrogations. Torn from her familiar environment, she dies and there is no beatification.

The third project takes a step forward. Based on a book by Mario Tobino (edited by Vallecchi, 1953), *Le libere donne di Magliano* (The Free Women of Magliano) is a rewriting of a diary that the author kept between 1949 and 1951 while he was a doctor in charge of the women's ward of Maggiano, the psychiatric hospital in Lucca, situated on a hill near Viareggio. Tobino explained, "My aim was to show that even in mental institutions there's a kind of order, that madness has its own laws, rules, and mystery—just like the life we all lead." Fellini is struck by this early vision of a "city of women"—a kind of circle of hell, where a slew of women unleash bestial fury while also expressing unexpected insight and kindness, all of it taking place in the middle of an agricultural society where the basic values of existence dominate, including a powerful sensual animalism.

Fellini and Tullio Pinelli visit Tobino at the hospital to see for themselves the incredible circumstance he describes in the book. Fellini is especially stunned by the "moss cells" where naked patients are sent when they start trying to tear up or destroy things. In this violent state of crisis, the only thing the women have to shelter themselves from the cold is the moss. This is the first time (and the only time, until *La voce della luna*) that Fellini, finding a genuinely sympathetic character in Tobino, makes concrete plans to adapt a current book for the screen. In the February 1957 issue of *Cahiers du cinéma*, there's a transcription of the director giving a long description of the movie, likely recorded over the telephone and mistranslated in sections. The story is so personal and engaging that it seems a pity it never becomes a movie.

While thinking about the adaptation, Fellini plans to cast the American celebrity Montgomery Clift, perhaps the most talented actor of his generation and certainly the most unfortunate. When Fellini is considering Clift, the actor still looks as handsome and expressive as he did in *Red River*. Sadly, he's involved in a terrible car accident on May 12, 1957, and half his face is mangled. Later, after undergoing plastic surgery, he will play the lead in John Huston's *Freud*, affirming Fellini's hunch that Clift would have made a good Roberto.

A young doctor (ten years younger than the character in the book), Roberto is a kind of *vitellone* exiled to a provincial mental hospital. The story is the account of a single year in which the doctor, like Marcello in *La dolce vita*, floats through reality, exposed to every sort of temptation. Roberto's days are spent waiting for six o'clock to arrive, when he can go play pool and chase women along with the other young doctors. At the stroke of six, he can finally escape to Lucca or Viareggio (he is always torn over whether to go to the medieval city or the carnivalesque resort capital). Yet gradually, Roberto becomes immersed in the parallel universe of the mental hospital, drawn to the notion that he might be able to create a deep and therapeutic rapport with the irrational sickness. It is this path that he ultimately chooses, driven by the conviction that he can help, a conviction that Fellini experiences while at Maggiano himself, sitting at the bedside of a miserable woman—blind, deaf, and dumb from birth—who nonetheless mysteriously senses Fellini's presence. In fact, she becomes agitated when he leaves. Unfortunately, Clift refuses the part, saying that the subject makes him uncomfortable, and the "movie about crazy women" comes to a halt. In 1975, Mauro Bolognini will direct a very Fellini-esque Marcello Mastroianni in an adaptation of another book by Tobino, *Per le antiche scale* (*Down the Ancient Staircase*), considered the sequel of *Le libere donne di Magliano*.

Another idea that sticks in Federico's mind, however, is taken from a story he read in the local newspaper over the summer: the horrifying discovery of a beheaded woman on the edge of the lake by Castel Gandolfo, in a zone named Acqua Acetosa, on July 12, 1955, quickly baptized as "The beheaded woman of Castel Gandolfo." It turns out that she was Antonietta Longo, a thirty-year-old Sicilian waitress who'd disappeared months earlier, after telling everyone that she was going to marry a "good boy." She cashed in her savings before she left and the money had obviously gone missing, much like the killer, who was never tracked down. Struck by the naïveté with which the woman had plunged toward her fate, Fellini makes a connection between this event and the stories he's heard from Wanda, a prostitute he met during *Il bidone* in a shantytown near Acquedotto Felice. Wanda leads a subproletarian life; she lives in a sort of chicken cage and fights with everyone. She's attempted suicide three times, always for love, but emerged each time with renewed vitality.

Another important element contributing to the development of *Le notti di Cabiria* is Fellini's encounter with Mario Tirabassi, aka "L'uomo del sacco" (the man with the sack), a former nurse from Orvieto who spends every night bringing food and clothing to scores of poor people, sack on his back, in a silent and solitary mission. These are the movie's inspirations. We know of other, more remote sources, such as the episode that Anna Magnani had rejected where the prostitute meets the actor, and of course Giulietta's character itself, already seen as Cabiria in *Lo sceicco bianco*.

Just like the doctor in *Le libere donne di Magliano*, Federico starts leading a double life. At night he restlessly cruises hubs of vice: like the Passeggiata Archeologica, the cafés and watering holes of the Roman periphery, the crevices of the Colosseum, and the banks of the Tiber. Piero Gherardi, the production designer, often goes with him. Gherardi is from Poppi in Tuscany; he's funny, curious about everything, and extremely talented. His name appears in the credits of *Le notti di Cabiria* for the first time, although he has been working with Fellini scouting locations and extras since *I vitelloni*. Fellini likes to think of him as Pinocchio's little friend "Lucignolo, greedy and childish," whom Fellini chases, enchanted (among other things) by Gherardi's knowledge of every hidden corner of Lazio. He's the perfect guide: one day they find a row of cypresses all leaning in one direction, the next day they find a colonial house next to a forest, and then the next day they see a hundred different shapes of Mount Soratte, depending on the angle from which it is viewed. "Piero has seen everything and remembers everything. He's like a diviner, out to find the physical version of something you think you made up."

Other times the director is accompanied by a young writer introduced to him by his dubbing director, Franco Rossi. Pier Paolo Pasolini had just stood trial and been absolved of obscenity charges on his novel *Ragazzi di vita*, and he often comes along as well, with the local brothers Sergio and

Franco Citti. They all do a lot of night wandering in the director's black Chevrolet or in the Fiat Seicento that Federico had the production company give Pier Paolo in return for his help. This is how Federico discovers new territory, like Guidonia, Tiburtino Terzo, Pietralata, the Idroscalo, where Pasolini will be killed on November 2, 1975. The writer, an assiduous expert on Rome's gutter life, introduces Fellini to unique places and characters, and he has a good ear and will work on Pinelli and Ennio Flaiano's dialogues, translating them into contemporary Roman dialect. For his part, Pier Paolo finds Fellini enormously interesting and takes advantage of the situation to study and revel in his character from up close. He particularly likes his voice: "The most curious phonemes ever to emerge from a blend of Romagna and Roman dialects—outbursts, exclamations, interjections, diminutives."

These all-nighters, some spent on a futile hunt for the "Bomba" (the bomb)—an enormous prostitute that Pasolini described as a variation on the whale from *Moby-Dick*—continue, each night different from the one before and also the same. Federico often returns at four in the morning, which worries Giulietta, who has taken an immediate dislike to the homosexual Pier Paolo as a corruptor of innocent young souls. Fellini's days are spent making the rounds of producers, and as before, the dance is a farce. He goes through a dozen producers before actually securing a contract—there are flat-out rejections, flashes of enthusiasm followed by a change of mind, problems getting advance money that ultimately become a sort of mortgage against the movie. Richard Basehart, in a well-intentioned lapse, finds an American producer who never makes a definitive decision. A quasi-gangster turns up bragging that he's an intimate friend of Lucky Luciano. A very rich Swiss man makes an appearance and then just as suddenly disappears. In the meantime, the ministry starts growing unhappy with the project. Why? Now that the threat of neorealism has been mitigated and *commedia di stato* (state comedy) is thriving, Fellini, the Catholic director, has begun rifling through the public's dirty laundry. Word is meanwhile leaking out that a movie about prostitutes in the Eternal City, the seat of Christianity, won't please the pope and the church. And producers grow even more cautious. They insist, for example, that if the director wants to go forward with a deal he has to agree in writing to authorize any cuts required by the censor.

Cabiria particularly alarms people because it's all happening in the middle of a debate concerning a new law proposed by Socialist senator Lina Merlin, demanding the abolition of brothels. The law is approved by the Senate on January 21, 1955, three years before it gets to the House, where it will pass on February 20, 1958. After tears and some bawdy rituals, the "houses" will close forever on September 20 of that year. Preproduction, the filming, and then the release of *Le notti di Cabiria* all happen during this critical time. But the director, despite having worked on *Persiane chiuse*, reveals no political interest in the issue of prostitution, and never joins in the proposal to legalize it as an alternative to the black market. Many people will in fact notice that Cabiria's profession is more asserted than practiced in the film and that the bighearted woman on the Passeggiata Archeologica is the most asexual prostitute ever portrayed on the big screen. She's practically a cartoon.

The millions of lire that Fellini has managed to round up from a variety of sources have mounted and the game is getting serious. It's spring and the project seems headed for cancellation. But De Laurentiis comes back into the picture. He reads a few pages of the script in a car—his only light coming from the dashboard—and makes one of his Napoleonic decisions: "I'll make this movie. When do we start?"

Preparations are interrupted in late May, however, when news arrives from Rimini that Fellini's father has had a heart attack. Federico runs to his side and finds him much recovered. Touched by the unexpected attention, Urbano asks from his hospital bed, "Why did you bother?" It would have been the ideal moment for a father-and-son talk but for the constant interruptions of the doctor. Feeling reassured, Federico goes to a restaurant for lunch, and in the middle of the meal someone runs in to tell him that his father has suddenly died. The event, later reinterpreted as fantasy in the screenplay of *Viaggio con Anita*, leaves him with a wound that will never heal, making it even harder to return to Rimini, which he does even more infrequently after that. In a television interview with Sergio Zavoli, Fellini's mother will later say, "In the cemetery scene of 8½, when the hero tells his father 'I regret how little we talked'. . . I would never want Federico to have to say the same thing to me."

Dear Aunt Giulia had died too, the previous year, and, now that the brilliant heart of the apartment on via Lutezia is gone, Federico and

Giulietta decide to leave. They move to a luminous garret apartment on via Archimede 141A in Parioli, the elegant neighborhood where all the movie people live. The move happens right before production starts on *Le notti di Cabiria*. And somehow, as these family figures start disappearing, the Fellinis really begin to live as adults. On the verge of yet another particularly hazardous test to their relationship, the couple's new house is a showpiece of financial security. When a friend compliments it, Federico replies, "Do you really like the apartment? I do too, but if someone were to ring the doorbell and tell me it was all a joke, I'd leave without an argument."

Filming on *Le notti di Cabiria* runs twelve weeks, from July 9 to October 1, 1956, at least according to the production schedule found in the archive of production manager Luigi De Laurentiis. But we should also take into account that work was suspended when Giulietta had an accident while shooting the last scene and the production went off schedule. According to Luigi's plan, they started in Acilia, a town near Ostia Antica along the via del Mare, where Gherardi built Cabiria's shack. Then they went to the Passeggiata Archeologica and the actor's mansion. The hallway and ground floor are shot in the home of Senator Renato Angiolillo, on the ring boulevard. The bedroom and bathroom are studio sets built on via della Vasca Navale. After the initial filming along the Tiber, they shoot the sequence at Divino Amore, but not without a real struggle to obtain permits from the church.

The sanctuary of the Madonna of Divino Amore, the protectorate of Rome, is located on via Ardeatina, near Castel di Leva. It was built in 1744 to honor a miraculous apparition of Mary dating to the fourteenth century, which was meant to have saved a traveler from assault by ferocious dogs. The devout go there from Pentecost Monday through the end of October. The prostitutes' pilgrimage to the sanctuary—a source of confusion for many Catholic viewers—is shot under the persistent threat that the priests might kick them out at any moment. The director worries Luigi De Laurentiis by shooting a lot of real pilgrims from various angles, but most of that footage is cut during the edit, avoiding in the process any explicit depiction of religious fanaticism. The next step in the shooting schedule takes them to the theater, where Cabiria gets hypnotized by the magician (Aldo Silvani); then there are the scenes with the evil suitor, and the tragic ending at Castel Gandolfo. The principal photography closes with some filter shots taken through a car window in the studio in Cinecittà.

There are contradictory accounts of Giulietta's accident during the final scene—what happened and how serious it was. The actress claimed she'd hurt her knee while playing the scene in which she suddenly discovers Oscar's evil intentions, and throws herself to the ground shouting "Kill me, kill me!" Luigi De Laurentiis remembered the scene being incredibly intense and laborious ("There were thirty takes"), but he didn't associate it with the accident. For the production manager, work on that scene was, instead, definitive proof of what so many had already seen in the past—that Federico was particularly hard on and impatient with Giulietta. That may have been because (as the director himself tried to explain on different occasions) every time Giulietta didn't get his direction right away, he felt it as a betrayal of his own flesh, like the sudden paralysis of a limb that wouldn't respond to a brain impulse. Federico, however, gives a homelier version of the accident: Giulietta hurt herself when she slipped in the bedroom and had to wear a cast for three or four weeks. Luigi didn't remember any cast, but, in any case, Giulietta was hurt. Fortunately it wasn't serious, and production moved forward serenely, laboriously, and with a final cost that didn't exceed the relatively modest budget.

Giulietta always thought of Cabiria as the role of her lifetime and would remember the making of this film as a party that lasted for weeks. While it had been a challenge to get into Gelsomina's character, she instantly liked Cabiria. Gelsomina made her feel anxious, while naïve Cabiria, always the loser, keeps bouncing back with that same charge of vitality that Fellini had seen in Wanda and that Giulietta recognized in herself.

Federico and Giulietta had genuine clashes over their divergent visions of the character that continued throughout production. He wanted a puppetlike Cabiria, whereas Giulietta felt that Cabiria was more of a melodramatic role. For example, in the scene where Oscar the accountant proposes to Cabiria—dressed up in her sailor's blouse—Fellini wanted her to fall apart ambiguously. But as played by Giulietta, Cabiria is so stunned by the proposal that she almost tries to talk her suitor out of wanting a wife like her—she paces, argues, and runs to the fountain to drink. They did many takes of this scene before it was perfect, and the expertise that François Périer brought to the set was a real asset. Périer had come to the project through Leopoldo Trieste. Fellini had initially wanted Leopoldo to play the role of Oscar, but the actor and former playwright was busy directing his own first film, *Città di notte* (*City at Night*, 1956), and wanted to be free to concentrate on that. Périer, a French stage actor (dubbed by Silvio Noto), is accustomed to playing large roles; he brings a hint of southern European and a sinister slant to the character. Though Fellini generally preferred working with small-time actors and even nonactors (he has them "recite numbers" rather than real dialogue, and then dubs them), he knew how to make the most of professionals, Périer included.

Amedeo Nazzari, a natural choice for the part of the big movie star, at first had "some justifiable hesitation" (to quote Federico) about the role. The most popular celebrity in Italy isn't entirely mistaken in this, as many of his personal habits, already well known to readers of gossip magazines, are on display here: his attraction to *la dolce vita* of nightclubs, the stormy love affairs, a passion for sports cars, his massive wardrobe, his butler, the many rooms and white telephones in his mansion (on via Cassia rather than on via Appia, as in the film) where he lives alone—just like in real life. In short, Amedeo senses that he's being mocked. What's more, the director doesn't dare suggest that they use his real name, like he did for *Apparizione*. In the screenplay the character is simply named "Actor," though once they start shooting he's baptized Alberto Lazzari, for practical reasons. Once Nazzari actually comes on board, however, he displays a good sense of humor and isn't at all opposed to being mocked. His only regret is that the episode finishes shooting in just a few days. He will go on to express another regret later in an interview: once the shooting was done he never heard from his friend Fellini again, not even a merry Christmas. But these are the sorts of things that go on all the time in the world of cinema. Great friendships are born on the set and last only as long as the film does.

Similarly, Franca Marzi (who plays Cabiria's friend Wanda) becomes Giulietta's best friend for a while. She's a nice person, engaged to the boxer Franco Festucci, and pregnant with her first child. She tolerates without complaint the way that Gherardi—goaded on by Fellini—pads her up, trying to emphasize her voluptuous shape in contrast to Cabiria's slightness; it's the same contrast between big and small that characterized Giulietta and Jole Silvani, the original prostitutes in *Lo sceicco bianco*.

Piero Gherardi is an invaluable collaborator. He tirelessly brings new inventions to the set and costume design. He's the one who recommends building a cube-shaped shack for Cabiria with no roof so that they can shoot interior and exterior shots with full illumination. The Tuscan architect's talent really shines in his surreal attention to detail, something he'll realize on a large scale for *La dolce vita*. In *Cabiria*, for example, he adds aquariums and a glass aviary to the movie star's mansion, and he builds huge closets to house the actor's extensive wardrobe with rolling doors that chime when they open. But Gherardi's most fanciful inventions are devoted to the costumes for Cabiria and her friends. They wear flashy, eccentric garments inspired by the outfits of real prostitutes. Some of Cabiria's wardrobe, like the kimono with two Mexican dancers on the back and the caplet made out of chicken feathers, become classics. Since both Fellini and Gherardi are used to drawing, they exchange drafts for the characters that make continual references to the animal world, like a cartoon strip. They understand each other with practically no need for elaboration; it's a sort of marvelous, charmed telepathy that will refine itself and endure for years to come.

When the time comes to pick things back up after the interruption of Giulietta's accident, the cinematographer Aldo Tonti is fired (various theories about why circulate, but it seems to come down to dissatisfaction with his work on the background of the scene at Lake Bracciano) and Otello Martelli takes his place for the closing sequences. This situation has happened in the past and will happen again—changing cinematographers in Fellini films was something like a ritual sacrifice offered up to quash doubt. In any event, the director had a positive experience with Tonti, and, perhaps thinking that he'd made a mistake, always regretted not having worked with him again. Born in Rome in 1910, Tonti is one of the inventors of neorealism—he worked on *Ossessione* and many other films in the postwar period. His black-and-white photography is slick, and he's an expert in the use of chiaroscuro and dramatic lighting. Beyond dependably perfect results, Aldo is also appreciated for his speed when adjusting lights, allowing the actors to maintain their momentum.

When shooting wraps, the director has 56,000 meters of film and, along with the editor Leo Catozzo, faces the problem of reducing it to feature length. Work with Nino Rota on the score also proceeds in an unusual way. They move a piano into the screening room and compose music to follow the rhythm of the images, just like an accompanist would have done in the days of silent film. Typically, Nino uses a lot of non-original material, drawing inspiration from everything from variety shows to the religious music of the pilgrims. But he also writes wonderful original music, like Cabiria's own motif and a jazz beat for the Passeggiata Archeologica, as well as the ditty "Lla-ri-lli-rà," which comes back in the final scene, when the children surround the heroine, miraculously still alive, and serenade her.

The offices on via della Vasca Navale would be brimming with optimism if it weren't for the rumors filtering in from the government ministry that Nicola De Pirro, general director of the Ministry of Entertainment, is highly concerned about the allegedly immoral and possibly even blasphemous content of the film. The mayor of Rome, Salvatore Rebecchini of the Christian Democrats, is already planning to protest the release of the film in the historic city center, which, he charges, the film depicts as a central artery of vice. It doesn't matter to him that prostitutes and pimps actually do frequent the area in great numbers and that there has been widespread attention recently devoted to the murders of women by the mysterious "hammer man of Passeggiata Archeologica"; in any event, it is unacceptable to depict this behavior in a movie clearly aimed at desecrating the Eternal City. A rumor is afoot that in one scene, inspired by Guy de Maupassant's *La Maison Tellier*, the prostitutes participate in a religious ritual. Meanwhile, charity organizations are concerned about the idealization of the man with the sack, an "unaffiliated" lone benefactor whose work is unsanctioned by the religious orders.

In order to enter the competition at Cannes, *Le notti di Cabiria* must receive a permit from the censorship board. The presiding commission, which convenes on March 9, 1957, is actually willing to grant the permit provided that it carries a warning prohibiting children under sixteen from seeing it. But the permit is opposed by prefect Adolfo Memmo, representing the Ministry of the Interior, who deems the movie "damaging to the decorum of the state," and requests that it be blocked. Faced with the doubly troubling proposition that he won't be able to go to Cannes and the anticipation of cuts before the film is even released in theaters, Fellini turns to a friend, a Jesuit priest he'd met through Brunello Rondi when *La strada* opened in Venice. Father Angelo Arpa (of Hungarian descent—his family name was Arpad), whom the director will later lovingly mock in the character of a Catholic film buff in *Toby Dammit* (1968), is an extraordinary person. He marries genuine spirituality with pragmatism. Later nicknamed in the papers "the Syrian Harp" (a reference to the 1956 Japanese film *The Burmese Harp* (*Biruma no tategoto*) and to his surname, which means "harp" in Italian), Father Arpa agrees to make an appeal to the Archbishop of Genoa, Giuseppe Siri (the youngest cardinal in Italy), a man who he happens to know quite well. According to Father Angelo's account in his book *L'arpa di Fellini* (Fellini's Harp), Siri was "a sort of vice-pope during Pius XII's last years. He presided over the Conferenza Episcopale Italiana, directed the members of Catholic Action, all of whom voted Christian Democrat, and had an honorary seat on the board of all the principal state interests." Arpa's idea was to organize a secret preview of *Le notti di Cabiria* for Siri. If he liked the film, then all of these obstacles would certainly fall.

The priest makes a phone call, and Federico races to Genoa with a copy of the film and loyal Gigetto Giacosi at his side. It's essential to set up an immediate screening for the cardinal, but the only small theater available is in the *caruggi*, the seedy alleyways behind the port. Can one invite a prince of the church to screen an allegedly blasphemous film in such a dodgy neighborhood? There's no time to lose, and in an attempt to create some dignity around the event, Giacosi runs to a furniture restorer and rents a golden throne, which he sets in the middle of the small orchestra pit. The agreement is that Siri will screen the movie at midnight, after the audience has left the last show. There is only one projector in the theater, so there will have to be a pause between each reel. Father Angelo recommends that Federico stay hidden, allowing the cardinal to avoid him if he doesn't like the film. "When we come out, I'll give you a signal."

Half hidden in a doorway outside the theater, Federico and Gigetto see the cardinal arrive with his entourage a few minutes after midnight.

They wait in the alley for a very long time that night, watching drunk sailors shout and fending off invitations from real-life prostitutes—while inside the theater the priests are watching their fake counterparts. After a number of pauses, the screening ends at almost three in the morning. The two filmmakers, huddling in the shelter of the doorway, peer anxiously into the darkness and catch a glimpse of Arpa's relieved smile, and then the priest beckons them to him. In two strides, Federico is standing next to the cardinal. The Jesuit makes a murmured introduction and Siri glances at the director, a distant look in his eyes. He says only three words, *"Bisogna fare qualcosa"* (something has to be done), and sighs. It's unclear whether he's referring in a political sense to the complexities of censorship, or as a shepherd of souls to the human and social issues raised in the film. As the archbishop's court speeds off into the night, Gigetto plays a nervous Sancho Panza to Fellini's Don Quixote: "What did his eminence mean? Can we do it?"

The answer comes indirectly—as it so often does in ecclesiastical matters—in the form of a very irritated phone call from the Ministry of Entertainment to De Laurentiis the next morning: "Did you have to go do that?" It is an episode that gives us some insight into the Italy of that time: because a cardinal had approved it, the movie had a right to exist. Monsignor Albino Galletto of the Centro Cattolico Cinematografico promptly confirms the "judgment of the Most Illustrious Prelate," though, after Cannes, the censoring board will come back to the producers asking them to cut the episode about the solitary benefactor. They're fine with everything but the man with the sack. Charity must go through legitimate channels. Fellini hesitates, but De Laurentiis goes into the editing room himself and, to use his own words, "steals the scene."

News of Fellini's visit to Siri provokes a storm of indignation from the leftist camp. Fellini's initiative is read as submission to ecclesiastical power. Can the church really be more powerful than the government ministry and the censorship board? Fellini, however, is completely indifferent to the criticism. He knows that he has defended his work in the most effective way he knew how, feels no remorse, and begins to prepare for Cannes.

The honorary president of the 10th Cannes Film Festival is Jean Cocteau. The jury is made up mostly of French academics: André Maurois (president), Marcel Pagnol, Jules Romains. Fellini's competition is stiff: Ingmar Bergman with *The Seventh Seal*, Robert Bresson with *Un condamné à mort s'est échappé* (A Man Escaped), Andrzej Wajda with *Kanal*, but, as often happens, the Palmes d'Or goes to a less important American movie—*Friendly Persuasion* by William Wyler. *Le notti di Cabiria* premieres on May 10, and receives the award for best actress with the peculiar explanation, "*Giulietta Masina, Italie, et son personage, avec hommage à Fellini*" and also "*Ce prix a été à l'unanimité.*" Giulietta, Federico, and Amedeo attend the screening; François sends a telegram from Tananarive. The outcome could not have been more extraordinary. Silvana and Dino De Laurentiis throw a party in their villa on Cap Martin—a whole train is rented from the state to transport the guests.

The Cannes effect has immediate reverberations among Italian critics, who receive *Le notti di Cabiria* quite differently than the polemical *Il bidone*. While there is no lack of negative opinions, pedantic arguments, and detractors, there is also no relationship between the critics and the universal chord that the movie strikes in audiences. Someone writes that this is Fellini's masterpiece. Others remark on the director's ability to keep an equal distance from excessively heavy-handed naturalism and overly compromising sentimentalism. Almost everyone praises Giulietta. But the most notable fact is that the moral concerns seem to have entirely dissipated—no one finds it vulgar, irreverent, or blasphemous. Fellini not only has a poetic gift but a political one as well, dealing innovatively with opinions and issues, and expanding the boundaries of freedom of expression. Every one of his movies leads to a breach of caution, but they never contain polemical grandstanding: he simply and concretely demonstrates that a certain something can and must be done. Fellini has always been the confirmation that cinema can blossom where there's freedom.

After Cannes, the movie becomes an international success, and Fellini's most universally beloved work. It is released in Italy in October 1957 and does well at the box office, in addition to winning four Silver Ribbons (Fellini, Masina, Franca Marzi, and Dino De Laurentiis) as well as various other prizes from around the world. The prizes in the apartment on via Archimede have become troublesome clutter, considering the quantity and size, and Giulietta decides to put them all together in one room that is covered with plaques, certificates, trophies, and medals of every

description. Upon first entering the room, it looks like a collection of vo-
tive offerings; thus Federico immediately defines it as the "sanctuary of
Divine Love," a self-ironizing name that will get picked up by the press.
That same month, the movie is released in the United States—the first
time that a Fellini film receives simultaneous distribution and a sign that
his work now commands international attention. Bosley Crowther's prediction in *The New York Times* is totally off base—"The movie goes on for
too long considering what it has to say"—but the majority of critics praise
the film. When they return to America for the launch, Federico and Giulietta receive yet another prize for *La strada*, this time from the Screen
Directors Guild. The prize was Frank Capra's idea; as president of the
guild, he doesn't like the fact the Oscar for best foreign language film is
presented to the producer rather than the director. The banquet is also
an occasion to lobby for increased awareness among American directors
regarding the property rights to their films (changes to the screenplay, final cuts)—rights that their European colleagues maintain. A group of Sicilian cooks bake and decorate a cake in the form of Gelsomina and
Zampanò's cart, and, once it is presented, the evening culminates in a
rather rambling speech by the venerable John Ford. Fellini has always
been a devoted fan of the director of *Stagecoach* (1939), but between his
heightened emotional state and scant knowledge of English, he will never
know what Ford said about his movie.

On March 26, 1958, *Le notti di Cabiria* unexpectedly wins the Academy Award for best foreign language film, just one year after *La strada*
won. At the Pantages Theater in Hollywood, Giulietta accepts the Oscar
from Dana Wynter and Fred Astaire. Federico, who has stayed behind in
Rome, can hardly believe it when he hears the news on the radio. The astounding popularity of Cabiria's story is later confirmed when it's translated into the musical *Sweet Charity* (1959), written by Neil Simon. Its
Broadway debut signals the arrival of a promising new director, Bob Fosse.
Gwen Verdon plays Cabiria on the stage, now a taxi dancer with an American name. Shirley MacLaine plays the part in the movie adaptation of
the show, directed by Fosse in 1969. Fellini, more surprised than he is
pleased by the event, never sees the musical, but when he catches the
movie on an airplane, his reaction is genuine bewilderment: "A movie inspired a musical that inspired a movie? Go figure."

22

A Journey with Anita
Viaggio con Anita

One of Fellini's favorite movies was made by someone else more than twenty years after he wrote it. *Viaggio con Anita*—also known as *Viaggio d'amore* (*A Journey for Love*)—is invention born out of intimate truth. The story is based on Federico's trip to Rimini in May 1956, when his father died. After the triumph of *Le notti di Cabiria*, Federico was all-powerful in the cinema world; he had his pick of movie projects. Grateful that he'd wrenched a long-term contract out of the director (which will never ultimately lead to anything), Dino De Laurentiis wanted nothing more from Fellini than his next masterpiece. Sophia Loren is in; she can't wait to start. A number of lengthy telephone calls from Loren to Fellini in the fall of 1957 all begin with her saying, "Hello, it's me, Anita." Gregory Peck signs on too, after listening to Federico describe the movie to him— through an interpreter—in a Los Angeles hotel room. Truth be told, the summit meeting with the actor, arranged by a restless De Laurentiis, didn't entirely convince Fellini. He got the impression that Peck was friendly, even warm, but also that he was mired in a kind of official man-of-cinema monumentality, which wouldn't necessarily lend itself to the autobiographical nature of the character that Federico will later find in Marcello Mastroianni. But the director also has faith in the magic of the Italian climate, and he's sure that in the breeze off the Adriatic, the impeccable actor-gentleman will end up like a member of the family, just like Tony, Dick, Brod, and François have before him.

Not surprisingly, Fellini's recitation of the plot leaves *Moby-Dick's* Captain Ahab a little perplexed. Once again there is a south-to-north road trip through Italy, like in *Paisà* and *Il cammino della speranza*. The itinerary starts on the Cassia highway and then veers off over the Passo del Furlo, up to Fano on the Adriatic. We could say that the screenplay is a love letter to Rimini prudently dressed as a letter to Fano, for the landscape is that of Fellini's home: the bridge over Marecchia, the Piazza Tre Martiri, the Malatesta temple, and the legal office of Federico's friend, Titta Benzi.

(It should be noted that Fellini used all of this material later in *La dolce vita*, *8½*, *Amarcord*, and other films, starting with the lead character's name and temperament. Guido, a well-known writer, like in the first draft of *8½*, is enduring an ongoing marital crisis, and has a lover he desires and fears simultaneously. This movie that never was deserves further discussion, because it can be construed as a genuinely autobiographical chapter, cloaked in the indispensable fabrications of narrative.)

The beginning of *Viaggio con Anita*—an absurd cocktail party being thrown in honor of a Chinese intellectual—anticipates a similar scene in *La dolce vita*. Upon returning home, Guido receives a phone call from his sister Gina in Fano. Their father is unwell. Guido doesn't leave immediately and he downplays the news to his wife, Gianna, hoping to discourage her from offering to accompany him. The hero leaves home in the middle of the night and runs to wake his mistress, Anita. He asks her to come with him. They drive a Cadillac through the night and the following day, stopping in Bassano di Sutri, and in the hills between Arezzo and Sansepolcro to admire the Piero della Francesca Madonna (which is the focus of Andrei Tarkovsky's 1983 film *Nostalghia*). Heading northeast, they arrive at a farm in the midst of festivities celebrating San Giovanni (the feast of Saint John the Baptist falls on June 24), where Anita makes friends with the local women who initiate her into a traditional ritual— rolling naked in the grass far, but not too far, from the men's eyes, under the moonlight. The couple gets back on the road, but when they stop to look at the sea, Guido's thoughts turn back to his father. Anguished, he calls home, only to learn that his father is getting better. Finally he tells Anita the reason for their trip.

After depositing his mistress in a hotel on the outskirts of town, Guido heads to his parents' home, but is suddenly beset by excruciating memories of a past he'd left far behind. He finds his father surrounded by doctors, his nervous sister, and his anguished mother. It seems that Mr. Giovanni will survive—thanks to treatment and prayers—so Guido leaves, but while he's down at the bar, a breathless, overwrought taxi driver arrives to tell him that his father has died. Guido is left to take care of everything—comfort his mother, call the nuns for the vigil, receive condolence visits, and prepare food. He doesn't get back to Anita until late that night.

The next day, Guido has to deal with the papers for the burial and se-lect a headstone. His friend Titta offers to help and, while they're to-gether at the town hall, affectionately recounts his own memories of the deceased. At a café they meet an architect who proposes a ridiculous monument for the grave—a tribute, really to the great fame of the son. Guido sleeps next to his mother in his father's bed that night, so that she won't be alone, and she asks about his marriage, prompting a long talk about the fact that he has no children and doesn't seem to be getting along with his wife.

During a walk on the beach, Anita decides that she wants to know Guido better, so she decides to secretly follow him: the writer takes his mother and sister to a restaurant for breakfast while the coffin is trans-ported, according to custom, to the cathedral. That night, at dinner with Anita, he tells her of his relationship with his father, the Oedipal battles and mutual incomprehension, and, as the night goes on, Guido feels an overwhelming urge to see his father again. The cathedral is closed, but he remembers a little door he used to sneak through when he was a boy (re-member the trapdoor in *Giulietta degli spiriti*), and he climbs up to the crevice where pigeons are nesting, followed by Anita. But the door is gone; it's been walled over. Guido and Anita embrace in that niche of his childhood, a symbol of the womb giving birth to a new life. At dawn, he feels like a new person, and vows to change his life and join destinies with the woman at his side.

At the funeral Guido notices a woman who seems excessively dis-traught—perhaps his father's Anita. He returns to the hotel to discover that his mistress is gone. Before leaving Fano, Guido stops at the ceme-tery, only to find Anita at his father's grave. After they exchange a few sad but peaceful words, he climbs back into his Cadillac to return to Rome. Anita stands at the cemetery gate and watches him drive away.

Everything seems ready to move on to the next phase (the script is dated July 1957), when trouble starts. After splitting up as partners, Carlo Ponti and Dino De Laurentiis have cultivated a mutual hostility, yet destiny has brought Sophia Loren, Ponti's girlfriend, into a De Laurentiis project. The two reluctantly begin negotiations, but spend more time torturing each other than actually working anything out: Ponti asks for an astronomical fee, far too much, for Loren, and De Laurentiis tells him to forget about it. Each phone call brings the situation closer to disaster. Meanwhile, Sophia marries Ponti by proxy in Ciudad Juárez, Mexico (September 17), causing a somewhat "irregular situation": the Department of Justice is starting proceedings against Ponti for bigamy. It's increasingly uncertain whether Sophia will even be able to come to Italy, but Fellini doesn't want any other actress for the movie. He's built the whole thematic structure with Sophia Loren in mind: man is culture; woman is nature; doubt is male; decisiveness is female; men think, hesitate, and lie; women live. In some ways, Federico will portray these dynamics through another Anita in *La dolce vita*, but at this moment he's convinced that any other actress, even one better than Loren, cannot fill the role. He prefers to postpone the project—he'll come back to it, casting Loren and Mastroianni, after the movie about via Veneto (*La dolce vita*). But every project has its season and then it becomes something else. That much is demonstrated by the flop that will eventually be *Viaggio con Anita* (titled *Lovers and Liars* in the United States), which Mario Monicelli eventually makes in 1979 starring Goldie Hawn and Giancarlo Giannini.

By the spring of 1958, De Laurentiis decides it's time to bet on a new horse. He talks to Fellini extensively about projects they'd discussed in the past: *Memorie di Casanova* (Casanova's Memories), *Decamerone* (The Decameron), *Don Chisciotte* (Don Quixote), *Un marziano a Roma* (A Martian in Rome)—from a famous short story by Ennio Flaiano—and even *Barabbas*, adapted from the novel by Nobel Prize winner Pär Lagerkvist. Fellini had once quite liked the Swedish author's book, and had originally told De Laurentiis to buy the rights, but the producer will end up giving the project to the American director Richard Fleischer in 1962. Zampanò's creator, Anthony Quinn, will play the lead.

In the end, De Laurentiis and Fellini decide to make *Moraldo in città*

(Moraldo in the City), which had been languishing in a drawer since before *La strada* was even made. Dino still thinks it's a viable project: a lively, young, adventurous movie, with fabulous characters that lend themselves to an international cast. The producer can already envision how to launch it so that it will attract friends and enemies alike: "Fellini returns to *I vitelloni*." Though Federico appreciates his friend's enthusiasm, he doesn't share it. For his part, Tullio Pinelli thinks it's a mistake to return to material that they'd already put aside, while Flaiano is, typically, totally against it. And while they're all discussing the possibilities, the great summer of via Veneto suddenly explodes.

23

The Summer of via Veneto
La dolce vita

Via Veneto, originally named in the last decade of the nineteenth century for the destroyed villa of Cardinal Ludovisi, nephew of Pope Gregory XV, was renamed via Vittorio Veneto after the Italian victory in the World War I. The neighborhood that the street passes through is called Ludovisi, also known as "the neighborhood of the regions" because of its place-names. The street runs up from Bernini's Triton Fountain in Piazza Barberini to the ancient wall at Porta Pinciana. There are two rows of plane trees, and bushes along it, flanked by the neo-baroque, ornate Liberty and Fascist architecture that had come into fashion. The idea of having bars in hotels dates to the late 1800s, but via Veneto took their place as the center of the worldly, intellectual society between the two world wars, with scores of cafés—like Rosati, Strega-Zeppa, Doney, and later, Café de Paris—setting tables outside in the spring and summer, and staying open late into the night.

Many books have been written about via Veneto, in large part because of the people who frequented its cafés—Ennio Flaiano being one shining example. The story of the street is a story of the literati at play. Though the cafés have now all become banks or fast-food restaurants, in the 1950s people associated with the world of entertainment and journalism enjoyed easy access to their cultural ambience. At Caffè Rosati you might meet renowned intellectuals and journalists, eavesdrop on the most current conversations, witty punning, and polemics about culture. Actors and movie people stick to the other side of the street; they're all at the Strega-Zeppa Caffè, or, even farther downtown, at Doney. At about one in the morning, small groups of people start to arrive, on their way back from first-run films or plays, rehashing what they've seen. The gossip is caustically ironic, takes pleasure in ripping things apart and roasting anyone who's not there (and sometimes someone who is). All is done in such a way that, years later, people who partook in those nights remember it as affectionate, even innocent. In the meantime, a young lady recently arrived in the city from Modena or Bisceglie strolls by, a stuntman from Cinecittà comes up to Marcello Mastroianni and hugs him, an agent patiently waits for the perfectly relaxed moment in which to steal an intimate moment with a famous director.

At the end of World War II, people say there's no real nightlife in Rome because "the pope doesn't want it." Pope Pius XII, an upper-middle-class Roman, is certainly wary of such things, and it's not entirely arbitrary to make a connection between his physical decline (he dies on October 9, 1958) and the explosion of a sort of street party that will rage for several years on via Veneto. Journalists, accustomed to late hours, pass through here on their way back from nightclubs on adjacent streets, or on the way to the nearby Excelsior or Grand Hotel. Rome has initiated a new custom of spending long evenings on this always brightly lit street, enjoying the northern breeze off the sea, and watching the celebrities try to escape the paparazzi—it looks like a corrida. Here are the "barefoot countesses"—named after the movie staring Ava Gardner, *The Barefoot Contessa* (1954)—and starlets willing to try anything. Here former King Farouk of Egypt delivers his classic line: "In a few years there will only be five crowns left in the world—four kings in a French deck of cards, and the queen of England."

Photographers morph from witnesses of reality to participants and creators of it. One pioneer in the field is the native Roman Tazio Secchiaroli, who will be Fellini's principal muse for *La dolce vita*. He's known for his brawls with Walter Chiari and for being attacked by King Farouk on August 14, 1958, having driven him to rage with flashbulbs. A whole new strategy of provocation blossoms: making important people lose their temper leads to more interesting photos, which then earn higher fees from the gossip rags. Traditionally engaged in a bloody competition, the photographers of via Veneto also occasionally form alliances. One photographer, for example, might approach a selected target and shoot him or her, allowing other photographers to swoop in and capture the violent response. Anita Ekberg and Anthony Steel are frequent victims of these skirmishes, what with their alcohol and jealous scenes. As soon as he gets a shot in, Tazio deposits the film with his buddy at the newsstand, so that when the prey demands the offending film, he can pass off a blank roll.

Gradually, after endless nights spent observing this spectacle, Federico starts to conceive of a new backdrop for *Moraldo in città*. The director now understands that it's a mistake to look to the past; the farewell ceremonies are over for now. Rimini is far away, the specter of his father has disappeared, and a new generation is emerging, one that didn't live through the war. It's time to open up and tell the story of what's happening in the world around him. Slowly Fellini passes from his nest of memories into a chronicle of the moment; from the faded diary pages, he moves into an "open space"—a concept that others are just starting to theorize about. As the writers get to work updating *Moraldo in città*, Tullio Pinelli balks. He's not entirely convinced that there's anything dramatic to say in this movie beyond the idea itself. Flaiano, instead, is more involved than usual. The idea of taking on his own environment stimulates him, and he likes Federico's concept of breaking the links between episodes: "We have to make a Picasso sculpture, smash it, then put it back together the way we want it."

As they work on the project, the three writers start liking it more and more. Dino De Laurentiis, however, can't drum up any enthusiasm. He liked the old *Moraldo*, a typical Italian comedy. The new movie looks fragmented, risky, full of unknowns. After reading the first version of the screenplay (written in three months), he rejects it. But he's not entirely sure, so he has Fellini solicit another opinion—actually, three more opinions—from Ivo Perilli, Luigi Chiarini, and the critic Gino Visentini. All three readers agree with the producer. Though some of their comments are justified, they primarily tend to retreat to old neorealist arguments regarding the script's lack of scenes depicting society's "healthy impulses."

The unhealthiness that specifically alarms Dino is the massacre at Steiner's apartment. A typical Neapolitan, De Laurentiis begs Fellini to rewrite the cruel scene, quoting the famous last line from *Filumena Marturano* by Eduardo De Filippo,* "*I figli 'sso figli*" (Your children are your children). In fact, because the movie already seems too long, he'd like the

---

*Eduardo De Filippo was a Neapolitan playwright of enormous consequence in Italian theater.

morbid intellectual simply written out of the script. But from Federico's point of view, Steiner is one of the cornerstones of *La dolce vita*, and without him, the meaning would change. This is, at least, how De Laurentiis characterized the debate. Fellini, on the other hand, would claim that Steiner wasn't even in the first draft.

One inevitable source of conflict between De Laurentiis and Fellini is the casting of the lead. Dino wants big stars like Maurice Chevalier, Barbara Stanwyck, Henry Fonda, Walter Pidgeon, Luise Rainer, and Silvana Mangano—he doesn't think that an Italian actor can feasibly carry the film. He wants Fellini to use Paul Newman, who has said he's available, but Federico is in love with the idea of casting Marcello Mastroianni. He doesn't know him well, but he asks him to come by, and, after they talk, Fellini can't imagine anybody *but* Mastroianni in the part. He immediately changes the protagonist's name from Moraldo to Marcello; the die has been cast, and there's no going back. Bully for De Laurentiis who doesn't like being contradicted.

And so the dance of the producers starts again. Fellini needs to come up with someone willing to pay 75 million lire to buy out the project from De Laurentiis. Franco Cristaldi at Vides Cinematografica might work, or even Goffredo Lombardo again—he's recovered finally from the shock of *Il bidone*. Lombardo wants to keep the budget to 400 million, though, and the movie already looks dangerously close to being more costly than that. Fellini runs into Peppino Amato in front of the Excelsior, where Amato lives and works, and it turns out that Amato is ecstatic about the idea of a movie set on his beloved street. Fellini has known Amato, a founding father of Italian cinema renowned for his films as well as his brilliant neologisms and surreal sentences, since *Avanti c'è posto*. Like Samuel Goldwyn, the creator of Hollywood "goldwynism," don Peppino was the inventor of a new lexicon for Italian cinema. He assures Fellini that Angelo Rizzoli is a "sure bet, absolutely sure, actually, even probable" for up to 600 million, and he predicts that the film will be "an emilian stone" (or a milestone) in the history of cinema. But the title, he says, must be *Via Veneto*. Fellini promises him satisfaction, even though he really wants to call the movie *La dolce vita*—despite the fact that it is also the title of a long-forgotten 1912 comedy written by Arnaldo Fraccaroli.

Federico gets a call from a German producer who offers to fund the movie if there's a part for Lilli Palmer. Another call comes in from a company based in Lombardia, and run by the journalist Arturo Tofanelli. At a certain point, the carousel of potential backers grows so confusing that even Clemente Fracassi, the production manager, can't figure out what's happening to this surreal project.

Amato proves a tough negotiator. He keeps insisting that the title should be *Via Veneto*. In every meeting with lawyers, he pushes the discussion to a point of frenzy, claiming that he'd rather drink ink than sign a contract with it, and then he does drink some ink. Another time, he tears up the papers with his teeth and starts chewing. In the final meeting, he accuses the negotiators of attempted rape, and then, in a gesture of surrender, he drops his pants. Apart from these quaint anecdotes, which Amato sometimes remembers fondly and other times denies entirely, he is one of the most experienced operators in Italian cinema. He can see a good deal long before the others, and Rizzoli trusts him. The old billionaire doesn't really care for the ultramodern, difficult movie that Fellini wants to make, but don Peppino presents it so skillfully that Rizzoli agrees to produce it.

When Rizzoli and Fellini meet, they both feel an immediate and profound mutual sympathy. Rizzoli is almost fatherly toward the director, and yearns to transmit some wisdom about life to the "dear artist" (which is how he addresses the director), perceiving that, if he wanted to, Federico could become the richest filmmaker ever. He treats him as a sort of renegade youngster, in the meantime developing the opinion that Flaiano is the bad seed. Rizzoli knows that Flaiano happily spread rumors about him (Ennio used to quote—correctly or not—Rizzoli as having said, "But that Tolstoy . . . isn't he *really* Dostoevsky?"). Thus, when Rizzoli reads the episode in the final screenplay where Steiner kills himself after shooting his children, he assumes it's Flaiano's idea and tells Fellini, "You could never have come up with such a dreadful thought, you have such a nice face." The truth of the matter, however, is that Pinelli was responsible for the suicide episode. He'd gone to school with Cesare Pavese,* and followed the writer's tragic story closely. De Laurentiis

---

*Cesare Pavese was a highly respected Italian novelist who committed suicide in Turin on August 27, 1950.

wanted "healthy impulses" in the film, and Rizzoli similarly insists there must be a "ray of sunlight."

In the interim, discussions about *La dolce vita* have shifted from via della Vasca Navale to via XXIV Maggio, and then to via Salandra, and finally to the Safa-Palatino studios in Piazza San Giovanni e Paolo. Fellini, not at all perturbed by the constant moves, keeps on taking meetings, collecting head shots, discussing the story with the writers and trusted friends. He is becoming methodical about his use of secret consultants. The director "kidnaps" the person he wants to share an idea with and drives him around the outskirts of Rome at night until the issue at hand is fully examined; Pier Paolo Pasolini is one of the friends who gets sucked into this interminable fox-trot. Fellini and Pasolini are very close, and the director often invites him to watch the auditions at Cinecittà and offer opinions.

Fellini likes Adriana Botti, a rich girl from Milan, for the part of Maddalena. He goes to Milan to ask the writer Elio Vittorini to play Steiner, but Vittorini refuses. While traveling, he hears about a young singer, Adriano Celentano, who has made a name for himself imitating Elvis Presley, and adds him to the cast. As for the part of the father, the director is considering several different stage actors, but when he meets Annibale Ninchi, the former star of *Scipione l'africano* (*Scipio the African*, 1937), who bears an uncanny resemblance to Urbano Fellini, it's a moment of revelation, and an intimate rapport will spring up between the two. Federico, who doesn't want to miss the chance to bring Luise Rainer back to the silver screen after twenty years, casts her in the part of Dolores the writer, Marcello's lover and protector. During revisions on the screenplay, though, the character grows hyperbolic, and despite the actress's desperation, Fellini cans the entire story line. Another scene, which he'd held out as a carrot to Rizzoli, is cut because of the excessive length and expense of shooting on Ischia, the island the producer adores— it was to have been a picnic on a boat gone haywire when a beautiful swimmer is burned alive in the water while surrounded by motorboats.

At 11:35 a.m. on March 16, 1959, the volunteer assistant director Gianfranco Mingozzi, a future director himself, calls the first take at Studio 14 in Cinecittà, where Piero Gherardi has reconstructed the spiral stairs leading up to the dome of Saint Peter's Cathedral. Anita Ekberg is on the set in her black dress and priest's beanie, feeling reassured about the production. Worried that the movie will be seen as a satire of her mundane married life, the former Miss Malmoe has made Fellini change the name of the character from Anita to Sylvia. Now that she's here, she's quite pleased to be the center of attention, charmed by Federico and Marcello, who nicknames her Anitona. The next scene, also shot at Cinecittà, is the press conference in the Excelsior. The director has called on a number of real reporters to participate in the scene, and he gives them improvised questions to ask just moments before shooting. The sequence with the American celebrity continues with a long scene in an open-air nightclub at the Terme di Caracalla. But the episode that sets everyone abuzz is the one where Anitona and Marcello, after a long, hard night, go into the Trevi Fountain. The scene, inspired by a photographic exploit of Pierluigi Praturlon, recalls the Jazz Age of the 1920s, when Zelda Fitzgerald jumped into the Union Square fountain in New York City on her honeymoon, inspiring her husband to later leap into the fountain in front of the Plaza Hotel in an effort to keep up.

At this point, Fellini's set has become a spectacle in its own right, a destination spot for tourists, and a real event for guests and passersby. The whole of Rome wants to see the crew working in front of the fountain and, of course, see Anita, the Nordic blond beauty who makes a cult out of this crazy party—immediately and forever, the symbol of an era. It is a historic event. In fact, fifteen years later, Ettore Scola, with Fellini's grumpy participation and Mastroianni's bemused approval, will reprise the event in his film *C'eravamo tanto amati* (*We All Loved Each Other So Much*, 1974).

The club where Marcello brings his father is constructed in the Acque Albule in the Bagni di Tivoli (the baths); the night scenes at Maddalena's swimming pool are set there as well. In the end, Anouk Aimée takes the part of Maddalena and joins the production on April 25. The actress is shy and Fellini's French is bad, leading to an embarrassing first meeting, but "Anucchina" quickly becomes a member of the family. She's not even terribly upset when a crowd of youngsters, expecting a glimpse of Anitona as they shoot the exterior of the prostitute's house at Tor di Schiavi, loudly express disappointment at finding her too tiny. In May the crew moves on to the aristocrats' party set in Bassano di Sutri, a town along the Cassia, forty-two kilometers outside of Rome. Livio Odescalchi's marvelous sixteenth-century villa provides the location. Guidarino Guidi, whose expertise and ability to define high society proves invaluable, helps round up the amazing cast of characters and Fellini acts the perfect host to aristocrats, both real and fake, princes, and extras. The background music is Kurt Weill's "Mack the Knife," though in the end the rights to the song will be too expensive. Nino Rota, undaunted, will compose his own similar tune.

After a series of delays, because the crew can shoot on via Veneto only late at night and with a plethora of regulations, the producer agrees to reconstruct a section of the notorious street in Studio 5 at Cinecittà. At a cocktail party on June 6, Rizzoli expresses concern over the ballooning costs. The sidewalk in front of Café de Paris is a perfect replica of the original, except for the fact that it's not set on a slope. Federico insists to everyone that cinema doesn't have to imitate reality but merely reinvent it, and praises Cinecittà's via Veneto as better and more real than the original. At a certain point later on, he'll decide that he always wants to reproduce everything and stops shooting on location.

It's not easy for Fracassi to keep up with the director's doubts, hesitations, and sudden decisions. Legend has it that one day Federico sped past the crew as they were walking toward a location, came to a screeching halt, and gesturing wildly, ordered them all to turn around. The location had changed. After endless scouting, they finally find the field where the fake miracle will take place; they settle on Bagni di Tivoli, near where the nightclub was shot. The scene, which requires hundreds of extras to withstand a cruel drenching from fire hydrants, calls for another series of unforgettable nights, inspiring more pilgrimages by friends and curiosity seekers eager to watch Fellini work. This episode is also based on real events experienced by the photographer Secchiaroli a few years earlier, in June of 1958: after reading a newswire about two children who claimed to have seen the Virgin Mary, Tazio rushed off to Terni to get pictures. The idea that *La dolce vita* is somehow a realistic movie about life on via Veneto has become so widespread that, when there's a fire at the Ambasciatori Hotel on June 21 and four coatroom attendants trapped in the flames are forced to jump out a window onto via Liguria, some newspapers report that Fellini has added the scene to his movie.

Meanwhile, Federico is still mulling over Steiner's character, entirely undecided between Alain Cuny and Enrico Maria Salerno for the part. He holds long auditions with both actors, forcing them to practically recite the entire role, but doesn't make up his mind until the last minute. Pasolini proves an important influence on this decision: he compares Cuny to a Gothic cathedral. Indeed, the grand background that Gherardi has already built seems to match the French actor's stunning poise.

The so-called orgy is shot in Cinecittà, after much concerned debate about exactly how naked Nadia Gray will get—she performs her striptease quite cautiously, and only after certain body parts have been prudently covered. Federico is now tired and irritated by the pressure of production. Having to defend real or alleged over-budget costs every day doesn't put him in the best of moods, but it's late August already and the exterior shots of the sequence are all that's left to shoot—after the partygoers leave the orgy and end up on the beach where Gherardi's leviathan (which the director didn't even bother to inspect beforehand) is pulled to shore. This scene too comes from a real-life fright when a horrible, unclassifiable fish washed up on the beach at Miramare in Rimini in the spring of 1934, winning a cover story in the *Domenica del Corriere*. For the film, the episode is set at Passo Oscuro, about 30 kilometers north of Rome on the Aurelia. After that, the crew takes some more shots from a helicopter, and, by early September, filming is essentially wrapped.

Because of its daily surprises, unexpected location changes, and the constant shifting of characters and scenes, production on *La dolce vita* will be remembered as a unique experience by those who were there. It was something of a long holiday for Federico, an impression enhanced by Giulietta's extended absence; she was abroad working on another movie. In mid-September, Fellini embarks on the delicate editing phase with Leo Catozzo, followed by the dubbing of hundreds of dialogues and the composition of the score. Rota would like to keep as many of the playbacks used during the shooting as possible, because he really likes the collage of sound, but he'll eventually be forced to overcome his laziness and write quite a lot of new music.

An extraordinary rough cut of the movie is ready that autumn. It still has the original soundtrack with all of the original voices, including the director's orders and a number of colorful expletives. At three hours and twenty minutes long, it's thrilling to watch. Over the course of a few weeks, intimate friends and acquaintances fill Cinecittà's private screening rooms, many of whom will report that the final dubbed and edited version of the film loses some of the rough cut's original charm. But that early copy is impossible to find today.

The final edit of *La dolce vita* runs three hours. Like many great movies—*Intolerance*, *Greed*, and *Ivan the Terrible*—the length itself is already an event. It isn't long because of any initial decision to make an exceptionally long movie, but because of the ongoing, progressive development of themes and characters over the course of five feverish months of filming. Fellini's initial concept was to show a series of anecdotes about an archetypal figure of society, the journalist. He ended up painting a grand portrait of the whole world. Some critics will foreshadow a future chapter in Fellini's filmography by labeling this picture the *Satyricon* of the twentieth century.

The seven principal episodes in this mosaic of a film are linked by the journalist Marcello Rubini: his evening with the heiress Maddalena; the long night spent with the American movie star; his relationship with the intellectual Steiner (this episode is split into three sequences: the encounter, the party, and the tragedy); the fake miracle; his father's visit; the aristocrats' party; and the orgy. The succession of these episodes is abruptly interrupted by the apparition of the angelic Paola, and framed by a prologue (the Christ statue flying over Rome) and an epilogue (the discovery of the leviathan), which are symmetrically symbolic. Through all the episodes there is the running story of Marcello's difficult relationship with his lover Emma, explored more deeply in the small scene where they have an explosive argument.

The movie's theme is predominantly café society, the diverse and glittery world rebuilt upon the ruins and poverty of the postwar period. It's a kingdom for the few carefree people who circulate between parties and cruises, scandals and follies. Yet, in truth, the film is a tragic allegory of the desolation lurking behind the façade of a perpetual carnival. The term *dolce vita* (sweet life, or good life) invites facile moral interpretations that are utterly alien to the director's intentions. Fellini had no other aim beyond depicting the matter-of-fact, and it doesn't matter to him that, to achieve this, he tells a disjointed story that eschews the tricks and tropes typical of more traditional dramas. *La dolce vita* is the "nocturnal diary" of a man living out the tension of attraction to and disgust with the world he lives in. He's an everyman in Mastroianni's interpretation—which is entirely in keeping with Fellini's intentions. Marcello has no real roots; he doesn't have anything to prevent him from falling into perdition at any time. But he's sensitive enough for epiphany. Marcello must contend with himself before all else—his impatience toward anything futile, temporary, or bad; and his repressed provincial desire for order and cleanliness. From a moral point of view, however, he's often a kind of deaf-mute. He has the same essential affliction as Zampanò and Augusto—it's not incidental that he ends up alone, just like Fellini's other heroes. The only difference is that this protagonist is an intellectual, in one respect entirely self-aware and in another an exuberant participant in the endless party.

Marcello's aspirations to change are personified in a number of characters he encounters, however briefly, as he seeks the help that no one can give him. Maddalena, the beautiful heiress, is too rich and spoiled to know what he wants. Emma, on the other hand, is too organic and possessive. His father is a stranger to him and the visit brings up only regret, remorse, and melancholy. Steiner is adrift on an unknown sea; he responds to a moment of fear with pride and commits murder worthy of a Greek tragedy. Marcello-Fellini is something of a little Faust, a man who ultimately wants to descend into the realm of the Mothers.* There are no real digressions in this galactic movie; every detail belongs to the larger design, a step along a definitive itinerary. As in medieval morality plays, the various episodes have a symbolic function. They each represent a path to peace for Marcello, yet the paths are all closed off. In the end, on the shore after the apparition of the leviathan—the apparent symbol of total evil—Paola calls to Marcello, but her words are lost on the wind. She has something to say, but Fellini's hero is deaf, as usual. Perhaps, though, we can read in the girl's enigmatic smile that this one path isn't entirely closed off to him.

People debate about whether Fellini's film makes any contribution to what is known about contemporary society, whether he's changing the world, and what side he's on. His enemies repeat—under their breath—

---

*A reference to Faust in the dark gallery of the Mothers.

that Fellini is incapable of expressing a sociopolitical judgment, that his inability to demonstrate a positive vision is pathological.

By now, after so many polemics, Fellini has arrived at a place where he is universally recognized in international cinema; the lines drawn in the sand around him are more distinct. Some people support the idea that art should be a means for teaching values, that it should come out of engagement and old-school neorealist ideas. But the predominant theme of this moment is that all art has transcendental politics. There's no need for explicit accusations or banner waving in order for a director to prove he's on the right side, because the right side, for an artist (beyond the problems he faces in real life), is fantasy, sincerity, and inspiration. This is the only way to explain why a film about pure disillusionment, such as *La dolce vita*, is not entirely morally bankrupt—which is to say, within the parameters of a complacent, macabre dance in a doomed world, that the movie actually depicts a lucid self-examination. Analyzed scene by scene, it certainly does appear to be a tale of failure—but how then to explain *La dolce vita*'s inherent serenity? How its broad meaning contrasts with the dark, bitter, and frightening atmosphere of the movie's individual scenes? The leviathan is also a fish. Many of our fears are born of illusion, rhetoric, and sentimentality. *La dolce vita* takes it all on, deconstructs and demystifies it. Fellini has reached a complete maturity, and he's inured to the temptation of satire, caricature, or desperation. With the understandable exception of the sentimental indulgence in the episode with Marcello's father (where the character of the prostitute with the heart of gold reappears), the movie is arid, virile, and absent of chicanery. The director seems to be saying: Let's try to see things as they are, and the clouds will disappear from the horizon.

The movie's poetry comes out of its respect for its characters, even the most notorious and undeserving ones. It comes from the measure of positivism that is part of the negative solutions that Marcello considers. It comes from the awareness that the paths to serenity are many. When Anita goes into the Trevi Fountain it is a purely organic, joyful moment of living. The crowd's fervor at the scene of the miracle masks a charge of spiritual tension, albeit behind the horrendous distortion. The aristocrats retain an aura of dignity in their wan survivalism. The ambiguity of *La dolce vita* doesn't, nonetheless, stem from an urge for self-protection or an attempt to sidestep judgment. It comes instead from the awareness that any human judgment is tenuous and reversible—no one is entirely good or entirely evil. Our perspective is always somehow biased. In this sense, the scene at Steiner's cocktail party is revelatory. The guests gather around a tape recorder listening to nature sounds, as the light outside the window seems to herald an unknowable new day. The relationship between nature, mankind, and the uncertainty of progress is expressed in the film with both apprehension and tenderness.

Federico might condemn every present moment, but that doesn't mean he hates or fears it. He simply depicts life as a source of nourishment and new experience. In a way, *La dolce vita* evokes a line of Eugenio Montale's: *"codesto solo oggi possiamo dirti / ciò che* non *siamo, ciò che* non *vogliamo"* (this, today, is all that we can tell you / what we are *not*, what we do *not* want). But the images of the movie are so exhaustive in their sum that they alter something inside every viewer.

La dolce vita is the manifesto for what can be called "the second liberation." The movie typified a time—the early sixties—when Pope John XXIII, JFK, and Nikita Khrushchev came onto the scene. People started talking about ecumenism, the new frontier, and internationalism. When viewed from this perspective, the film contains multiple spectacles: the authentic expression of an omnivorous culture that has long hungered for experiences denied it. *La dolce vita* was born out of existential curiosity and nurtured by a shattering desire for freedom. It's a film that refuses any moralistic schemata for analyzing events and characters: it chooses an antimetaphysical position (which will later be called "weak thinking"). This movie is a momentary victory of ego over superego and its conditioning. It's an invitation to pause, but with eyes and ears open wide. It looks quite simple, but the Italy of the late fifties and early sixties is still provincial and responds pathologically to such suggestions.

24

Public Sinner

The applause lasts all of twenty seconds and there are even some catcalls at the premiere of *La dolce vita* in Rome, February 3, 1960, at the Cinema Fiamma. The usual bevy of photographers circles Anita Ekberg. That very same night, in a morbid coincidence, the popular singer Fred Buscaglione dies in a car accident in Rome. After the opening, attention shifts to Milan, a notoriously difficult market, and the gala planned for February 5. Angelo Rizzoli is being inundated by complaints from Riama Film, the producers, and Cineriz, the distributor. Both companies fear the worst. The new Fellini movie cost too much and they're afraid it won't earn back the money. Rumors are also circulating about a possible intervention from the censorship board and even the courts.

Italy is about to move into a dreadful period of censorship. Soon, the attorney general of Milan, Carmelo Spagnuolo, will call a release blackout on Luchino Visconti's *Rocco and His Brothers* (1960) for scenes of sex and violence, and the previews of *La dolce vita* in the days running up to the release give no cause for optimism. At a screening in a private room of Rizzoli's palazzo on via Crocifisso, the elite of Milan and friends of the producer seem indifferent. Perhaps the movie is too Roman and they are simply affirming the historic hostility between the two metropolises, or perhaps they are disappointed—after all the alarms, they might have expected something more boldly erotic. The old patron embraces Fellini resignedly and says, "My dear artist, you made something good, but you can't expect to be praised by these people," as he cheerlessly indicates his guests. As to the other preview, at the Centro San Fedele on January 30, the storm over that event will go down in the history of the Compagnia di Gesù. But we'll come back to that.

Cinema Capitol holds a free screening, which is the worst kind of public you can hope to view a new release. The well-heeled Milanese find the movie long, not funny enough, and, worst of all, immoral. The orgy scene provokes the audience, and calls ring out: "Disgusting!" "Stop it!" "Shame on you!" There is only a smattering of applause at the end and some hoots. As Fellini is walking down the stairs from the balcony, he feels something slightly wet on his neck, and turns to see the red face of someone who'd just spat on him. In the meantime, others are attacking Mastroianni: "Coward." "Vagabond." "Communist!" Meanwhile, fans race up to the director, fighting each other to shake his hand. Federico has a cold and is slightly disoriented under the effects of antibiotics. In the end, he remembers it as an entertaining evening.

The next morning Fellini and Clemente Fracassi, the production manager, are back in the lobby of Cinema Capitol looking at posters for the first show at two o'clock. Fracassi repeats that he thinks it's a beautiful movie, just like a book of poetry, a concert, an art show for sophisticates—how can you expect regular people to understand it? Federico shrugs, as if to say, let's see what happens. They head off for risotto with saffron at Biffi Scala, and try to talk about other things over lunch. While drinking their coffee, Fracassi suggests they return to the cinema to see what's happening. Emerging from Piazza della Scala, they see a crowd gathering at the far end of via Manzoni by the corner where the Grand Hotel et de Milan is. Federico grows pale and exclaims, "My God, something must have happened!" The crowd has broken through the glass door; hysterical, they want to see the movie before the censors seize it. The ones left out on the sidewalk are protesting. The prefect of Milan immediately takes advantage, threatening to close the theater to protect public order. Rizzoli calls his lawyers. But it's all just grandstanding—the conquest is unstoppable. The crowds waiting outside the Capitol grow and the excitement quickly spreads throughout Italy. *La dolce vita* breaks box-office records, despite the fact that ticket prices have just gone up to 1,000 lire. Sales in other cities and towns exceed all expectations.

One significant contribution to *La dolce vita*'s allure is the hostile campaign against it being waged by the right wing in newspapers like

Il Secolo d'Italia (which runs an article under the headline SACROSANCT HOOTS IN MILAN! SHAME ON YOU!), in collaboration with the conservative clerics. The Fascists take the case to the House on February 9, with a claim that could have appeared in a satirical newspaper: the film causes "clear offense to the virtues and probity of the population of Rome," and launches "a banal mockery of Rome's highest mission as the center of the Catholic world and ancient culture." This line of argument, that the film is an attack "on the prestige of the city," is variously adopted by other politicians in parliament, but the vice secretary for tourism and entertainment, Domenico Magrì of the Christian Democrats, voices his noble defense on February 17. In the meantime, the Centro Cattolico Cinematografico, which had classified the film as "not recommended," revises the classification to "should not be seen." The diocesan board of Catholic Action in Rome asks for the censorship board to reexamine the film. Under the directorship of Giuseppe Della Torre, an old count, the Vatican newspaper *L'Osservatore Romano* also lobbies for censorship. Della Torre hasn't seen the movie, which he freely confesses to Father Angelo Arpa, saying, "One doesn't need to see filth to condemn it." At the end of the month, the *L'Osservatore Romano* reiterates its complaint in a series of unsigned articles calling the movie "the obscene life," and pleading for someone to "stop it!" The anonymous author calls for government intervention, criticizing Father Arpa's liberalism. In later years, the articles would be attributed to Oscar Luigi Scalfaro, future president of the republic, and he never would deny writing them.

In the midst of this noisy debate, there is a particularly unhappy incident involving the Jesuits of San Fedele in Milan. For the occasion of a preview held in that institution, Father Arpa had returned from Genoa without what some people had come to think of as "the purple seal" of approval. Cardinal Siri had again privately screened Fellini's movie—not in a back-alley theater this time but in a room of the Arecco Institute—and he was typically reserved when he emerged from the screening. He didn't have a necessarily negative opinion of the film, but he wasn't ready to come to its defense as he had for *Le notti di Cabiria*, a maneuver that had cost him too much criticism already. He doesn't want to further strain his relationship with the curia of Milan, and for good reason: he'd heard that the cardinal of Milan, Giovanni Battista Montini, his future opponent in a conclave for the papacy (Montini will be named Pope Paul VI), is preparing an edict against *La dolce vita* under the apparent urging of the president of a group that constructs churches. Thus, Father Arpa may refer to the archbishop's "not negative" opinion only when informally asked to describe it to the president of the republic, Giovanni Gronchi, leaving the film open to attack and possibly inappropriate for the Jesuits of San Fedele.

On February 15, Cardinal Montini calls Father Alberto Bassan, the father superior of San Fedele, into a meeting and orders him to publicly reverse the monastery's positive response. Since Montini hasn't seen *La dolce vita*, Bassan offers to organize a screening for him that very night, but at the appointed time, the cardinal's secretary appears in his place. The following morning a letter from Montini arrives at San Fedele. Coming right to the point, the letter instructs Bassan "to find a way to comfort the souls of those who have seen the movie or will see it, and to do so from a position of moral reservation and reprobation. The widespread impression that Jesuits ratify such film productions and representations must be corrected."

The brothers of San Fedele—as demonstrated in a courageous article published by Father Alfonso Scurani in 1959—claim that they cannot comprehend the archbishop's harsh position: "Who instigated it? Someone in the Sant'Ufficio? Roman nobility? Aristocrats who pressured the Vatican?" Though distressed, the Jesuits refuse to be silenced, and publish a review of the movie in an early March edition of the magazine *Letture*. In the review, Father Nazareno Taddei explains how the representation of evil can be a means to communicating a positive message. A second, harsher letter from Montini then arrives, deploring Taddei's position and ordering the monks to desist publishing *Letture*. Montini also orders the Jesuits to stop attending public screenings and claims that Taddei must not only publicly retract his review but never publish again or watch movies. He also must stop directing the religious program he has on RAI TV and move to Munchen in Bavaria. Father Bassan is unseated as abbot and exiled to Padova.

Father Arpa receives an admonishment by the Supreme Congregation of the Sant'Ufficio. Taddei remembers, "Federico Fellini was the most upset about this. He said, 'I was wrong after all. My movie causes evil, and I thought I'd made a Catholic movie.' He asked to meet the cardinal and was told that His Eminence was very busy. He waited patiently and kept trying for about two weeks. Finally he got the point and gave up." As it is to be expected, however, the stories about Fellini's second visit to a prince of the church diverge. In his book *L'arpa di Fellini*, Father Arpa, who accompanied the director, writes,

> After two and a half hours in the waiting room, the cardinal canceled the appointment through his secretary without any kind of explanation. I still remember how Fellini suffered this poor treatment. He couldn't resign himself to the situation and told me, "Angelo, if you ever meet Cardinal Montini, you can tell him that his refusal to see me hurt a lot."

The Charlie Chaplin club in Rome held a public debate on the movie on February 17. The next day the paper *Paese Sera* reported that "more than 2,000 people filled the room, the halls, and the stairway of the gallery L'Incontro." The article continues, "Many spectators had to give up trying to get in and the police had to intervene to control the overflow and maintain order, although they couldn't prevent some incidents." Alberto Moravia opened the debate, ceding to Pasolini, who claims that *La dolce vita* is a Catholic film. He celebrates the film's "beauty, at times shocking, sometimes monstrous, often angelic," and attacks *L'Osservatore Romano*. On another occasion, after disagreeing with editors of the weekly *Reporter*, where Pasolini is movie critic, he storms out of the office, slamming the door behind him.

The left wing, at this point, makes a historical position shift, almost as if they'd entirely forgotten about the insults they'd hurled at Fellini from *La strada* onward. The Socialist-Communist newspapers and parties race to his defense. The movie is being attacked by the general assembly of the Board of Roman Parish Priests, and by the Genealogical Board of Italian Nobility, who harshly criticize Livio Odescalchi for renting out his palazzo in Bassano di Sutri for the production. Some of the aristocrats who actually appeared in the movie suffer a crisis of repentance and write to their papers, claiming they were tricked. One reader writes to the Vatican paper, calling for Anita Ekberg's prosecution under Article 498 of the Criminal Code that prohibits anyone from abusing priestly vestments (referring to her hat and cape in one scene of the movie). Practically everyone writes, talks, and debates *La dolce vita* in the months after its release, but perhaps the most intelligent and serene voice comes from right-wing Indro Montanelli, who publishes a lucid defense of the film in *Corriere della Sera* on January 22.

Overwhelmed by mail, clippings, and phone calls, Federico is constantly being stopped in the streets, interviewed, praised, insulted, and put on a pedestal. In a 1989 interview he recalled several specific incidents:

> I remember a big poster on the door of a church in Padova. I was waiting for the train and I came out of the station to take a little walk. I wanted to see the famous Caffè Pedrocchi. But I happened by a church, I don't know which one it was, with an impressive façade and a huge sign on the one of the main doors—a big white square framed with a black line, like a death announcement. I thought I recognized something about it and went closer. To my surprise, I read there: *We pray for the soul of the public sinner Federico Fellini.*

Back in Rimini, Fellini's mother, Ida, doesn't dare see the movie, but she worries about her son. Fellini continues:

> I knew she'd been publicly chastised by the archbishop and so I decided to go speak with him. I knew the building, we used to pass by it when we were students. We used to think we could see the priest through the window and we'd all stop and chant, "Blessings, blessings!" I don't know whether he was the same archbishop. I don't think so. Anyway, this one was really old, sunken and retreating into his armchair, not entirely coherent . . . He asked me in a barely audible voice, "Are you from Rimini?" He dragged the conversation out for a few minutes and I never got to discuss my mother. As I was leaving, I turned around and surprised the old man in the act of trying to bless me.

Though such events seem quite funny today, they do provide a good portrait of Italy at the beginning of the 1960s, as well as a confirmation of the film's revolutionary role in the way people thought about their society. The same is true elsewhere. Internationally, some countries wouldn't allow the movie's distribution for decades: in Spain, the film wasn't released until June 18, 1981, more than twenty years later.

At the Cannes Film Festival, the jury is divided. The president of the jury is Georges Simenon, one of Fellini's favorite writers. The mutual admiration between Fellini and "Sim" grows into a fast friendship; they take frequent walks arm in arm along the sunny Croisette. When it comes time to select a winner, however, Simenon writes in his *Mémoires intimes*, "Robert Favre Le Bret, the director, with obvious intentions, lets me know that, for diplomatic reasons, the Americans must get at least one big prize." Michelangelo Antonioni's *L'avventura* is also among the movies in competition, having regained some prestige after a debut that degenerated into total mayhem. Some jurors prefer Michelangelo to Federico; they consider him "more of an artist." But Simenon wins Henry Miller over to his side, and, because of that vote, manages to give the Palme d'Or to *La dolce vita*.

> When I bring the roster of winners to Favre Le Bret in the hallway, he's not alone. He's with a representative of the Foreign Ministry, a cultured man, a fan of cinema . . . But he's not at all happy with our selections. At the time, it was up to the president of the jury to announce the names of the winners during the gala. I received criticism and hoots, people had brought tin whistles. Giulietta is waiting for me backstage, she has completely fallen apart, and she cries on my shoulder. I was never again asked to preside over the jury, and I'm relieved. I'm quite pleased that Fellini, who has become my dear friend, is universally recognized today as the greatest director of our times.

At the Academy Awards, Piero Gherardi wins the prize for best costume design in black-and-white, and accepts the prize from Eddie Albert and Dina Merrill on April 9, 1962, at the Santa Monica Civic Auditorium. Federico, who stayed behind in Manziana to work on the screenplay for 8½, is pleased for Piero and doesn't feel the need for more recognition. *La dolce vita* has already collected half of the major and minor awards on the planet. Strangely, the Silver Ribbons are scarce; it only wins three: for best screenplay, best leading actor (Mastroianni), and best art direction (Gherardi).

25

The Big Bishop of Federiz

In the weeks following the release of *La dolce vita*, Fellini enjoys a sort of provisional existence; he travels Italy, sometimes without any real reason. He takes meetings, attends debates, gives interviews, sits for photo shoots, lunches, and receives phone calls. This is his way of relaxing; he rides the tide, alternating easily between active and passive. He floats. The convulsive mobility between Rome and Milan, passing quiet nights in the noisy solitude of sleeping cars on the train, provides him with some respite, and he slips happily into it. He eats in restaurants, sleeps at friends' houses, and only occasionally listens to conversations. He arrives in northern cities at night in the fog, and sometimes finds it gratifying to stop and watch a crowd line up at a movie theater to see his film. In Rimini, he's spied walking on the wind-beaten winter beach with Marcello Mastroianni.

The movie's success has taken the director by surprise, but he's even more bewildered by the intense polemics surrounding it. People stop him on the street and ask for clarifications—"Is it true that at the end Paola wants to jump into the pit and join the orgy?" asks one girl. It's clear that everyone is putting his or her own interpretation on the film, finding whatever they want to find in it. Fellini is taken aback by some of the hostile, even menacing looks sent his way as he walks down the street, stops at a newsstand, or sits in a bar. He discusses it with Pier Paolo Pasolini, who is a professional political lightning rod himself, and eventually comes to the conclusion that the reasons people support him are often as embarrassing as the reasons they don't. When people encourage him, "Bravo! Keep it up!," Fellini wonders, "Keep *what* up?"

La dolce vita was seismic. It ruined old friendships and built new ones. Most of the cinema world takes issue with the movie, and envy, a sentiment that pathologically dominates the environment, keeps the majority of his colleagues from forming any lucid opinions. As for the intellectuals, once the movie realizes success, they claim that it's been cleaned up, dubbed, and edited to be less beautiful—and Steiner is a totally untenable character to boot. Pasolini and Alberto Moravia, each with his own personal take on the film, manage to worry the director more than reassure him. He doesn't like the label "neo-decadent" and is totally perplexed by the comparison drawn between him and the poet Giovanni Pascoli. He thought he was doing something completely different and much more basic—a made-up magazine, a magazine film.

Sophia Loren emerges from a private screening of the movie and crawls into Federico's car murmuring, "Poor you, what do you have inside of you?"—a line from *Viaggio con Anita*. They start exploring that project again, but *La dolce vita* has accelerated the director's life to such an extent that he has no desire to return to previous ideas. Something has definitively shifted in him, and a lot of things have to change in his life and work. The tabloids have their own read on the signals and report that Federico is leaving Giulietta, but, as usual, there's no truth to the rumor. Federico scrupulously denies the gossip not only about a possible breakup but also that the couple has suffered an artistic split. He's working on many ideas that involve Giulietta and he's decided that they'll make another film together soon. There may be no change in his family life, but he does have a strong urge to change his relationship with his producers. It's Angelo Rizzoli, the most paternal of all the financers, who offers a practical solution: they'll start a company together, half owned by Rizzoli and half by Fellini and Clemente Fracassi. The plan is to start thinking about the next movie as well as looking to produce other projects, supporting young directors, respected friends, and artists who are shut out by traditional producers.

In the only interview they gave together (in *Settimo Giorno*), Federico and Clemente are honest about the subject. The director brings up the risks of being a filmmaker.

FELLINI: Exhaustion, crisis, burnout . . . Really, thinking about this apocalyptic future, I decided to come up with something less

murderous that would also provide me with the chance for economic survival—doing a job I like and avoiding the responsibilities
that would drag me down.

FRACASSI: Federico is speaking in terms of self-interest because
he's being modest about the Don Quixote aspect of the project.

FELLINI: I have to say that if I hadn't met Clemente Fracassi I
would never have dared to undertake this venture. I don't even
know how to manage the money in my pocket—can you imagine
me managing a company? And we should also add that we want to
help out young directors. They find themselves in such subordi-
nate positions when they face a producer today.

FRACASSI: You know, the typical authoritarian producer. He asks
a director to make something. Then he watches over him, spies on
him, and scolds him if he exercises any freedom.

FELLINI: And *then* he changes the end of the movie. That's it. We
will not change any endings! Usually what happens is that a producer calls a director and says, You have to make this movie. We're
going to call the same guy and ask, What movie do you want to
make?

FRACASSI: That's actually why we can't find any directors. The
minute you offer them complete freedom, they all run away, terrified by the crises and self-doubt.

A name for the new company is easy to come up with; it will be
called Federiz, a synthesis of Federico and Rizzoli. They open a nice office in a building at via della Croce 70, with two large bearded statues
guarding the front door. By September, Fellini is happily decorating his
new nest "with the pleasure and pride of a young man," as Pasolini wrote.
He puts in three long monastery tables and white curtains with green
stripes.

Italian cinema is in full recovery. Michelangelo Antonioni brought
L'avventura to Cannes. Luchino Visconti is filming *Rocco and His Brothers* in Milan. There's a boom in independent projects, as Fellini's success
has brought legitimacy and charisma to the role of the director. This is
the most fervid period in auteur cinema, and theories abound about the
nouvelle vague: the director is the sole author, budgets are low, and the

camera work is *caméra-stylo.** The rejection of *La dolce vita* by so many producers has hurt the reputation of the entire industry, prompting producers to return to their roles as organizers, fiscal and business managers.

Some debates at via della Croce circle around these very topics and, for a brief time, the company is like Lux Film just after the war. Federiz is where aspiring directors, screenplay in hand, gather alongside journalists and friends.

Federiz announces the debuts of director Rodolfo Sonego of Friuli (who wrote Alberto Sordi's screenplays) and documentary filmmaker Giulio Questi of Bergamo (who played one of the aristocrats at Bassano di Sutri), but in both cases the ideas are too disorganized to be realized. Pasolini, however, has no doubts. He wants to direct his first film, to be titled *Accattone* (*The Scrounger*). He's already thought the screenplay through and set the film in the periphery of Rome. He also wants to cast his friends in it—sticking extremely close to reality, as a rebuttal to the elegant packaging that director Mauro Bolognini (*La notte brava* and *La giornata balorda*) imposed on Pasolini's screenplays. With these attributes, *Accattone* seems perfect for Fellini's company, and in just a few weeks, in late 1960 and early 1961, they take on two more impoverished but beautiful projects. The first, documentary filmmaker Vittorio De Seta's self-funded film *Banditi a Orgosolo*, set in Sardinia, which had been aborted midway when the money he'd earned by selling two apartments ran out. In Milan, Ermanno Olmi has finished the second: a screenplay, *Due fermate a piedi* (Two Stops on Foot), later retitled *Il posto* (*The Sound of Trumpets*), for which he needs funding and help finding a distributor. *Accattone*, *Banditi a Orgosolo*, and *Il posto*: this is the manifesto of new cinema to be presented in Venice in August 1961, kicking off a brilliant movement that the Americans will call the "new Italian Renaissance." At last there's a new cinema to follow neorealism and, for a few weeks, the fate of these three movies rests with Federiz—which is to say it rests with Fellini and Fracassi, because Rizzoli, well aware of his limitations, stays out of artistic decisions.

Caméra-stylo is a term coined by the theorist Alexandre Astruc in 1948 proposing essayistic film, an approach in which the camera becomes a pen, and the images build a story or argument as much as the dialogue, an important idea in the evolution of the French New Wave.

Federiz was created expressly for such projects, yet unexpectedly failed them all. The wedge is Fracassi's temperament. Clemente is so bent on identifying the weak points in each project that he manages to discourage everyone. Pasolini is a poet, a novelist, an essayist; he can be very helpful as a screenwriter, but what makes him a good director? *Banditi a Orgosolo* is set in Sardinia—everyone knows that the island is a jinx in cinema. And *Il posto* is a movie about office workers! Is this really the moment, in the middle of Italy's industrial recovery, to poke fun at the world that Courteline and Gogol already wrote about so aptly?

Fellini, barely listening to his associate's thoughts, doesn't dare confess that after the first blush of excitement he has no interest in these, or any other, projects. He's too focused on his own work to even read anyone else's screenplays. And beyond that, sitting around in the office bores him, and going there starts to feel more like a duty than a pleasure. Not to mention the fact that having to make decisions makes him want to run away. In rare moments he opens up to some intimate friends, admitting that he got involved in this company only as a way of filling the empty spaces between one movie and the next, and because he wanted a place to meet people. But now he's realized that there are no empty spaces, just like there are no hobbies or holidays. He realizes that he voluntarily condemned himself to always having an idea going—that, coupled with the monomaniacal need to achieve the next thing. So, just after completing one movie, he's already immersed in a new one, which, typically, springs from the previous one, from an encounter he had or an emotion he felt on the margins of the set. He has neither the time nor the desire to think about other people's movies. Federico never wanted to watch them anyway, why should he care about helping make them? He doesn't have any objections to Fracassi making all of the decisions, but the problem with Fracassi is that if he's unsure about something he tends not to do it—and when he's unsure, he moves slowly. Perhaps he's unconsciously projecting onto others his own experience. Fracassi left directing after his film *Andre Chénier* flopped. He was known to say, "In this business, either you're Fellini or you're nothing."

As for Pasolini's project, Federico is confused and paralyzed when confronted with his "little brother's" easy self-confidence about stepping behind the camera. Looking at the sudden birth of Pasolini's directorial vocation, Fellini feels with some regret that a lovely period is coming to an end and that their relationship, based on total dedication and affectionate intimacy, is already over. Maybe he also senses that Pasolini's movie is an invasion of his territory. But who even knows if Pasolini is technically competent to make a movie, manage a crew, adhere to a schedule? The only way to find out, suggests Fracassi, is by testing him. Federico suspects that this is just a ploy to postpone the decision, but Clemente uses it as a pretext to cancel the project. In the beginning of October, Clemente gives Pasolini a small crew for three days. When Pasolini had been working on the project for another producer, he'd considered Franco Interlenghi (Moraldo in *I vitelloni*) for the lead, but in the context of this test, he resorts to calling on his friends from Torpignattara. While testing Franco Citti on the set, he decides he's perfect and casts him. Pier Paolo shoots two scenes: one in the pine grove on via Fanfulla da Lodi and the second one outside Castel Sant'Angelo where swimmers would sunbathe. Once they were edited, the sequences were screened in semi-secrecy at the Istituto Luce and the initial response was that they were disappointing, rough, and, for some, inscrutable. Fracassi is convinced that the moment for action has come; back at the office, he says, "It's time to get the dead cat out from under the table," a directive to Fellini that he must assume the role of his least favorite character, the producer.

Pasolini is very upset. In his October 16 column in *Il Giorno*, published right after the debacle, he makes fun of Fellini, the big bishop with his entourage. Pasolini concludes the column with the prophecy: "It's entirely likely that Federiz won't end up producing anything but Fellini films." A few days later, during one of their car adventures to Tor Vajanica, Federico tells Pier Paolo his idea for 8½, a sign that he's already thinking of something other than producing movies, including *Accattone*. In that last trip together, the two friends act as if nothing has changed, but Federiz's rejection of Pasolini's movie has driven a permanent stake into the heart of the friendship. For Fellini, after an idyllic five years, Pasolini has become a brother but not a colleague. For Pasolini, Fellini is a brother but not a friend.

It's a shame that the ideals of Federiz were so quickly lost, yet something else happened in those offices that perhaps wouldn't have otherwise come to pass. A director, Vittorio De Seta—a messenger of destiny—came in and mentioned the name of his psychoanalyst, Ernst Bernhard, to Fellini.

26

The Dream Man

La dolce vita signals a shift from the old Fellini to the new, from the young man engaged in the ceremony of farewell (and the episode with Marcello's father is a poignant extension of that) to the adult Fellini, newly emancipated from the conditioning of childhood and able to face reality. The early 1960s is the dawn of a new phase and, along the path of this existential transformation, Fellini meets Dr. Ernst Bernhard, born in Berlin in 1896. His Hebrew name is Haijim Menahem (which means life and solace). His family was originally from Galicia, but they followed their rabbi to the German capital. After having studied analysis with Otto Fenichel and Sandor Rado, Bernhard attended Carl Gustav Jung's school in Zurich, and was then forced to escape the Rhineland. After being kicked out of England, he came to Rome in 1936, where he would live for the next thirty years. His name plaque still hangs outside the door at via Gregoriana 12, apartment 15, due to a strange coincidence. Dante Ferretti and Francesca Schiavo, both associates of Fellini's, ended up living there, and, though the place is now completely renovated, they decided respectfully not to remove the plaque.

In 1940 Bernhard married the psychoanalyst Dora Friedlaender (born in Vienna in 1896, she died in Rome in 1998 at the age of 102). When the couple lived on via Gregoriana, the house was a labyrinth with big white curtains covering windows overlooking the city. The scholar occupied two rooms. In one, the most secluded part of the apartment, behind a divided screen and over the bed, hung a reproduction of the Holy Shroud. In the other room, his office, Bernhard would sit behind a desk he'd built. Everything seemed perfectly calibrated to give a visitor the sense that he was being initiated into a mystery. The doctor would ask his patients to sit on a little couch next to him, rather than have them recline as Freud did. There weren't set times for therapy and sometimes patients would have to wait if the session before theirs ran long. He often offered his patients tea and cake, believing that eating together was a good way to get to know a person.

Bernhard also believed in a kind of psychological ecumenism ("Psychologists of the world unite!" was his motto). He liked to meet often with Freudian psychoanalysts such as Edoardo Weiss of Trieste, among others. As a Jew, Bernhard had faced difficulties during the war. He was imprisoned in a concentration camp in Calabria in 1940, and then had to hide in the apartment next to his in Rome. Those were years for reflection, and it was during that period that the intellectual refined his ideas, techniques, and rituals. Everything has an archetypal source according to Bernhard— as Goethe says in *Faust*, "everything is a symbol"—and every symbol is either "pregnant" or "fully developed," the content of which is nevertheless myth. To begin one's *Mitobiografia* (Mythobiography, which is the title of a posthumous collection of Bernhard's essays, published in 1969), one must coax the "mythologem" at the heart of one's destiny into the light. It is history that makes people's myths come true, just as reality gives concrete context to dreams. For Bernhard, dreams are as important as, perhaps more important than, waking thoughts. Dreams and the interpretations of dreams are the basis of every thought that a man can and must have about himself. The doctor is also curious about the occult and consults the *I Ching*; further, he explores the world of magic and esoterica.

In Italy, he discovers a profound consonance between his Jewish roots and the Latin world, dominated by the Great Mediterranean Mother. Bernhard is not a pure psychoanalyst, for he avoids the strict parameters of analysis, opting for a looser treatment he calls "psychological interviews." The director Vittorio De Seta is a frequent visitor to the German's office, and he tells Federico about him, convincing him that he must meet this doctor.

In his book *Jung e la cultura italiana* (Jung and Italian Culture), Aldo Carotenuto tells the story of Fellini's first encounter with Bernhard by adopting the fairy-tale mode that the director himself would use: Bernhard's telephone number languished unused in Fellini's pocket for a long time, until one day he dialed it, thinking that he was calling a woman named Maria. Reflecting on the name, a mythographer might make a connection between the name Maria and the heavenly mother (a more or less Mater Matuta figure). When Bernhard answers the phone, he's not at all surprised to hear from Fellini, who immediately intrigues him. "Creativity and play are very similar to each other," wrote Jung. Bernhard, a Jung disciple, immediately understands Fellini's unusual psychology. And, for his part, Fellini immediately felt that his interlocutor could have a stimulating and positive effect on him. Soon Fellini's meetings with Bernhard become a habit and the director is a regular at the office on via Gregoriana.

According to Giuliana Marinangeli, who studied Bernhard's life and work and is a devoted custodian of part of his archive, Fellini was in regular analysis, three times a week, for four years. The director is certainly paying for the sessions, because "Dora and Ernst were attentive about money." Sometimes they would meet in a pizzeria near the office, a more amiable environment. The psychologist recommends some of Jung's books, which Federico reads with his typical chaotic voraciousness, the most influential being *Memories, Dreams, Reflections*. The director will also visit "Jung's tower" in Bollingen, "the site for gestation, a mother's womb," constructed by Jung in San Meinrad, near the upper lake of Zurich. When Fellini arrives, Jung's grandson brings him into the sanctum sanctorum, a room for relaxing and playing, full of paintings and souvenirs. Being there helps Federico understand Jung's personality, which he finds similar in many ways to his own.

Ever since he was a child, Fellini has liked to let his mind wander, to fantasize and float in a half-sleeping, half-waking state. He takes the habit up again in 1953 and 1954 while developing *La strada*, and, under Bernhard's tutelage, Fellini learns to understand the psychology of what's drifting through his mind beyond the conscious level. He learns to stop thinking of the unknown as a threat, understanding that it's essential to develop some comprehension of a life that exists inside the mind and beyond everyday awareness—because this kind of knowledge broadens knowledge and gives courage. Fellini writes to Bernhard about several séances he has participated in, but the analyst is rather skeptical (we'll come back to this when we discuss *Giulietta degli spiriti*). Through their discussions, the director learns to control his extrasensory perceptions, to use the *I Ching*, and, most important, to memorize, write down, and illustrate his dreams using the techniques that Bernhard recommends to all his patients. Fellini's work in the early 1960s develops under this influence, and has its own personal resonance. According to Carotenuto, Bernhard is a "father in the real sense of the word" to Fellini, with all that this entails.

Federico is guarded about his relationship with the German doctor and doesn't even discuss it with his closest friends. When it's time to go to via Gregoriana, he just disappears. He's protective about those fragile meetings and doesn't want them sullied by curious gossip or misunderstandings. This is an example not only of his tendency to socialize intensely with "one person at a time" but also of his determination to protect this very special bond from pollution. Unfortunately, Fellini's clinical record has disappeared from the analyst's archive. Some thoughts about his analysis, however, can be found in Dora's diaries, which are written in German and, until some time ago, in the possession of an old friend in Vienna. According to Marinangeli, who talked to Dora about Fellini, the problem was his humanity. Bernhard saw in Fellini the embodiment of the *puer aeternus* (literally, the eternal child)—not a child, however, but a rebellious young man—and he helped Fellini see that. Federico, for example, was excited and thrilled when the first student demonstrations broke out in 1968, before the movement became politicized in a way that he found intolerable. Through their work together, Bernhard helped Federico see his own puerile nature as acted out in everyday life, like the bizarre fury with which he'd tear up mail, the typical destructive behavior of a child.

For Fellini, the trauma of Bernhard's death was preceded by a prophetic dream. In the dream, Federico arrives at via Gregoriana, and a pale man he doesn't know answers the door, all dressed in black. Ernst is lying dead in his study, but when the director approaches to look at the body, the supposedly dead man raises his arms and clutches Fellini's wrists. Though the dream seems like a horror movie, the end is reassuring, as if Bernhard is saying, "Don't think I'm dead. I will never die." When Bernhard does die on June 29, 1965, Fellini stops filming on *Giulietta degli spiriti* for several hours in order to go pay his respects. The man at the door on via Gregoriana is the same man he'd seen in his dream—the journalist Antonio Gambino, a complete stranger to Fellini. On his deathbed Bernhard was as lucid as he was throughout his life, offering a final lesson to his disciples: "Suffer your death in full consciousness." During the summer of 1965, Fellini writes a tormented screenplay with Dino Buzzati, *Il viaggio di G. Mastorna*, which turns out to be a kind of illustration of the master's last parable. But the most immediate and tangible fruit of Fellini's relationship with Bernhard is that he starts keeping his legendary Dream Book.

The Dream Book is actually not one but several books that the director keeps in a drawer in his desk at his office. It's supposed to be a secret, but Fellini doesn't keep the secret at all. Many of his friends are offered the privilege of looking at these huge albums or encouraged to take their time reading entire sections. A few of the writing- and drawing-filled pages are even photographed for publication in magazines. The format is similar to a comic strip, with the text handwritten in Fellini's very recognizable, quick and clear calligraphy, which wraps around big black-and-white or color drawings, sometimes even cartoons. There is, for example, a comic strip featuring one dream where Federico goes to Rimini with Totò to see one of the comedian's shows. In these drawings, the dreamer often represents himself as a character, sometimes a caricature. Imprecise and vague about real events, Fellini is extremely rigorous when representing his dreams, and he almost always keeps a record of the date as well. Consequently, when he wants to recall important daytime events, he uses his "night diary"—making a connection between the dreams about which he has perfect recall and whatever was going on during the same period.

He started his dream collection on November 30, 1960, but wrote less as time passed. When I had the chance to look at the final volume, with the author watching over my shoulder, the last dream he'd written and drawn about was from August 1984. Even though it's not really a secret, it's still rather embarrassing to be allowed to read the Dream Book. You feel as if you're spying on someone else's private life, and perhaps you fear finding yourself depicted or mocked in some corner of Federico's vast dreamscape. Fellini pasted two death notices for Bernhard into the book that were published in *Il Messaggero* on July 1, 1965. One is in German, from his wife and family: "*Mein lieber Mann, unser Vater, für immer von uns gegangen"* (Dear husband, our father, who has forever left us). The other is from his disciples and friends, announcing a wake at the Italian Analytical Psychology Association.

We will talk at greater length about the group of dreams that precede and accompany Fellini's illness in the chapter on *Il viaggio di G. Mastorna.** But let's review some of his other fantasies here:

May 1968. He was deeply troubled about whether or not to make *Satyricon*. He has two dreams that mean the same thing: he has to abandon an airplane by jumping out of it into the void with a parachute; then he explores the deep sea in a diving suit.

December 1974. Fellini is flying in a hot-air balloon basket without a balloon in the company of Pope Paul VI, who is wearing his red velvet hat. They fly over a crowded Rimini beach. A marvelous giant woman in a bathing suit appears and the Pope describes her as "the Great Maker who dissolves the clouds."

March 13, 1975. Federico has no legs and he's sitting on a little cart. He wonders, "Where can I go like this?" The actress Silvana Mangano (De Laurentiis's wife) tells him that Dino (seen in a round frame to the side) is completely paralyzed and that they're taking him to a clinic and he may die. But Federico should be careful too. On the margin, a white owl flies over a woman standing in front of a sink, her huge naked ass brilliant in the candlelight.

April 1, 1975. He dreams of a naked woman with cool skin who is sitting on a cloud in a bright sky; she blows on a cloud and says, "It's time to make fertility down there." Propelled by her breath the cloud travels through the sky, and, holding her breasts in her hands, she makes a bright, soft rain fall. The dreamer comments, "Well."

February 1982. He dreams about a black boat that turns into a submarine.

After 1982 there are many explosions, flashes, and boats, anticipating the images in *E la nave va* (*And the Ship Sails On,* 1983).

There are other interesting encounters here and there, scattered through the days or undated. He dreams of Picasso, who is in a bad way but lively and talks with animation about his work. There's a dream where Fellini re-

*See Chapter 30.

sponds to someone criticizing him for accepting an award: "Isn't it better to be admitted to the French Academy than to be a clown?" There's also a slot machine named "father machine." Federico tries to work it even though he knows that if he pushes the wrong button the whole building will explode. The dreams are, of course, also a real "city of women," and most of the women here are his type, voluptuous and exuberant. But there are also dreams in which he's forced to have mortifying sex with very ugly women.

Meeting Bernhard reinforced Fellini's contention that dreams, which produce fantasies, must be considered more important than waking activities. In a 1964 interview Fellini claimed,

> Dreams are fairy tales that we tell ourselves. They are the small and big myths that help people to understand. Of course, you shouldn't ask your dreams for instant or constant help in changing your daily behavior. And you shouldn't completely abandon yourself to the pleasure of this night spectacle. The insensitive dreamer risks spending his days doing nothing, surrounded by brittle, evanescent things. Sometimes people are so immersed in that reality they dream only at night—but by then it's too late for images.

Note the pragmatism of this sentiment, a familiar notion in the world of cinema: movies are dreams with open eyes that are constructed extremely carefully. Reality and delusion, existence and representation, life and fantasy all coexist. For movie people, dreaming is a useful activity.

Fellini started keeping his Dream Book between *La dolce vita* and *8½*. It will mark an important turning point in his work, which after this will be primarily oneiric. In a way, the director bids farewell to reality, taking the gesture of cutting the umbilical chord to the extreme—distancing himself from his birthplace, his family, his adolescence, and every other aspect of his history and social background (particularly the education, or rather ignorance, that he'd acquired at school under fascism). In the early 1960s, Fellini has nothing more to say on these subjects. He's paid the debts of his free education in the university of neorealism. His vision has transcended those theories and teachings and entered a broader, evanescent, and intangible dimension. From this point on we can say that for Fellini, life is but a dream.

27

The Moralist

Boccaccio '70, Le tentazioni del dottor Antonio

He refers to it as a "silly little thing," like a story in *Corriere dei Piccoli*. And it all starts in January 1961 with a phone call from producer Tonino Cervi, asking Fellini to direct an episode for a collective movie protesting censorship, *Boccaccio '70*. At the time, Fellini is working on a project that still has no title and no lead actor. He keeps saying that what he needs is a "forty-year-old Chaplin—an actor that doesn't exist," as he looks list-lessly through more head shots. There are sketches for Piero Gherardi on the blackboard in the office where Fellini's assistants work, and where a small crowd of aspiring lead actors waits to be seen. But Fellini sits in the back, sketching with watercolors and tormenting Clemente Fracassi over this problem of the protagonist.

Fortunately, *Boccaccio '70* rescues the director from having to make any decisions. Fracassi had just booked him on a flight to New York City to meet with Sir Laurence Olivier, where, as if they were diplomats, they were supposed to avoid talking about the film, giving Federico the chance to look the great actor over, observe him, and figure out if he might suit his character. Federico is very happy to cancel the trip, neatly avoiding the man who he worries will be too much of a "theatrical monument." He's happy to throw himself, instead, into *Le tentazioni del dottor Antonio*, the title a twist on Flaubert's *The Temptation of Saint Antony*. Fellini's section, the second act of *Boccaccio '70*, will run an hour, and Federico devotes his full attention to it, ignoring Angelo Rizzoli's pained lament: "Federiz is almost one year old and we still haven't announced any titles and you go to work for someone else." But when the mogul joins the team of producers, he's a full partner from the word "Action!" In the meantime, Carlo Ponti comes on as producer of the whole project, in association with two French companies.

Fellini is reserved as he heads into development, saying only that he's enthusiastic about the collective project, spearheaded by Cesare Zavattini, like *L'amore in città*. He's pleased that Luchino Visconti, Vittorio De Sica, and Mario Monicelli are also involved. He'd have liked Roberto Rossellini and Michelangelo Antonioni to be part of it too—for him, the project's aim is to declare that freedom of expression belongs to cinema, in much the same way that it belongs to great literature. Even the title, *Boccaccio '70*, comes out of this aim; it's a polemical statement against the "popular morality" that is trying to quash free expression through the right-wing media, censorship, and the courts. Fellini, who in the past has solicited the indirect help of church officials, believes the time has come to form a unified front. The same belief will have him lead, many years later, an impassioned campaign against the corruption of movies on television through advertising. Fellini, frequently considered an apolitical individualist, is actually able to take courageous and risky stands when fundamental values, like full respect for creative work, are at stake.

Initially Fellini's demands to Cervi are explicitly moderate. He wants only one actor, Romolo Valli, who had dubbed Steiner for *La dolce vita*, and he wants to put him under a huge poster in the Eur section of Rome. On the poster he wants a picture of Anita Ekberg in a low-cut dress holding a big glass in her hands, with the title "Drink more milk." Thrilled with the opportunity, Valli starts studying Giulio Andreotti's ambiguous physiognomy and manners in order to develop the character. It is, however, difficult to secure a contract with the actor, because he's currently working in the play *The Aspern Papers*, adapted from the Henry James novel. The problem is resolved when the show's director, Giorgio De Lullo, generously offers to switch him out of the run at the Teatro Manzoni in Milan, but the real and impossible challenge to negotiations is the money. Valli wants too much. When Fellini calls to ask him to do it for less, the actor says, "Let me fight my battle." The director immediately realizes that it's hopeless and, as soon as he hangs up, calls the producers: "Let's get Peppino De Filippo instead." Romolo will, of course, accuse Federico of betraying him; Federico will reply the same. Both of them are bitter over having missed the chance to work together on another project, an opportunity that will never present itself again.

As he proceeds, Federico realizes that he needs more than just Anita's picture—he needs the real actress. His idea is to have her descend from the poster, as giant as her image, in order to create a juxtaposition with the little man. Cervi, who thinks it's a great idea, doesn't know how they'll pull it off—but Fellini has already thought of that. They have to work with a special-effects technician, rebuilding the whole neighborhood in miniature. This was how a new adventure was launched—somewhat like *La dolce vita*, but on a smaller scale. For several weeks during the summer of 1961, Federico plays with setting Anita in the perfect reproduction built for him by Piero Zuffi. The little *Corriere dei Piccoli* story has turned into a Swiftian satire, an allegoric moral tale to challenge the Philistines. Peppino's character, a representation of the grotesque insecurity of professional moralists, is obsessed by Anita's explosive image. Dr. Antonio Mazzuolo is a self-important man wearing glasses and dressed in black. At night he thrusts himself between kissing couples ("Shame on you! That's immoral; you should get married first!"). He finds lovers who are meeting in cars and calls the cops on them. During a variety show, he runs onstage in the middle of a dance performance and stops the act. Eating breakfast in a restaurant (in a scene shot in silent-film style), Mazzuolo rushes to cover a woman's cleavage with a napkin.

It's worth a short digression here to explain that this scene references a real and notorious event on July 21, 1950, at the trattoria Chiarina on via della Vite in Rome, when a young Oscar Luigi Scalfaro of the Christian Democrats approached an attractive lady showing a bit of cleavage and asked her to cover herself. Her name was Edith Mingoni Toussan, and her case ended up before parliament. Some people say that in mocking the event Fellini is taking revenge against the critical articles that Scalfaro allegedly wrote against *La dolce vita* in *L'Osservatore Romano*. Significantly, Scalfaro didn't interfere in the making of *Le tentazioni del dottor Antonio*—he wanted people to forget the embarrassing incident—and neither did the censorship board, though they did impose cuts on the Visconti and De Sica episodes. It's probably due to the long, tacit antipathy between the politician and the director that, when he became president, Scalfaro ignored the repeated and ardent nominations that Fellini be made an honorary Senator for life.

Regardless, Anitona is tense on the set. She's no longer the happy-go-lucky Viking of *La dolce vita*. She's an international movie star now, and well aware of it. Her fame has changed her personality; she is more difficult to deal with. Eventually she will claim, "Fellini ruined me," but not even the most skilled magician would have been able to convince her to dance barefoot at the Terme di Caracalla all night long, or to walk into the Trevi Fountain fully dressed. In fact, of all the citizens of the mock Eur, Anita is having the least fun. They say she's upset because she didn't know that her part was supposed to be only a picture on a billboard—she wanted a real role. Anitona spends most of her time in her trailer watching TV, but on the set after Fellini shows her how to walk around the miniature houses and streetlights, she returns—the incarnation of eternal femininity. According to the inner circle, Fellini's section will be a small, biting classic. Critics instead start saying that it's an exaggeration and that Fellini's work style carries a price tag that is much too high, unless, of course, this picture makes as much as *La dolce vita*.

The audience's response to *Boccaccio '70* when it is released on February 22, 1962, at the Cinema Capitol in Milan isn't exactly what you might call a sweep. They like the movie—with reservations—and critics prefer Visconti's section, *Il lavoro* (*Work*), which features an acclaimed performance by Romy Schneider. Opinions are split over *Le tentazioni del dottor Antonio*, but almost everyone agrees that the first part is better than the second. They say that Fellini was too complacent with his project, that it lacks consistency and is too baroque, too complicated, too self-satisfied, and too long. Some comment that the section is like a big satirical comic strip and that, in a way, Fellini seems to be returning to his *Marc'Aurelio* days. The film's episodic quality may not ultimately be the most congenial format for Fellini's creativity, but there are other factors working to compromise the success of his little fairy tale, which is, after all, rather likable. Perhaps it is due to the special effects that aren't up to Hollywood's standards (the same problem that beset another fairy tale, De Sica's *Miracolo a Milano*). Peppino also seems slightly put off by the complex character he plays; he's very effective at conveying Antonio's meanness, but not his sexual frustration, a quality that the director sought in vain to create, this spark of conflicted eroticism between the small man and the giant woman.

Boccaccio '70's premiere at Cannes on May 7, the opening night of the fifteenth festival, provokes a small scandal. A few minutes after the start of the screening, an agent from the local court arrives to seize the film. Monicelli had filed a lawsuit after his section, too long, had been left out of the final version. Even though *Boccaccio '70* is not in competition, one of the jurors, Mario Soldati, resigns in an act of solidarity. Ponti tries to justify the omission of Monicelli's episode, claiming that it was a matter of artistic difference, that the section was too neorealist and out of sync with the collection's overall style. In the end, the court of Grasse allows the screening to go forward, saving the gala, and Robert Favre Le Bret, the director of the festival, plays mediator and convinces the producer to reinstate Monicelli's section. Despite the dramatic turn of events, the audience's response is muted and critics are divided. In the United States, *Boccaccio '70* is put on the blacklist of the Catholic Legion of Decency, yet it still doesn't attract large crowds.

28

The Conscience of Guido

8½

Nasty rumors about what has happened in the offices of Federiz have created a general antipathy in the movie world toward Fellini. Compounded with the envy that people already felt over the massive success of *La dolce vita*, the gossip has turned into a ruinous flood.

It's said that Fellini is exhausted and out of ideas, and that he's taken on *Boccaccio '70* in order to avoid facing his creative block. This is the backdrop—ephemeral, like everything having to do with temperament—that sets up the premise of *8½*. In the meantime, Fellini and Clemente Fracassi, the producers at Federiz, have lost faith in each other. All three movies that they had rejected were hits in Venice. *Accattone* was produced by Alfredo Bini in the end, while *Banditi a Orgosolo* and *Il posto* went on to be the jewels of Titanus's vault, proof positive that Goffredo Lombardo was actually prepared to invest in new talent. The partners at via della Croce have only each other to blame: Fracassi accuses Fellini of wanting to produce only his own movies, while Fellini says that Fracassi doesn't want to produce anything. They're probably both right. Even Giulietta is upset, because Fellini didn't take on a project Salvato Cappelli had written for her, a movie about Madre Cabrini, the patron saint of immigrants. Meanwhile, Federico is burning with regret over having ruined his friendship with Pier Paolo Pasolini, an incident that first publicly revealed the crisis state at Federiz.

In a burst of sudden excitement, Fellini becomes interested in a new Ermanno Olmi project. After having left the cinema branch of Edison-Volta, Olmi had founded a company with friends called 22 Dicembre in

Milan—the name was the date that a notary ratified the company in 1961. The young turks in Milan are planning a similar enterprise to that of Federiz: produce young filmmakers on low-budget projects, giving them total artistic freedom. Fellini is struck by the affinity of their ambitions, and wants to team up, perhaps merging Federiz with 22 Dicembre and taking on Angelo Rizzoli to manage the financing. But it comes to naught. Fellini puts forth the idea and then instantly loses interest. In point of fact, he's become immersed in what will turn out to be the most sensational confessional in the history of cinema.

In August 1961, the director oversees dubbing and editing on *Le tentazioni del dottor Antonio*. Then he starts scouting locations for his next movie, traveling extensively throughout Italy. He keeps saying that he'll start filming in October but no one believes him—he doesn't even believe it himself. Fellini has changed, just like Anitona. He's more mature now and more meditative. He doesn't like to talk about his work and even avoids conversations. When journalists manage to pull some comments from him, the comments serve only to reveal Fellini's confusion.

Does the big confession start with a lie? "Not only is 8½ a bad title, but it's also incorrect," Pietro Bianchi, an accomplished critic and friend of Fellini, used to say. If we include *Luci del varietà* in Fellini's filmography, he's made only eight movies when he gets to 8½. But if the half is meant to include the episode in *Boccaccio '70*, then how do we count the other half movie, *Un'agenzia matrimoniale* in *L'amore in città*? Perhaps *Luci del varietà* is the half movie, and the two short films put together make one; if that's the case, then the math works out. But math is only one of many interpretations, and even the director isn't sure what he means by it. The title is selected at the last minute under pressure from Cineriz. For a while, Federico had been attracted to Ennio Flaiano's idea that the movie should be called "The Beautiful Confusion," but then he had the simpler idea (which proved entirely wrong) to call it "Comedy." Fellini is so invested in the idea of an amusing film that he'll affix a sign to the camera that reads, "Remember, this is a comedy." Intentions aside, however, he feels like he's on the brink of tragedy, a total collapse something like what he felt at the end of *La strada*—a feeling he'd once described as "falling from the Great Wall of China."

Federico plunges into preparation like he did with *I vitelloni*, just like in the good old days. He drives aimlessly through the city streets, involving collaborators and friends, bringing them along with him one at a time. *La dolce vita* was a gallery of locations, but for this picture, the director wants to focus on the main character's personality. Fellini returns from the spa at Chianciano Terme with an idea for a short scene: an average forty-year-old man, facing a midlife crisis, interrupts his daily rhythm by going to the spa for a cure. While he's immersed in a kind of a limbo of mud and steam, he reflects on his problems and interacts with other people. His wife and his mistress both show up to visit at the same time and he can't seem to escape his work. Who is this man? What's his background? What does he think about life, having already used up half of it, as he prepares for the next half? Can he hope to find happiness? Can he change his destiny? Can he change the world around him? Most important, can he change himself?

At the end of the summer of 1961, having packed off the master cut of his section of *Boccaccio '70*, Fellini is working out his next protagonist, which is to say, his ego—in Jungian terms. He thinks he's looking for an actor, but what he's really looking for is a human mirror, someone who can reflect his own image. He tries to solve the problem by looking for the perfect actor. Having abandoned the idea of casting Laurence Olivier (too theatrical, too English, too aware of his own genius), Fellini obviously chooses Marcello Mastroianni, who has been waiting in the wings for months, keeping a low profile and not pressuring the director. The pair enjoyed a very strong friendship, seeing each other daily, especially during *La dolce vita*. At the time, Marcello was already a celebrity of Italian cinema, particularly well known for the comedies he'd done with Alessandro Blasetti. Mastroianni had also seen a great deal of success onstage with Luchino Visconti's company, performing in plays by Tennessee Williams, Arthur Miller, Anton Chekov, and Carlo Goldoni. And, even though he'd come of age artistically in Visconti's cultural world—the opposite of Fellini's—the actor was utterly open to Federico. Their meeting each other was a sort of revelation for both: they'd had a kind of symbiotic existence for months, sharing and competing for everything—the fastest car, the craziest female fans, the greatest popularity. Even though neither of them was particularly interested in such mundane things, when together they'd compete for the pure fun of it. From the start, the pair had invented their own private lingo, made fun of each other, and laughed about every-thing and everybody. They also got to know each other's families, growing ever more intimate. The actor visited Fellini's parents in Rimini. The di-rector enjoyed Mastroianni's mother's famous meatballs. In short, the two felt peculiarly alike despite their differences.

This is important considering that Mastroianni would become Fellini's cinematographic alter ego: a first-person narrator within whom there ef-fortlessly lies a second person. Marcello is as quiet, lazy, and fatalistic as Federico is exuberant, hardworking, and authoritative—at least in appear-ance. In truth, the opposite is often the case. Mastroianni loves being overwhelmed by his passions. His life is complicated to an enormous de-gree by love affairs (both with celebrities and not) that frequently come to tragicomic end. Fellini, instead, tends to avoid sentimental quagmires and lives his affairs in total secrecy. Marcello feels fortunate that he can play at something he likes, the movies, call it work, and be well compensated for the gratification. Federico may think of cinema in some respects as a game, but he also feels that it's a means of expression critical to his sur-vival. All that said, Mastroianni manages to be an utterly serious actor and Fellini, as a director, knows how to joke around.

Despite the teenage-style rapport, the two friends are also extremely discreet about their feelings. Marcello in particular thinks that meeting Fellini, the extraordinary phenomenon of creativity, is a gift of fate, and he wants to live up to it. He also likes provoking Fellini's jealousy by working with other directors, not calling, and playing hard to get. Mar-cello's sense of pride keeps him from taking advantage of the friendship to find out about Federico's next movie or its cast. He is, however, always prepared to cancel a deal; he's always available, should Fellini want him. He'd like to be in all of the great director's films—especially in the roles that Fellini thinks aren't right for him—so much so that, every time Fellini offers him a role, he becomes so nervous that he doesn't ask about details, or to see the script, or even what the dialogues for the next day will be. Mastroianni claims that it's amusing to arrive on the set knowing nothing; he also points out that it would be useless to study ahead of time anyway: "Once he starts shooting, Federico always changes everything. Then he rewrites lines during the dubbing and then changes everything again." That style of working is risky, but never boring.

Fellini is so pleased with Mastroianni's work that he casts him for five major roles in twenty-five years—and yet continues pretending that he's not satisfied. He says Marcello eats too much, looks like a Goody Two-shoes, that his eyes are too honest or sometimes too red. He'd prefer a thin, sinister, almost wicked Mastroianni. He's always tempted to put tape around the actor's eyes and fake eyelashes, as in the first scenes of *La dolce vita*. During the rehearsals for 8½, he tries to make Marcello look stranger by streaking his hair, darkening just one eyebrow, or painting bags under his eyes. He wants him to look older, grayer, balder. He wants him to wear glasses. Also, knowing that Marcello doesn't like to get undressed on camera because he thinks his legs are too thin, Fellini threatens to shoot the scene at the baths with him completely in the nude. During the tryouts, he invents ludicrous threats: "Remember that the sheet is going to slip and you'll have to show your ass." Marcello launches a mild resistance: "But that would be in bad taste, no?"

All Mastroianni knows at this point is that he's to be the protagonist in a funny movie, something like "Charlot at the spa." He knows that the character will talk about himself with brutal honesty, and that the movie will be a total invention made out of Piero Gherardi's imagination and technique, Nino Rota's music, and the bold photography of an amazing new friend, cinematographer Gianni Di Venanzo—whom Fellini met on the set of *Un'agenzia matrimoniale* and then again for breakfast in Fiumicino.

The secret meeting between Di Venanzo and Fellini was set up by a mutual friend. Secret, because things might turn tragic if Otello Martelli were to ever find out. During the filming of *Le tentazioni del dottor Antonio*, Fellini had grown bored with Martelli's recurrent "You can't do that . . ." and, though he loves and respects him, the way one loves a part of his life, he's ready for a change. Di Venanzo has worked on Francesco Rosi's *Salvatore Giuliano* and on *L'eclisse* (*Eclipse*) by Michelangelo Antonioni, two jobs that earned him top ranking among Italian cinematographers. He is one of the last masters of black-and-white, and maybe the best. He's also congenial and sensitive and has integrity. Audacious in the face of technical challenges, he loves puzzles, extreme backlighting and camera angles, close-ups in silhouette, and partially lit shots—pitch-black if necessary. With this kind of collaborator, Fellini will be able to create a much more conscious "set designed out of light," as he sometimes described it, and push the limits of avant-garde film—such as the use of solarization in the scene at the baths. Filmed on the threshold of color's dominance, 8½ is the perfect way for the tenth Muse (cinema) to bid farewell to black-and-white.

But none of that happens until later. For the moment, Fellini still hasn't figured out his movie. His searching will be long, as it so often is when the answer is so evident. Picasso said, "I don't look for it, I find it." Fellini might reply, "I already found it, but I keep looking." He knows for certain who will play the mistress, the soprano Marcella Pobbe, whom he'd just met and been courting for the part. That doesn't stop him, however, from practically broadcasting throughout Italy his search for a woman "who looks old-fashioned, a plump chatterbox." He issues a verbal identikit describing a Rubenesque woman, or Titian's *Venus Reclining*, or Palma il Vecchio's *Venus at Rest*. The candidates amass and, wanting to see them all, the director organizes a tour of Italy to find his unknown beauty. It's just an excuse to travel through, to alleviate the stress and recharge his batteries. It's also one of his favorite rituals about moviemaking.

There's some concern over a smallpox epidemic in February 1962, and in the Milan offices of 22 Dicembre, Fellini interviews candidates while simultaneously getting an injection of antibiotics. The next day, maybe because of the slight fever he was suffering, Fellini has a prophetic vision while at the train station on the port in Trieste. He finds himself bewitched by a lighted transatlantic steamer, and, though he would like to go aboard, it's simply not possible. In anticipation of the movie he will make twenty years later, *E la nave va*, he mutters to himself, "If you wanted to shoot a movie on that, you'd have to build it in the studio."

Fellini's clan, already deep in the new adventure, finds itself more than ever at the mercy of his mood swings, sudden urges, and reticence. There has never been such a large production built on such shaky pillars. But Fracassi goes forward, making deals, hiring actors and technicians, setting deadlines he won't be able to meet. Everyone thinks Fellini is taking it too far—the movie is still a complete mystery, not only to strangers, people not on the payroll, but to the director himself. Those inside the circle fret, "This time, he really doesn't know what he wants."

Rushing the preproduction seemed like a tactic to force the director to resolve his haziness, but starting to build the set actually brings up some serious concerns. Fellini is tormented at this moment of his life and is apt to behave neurotically. He arranges for an escape under the cover of darkness from the via della Croce offices, asking the moving trucks to come after midnight and convincing them, with absurd explanations, to drive around magic locations (churches, obelisks, historical sites), all in an elaborate ploy to unjinx the new office on via Po, which is actually a familiar, lucky place, where I vitelloni was born. What if the set, already constructed in the studios on via Scalera near the Appia Nuova, will languish unused? As the days pass, the director feels like he's forgotten what movie he wanted to make, the same way you forget your dreams.

Then one fine day, while shut in his office, Federico reaches for a pen and paper and starts writing, "Dear Angelino . . ." In the letter to Rizzoli he confesses that he can't go on and wants to give up. Luckily, someone knocks on the door. It's a worker from the set come to fetch him. In the studio they've organized a toast to celebrate Gasparino's birthday. (Gasparino is the hulking technician who will play himself in I clowns.) The crew welcomes Fellini affectionately. Everyone is drinking to Gasparino, but they're also celebrating the masterpiece in progress, and its success. When he sees all of those men who depend on him to pay their rent, Federico is ashamed, and once the party is over, he returns to his desk and rips up the half-written letter. But the problems, many problems, haven't disappeared.

The most urgent problem is the question of what the protagonist does for a living. Fellini is undecided among several possibilities. He could be a professor working on an encyclopedia entry about Messalina or Saint Francis. Or an architect, a novelist, a screenwriter. Gherardi has been asking for some input to design Mastroianni's wardrobe. Fellini thinks about it night and day, but doesn't have an answer. He feels like he's always known this character; he can describe his behavior in detail, the tics, the verbal mannerisms, even tiny character traits. But he can't see him as a whole. Then a light comes on, a flash. At some point, the solution to the mystery has already become clear to everyone involved in the production—everyone but Fellini. The protagonist of 8½ has long ceased to be a man without a face and Fellini, still racked with doubt, is the only one who hasn't seen it yet, but slowly he begins to see it too. He asks a very worried Fracassi, "Don't you think that he could be a filmmaker?"

After that, he might have mentioned the notion to the other screenwriters, but he never says openly: "I have realized that I am Guido Anselmi." He will start to admit this only once the movie is completed.

But once the decision about Guido's job is made, all of the life energy that has been missing from the movie surges forth. Such energy was something that the director always considered essential: "It doesn't matter to me whether a film is lovely or ugly. What's important is that it's alive." He has opened up his consciousness and revealed his deepest secrets—the problems he was facing on this very film, his recurring concerns about his creative impotence, and ultimately the carnival of cinema itself.

Finally he was able to give Gherardi some ideas for Mastroianni's costume: a black suit, a black wide-brimmed hat. Those were the clothes that he himself tended to wear at the time, deaf to the protests of his maid, who argued, "But, sir, you never wear the brown suit." This is the reason why 8½ is one of the most admired and praised works in the history of cinema, because it teaches bravery and (with difficulty, effort, pain, and joy) how to say "I."

Fellini's eighth and a half movie is a bracing explosion of genius; many still consider it the high point of the director's career. Some critics found echoes of the early twentieth century in it, a period that Fellini doesn't know much about but comes to instinctively as an artist, reawakening it with the verve of an entertainer. And 8½ brought forth references to Proust's memories, and Joyce's open work, a return to the great days of surrealism, complete with citations from Pirandello's *Quando si é qualcuno* (*When Someone Is Somebody*). But the real points of reference for this movie can be found in the psychoanalytic novel and the cinema it inspired. Not incidentally, Bergman's *Wild Strawberries* is one of the few films that Fellini did see and enjoy. Fellini never, however, read the novel that most readily comes to mind, *La coscienza di Zeno* (*The Confessions of Zeno*) by Italo Svevo. This author, too, had a strong identification with his character and assumed all the risks that this entailed. He started by looking at the unconscious and arrived at a general portrait of all of mankind. *La coscienza di Zeno* is Svevo's confessional novel, an experiment that the writer attempted on his own skin—just as in 8½—and here too the tragedy of the end is overcome through the supreme gift of humor.

A few years later, when Fellini saw a theatrical version of *La coscienza di Zeno* with Alberto Lionello as the lead, he was irritated; he felt almost as if someone had plagiarized his work. Svevo is absolved of all guilt, however; he died in 1928.

There are two ways that 8½ can be interpreted, and the first is mostly available to Fellini's intimate circle of friends and acquaintances, those who can recognize the biographical references at more than one level, and who have fun cracking the code of the story. For instance, they can identify Carlo Ponti and Sophia Loren in the characters of Mezzabotta, a producer of a certain age, and his young girlfriend. There's no malice in this caricature; in fact, Mezzabotta is played by a favorite actor of Fellini's, Mario Pisu (who will also play the husband, another alter ego, in *Giulietta degli spiriti*). In the neurotic temperament of the foreign actress, played by Madeleine Lebeau (Tullio Pinelli's future second wife), they can see a portrait of Luise Rainer, who used to involve Fellini in futile discussion on the set of *La dolce vita*. In Conocchia, the executive producer (played by the lawyer Mario Conocchia, who was also the lively bon vivant with a bra on his bald head in the orgy scene of *La dolce vita*), we have a half-insulting and half-sentimental portrait of Gigetto Giacosi. Giacosi was so offended when he saw himself portrayed onscreen that he asked to be paid for it.

You could go on decoding characters and events like this forever, pushing every boundary of privacy. But it's important to remember that in 8½, objectivity and autobiography coincide, and that truth and lies are two sides of the same coin. The picture is so realistic about Fellini's life and problems that it turns totally fantastic. Marcello's wife, as played by Anouk Aimée (Federico calls her Anucchina), is nothing at all like Giulietta, but she is, at least, a cautious idealization of her. The character of the mistress, on the other hand, really does reflect Anna Giovannini, who Federico had already been seeing for years, and the actress playing that part, Sandra Milo, was also a perfect physical match. Milo had met Fellini through Flaiano when they ran into each other at the Villa dei Pini in Fregene.

Born in Tunisia in 1932, Sandra Milo (née Elena Salvatrice Greco) made a career for herself as an actress in Italy and France with the help of her companion Moris Ergas, a Greek producer. He commissioned Roberto Rossellini to make *Vanina Vanini* with the intention of launching her as a prestigious actress, but it ended up being the biggest flop of the 1961 Venice Film Festival. After that catastrophe, Milo decided to stop working in the movies; when Fellini invited her to call him, she simply never did. Intrigued by her unexpected evasiveness, Fellini, having conspired with Ergas, bursts into their house with Gherardi and Di Venanzo and a camera in tow to stage an impromptu audition, which goes perfectly. Fellini has no hesitations when he offers her the role of Guido's mistress. Even beyond the fiction of the film, she will be sucked into Fellini's universe. They will embark on a long habit of friendly trysts, described by the actress as "seventeen years of love," an exaggeration. During those years, Sandrocchia, as Fellini used to call her (or sometimes "Bamboccia," which means happy doll), will find time, after divorcing Ergas, to marry again, have children, and write a tell-all autobiography. After Federico's death she took every opportunity to play the role of his pretend widow.

There's a second way to interpret 8½, which is available to the common spectator, and it holds up equally as well. The world and its fauna, depicted in bright, comic nuggets, are secondary in this interpretation. The heart of the film is existential: Why are we here? It may seem daring for Fellini to put Mastroianni in his clothes and give him his lines to deliver; and there's no doubt that every time the hero hides his face under the famous black hat, so does Fellini. He handles the risk in his own way, not trying to conform to rigid cultural norms that he doesn't feel in command of. His private universe, similar to the private universe of any Italian male, is revealed in its entirety here: the painful, oppressive parents (Urbano again played by Annibale Ninchi); his wife and "all the other ladies," to use Bergman terminology; the circus of ambitions for his career; and the Catholic church—merely a construction, or hope for salvation. Guido is a director making a movie that he can't focus on. At his side, there is a mean but not stupid intellectual who pushes him toward an abyss of doubt and reveals his presumed creative impotence. Some people go so far as to say that this character, Carini, is a caricature of the critic Guido Aristarco, a righteous soldier of pure neorealism and a harsh opponent of Fellini's heretical deviations from it—though the writer Jean Rougel who plays Carini doesn't look at all like Aristarco. At the other extreme is Maurice, a performance fortune-teller (played by Ian Dallas, a

Scottish writer of comic plays, who later got interested in mysticism) who can read the protagonist's mind and extracts the enigmatic *"asa nisi masa"* (Italian pig Latin for *anima*, or soul). For this tuxedo-wearing clown, show business is the only natural way of life; it connects him to the "Mystery." Talking about the impossibility of fully comprehending his magical games, he explains, "There's something in it . . ." Guido has the hypercritic hung and accepts instead the clown's choice, deciding at last to identify with him. The inextricable blend of reality and fantasy comes to a wild close with an extraordinary procession of 152 characters from life and the film, crowded onto a merry-go-round, while a band of clowns plays a fanfare under the direction of a child dressed all in white.

The great novelty of 8½ lies in the grace of its conclusion, one no longer based on faith or temporary resolution, as in the earlier films. Here there is a character who can be seen as the embodiment of "grace" or "inspiration"—Claudia, played by Claudia Cardinale. She has an easy, earthy quality. Religion, as a decrepit cardinal explains, doesn't offer simple solutions: instead, it speaks an incomprehensible language (as the bishop of Rimini did during *La dolce vita*) and requires total abandon. But hell isn't scary anymore. In the gorgeous scenes set in the boarding school, where little Guido is punished by the priests for having gone to visit the prostitute on the beach, it's clear that the sympathy is all with poor Saraghina. She's so monstrous and innocent against the background of the sea that she can't possibly be the devil.

For the first time, a Fellini film doesn't end in anguish or with the sudden rediscovery of hope, but rather with the stoic, playful acceptance of life's assaults. The director transcends mythology, incinerating it by fully representing it and accepting all of its contradictions. This is all a perilous high-wire act. The confessional acrobats are Federico and his alter ego, both ready to break their backs for a show in which everything becomes part of a total visual delirium. Rarely has an artist recounted his crisis with such lush invention and imagery, freedom of voice and associations.

They say that every Fellini movie has its own unique spirit, a prevailing mood brought to the project by the director, which stays with the movie from start to finish. If that's the case, then 8½ is at once a movie of both doubt and determination, marked by a constant temptation to give up and by an exasperating perfectionism. The project was foggy in its inception and fiercely accurate in its execution. "The lucid dreaminess must be perfectly in focus," dictated the director. His idea seems to be that the answers to all of his problems were going to be solved through craftsmanship. Throughout preproduction, the director would repeat thoughts like "I feel like a train conductor who's sold all the tickets, lined up all the passengers, tucked the bags away. But where is the track?" His relationship with Gherardi, while destined to fall apart during *Giulietta degli spiriti*, is perfectly intact now. The art director can anticipate and elaborate on all the director's desires. He labors to create a Liberty-style hotel and reproduce, loosely, women's fashion from the years between the wars. He's an eclectic, and bases the farm in the movie on the house where he was born in Tuscany; the spaceship is inspired by Brueghel's *The Tower of Babel*. This is the first project for which Fellini doesn't want to shoot anything on location; he demands that everything be reconstructed, a trend he'd begun by rebuilding via Veneto for *La dolce vita*. His obsession with manipulating reality is so intense that he wants to transfigure his actors as well: Sandrocchia has to gain fifteen pounds, Anucchina has to lose fifteen.

The shooting begins on May 9, 1962, and continues through October 14. The exterior scenes are shot in Tivoli, Filacciano, Viterbo, Ostia, and Fiumicino. One of the first scenes shot in the Titanus Appia Nuovo studios is the production room with the girls on a bed. The next one is a little eucalyptus forest in the Eur neighborhood, which is supposed to be a park at the spa. Over the summer, the cast and crew film, more or less in this order, the descent to the underworld, the lobby of the hotel, the main street of a little town fashioned after Cecchignola, the scenes with Sandra Milo, the farm with the children, the cemetery with Guido's parents (also shot in Cecchignola), and the women's farm.

Something new, in fact, has been incorporated into Fellini's methodology. There was a long strike in the photography labs that started only a few weeks into shooting, so the director was unable to screen the rushes. He reassured his worried collaborators, "It doesn't matter. We'll go on anyway." Then, once the strike has ended, and the film is printed and ready to be seen again on a daily basis, Fellini still doesn't look at it. He sends Di Venanzo in his place to check for technical quality. He will later report,

I made the entire film in darkness, like a long night flight, and from that point, I developed the theory that it's better not to look at each scene as you shoot day after day. You must be bound to the illusion of the movie as you imagine it. What you are doing won't come out how you dreamed it, and so if you look at what you've done, you might change direction. I also think this is a good theory because Hitchcock doesn't look at rushes either.

In September, the moment arrives for shooting the end of the film as it had been initially conceived. Guido and his wife are returning to Rome, and they're sitting in the restaurant car of the train. Suddenly the protagonist looks up and sees all of the characters from his life (and his movie) sitting at the other tables. They smile at him benevolently or ambiguously. Once this scene is completed, Fellini also has the idea of shooting another short scene (four minutes) around a spaceship on the beach at Ostia, with the intention of using it as a trailer. It's yet another gathering of all the characters, and the scene is shot with eight cameras. During a prescreening, the beach scene turns out so exuberant and fun that they decide to make it the end of the movie, though the restaurant-car sequence is put aside with lots of discussion about keeping it safe because it's so beautiful. (Before long, the negative's whereabouts are forgotten.) The new final scene had been shot while listening to *Entrance of the Gladiators*, so for the closing procession, Nino Rota composes a march that will go on to become the anthem of Fellini's cinema, played at every public celebration of the director. (For the fanfare of the clowns, Rota composes a nostalgic *Ricordo d'infanzia*, a childhood memory, which will be very popular as well.)

For the first time Fellini's name appears above the title in the credits, which Gherardi sets in a flowery type. The movie is released on February 14, 1963, with a running time of two hours and fifteen minutes. It's highly praised critically—much more so than *La dolce vita*, where political issues had precluded any artistic judgment. The superlatives that stud all the reviews will quickly spread to the international press: Fellini is called a magician, a genius; it is said that he has a magic touch, a prodigious style, that he's inspired; and the compliments go on. There is also some negative criticism, but it's typically respectful and quite a change from the flat-out pans that *La strada* had received. Some critics complain that it's discursive, narcissistic, histrionic, and exhibitionistic, and that it doesn't engage the audience. Alberto Moravia's review echoes accusations that the director himself admits to: "Fellini's character is obsessed by eroticism, he's a sadist, a masochist, a self-mythologizer, he's scared of life and wants to go back into the mother's womb, he's a clown and a liar and a cheater." Moravia adds, "Some of these traits align him with Leopold Bloom in Joyce's *Ulysses*, which it's clear from various sections of the film that Fellini has read and thought about." Though Moravia's theory was certainly feasible—the first Italian translation of the novel came out in 1960—the people who knew Fellini at the time recognize that he most likely wasn't referencing *Ulysses* at all. Alberto Arbasino's criticism is more on target; he notes that 8½ "lands on our literary world at a time of extreme friction between the conventional and the avant-garde and gives a good shove in the direction of experimental. This is the future." In the same year of the film's release, a group of young writers form Gruppo '63* and reviewers and critics alike claim that the movie has inspired writers around the world. Christian Metz defines it as "a potently creative meditation on creative impotence." It does well at the box office in Italy especially, a surprise considering what a difficult movie it is and how little it is understood. Movie buffs are outraged that, in the provinces, the movie is shown with the flashback sequences tinted sepia to make the time changes more comprehensible to the audience.

On June 3, 1963, Pope John XXIII dies. He was the only pope that Fellini felt a filial devotion to. Sometimes, during his night crawls through Rome, the director would drive to the square at Saint Peter's to look affectionately at the Pope's lit window, and some remembered him saying, "I feel reassured knowing he's there." Even though they never met, Federico will miss Angelo Roncalli.

Later in June, the director and Marcello head to New York for the American release. Joseph E. Levine has bought the rights sight unseen, and the screening is held at the Festival Theatre, to be followed by a cel-

---

*Gruppo '63 is a literary collective of the *neoavanguardia* made up of poets, novelists, and critics protesting the mainstream, the establishment, and neorealism, and working off of artistic values expounded in Umberto Eco's seminal essay "Opera aperta" (Open Work).

ebration at the Four Seasons. Everyone praises it, except for a few critics. Pauline Kael calls the film a "structural disaster," while John Simon claims it's a "fiasco," but these illustrious critics don't anticipate the audience response. Success is so widespread that one company wants to mass-produce Marcello's black hat—8½ had clearly already conquered half the world and was preparing to conquer the other half.

Selected in the competition of the Moscow Film Festival, the film is presented to an audience of 8,000 in the Kremlin's conference hall on Thursday, July 18, 1963. The technical circumstances aren't up to snuff: the sound is too low and the simultaneous translation is poorly done. To the Soviets, 8½ is a political embarrassment. They worry that audiences will like this example of Western decadence too much. Sergei Gerasimov, an authority on cinema as well as a director (*The Young Guard*), had already warned Fellini at the airport, murmuring, "Don't be too happy. The more applause you get, the less likely you are to win." Yet some members of the new Soviet cinema are enthused before the lights even go down. Federico will have three devoted musketeers at his side for his whole stay in Moscow: Vladimir Naumov (who cowrote *Mir vchodjašćemu* [*Peace to Him Who Enters*] with Aleksandr Alov), Tengiz Abuladze, and Marlen Khutsiyev (who will have success in Venice in 1965 with his film *I Am Twenty* (*Mne dvadcat' let*), which was contested in Russia); the latter two are both from Georgia. While Gerasimov is exuberant, though clearly still a party-line man, the young directors all openly express the hope that 8½ will help push Russian cinema toward a greater freedom of expression.

When the time comes to address the audience, Federico is fully aware of his responsibility. He tries to say simple things: "I'm from another country. You don't know me and I don't know you. In this movie, I talk about myself to you. Maybe we'll find some similarities." Though the movie is received warmly, the mood in the screening room seems cold. Nevertheless, the three musketeers force Fellini to stay through the show and not run away as he would like. They are right to do so, because at the end, the applause is an explosion, a roar that seems as if it will never end. The delirium is a way of saying that the audience not only liked the movie but something more, something that alarms the festival authorities: the applause is a cry for freedom.

That night there's a reception on the seventh floor of the Moskva Hotel. A highly placed official by the name of Vladimir Baskakov seems embarrassed, but many others approach Fellini and more or less furtively shake his hand. The astronaut Gherman Titov pays homage to the movie, saying that "8½ is more mysterious than the universe." Poet Yevgeni Yevtushenko is pleased—he'll go on to make his own 8½ many years later, which will be called *Detskiy sad* (*Kindergarten*, 1983). The opinions about the film are clear, the audience loved it. Gerasimov falls in between those who loved it and the opposite camp; he likes it but is scared by it. The Soviet director then pulls Fellini into an all-night man-to-man discussion, but gets so involved that he starts speaking Russian and his Italian guest doesn't understand anything other than the director's preoccupations. The next day, Rotislav Jureniev, a respected critic, attacks the movie in *Sovetskaya Kultura* as an individualistic, asocial, politically ambiguous movie, too far removed from the people.

As the festival comes to a close, there is some complicated maneuvering to influence the jury's decision. The festival organizers struggle to include Nanni Loy's *Le quattro giornate di Napoli* (*The Four Days of Naples*) in the competition, so that they may give the prize to another Italian film. Grigori Chukhraj, director of *Ballad of a Soldier* (1959), is leading the fifteen-person jury, of which seven members are foreigners. Representing Italy is Sergio Amidei, an undisciplined, moody Communist who'd written the screenplay for *Roma, città aperta*. He recognizes the concerns that the Soviets have—they're still in shock from Nikita Khrushchev's March 8 speech declaring the end of the cold war—but he's also aware of the fact that it's in everyone's best interest to fight some battles openly. When Chukhraj, with the support of a Russian jury member, proposes giving 8½ a special prize that will exclude it from eligibility for the grand prize, Amidei explodes in his typical fashion and invites the foreign jury members—including Stanley Kramer from America, Jean Marais from France, and Satyajit Ray from India, director of *Pather Panchali*—to walk off the panel. It is Ray who, on the afternoon of Sunday, July 21, returns to the Moskva Hotel to announce that Amidei scared the Soviets to death and managed to secure the festival's most prestigious award in a unanimous decision for 8½. This is the last festival that one of Fellini's films will compete in. From this point forward, the director, who'd long had his doubts about the festivals, will always screen his films out of competition.

In July 1963, the movie has another success at Saint Vincent, where the jury of the Grolle d'Oro gives it the grand prize, over Luchino Visconti's *Il gattopardo* (*The Leopard*). Another source of pleasure for those who still hold fast to the idea of a contest between the two directors comes when Fellini also beats out Visconti for the Silver Ribbon. Seven prizes are awarded to Fellini's film (and only three to *Il gattopardo*) for director, producer, original story, screenplay, music, cinematography, and best supporting actress (Sandra Milo). Later the New York Film Critics Circle also names 8½ the best foreign language film, and, in April 1964, it's Oscar season again.

Rizzoli heads up the expedition from Rome to follow the destiny of the movie's five Oscar nominations. Federico, Giulietta, Fracassi, Flaiano, and Milo, along with her husband, Ergas, also join the group. The most fruitful part of the trip was the half-joking question that Ergas presented to Fellini as they were landing in a misty New York City: "How much do you want for making a movie about the hereafter?"

Fellini probably conceived *Il viaggio di G. Mastorna* from this spark of Gothic humor. In Hollywood, while strolling at night as he usually does, Federico is stopped by the police. When he explains that he's Fellini they don't believe him. Later, when he visits the picturesque cemetery of Forest Lawn, he inquires as to the price of a mausoleum with all the amenities, including music: $35,000. Federico asks, "If I get it without music, can I have a discount?" Discount or no, on April 13, 1964, Fellini triumphs again at the auditorium in Santa Monica—though he wins only two out of the five nominations: one to Gherardi for costume design in a black-and-white picture (Gherardi's second Oscar; his first was for *La dolce vita*), and the other for best foreign language film. When he accepts the statue from Julie Andrews, Fellini seems a little stunned. Later he will explain that he didn't know what to say when he heard "Fratelli d'Italia," the Italian national anthem, being played instead of the usual musical accompaniment. When he returns home he has to turn the Oscar over in order to reaccept it from the hands of Aldo Moro, the prime minister of Italy.

The most striking effects of the film will resonate in the years to come, as imitations of 8½ pile up by directors all over the world. The list of movies it inspired is extremely long: *Mickey One* (Arthur Penn, 1965),

Alex in Wonderland (Paul Mazursky, 1970, in which Federico appears as himself), *Warnung vor einer heiligen Nutte* (Rainer Werner Fassbinder, 1971), *La nuit américaine* (François Truffaut, 1973), *All That Jazz* (Bob Fosse, 1979), *Stardust Memories* (Woody Allen, 1980), *Sogni d'oro* (Nanni Moretti, 1981), *Parad Planet* (Vadim Abdrashitov, 1984), and *La película del rey* (Carlos Sorin, 1986). In Eastern Europe the movie is seen as a model of contemporary style following its victory at the Moscow Film Festival, and it proves an influence on many Czech movies of the Prague Spring. The movie also inspired the successful Broadway musical *Nine*, by Mario Fratti, with a libretto by Arthur Kopit, and lyrics and music by Maury Yeston. It debuts in New York on May 9, 1982, at the 46th Street Theatre after a six-month run across America, and goes on to receive twelve Tony nominations. One of those nominations went to Raul Julia for his performance as the Italian director Guido Contini, juggling a harem of twenty-two women. The rights to the adaptation were easy to obtain from Fellini; his only condition was that neither his name nor the title 8½ should appear on the poster.

There's a sad side to the happy story of 8½, however, that not many people know about. A few years after the film, Marco Gemini, the young actor who played Guido as a child dressed in his white boarding-school uniform, the embodiment of Fantasy, died of an incurable disease, leaving everyone who'd known him in grief.

29

The Woman in the Shadows
Giulietta degli spiriti / Juliet of the Spirits

In the summer of 1964, Fellini, king of cinema, is directing *Giulietta degli spiriti* in the studios of Safa-Palatino. His *8½* is an international success and recognition of every description has rained down on him, from Moscow to Hollywood. On June 2, at the celebration for the feast of the Republic, he was named Grande Ufficiale and Giulietta received the title of Commendatore. Photographers, television crews, and journalists with microphones flurry around the director on the movie set, dressed in black, just like Guido Anselmi. Desperate to discover his artistic process, his magic tricks, they listen to and tape-record what he says, what he whispers, even what he thinks. The only thing missing from the scene is a march by Nino Rota. Fellini feels like he's living a remake of *8½*, but as an actor this time, rather than a director. Making a movie in such circumstances means writing, thinking, and rewriting with a crowd constantly on your back, watching over your progress. Working on a movie has become public, and Fellini's public is about as varied as you can get. People make dates on the set of his movies, his friends come along to root for him, enemies come to spy. Fellini's set is where people gather to discuss the day's events and where interesting people meet, new friendships are born and old ones lost. Federico claims to really hate this salon atmosphere, but he's trapped in it. This has become how he works and lives, and that will never change.

Anyone who visited Fellini's house in the pine grove in Fregene (Giulietta helped design it) will immediately recognize it in *Giulietta degli spiriti*, embellished and stylized by Piero Gherardi and based on drawings by Antonio Rubino. The studio used for the interior shots is as humid as a tropical jungle. The producer had left orders always to keep the grass in the garden wet, and never to let air filter through the small openings in the huge dark landscape surrounding the set—as if to protect this fantastical island from the contamination of the real world. Federico feels entirely at home here. *Giulietta degli spiriti* (a title that Fellini invented on the fly to satisfy a pushy journalist) was conceived of in the winter of 1963–64 with passionate although intermittent inspiration.

The idea for the movie comes out of the need to find another part for Giulietta, who hasn't worked on a film with her husband since *Le notti di Cabiria* seven years ago. In those years since her brightest success, the actress hasn't enjoyed any further recognition. Dino De Laurentiis had eagerly offered her the lead in another Fellini/Pinelli-authored film, *Fortunella* (1958), about a street vendor caught in the clutches of a Zampanò-like character played by Alberto Sordi. Though the film had many Fellini ingredients—including Rota's music, later used for Francis Ford Coppola's *The Godfather*—*Fortunella* didn't attract a big audience. Also in 1958, Masina appeared in Renato Castellani's *Nella città l'inferno* (*Hell in the City*), but had an unpleasant experience with her costar, Anna Magnani, who played a hardened criminal to Masina's wrongfully imprisoned innocent. The movie is based on a nonfiction book by Isa Mari, script supervisor on *La dolce vita* and daughter of the actor Febo Mari, and it recalls her experiences as a victim of a miscarriage of justice. Federico knows about the conflict between the two actresses, but finds it difficult to take sides, torn between solidarity with his wife and the enduring affinity he's had with Magnani since they worked together on *Il miracolo*. While Fellini is still working on *La dolce vita*, Giulietta and Richard Basehart fly together to Poland and then Germany to work on the film *Jons und Erdme*, which doesn't prove a big success. She goes on to Berlin and Düsseldorf for another project, *Das Kunsteidene Mädchen* (*La grande vie* or *The High Life*), an Italian-French-German coproduction, where the director, Julien Duvivier, tells Masina outright that he doesn't like how Fellini directs her. He wants her to bleach her hair platinum blond, like Marilyn Monroe, and in one scene, directs her to emerge naked from a bubble bath. When she refuses, Duvivier is convinced that Fellini has intervened and he complains that Italian husbands are too jealous. It's not Fellini's fault, thought—it's Giulietta's religious upbringing and her shyness about "love scenes, kisses, and all that stuff." Despite disagreeing about the nudity, Giulietta and Duvivier get along and she calls him "mon oncle chinois." But this movie is a failure as well. After so many disappointing experiences, Madame Fellini grows suspicious and makes two big mistakes, one after the other: she turns down both a Pietro Germi project and the lead in Michelangelo Antonioni's *La notte*, which will go to Jeanne Moreau instead.

While all of this is going on, Federico is still working on *La dolce vita*, a train wreck in the Fellini household. The rhythms are a whirlwind and Giulietta puts her own career aside to help Fellini with his business and trips. But the time soon comes for them to work together again. The Fellini-Masina team has been successful in the past and Angelo Rizzoli wants more, even though the big budget expected for the new movie has tempted other producers at Cineriz to enhance the director's brand by coupling him with an American celebrity. They secretly consult Katharine Hepburn about the project, but Federico is so angry when he finds out that, from that point on, no one dares to question Giulietta as the lead.

The fact that the producers went behind his back is evidence that Fellini's films are no longer born in a splendid atmosphere of enthusiasm, absolute loyalty, and friendship. In the world of entertainment, failures lead to recriminations and conflicts, but success has its own share of difficulties. Personal issues are exacerbated, people get territorial, and the conflicts that come up over days and nights of tension are ultimately difficult to resolve. Since he started working on the screenplay for *Giulietta degli spiriti*, Federico feels as if he's surrounded by people who don't understand him or trust him. Though he has the impression of being dangerously isolated, people say that he's the one who's changed—what Conocchia tells Guido in 8½. They say that he's impatient, closed off, engrossed in personal problems he doesn't want to share. It might be that he's getting older, or maybe he just needs to meet new people, but those old relationships won't erode until after *Giulietta degli spiriti*. Meanwhile, he goes forward as best he can, even without the idyllic atmosphere of previous sets: the writers are lazy, the director's ideas seem confused, his silences are exasperating. Gherardi suddenly starts making decisions on his own and presents Fellini with set designs before they've ever talked about them. Federico and Piero never really talked much, but in the past they'd shared an unspoken understanding, which for some mysterious reason—be it burnout, pigheadedness, or differences of opinion—has now vanished. Piero and Giulietta aren't getting along either. Even though she recognizes his talent, Giulietta worries that Piero's concepts will overwhelm her character. Beyond that, there is the natural pleasure that Gherardi seems to take in stirring up trouble—his decision, for instance, to force Giulietta, who's not very tall, to wear a mushroom hat that only reinforces her diminutive stature.

One recurring point of discussion is the use of color film. This is the first time that Fellini has worked in color for a feature-length film. Unhappy with the tests and rushes, Fellini insists that "color pictures" are a contradiction in terms. Cinema is about movement, while color is static. The cinematographer Gianni Di Venanzo, a master of black-and-white, is inexperienced in color and feels hampered by the fact that everything is essentially an experiment. For several weeks, before they arrive at an agreement that enables them to finish the movie, Fellini and Di Venanzo complain about each other to the rest of the crew, both saying precisely the same things: "He thinks that color is just like black-and-white, and he has to realize it's not." Giulietta doesn't like the way Di Venanzo shoots her, and when the movie is almost done, rumors circulate that she's secretly called in Otello Martelli to reshoot some of her close-ups at night (true or false?—we don't know).

There is also disagreement, traces of which appear in the final product, over what part of the story should be emphasized: the real life (middle-class wife, adultery, separation) or the fantastical. Giulietta lobbies for the human part, because she's sure that women will identify with it and be interested and moved by it; while Federico is attracted to the magic. Like in Le notti di Cabiria, the lines of communication between husband and wife are not entirely perfect. They disagree constantly over the meaning of the new picture, and if their conflict isn't apparent to the others on the set, it's only due to Masina's professional, highly disciplined demeanor.

Another element that seems to distance Fellini from his usual clutch of collaborators is his growing interest in the supernatural. The director talks quite openly about it in interviews. He tells *Planète*, "I believe in everything; there's no limit to my capacity for surprise." In the same interview, he reveals his lifelong tendency to "get lost when experiencing the magical aspects of reality." He also discusses the connection between magic and work. "The art of cinema is particularly adept at perforating daily reality and revealing another, the metaphysical, the ultra-sensory."

During 8½, Fellini made the rounds of magicians and mediums, but the most important encounter was with Gustavo Adolfo Rol. Rol was born in 1903 in Turin and had studied law, but eventually became a painter and dabbler in white magic, though with no professional aspirations. He has an encyclopedic mind and is an expert in Napoleonic history. Primarily a restorer of old paintings, he can often be found laboring away in his dark house on via Silvio Pellico 31 in Turin. He claims unknown forces of nature guide his hands. Quirky Gustavo is able to do tricks that would impress anyone: he can read closed books, move objects from one room to another without touching them, telepathically eavesdrop on conversations taking place hundreds of miles away, and shuffle cards with hallucinatory speed, making them change color and suit in the process. Federico is enthusiastic about the one-man show, as well as Rol's broad generosity (not unlike Federico's own) in using his mysterious talent to entertain others. Rol's tricks are beyond the limits of human comprehension; Fellini never tires of them. In his modern fairy tale, *Giulietta degli spiriti*, the director sets out to challenge those very limits, especially when they repress behavior or become barriers linked to social status.

During this same period, Fellini also experiments with LSD 25, a synthetic drug fashioned to produce the same effects as the hallucinogenic mushrooms used by Mexican tribes. The psychoanalyst Emilio Servadio, who cured Fellini for a short period after *La strada*, suggests that he try the drug under a doctor's observation. As Fellini tells the story, the whole event happened secretly one Sunday afternoon with a psychologist, a cardiologist, a chemist, two nurses, a stenographer, and many microphones in tow. With some apprehension, the director–lab rat has an electrocardiogram and takes the drug with a sugar cube. The effect lasts quite a bit longer than the usual seven or eight hours, but the entire time, Fellini talks and paces up and down the room. At a certain point, to keep him from getting too agitated, he is injected with a tranquilizer. Once the nurses take him home, he sleeps soundly and doesn't remember very much of the experiment the next day, nor does he have any interest in listening to the recording of himself or hearing the diagnoses, theories, or conclusions of the doctors. The whole experience, according to the director, has left him somewhat embarrassed over the stupid things he may have said.

Servadio's version of the story, as he told it to his colleague Simona Argentieri when he was well over ninety years old, is, not surprisingly, very different.

> There were just three of us: Fellini, a former student of mine who was also a psychoanalyst, and me. During the experiment, Fellini communicated at length with the spirits he believed in, and then, with my help, he reflected and realized that the spirits were his projections, which is how he abandoned the séances he'd been going to and came up with *Guilietta degli spiriti*—an abandonment of spiritism.

Some of Fellini's former girlfriends, particularly the cast-off ones, indirectly described some of those séances in their Fellini memoirs. Anna Salvatore, a painter of some repute, appeared in *La dolce vita* as one of Steiner's guests, and having made friends with Giulietta was later a frequent visitor to the Fellini house. In 1966 she published *Subliminal TU!* (*Subliminal You*), a "fantastic tale," according to the jacket, "that's also a novel of customs. It is the story of a group of people in contemporary Rome, who half playfully, half seriously take up séances, revealing their passions and weaknesses as if by an X-ray." The group that Salvatore writes about is easily recognizable and she blithely exposes their personal stories, claiming that the project came to her "as a gift of automatic writing."

At the head of the table sits Big, flanked by his wife Lietta (Giulietta), Count Fifty (Salvato Cappelli), and the narrator, Anna Salvatore. "Lietta was a strange person . . . shall we say she was extremely childish—quite different from Big, and their personalities clashed in a fascinating way. Over time, because of the peculiar relationship we had, I did a favor for Lietta that changed her life definitively. Big was always off somewhere else, chasing clouds, and she was frequently left alone. I happened to introduce her to a man I knew, a typical upper-class *charmer* who fell for her hard and became her constant companion." Big has difficulty accepting Count Fifty's constant presence in the house—"he's always there, underfoot, like a big, friendly dog"—and copes by organizing party games: operator, charades, mind reading, and playing with spiritualistic experiences. According to Salvatore, "Big and Lietta hardly even share a friendship anymore . . . They don't talk . . . they haven't had sex in eight years." Lietta drinks too much whiskey and then cries. While Count Fifty rushes to her defense, Big "sees his mother in his wife, suffering the infractions of his cheating father," and plays the part of the "sincerely apologetic husband."

On the brink of indiscreet and rife with inventions, the author defends her book:

> I don't think I'm doing anything wrong with my thinly veiled depictions. Big talks about his personal life in his dramas [read: films], as well as mine and his wife's, and the lives of anyone who has ever had something to do with him. He's extremely open, autobiographical; his references are obvious, he even quotes us directly! Considering how much he's read and seen, it's in fact quite common to meet a stranger who remarks, "Oh, you're the painter that Guido X talks about! The one who wants to love God in all his physical power!"

Verbose and imbalanced (more than seven hundred pages long), when Salvatore's book isn't adrift in delirious descriptions of spiritism with the "Friends" (astral creatures constantly invading the tableau), it describes—with some malevolence—the Fellini household, which is less haunted by spirits than by their human counterparts. It is in this sense that the book, while to be taken with a grain of salt, can also help us to understand some aspects of *Giulietta degli spiriti*.

Federico evokes the hereafter without much conviction and, in fact, with a great deal of reservation "for the scent of chrysanthemums surrounding these kinds of practices."* He tires quickly of the parlor games, though Anna, Salvato, and even Giulietta are still deeply engrossed.

---

*Chrysanthemums are a traditional funeral flower in Italian culture.

Fellini is still seeing Bernhard at this time, and in order to concentrate on the Jungian therapy, he must devote his attention to his nighttime fantasies. To this end, he has a strange dream while working on *Giulietta degli spiriti*:

> Giulietta is alone in the middle of an empty space and the camera is circling her on a trolley. The trolley is packed with people shouting—they're like clowns. I try to give orders, direct, but the people on the trolley are making too much noise and drowning out my voice. Then they all fall to the ground. Perhaps the dream means that I'm circumscribing the heart of the matter, and the risk is one of total collapse. When I woke I sensed danger, the possibility of a shipwreck.

The dream's significance lies in the shipwreck image associated with the trolley full of clowns—a tableau not unlike *Ship of Fools* (*Stultifera navis*), the painting by Hieronymus Bosch that later inspires *E la nave va*. Fellini had recorded yet another disturbing dream the week before starting work on *Giulietta degli spiriti*.

> Suddenly, someone takes out my right eye with a spoon. It doesn't hurt; it just takes me by surprise. What does that mean? I really don't know. Maybe it means that you don't need your right eye to make a movie, you don't need a concrete, earthbound vision, but only the transparent, fantastic vision of your left eye. Or maybe it's just a warning: you're going to mess up. You don't have your right eye anymore; you only see things halfway.

It's clear that the years between *La dolce vita* and *Giulietta degli spiriti* represent the most difficult period of Giulietta's life. She's in crisis over turning forty and having a hard time accepting growing old. Sometimes, even when there are guests over, she openly vents about her feelings of inferiority with respect to the *maggiorate* (buxom actresses), like Gina Lollobrigida and Sophia Loren, with whom she competed for roles throughout the fifties. "What do they have that I don't?" she asks, risking an obvious answer. She begins to obsessively challenge the official birth dates of her rivals, claiming that Magnani was born at the turn of the century. Dinner parties at the Fellini house are frequently tense: he obviously wants to escape, she can't control her free-floating anger. Even when they have company, she can be harsh with Federico and his family—including Riccardo, who Giulietta accuses of borrowing money without paying it back. Sometimes her husband scolds her for drinking too much, but Federico doesn't drink at all and two whiskeys can look to him like the evidence of alcoholism. All facts are pointing to the fact that Madame Fellini is in the midst of a meltdown—an isolated moment in an otherwise very orderly and consistently rational life. Later, when she's older, Masina will come to accept the inescapable primordial urges that drove Federico's dissatisfied rebellion, just as he will later find comfort in Giulietta's serenity, sustained by profound religious faith.

Giulietta degli spiriti is another chapter in the director's trajectory that doesn't follow in anyone else's footsteps. It's the portrait of an educated middle-aged woman. The plot is fluid and convincing, even from the psychological perspective, but it tends toward the fantastical with a stylistic intensity that Fellini had perfected through the dialectical, carefully modulated 8½. Through myth and ironic self-exploration, *Giulietta degli spiriti* is the bridge between *La strada* and 8½. The influence of psychoanalytic literature is strong, as well as a sense of urgency to return to historical roots and logically examine archetypes. The director has reflected for years on the theme of marriage and has come to think that Gelsomina's mistake was to live in the shadow of Zampanò, for the Gypsy's metaphysical redemption is no compensation for Gelsomina's human sacrifice. Giulietta, a bourgeois Gelsomina, has learned how not to be a martyr, how to stand on her own two feet, how not to depend on her husband, how to do away with the residue of a difficult upbringing and a childish dependence on her mother. These lessons are the only way to chase away the ghosts who persecute her, spirits that haunt the house and make themselves felt, as solid as dreams.

Fellini's creative inspiration is unleashed in a picture that tests the limits between delirium and reality, so much so that real people and things assume forms that are in one moment troubling and in the next spectral, as if there weren't a true boundary between the ego and the id, and dreams and visions are just another aspect of everyday life. With *Giulietta degli spiriti*, Fellini, once an analyzer of crisis, comes instead to a definition of morality that is neither vague nor uncertain. The world changes with incredible rapidity and people need to have a solid and conscious sensitivity to the changes—to stop wasting time in an attempt to heal the wounds of childhood. Everything must be discussed, put in its place, and rebuilt, including tradition, habit, and the whole list of rules handed down in school or from the family. It's far worse to keep those devils in than to build up the strength to let them emerge. Only once Giulietta has exorcised her devils does the old Fellini, vaguely faithful and still believing in miracles, come back out. The director is still affected by his Catholic education and finds consolation in grace. After letting Giulietta progress in terms of awareness, he brings her back to the solution that he'd already found for Cabiria. Perhaps he isn't ready to accept that Giulietta should let the spirits stay, grow inured to them, make friends.

Giulietta degli spiriti aims for a light colorful mood, like the drawings in *Corriere dei Piccoli*, but the film comes off instead as heavy and not at all childlike. The fact that Fellini surrenders to a fascination with the world of magic does not mean that he's given up on rationality. Rather he's recommending that modern man should sharpen his perceptive abilities, signifying a return, in a drastic and definitive way, to antiquated methods of thought, just at the point where science and the conquering of physical barriers are making people forget them. Along with the so-called decadentism—the mocking, grotesque imagery that we already saw in *La dolce vita*—*Giulietta degli spiriti* has an affectionate message, a life lesson. After the troubled wandering and impatient disorder of his youth, Federico is perhaps becoming wise.

The idea of the film, also a moral tract, is clearer than its form. And, in fact, when the character Susy (Sandra Milo) comes on the scene, the pleasure of fantastical evasion overtakes the director, which also leads Gherardi into superfluous whimsy. Without a doubt, the realization of the marriage crisis is the better part of the film, with all its cruelty and tenderness, despite the fact that it's played out in the context of memory and fantasy. Masina is clearly a lot more at ease in this candid homely environment than she is in her scenes with Susy the temptress. Throughout the film, the actress displays incredible strength in bringing a very personal situation from her own life—such as when Giulietta, the character, hires a private detective to follow her husband and film him because she suspects he's cheating on her—to the screen. It's no mystery that the event reflects reality, but the director puts this story into his screenplay, along with other stories from the couple's real life. Giulietta accepts it without argument.

This isn't to say that there wasn't tension under the surface. Mario Carotenuto, the great actor playing the detective, had to pay most for it. Federico was unhappy with him from the first day, a perplexing reaction given that Mario was exactly the kind of variety-show character actor that Fellini loved. But the director was unusually hard on him, wearing him out with endless repetitions of the same scene, and plying him with incomprehensible directions. And so we come to that always painful moment known in movie jargon as the "protest," the replacement of an actor deemed not to be up to the part. It was, to be sure, a recurring dynamic on Fellini's sets, but in this case a particularly unjustified and jarring call. Fellini replaced Carotenuto with Alberto Plebani, an amiable minor actor, yet asked nothing special of him. Instead of lines, the director had him recite numbers—and poor Carotenuto probably never knew the real, psychological reason for which he was humiliated and sacrificed.

Giulietta degli spiriti was scheduled to be screened out of competition at the 26th Venice Film Festival in the summer of 1965, but what actually happened was a sensational retreat. The director of the festival, Luigi Chiarini, had programmed Fellini's new film after rash promises from the director that it would be ready. But as the deadline approached, it became increasingly unlikely that the movie would be finished in time. The dubbing is still incomplete and Sandra Milo, who has yet to dub several of her scenes, has had a breakdown. Fellini seems quite happy to have a reason to skip the festival he's been avoiding for ten years, but Chiarini is stubborn and won't let go. There's an argument and insults are hurled. Chiarini accuses Fellini of betraying him and then they both threaten each other with lawsuits. Legal action aside, the first cut of the movie is simply not available and it is thus clearly impossible to show the film. This is the first time that a Fellini movie skips the festival circuit and goes directly to theaters, where it opens on October 22, 1965, in Italy and France and on January 4, 1966, in New York City. There's preview in November before the American release and a party at Jacqueline Kennedy's Fifth Avenue apartment, which Federico and Giulietta attend.

Both in Italy and abroad, reviewers can't hide their disappointment over the film. Negative opinions run along the lines of exterior, vague, chaotic, fake, uncontrolled, too long, outsized, heavy, schematic, frigid. Of the positive reviews, only a few make the claim that the film is a masterpiece, and the majority try to defend it against itself as coherent, studied, capable, not banal, unusual, difficult, important. The Centro Cattolico Cinematografico is harsh; people are advised not to see the movie because it's "extremely confused and ambiguous because of the unpleasant blur between the sacred and profane; and for the apparently biased and unjust condemnation of Catholic and religious education; and not least for the self-satisfied and gratuitous presentation of lascivious images." With this film, Fellini lost many friends among the Catholics.

His own vague dissatisfaction with the results is fed by the clashes that he experienced on the set and the relationships destroyed in the process of making the film. After fifteen years, his relationship with Ennio Flaiano is souring. Federico still appreciates the screenwriter's irony, but he has also suffered its repercussions. Flaiano has been not merely critical but openly hostile to some of Fellini's projects. He's bright and talented, but also temperamental and hypersensitive, and whenever Fellini introduces a new collaborator, Flaiano feels threatened. He doesn't like the understanding that Federico has built with Brunello Rondi, a cultured friend who comes up with scenes and ideas that are frequently quite stimulating, but the one that Flaiano plainly refuses to deal with is Pier Paolo Pasolini. He doesn't understand Pasolini's artistry and deplores his growing success. When Pasolini comes in on *La dolce vita* it irritates Flaiano to the extent that he writes a parody, "*La dolce vita* According to Pasolini," but doesn't publish it at Fellini's ardent urging. There's also an ugly episode in April 1964 during their trip to Los Angeles for 8½. Flaiano happens to be sitting in coach, which is where Rizzoli's office put him, and he is furious because he thinks it's Federico's fault. Though there's no truth to this suspicion (Federico didn't organize the trip, he was a guest too, and certainly didn't foot the bill), the idea that the director made the writer sit in economy was the gossip of the decade, and swallowed whole by those intellectuals who were convinced that Flaiano was the secret, humiliated author of all of Fellini's films. Throughout *Giulietta degli spiriti*, things continued to be tense between the two friends. Flaiano accepted the job with the sneer of an intellectual vehemently opposed to the encroachment of cinema into the literary world; as if to say, let's avoid the themes that only the psychoanalytic novel should tackle.

Fellini gradually starts to believe that Ennio is harboring a strange jealousy—not personal so much as abstract, like that of literature versus cinema. The writer tells everyone that Fellini is a megalomaniac. They hardly ever see each other during *Giulietta degli spiriti*, and grow further apart. Ennio complains that Federico never asks his opinion, while the director claims that his writer doesn't write. After *Giulietta degli spiriti* is finished, Flaiano sends an ugly letter full of criticism and complaints. Federico throws it in the trash before he even finishes reading it.

After that, they very rarely meet. In private they complain about each other, sometimes to each other's friends, and occasionally they exchange jabs publicly. In the avant-garde film *La decima vittima* (The 10th Victim, 1965), written by Flaiano and directed by Elio Petri, there's a street named Lungotevere Fellini,* an open mockery of the growing cult of personality that surrounds the great director. (After Fellini's death, there was in fact a square named after him, Largo Federico Fellini, at Porta Pinciana.)

A few years after *Giulietta degli spiriti*, however, Flaiano has a stroke, his first, and goes to live in a boardinghouse on via Isonzo, a short walk from Fellini's office on corso d'Italia. They begin to see each other regularly again; the differences are eventually overcome and the friendship will endure until Flaiano's death in 1972. On that occasion, Fellini describes his friend with both admiration and regret for the loss: "He was a mix of complicity, solidarity, and hypersensitivity. We weren't friends for years because of a ridiculous misunderstanding—he took offense over something and then I took offense that he was offended and it was impossible to work out. Ennio had the capacity to shamelessly destroy you, but he could reconcile with the same passion. He was a very dear friend."

A year after *Giulietta degli spiriti*, on February 3, 1966, another collaborator, the cinematographer Gianni Di Venanzo, dies suddenly of viral hepatitis. Fellini learns of his death while he's in Milan lunching with

*Lungotevere is the generic name of the streets that run along the Tiber in Rome.

Marcello Mastroianni at Biffi Scala. He's quite sad about it, not only because of their work together on 8½ but also, perhaps, because of their
quarreling on *Giulietta degli spiriti*. Tullio Pinelli is yet another casualty;
now the writer works with Giulietta only on projects for television. Gherardi, too, keeps his distance and is unkind when he speaks of Fellini.
Clemente Fracassi has become the right arm of the producer and is unable to maintain a close relationship with the director. Fellini is at a point
in his career in which he feels like a general who turns back to look at his
army and finds that he's alone on the battlefield. This is the end of his
partnership with Rizzoli as well—a collaboration that began with *La dolce
vita* and lasted five long years. Even after years have passed, the director
will be reluctant to talk about this dark period of splits and separations,
making comments such as "Sometimes excessive trust results in the betrayal of affinity. Just when you think you really know another person
well, you suddenly don't recognize him anymore."

30

La Dolce Morte

Fellini and Angelo Rizzoli have a meeting, and the producer makes the un-forgivable mistake of complaining too much about the budget overages on *Giulietta degli spiriti*. Angelo is troubled by the news that Fellini has plans to sign with Dino De Laurentiis, "the guy from Naples." Clemente Fracassi attempts to comfort Rizzoli, claiming that Fellini "will eventually come back to us anyway," but Federico won't, in fact, work with Rizzoli again.

At forty-six years old, Fellini has already seen the pinnacle of his career with 8½, and now he finds himself saddled with a film that he's unsatis-fied with. He's even less satisfied with the critical reception the film has received. It's true that his attempt to understand women, to make a "women's movie," is only partially successful, but neither women nor men are even acknowledging his effort. In his stubborn defense of the project, the director had sacrificed almost all of his collaborators and friends, but the ever-savvy De Laurentiis steps in to take advantage of the director's isolation. In January 1964, the producer had opened his new monumental studio on via Pontina, proudly naming it Dinocittà. He had *The Bible—In the Beginning* as well as other big productions under his belt, but wouldn't be satisfied until he could add Fellini's new movie to his treasure trove. Federico complies, and signs a contract with Dino to make a movie called *Assurdo universo* (*What Mad Universe*) based on Fredric Brown's science-fiction novel *What Mad Universe*, which the director had read while working on *La dolce vita*. It seems that at least early on, Fellini had ex-pressed his interest in adapting the book to De Laurentiis, but he soon changes his mind. There's a more ambitious picture he wants to make.

The idea behind what will be (or rather, will never come to be) *Il viaggio di G. Mastorna* goes back almost thirty years. In Federico's last few months in Rimini, he devoured the short serial novel *Lo strano viaggio di Domenico Molo* (The Odd Journey of Domenico Molo) by Dino Buzzati, published in the weekly magazine *Omnibus* in October of 1938. It's the story of a twelve-year-old boy who, having died, ends up in a Limbo where trials are held and punishments meted out. The child proceeds to go on an odyssey of the hereafter and, finally, instead of going to Heaven, he returns to Earth, having learned the secret of life.

In the spring of 1965, Buzzati receives a telephone call from Fellini, who is in Milan and wants to meet him. The two have never met but share a mutual respect. The writer is a little out of sorts, having just returned from Bombay where he was interviewing magicians, but he doesn't want to miss the chance to spend an evening with the director. They meet at a famous fish restaurant and Almerina, Buzzati's young wife, remembers how strangely excited Fellini became when he recounted how much he'd liked *Lo strano viaggio di Domenico Molo*—so much so that he wanted to turn it into a movie. Fellini is tired of the writers he's been working with and he wants to do something new. His proposition is that Buzzati, most famous for his novel *Il deserto dei tartari* (*The Tartar Steppe*), join him in writing the screenplay for *Il viaggio di G. Mastorna*. Dino's spontaneous response is "This proposal is an honor and I am flattered"—a happy start to a collaboration that (perhaps jinxed) would lead only to a series of insuperable obstacles . . . the first one being the dinner at hand. Only Buzzati, who didn't eat the fish, escapes unscathed. Almerina wakes at four in the morning with terrible abdominal pain and is hurried to the hospital, where they proceed to pump her stomach. When she returns home at seven, there's a call from Federico at the Hotel Continental; in a moribund voice he reports that he's going back to Rome after a god-awful night spent vomiting and in pain.

The affectionate symbiosis between Buzzati and Fellini continues for more than a year. They speak almost every day, though the director's habit of calling very early in the morning disrupts the life of a couple that tends to keep late hours. While discussing the film project they also start plotting other projects, often referring back to the world of magic and metaphysics. Buzzati is working on a series of articles under the title "In cerca dell'Italia misteriosa" (Searching for the Mysterious Italy), later to be published in book form as *I misteri d'Italia* (The Mysteries of Italy), and he asks Fellini for suggestions. On July 21, they travel together to Turin, where Federico introduces Dino to Gustavo Adolfo Rol. Later on, Fellini will visit Rol quite often in order to discuss his growing doubts about *Il viaggio di G. Mastorna*.

In one of his tales—there's always a seed of truth in them—Fellini reports that he had also brought Buzzati to meet Pasqualina Pezzolla, a fortune-teller who lives in Porto Civitanova in the Marche. Her house was a kind of Lourdes; she would sit behind a table in a parlor filled with sacred iconography and receive guests while, in a trance and as if protecting her eyes from a great light, she would lay her hands on her visitors. Claiming to be able to feel signals and emotions, she would then translate them into enigmatic drawings. Buzzati tried it at Fellini's behest, but the woman was so embarrassed by what she saw that she took the director aside, instructing him to look after his friend because he was sick. (The writer was already in treatment for an illness that would take his life in January of 1972.) In his August 1965 reportage about the trip, however, Buzzati tells the story very differently, not mentioning Fellini's presence. Almerina, too, claims that she was the only person with the author when he visited Pezzolla, but the conclusion of Buzzati's article is not entirely at odds with Fellini's version of the story: "Pasqualina's warmhearted and understanding smile stays with me. Was she hiding something? Could she see my fear, and so kept the truth from me? I still wonder." Facts aside, these "magical trips" brought Buzzati and Fellini closer together, and they meant quite a lot to Dino, who would later write about them in his book *Poema a fumetti* (A Poem in Comics).

Fellini writes a long treatment for the movie in the form of a letter to De Laurentiis; it's undated, but was probably based on the concept that Fellini had written in the summer of 1965. He's working from his new house on via Volosca in Fregene, which was similar to but bigger than the one Federico and Giulietta had occupied before. (The couple had abandoned their apartment on via Archimede, planning instead to live in Fregene forever.) Even though he'll change his mind when real problems start to arise on the film, Federico first casts the story in a realistic setting and plans for minimal props. Here's a list of the settings he imagines:

"airports, train stations, subways, ports, modern streets and old city streets, marshes, the beach, and then neighborhoods in Rome, New York, Amsterdam, Berlin, the Vatican, little towns in Lazio, and Venice . . ." Imagining the ruinous calculations that such a list would spark in the mind of a producer, the director rushes to qualify that he's thinking of "economical" sets. As with 8½, Fellini has a hard time settling on the profession of G. Mastorna (the G. stands for Giuseppe) and ends up deciding that he plays the cello, "the precious instrument with the womanly hips." But he could also be "a businessman like you, dear Dino," writes Fellini, "I mean a person who's busy trying to make something of his life, someone full of enthusiasm and resources." Maybe this attempt to seduce the producer by identifying him with the protagonist is a little off the mark—after all, the movie tells the story of Mastorna after his death, and we can easily imagine that when De Laurentiis read this, he tried to shake off the jinx. Meanwhile his partners, brothers Luigi and Alfredo, like the movie a lot. This is one of the few times that the De Laurentiis brothers disagree about a project, for Luigi, who is interested in the occult, is particularly enthusiastic.

The letter goes on to describe the beginning of the movie: an airplane flies into a snowstorm, the pilot loses control, and the passengers panic. Then, suddenly, everything grows terribly quiet. They land silently in the square of an unknown city, in the shadow of a Gothic cathedral. The passengers dismount the plane into the wind and snow and walk down dimly lit streets to a bus. Fellini says that he will try to represent "an ineffable, mystical experience, [and] convey the feeling of totality," but he has no idea about the ending yet. Despite the morose subject, the director insists that the movie will be funny—regressing to the illusion he'd maintained on 8½.

The producer, who'd signed on for a science-fiction movie, has a perfectly good reason to reject the idea, but he doesn't. He still regrets having passed on *La dolce vita* and wants to avoid making the same mistake. After mailing the letter to De Laurentiis, Fellini travels to Milan to meet the other Dino and to talk about the story. But it seems that the best part of this new relationship has already played itself out. Federico realizes that Buzzati's robust narrative lines and his tendency to structure even situations that are mysteriously uncontextualized don't cohere with his own ideas of an indeterminate and allusive cinema. They forge forward nonetheless, are cordial, and try to work with what they have in common, diplomatically ignoring what they don't.

For decades Fellini would be very reserved when discussing *Il viaggio di G. Mastorna*, for two somewhat paradoxical reasons. First, he continued to think that he would make the movie one day and therefore kept the plot a secret. Second, a kind of superstitious fear had crept into the project. Every so often, in a moment of confusion, the director would list the misfortunes surrounding *Il viaggio di G. Mastorna*, including the losses suffered along the constant detour, and entertain shocking fantasies about what could come out of it.

The screenplay reveals the seeds of several movies that Fellini would go on to make, for, once the project failed, the director would use bits and pieces of it in other films: The dirty, alienating motel invented for *Mastorna*, for example, appears in *Ginger e Fred*. The story posits a dreamlike atmosphere reminiscent of settings and scenes we'll see in *Amarcord*: the old school, the Fulgor, the priest who teaches religion and then turns up in a police station, the philosophy professor De Cercis, and Margherita (aka Bianchina), the girl next door, in addition to the familial scene where the father dictates an order ("Brunello Casati, Cesena, 400 kilos of coffee, 10 bags of rice, 200 kilos of jam . . .") and then lectures the hero on how wrong it is to pursue a career as an artist and how essential it is to find steady work while the mother repeats, "You'll make me die of a heart attack."

Gathered around a U-shaped table, Mastorna's entire entourage both reflects and becomes fodder for the director. Later, Mastorna will see a film of his life, starting with himself as a fetus. His passport to another, better world (Paradise?) will be conceded to him only after he watches himself on the screen, caught in the act of sticking his tongue out at a dog through a car window while stopped in traffic. The crowd around the table claps: this is the most personal gesture that the protagonist has made in his entire life.

At last, Mastorna heads for the airport (on a bus quite similar to the one Ginger arrives on), where he finds a man and a woman, friendly parents, demonstrating such total forgiveness that any kind of relationship might be possible between the three travelers, even a homosexual one, though the screenplay does not suggest it. After this final flight, the airplane lands in a valley surrounded by tall mountains. Two customs officials are there. (Fellini wanted the comedians Franco Franchi and Ciccio Ingrassia to play these parts; Ingrassia will play the crazy uncle in *Amarcord*.) A stewardess (the singer Mina if Fellini had gotten his way) leads Mastorna through the cold, bright night. The journey concludes in Florence, with Mastorna walking; it's a beautiful sunny day and he's anxious to be on time for an orchestra rehearsal. The mandala of his life has come around again after death—Mastorna has been to Hell and back.

Driven forward on this project by the emotion of Dr. Bernhard's recent death, *Il viaggio di G. Mastorna* is Fellini's destination at the end of a tormented road. It's a metaphor that extends the meaning of 8½ and *Giulietta degli spiriti* in a breath of cosmic serenity: accepting yourself, befriending yourself, or simply living requires accepting the past, present, and future, as well as welcoming death as you welcome life. One without the other is senseless.

But why wasn't this film ever made? Sometimes Fellini would speak of a "thick fog with undefined and threatening parameters." He would remember having felt, over the course of those two years, a sensation of inadequacy. Perhaps the film had entered his subconscious as a final "testament," complete with all of the sinister implications borne by a word in some sense final. Perhaps Federico was unhappy to have arrived somewhere and preferred instead to keep looking. Perhaps, as he so often said, he preferred the journey to the arrival.

In the late spring of 1966, production manager Luigi De Laurentiis hires Pier Luigi Pizzi for the art direction of the film. In June, they start scouting locations in Naples and Milan. Fellini had already been to Köln with his cinematographer, Giuseppe Rotunno, and shot the cathedral. Rather than working in Dinocittà, which he claims he doesn't like, calling it "a space station, an inaccessible checkpoint," Fellini opts to work alone in a small office at via Nazionale 36, where he begins the usual ritual of looking for faces. But then it's time to return to via Pontina, where Pizzi has built the central set—a square with a dome like the one in Köln—and to other locations. The director plans with Rotunno to shoot the movie in a black-and-white just barely dusted with dim colors. Even the costumes, more than 2,000 of them, should be gray, pitiful, and ashen.

The characters who will wear them should also represent all origins and extractions—the wardrobe manager has an enormous task before him. Fellini even wants Slavic extras, as they will give the crowd scenes in the movie an indefinable ethnicity.

The director is in an awful mood during this period. He keeps insisting that he doesn't want to make the movie anymore, but those who worked on 8½ have seen this before. One day, Fellini is alone in an office on via della Vasca Navale when he has an inexplicable and terrifying daydream. For a moment, he feels as if the cathedral of Köln is collapsing on him, brick by brick, and when he wakes, he realizes that he's leaped four meters across the room. The episode leaves him baffled and frightened.

In the meantime, the hunt for the lead actor had turned almost pathological. No Marcello Mastroianni: Fellini doesn't want to repeat himself, and must explicitly counter the opinion that *Mastorna* stands for *Mastroianni ritorna* (The Return of Mastroianni). Marcello isn't available, anyway. Since January he's been playing Rudolph Valentino in the successful musical *Ciao, Rudy* at the Sistina, and has been scheduled to return in the fall season. Federico is openly jealous that Mastroianni is acting for someone else; he thinks that his alter ego is being deviant, writes the behavior off as a workplace casualty, and tries to convince his friends not to go applaud him. There are other candidates for the part, like Laurence Olivier, but Fellini doesn't want him for the same reasons he didn't want him on 8½. Steve McQueen might be good, but he doesn't know him personally and he doesn't want to be committed to such a famous actor. Giorgio Strehler, who became Valentina Cortese's consort after she separated from Richard Basehart, and who is part of Fellini's clique, is secretly quite anxious to land the role. Fellini likes Strehler, though he hasn't seen all his plays, but it doesn't occur to him that he might want to be in the movie. Giorgio doesn't hold it against him; instead, he becomes one of Fellini's biggest fans, an actor who will go on to re-create some of the maestro's characters and situations for the stage. In the 1990s, toward the end of his life, this giant of theater will futilely propose his movie-directing debut by making *Il viaggio di G. Mastorna*.

In August, Federico's bad mood degenerates into an honest-to-goodness intolerance for Dinocittà—and, to make matters worse, he's realized that he actually does want Mastroianni for Mastorna. Fortunately, the actor is prepared to abandon the musical and even pay a hefty fine for breaking the contract. Fellini retreats to Fregene and will talk only to his assistant director, Liliana Betti, and Pizzi, both of whom are growing increasingly worried about the state of things. He tells them, "Let's slow down; we can make the movie somewhere else." Some people say that Rol the magician left a note in Fellini's pocket: "Don't make this movie." Dino De Laurentiis remains calm, however. He thinks Federico is just "a big baby who believes in the paranormal," and that things will get better soon.

On September 14, Fellini records a nightmare in his book. A train leaves at 8:30 (a reference to 8½, perhaps?), and, even though Fellini was at the station an hour beforehand, he misses it—just like Mastorna. The director manages to jump on one of the landing steps and cling dangerously to the outside of the speeding train, but he can't jump off, and he can't open the doors to get inside. The last word is "Help!" It might have been this dream that drives Federico to send a letter by registered mail that very day to De Laurentiis explaining his loss of enthusiasm for the film.

14 September 1966, Rome

Dear Dino,

I must tell you something that I've been struggling with for a long time and only now have reached a conclusion about. It is a serious decision and I don't mean to be dramatic about it, but it is the only honest answer for my spirit, which is tired of this ongoing attempt to placate deeper and truer feelings because of an implied feeling of obligation to friendship. I can't start this movie, because after everything that's happened, I couldn't make it. Don't misunderstand me. I have no doubts about the movie itself. But a long series of oppositional signs have been plaguing this film, from its conception to its development—in an atmosphere of obstruction and stagnation. I'm disarmed and exhausted. Under such conditions, I cannot make my movie.

As if it had been prophecy, De Laurentiis behaves just like the producer at the end of 8½, who threatens: "I'll ruin you if you don't make this movie." In the meantime, De Laurentiis releases a public statement explaining that, after a year of preparation, they were going to start *Assurdo universo* on September 5, but have postponed the production to October 3, because the director is unwell. In the meantime, "gigantic sets" have been mounted at Dinocittà and on via della Vasca Navale and the cost of the movie has gone up to 600 million lire (part of which is the 45 percent director's fee, already paid). Later that same day De Laurentiis receives Fellini's letter and decides to take legal action. He claims he's lost 1.1 billion lire: 600 million in expenses and 500 million in lost profit. There is a note claiming that due to Fellini's irresponsible behavior, seventy people will lose their jobs. A special court judge awards De Laurentiis a settlement for 350 million. On September 24, agents show up at the Fregene house with an order to confiscate "several paintings and art objects." The next day, newspapers report that "nonetheless the price of the settlement hasn't been reached." Exasperated, De Laurentiis persists; he wants to put a lien on all monies owed to Fellini, principally by Rizzoli.

Boarded up in his house, Federico doesn't talk to the press, and Dino is otherwise occupied with preparations for the opening of *The Bible* on October 11 at the San Carlo in Naples. Such a big hometown success somewhat mitigates his fury, which continues to be directed at Fefè (Fellini)—even though his brother Luigi is attempting to convince him to see the situation in a less tragic light. Dino is beginning to think that he went overboard with the confiscation, an act that hurt Giulietta more than Federico. After all, if De Laurentiis is the "Italian DeMille," as *Life* magazine claimed, then Fellini is the most important director in the world.

Then the newspapers announce that Fellini has founded a new company, Fulgor Film, and that American studios have started to express interest in producing *Il viaggio di G. Mastorna*. In early February 1967, Federico flies to London and announces that he's seeing English actors. He adds that, because Mastroianni is not available (he committed to a Luchino Visconti project called *Puccini*, one that will never be made), he has chosen Enrico Maria Salerno for the lead. (The actor had competed with Alain Cuny for the part of Steiner in *La dolce vita*.) De Laurentiis, worried now, sends his lawyers out to try to broker a deal. The reconciliation between producer and director happens one foggy morning at Villa Borghese. Dino and Federico both arrive with their legal escorts—they look like Mafia bosses—but the lawyers remain in the car while the two embattled friends walk alone to the appointed meeting place, and then continue strolling side by side. They walk back and forth several times, talking heatedly and waving their hands. Then they stop and hug. The lawyers cheerfully leap from their cars and immediately set about translating the hug into legalese. According to De Laurentiis, however, the meeting took place during an endless car drive.

Starting shooting at this point turns out to be very problematic, as most of the crew is now already engaged on other projects and must be replaced. The biggest problem is the lead, because for De Laurentiis, Salerno is just not well known enough. The producer is still fantasizing about an American actor for the film, but they'll have to start shooting on April 20—May 15 at the absolute latest—and it's unrealistic to think they can get a star like Oskar Werner, Gregory Peck, or Paul Newman in that time. Dino and Federico engage in circular discussions around the matter and some anger emerges over the fact that Federico has already announced his next project, *Satyricon*, with De Laurentiis's competitor Franco Cristaldi, and with Alberto Sordi as Trimalcione. In the end, Federico agrees to cast Ugo Tognazzi as the lead in *Il viaggio di G. Mastorna*, and the actor signs the contract in March.

Tognazzi is at the height of his career, yet enormously gratified at the prospect of starring in a Fellini film. He admits to a journalist, "I was so happy. All I could think was, who should I tell? So I called my dad." Even though Tognazzi is another actor who grew up under the spell of variety, Fellini is not entirely happy with him as his protagonist; he thinks his cello player should have a crazed, neurotic glint in his eyes. He had harbored the hope that Tognazzi would reject the offer or be too busy to accept, so that the director would have had more time to think.

Eventually, the Fellinis leave Fregene—life was impossible there (too humid)—and go to live in the Grand Hotel in Rome's Eur neighborhood. Dinocittà is close by. But as the moment to start filming approaches, Fellini grows nervous and is barely sleeping. He starts to record crazy dreams in his book, full of stop signs, barriers, level crossings, customs stations, catastrophes, and the word for "good luck," *auguri,* split down the middle.

On Monday, April 10, 1967, *La strada* is broadcast on television (RAI 2). That night, Federico isn't feeling well. He had contracted bronchitis while walking by the sea in Fregene and he's preoccupied because the next week he's scheduled to go with Alfredo De Laurentiis to check out final locations in Bologna, Naples, and Stuttgart. Giulietta is watching the movie at her sister's house, and the director is in bed. A doctor wearing a tuxedo comes to give him an injection to loosen the mucus. At ten, Fellini feels an unbearable pain in his back and chest, and collapses onto the floor while reaching for the phone. The last thing he remembers thinking is that he should write a note to put on the door: "Giulietta, don't come in if you're alone." He remains unconscious on the carpet for a long time, inhaling so much dust that he'll develop an allergy that, over time, will often make him feel as if he's suffocating. When he regains consciousness he feels totally lost, as if he were on the ocean floor. He remembers that he could hear someone trying to break down the door, then come into the room and lift him; he understands that he's being taken down the stairs and through a hallway full of elegantly dressed people. Obviously there's some sort of party. Fortunately, the doctor in his tuxedo is there too, and Fellini is put in the doctor's car. They drive away. There's a violent stop, and a crashing sound, and through the window, Fellini can see a yellow traffic light and hear people arguing. He can hear the doctor saying in a stern voice, "Let me through, there's a man dying in my car." Federico is still feeling the pain when competent hands lift him onto a cot and then he's inside a clinic, where they start to administer CPR; he's in a quiet, dimly lit room, and the pain abates once they've given him a tranquilizer.

On Wednesday, April 12, *Il Messaggero* reports his emergency hospitalization: "It's being said in the art world that Fellini suffered a severe respiratory problem, pleurisy, or a traumatic pleuropneumonia." De Laurentiis is obviously skeptical and sends out a team of his doctors to investigate (just as in a Molière play), but the doctors return with long faces and bad news. They think it's cancer and Dino weeps. Meanwhile, in room 105 on the first floor of the clinic Salvator Mundi on the Gianicolo hill in Rome, hundreds of telegrams are arriving, despite the "do not disturb" sign on the door. Angelo Rizzoli shows up with a bunch of roses, as full of trepidation and affection as if he were Federico's own father. He's forgiven him everything. Marcello, Strehler, and Titta Benzi also come. Each one is allowed to stay for only a few minutes. Others arrive to express their regrets, heads lowered, pausing at the doorway—even former friends turned enemies, like Piero Gherardi. The mere fact that Gherardi shows up makes Federico realize how sick he must be. He receives a message from Pope Paul VI, who seems to have forgotten that, as bishop of Milan just a few years ago, he refused to see Fellini, the public sinner of *La dolce vita*.

Some people insist that it's just a tactical illness, a way to get out of making the movie, but alarm spreads. Newspapers start commissioning Fellini's obituary. But after endless analyses (apparently he underwent 128 X-rays in seven hours), the official diagnosis is comforting: acute pleurisy. After a few days, Fellini is strong enough to smile at the news that De Laurentiis has been hospitalized in the meantime for appendicitis. On April 20, he records the dream he had on the first night in the hospital in his Dream Book: a man is swallowed up by an elastic breathing tube; he doesn't get mashed or crushed, but the director thinks, "When will I see him again?" On May 3, he dictates a business letter to De Laurentiis: he will start shooting in August unless he doesn't get a clean bill of health at his checkup scheduled for June 15.

The producer agrees that Federico's health is the most important thing for the moment, but his recovery is slow. Then Ercole Sega, an old school friend from Rimini who has become an important physician, comes by for a visit. He takes one look at Fellini's chart and comes up with another diagnosis. Fellini is suffering from Saranelli-Schwarzmann syndrome. Although the doctors at the clinic are skeptical, they begin treating him for Saranelli-Schwarzmann; he starts getting better right away and is able to leave the clinic soon after.

He goes to Manziana to recover, where he is visited by Paul Newman, who De Laurentiis sent in to discuss possibly working in *Il viaggio di G. Mastorna*. In the meantime, Tognazzi reads in the newspaper that Fellini is actually suffering from *tognazzite*—an allergy to Tognazzi—and, scared, threatens to sue. After a period spent relatively worry free in Manziana—where he starts putting down on paper some of his memories to be published later in *La mia Rimini* (My Rimini) and which will be the basis of *Amarcord*—Fellini moves to Fiuggi. Meanwhile, from his top-floor office suite, Dino De Laurentiis can still see the dome of the Köln cathedral lording over the Dinocittà studio. He worries that *Il viaggio di G. Mastorna* will never be made. On August 21, 1967, Fellini is healthy enough to sign a three-movie, five-year contract with De Laurentiis that will take the place of *Il viaggio di G. Mastorna*. The contract also accounts for the more than 500 million lire already invested in the project, which Fellini will have to repay. It's a mess, but what else can they do? On the same day, Federico has a strange dream, but not really a nightmare, in which he's "decapitated while driving" in an attempt to save some children. He will, in fact, save his movies-to-be (his children) by beheading the driver (Mastorna), as well as *Toby Dammit*, the character in an Edgar Allan Poe adaptation about a man who bets his head with the devil.

This new, adventurous idea starts where *Mastorna* ends: born, as usual, in the amusing accidental manner typical to Fellini. One summer day in 1967, at his house in Eur, a man named Grimaldi requests a meeting with Fellini. Federico, assuming the man is just there to harass him, replies that he's not in. But Alberto Grimaldi, a lawyer from Naples, just like De Laurentiis, has an idea and he won't back off. He waits for the director out in the hallway and introduces himself as a businessman who has already had some movie experience, having produced a couple of successful Westerns with Sergio Leone. He wants to make a movie with Fellini now. The director can make any movie he wants. Even *Mastorna*? Why not? But that movie belongs to De Laurentiis, and in order to secure the rights, Grimaldi would have to shell out hundreds of millions. Grimaldi is unruffled: Let's see what we can do. He thinks that producing a Fellini film is worth some sacrifices. Half an hour later, the two men are already talking about personal matters: Fellini's illness, their families, and life in general. They quickly form a friendly relationship, a genuine sympathy that will survive time as well as some calamitous crises.

Fellini calls on Enzo Provenzale, an old friend/enemy from *Lo sceicco blanco*, in an attempt to figure out what can be done with the aborted movie. The set is still in Dinocittà, but could be used there. The budget would have to be updated, but shouldn't be too high. Basically, Provenzale, a confirmed pessimist, concludes that it can be done. De Laurentiis has grown very nervous in the meantime, and he's jealous that another Neapolitan is stealing Fefè from him. He's also a little shocked at how much money Grimaldi is willing to pay for the project. On September 13, De Laurentiis hands down an ultimatum: they have to buy the movie by

September 25, they have to pay 435 million lire up front, and they must compensate Tognazzi in full for his contract.

Grimaldi goes to Dinocittà to pay off De Laurentiis, becoming the new owner of *Mastorna*. When De Laurentiis has the check in his hands, according to Federico, he falls to his knees, shouting, "Saint Gennaro does exist and he's standing before me and his name is Alberto Grimaldi." He will later add, "Not even Saint Gennaro managed to perform the real miracle of getting Fellini to make that movie." Now there are no more obstacles. Everything is set to go. The American producers read the screenplay and sign on; Provenzale redraws the budget and begins setting up the shooting schedule. Designer Mario Chiari is busy planning some adjustments to the set. Mastroianni is free again and happy to be onboard. Then Fellini takes off his mask: he *really* doesn't want to make the movie. In order to get out of it he offers a series of alternative projects to Grimaldi, all of which are intriguing: the history of the Merovingian Dynasty, something from Giovanni Boccaccio, or *Orlando furioso*, or perhaps the adaptation of *Satyricon*, which he'd already been plotting out with Franco Cristaldi. Grimaldi is up for anything; the only condition being that his troublesome hire shapes up, chooses a project, and starts working. The dilemma, as we'll see, is resolved more quickly than expected when an offer comes in from France and *Il viaggio di G. Mastorna* is pushed aside again.

The next year, after Fellini has finished *Toby Dammit* (an episode in *Histoires extraordinaires*) and just before starting work on *Satyricon*, the director makes an "epitaph" to *Il viaggio di G. Mastorna*, a one-hour documentary, produced by Peter Goldfarb for NBC under the title *Fellini: A Director's Notebook*, in which he bids farewell to *Mastorna* and announces a new movie about ancient Rome.

A Director's Notebook begins on the scraggly lawn outside of Dinocittà. A bunch of hippies (it's 1968) are camped out in the shadow of the cathedral. It's clear from the first shots that the documentary is riffing on the Andy Warhol style popular at the time (Fellini always claims he doesn't watch other people's movies, but he's very informed about what's going on.) He has a friendly conversation with the hippies, but then Mastorna appears out of a windstorm, looking just like the director in black in 8½. A number of digressions follow: there's a scene in a warehouse in

Cinecittà, where the material for the set is piled up in storage; another one near the Colosseum, following the gimpy nightlife of the transvestites and gays. Giulietta introduces the man with the sack—the scene cut from *Le notti di Cabiria*. There's a silent-movie section about the Forum, and other funny clips about ancient Rome, which are being shown in a 1920s style theater. A child is there, watching, dressed as a sailor and sitting on his father's lap. Montage that it is, *A Director's Notebook* definitively links Fellini's previous work to the new movie *Satyricon*. Federico goes around the catacombs under the Appia Antica with his new writer Bernardino Zapponi to "listen to the dead," a Gothic and disturbing ritual that people actually participated in. Another scene of ancient Romans walking through the tunnels was shot through a subway window. An enactment of the rape of the Sabine is also included, in which truck drivers kidnap some costumed prostitutes and take them out to a field. Another scene visits Mastroianni in his new house in Porta San Sebastiano on via Appia (his real house). After some joking around, Marcello dons Mastorna's costumes and pretends to play the cello. At the end of the documentary, there is a visit to a slaughterhouse in pursuit of "dark, bloody atmospheres and typical Roman ferocity"; a lineup of strange, dangerous-looking faces Fellini is considering for *Satyricon*; and a screen test with the American actor Martin Potter, who will play Encolpio. This disorderly but intelligent adventure ends with Rota's march from *8½*, and receives some interest from American audiences. It shows a bold Fellini, a director who enjoys little gimmicks while admitting that really big stunts are mysteries to him as well—just like when the magician in *8½* reveals to Marcello that "there's something" in the magic that even he doesn't understand.

A Director's Notebook isn't the solution to the problem of *Il viaggio di G. Mastorna*, however. Between one contract and another, though, Fellini manages to repay Grimaldi; he finally owns the rights entirely in 1971. In 1976, after *Il Casanova*, he starts talking about resurrecting *Mastorna* with writer Tonino Guerra, but a refined and updated resurrection. Yet once again the director runs into obstacles that he takes to be coded warnings not to proceed. One day while he's discussing the story with Tonino in an office on via Sistina, he receives a phone call relaying bad news, at which point he closes the screenplay, then throws it into a cupboard and locks the door. He won't talk again about the film that, once upon a time, Buzzati had wanted to call *La dolce morte* (The Sweet Death). In an interview, Federico would conclude that "*Mastorna*, like the relic of a sunken ship at the bottom of the sea, would nurture all my movies that came after."

31

Edgar Allan F.
Histoires extraordinaires, Toby Dammit

The solution to the problem of which movie to do with Alberto Grimaldi instead of *Il viaggio di G. Mastorna*, as we've already said, came from elsewhere, in the form of producer Raymond Eger. The Frenchman, who works with Les Films Marceau, asks Fellini to make an episode for his omnibus *Histoires extraordinaires*, based on the short stories of Edgar Allan Poe, boasting of having secured arrangements with Orson Welles, Joseph Losey, and Luchino Visconti—all of which, for one reason or another, fall through. Still, Fellini finds himself in the company of Louis Malle (*William Wilson*) and Roger Vadim (*Metzengerstein*) and Grimaldi agrees to coproduce Fellini's segment with the French studio. The director is happy to be working again on something short—essentially predigested and ready to go—after two years away from the set.

Now the problem is which Poe story to do. Eger proposes "The Tell-Tale Heart," the story of a murderer whose victim's heart continues to beat after he cuts the corpse into pieces and buries it under the floorboard. The director knows the story but can't imagine how to transform it for the screen, so he rents his first private office at via della Fortuna 27 and hires Liliane Betti to read and quickly sum up all of Poe's work. Summations in hand, he discusses various possibilities with Bernardino Zapponi, a writer whom he met through Goffredo Parise and who will go on to write many screenplays for him. Zapponi is forty and an expert in literary innovation. He's the editor in chief of the clever magazine *Il Delatore* (The Spy), and has just had a collection of stories, *Gobal*, published by Longanesi. Initially, Fellini thinks he might prefer to adapt one of Zapponi's stories instead of Poe—he goes so far as to have someone translate "L'autista" (The Driver), a story of a man who destroys a car he's paid to drive, into French and sends it to Eger—but the producer wants nothing to do with it. He wants Poe.

The search for the right story continues, though Fellini, rather than reading the complete works, relies instead on Betti's summaries. He becomes fascinated by "The Premature Burial," and thinks about setting it in Naples, having Alberto Sordi play the man plagued by a fear of being buried alive. But while he's scouting at night with Zapponi, they come across the bridge of Ariccia, recently collapsed, which reminds him of yet another story, "Never Bet the Devil Your Head." The tale is narrated in the first person by an apparently sympathetic, but ultimately quite cynical, character who complains about his friend Toby Dammit's tendency to say, "I'd bet the devil my head . . ." When the devil finally appears, he is an old man standing on one side of a bridge closed off by a gate. Toby bets his head that he can jump over the gate, but a sharp steel wire suspended in the air decapitates him and the devil wins the wager, taking Toby's head with him.

This time around, Fellini knows nothing but the movie's ending. He doesn't look for the rest of the film in Poe's story and won't actually read it until he's finished shooting. His thoughts turn again to Mastorna's journey through Hell and he reflects on his own personal memories—maybe he's reminded of Broderick Crawford's crazy behavior working on *Il bidone*—this time without the humor that he used to bring to the experience. Fellini develops his protagonist as an English actor, wavering between reality and hallucination, who's come to Rome to act in the first "Catholic Western," produced by a priest who is a satire of his former defender, Father Arpa. It takes the director and Zapponi only a few days to write the screenplay, with Peter O'Toole in mind for the lead. The actor is initially quite interested and very friendly when they meet in London, but when the former Lawrence of Arabia reads the screenplay in translation, he grows worried about being identified with the protagonist. O'Toole and Fellini end up exchanging insults over the phone: the former shouting "Fascist!" and the latter responding "Fuck you!" There is a crisis moment back in the office of P.E.A., the production company on Largo Ponchielli: they need to come up with a replacement—Richard Burton,

James Fox, or Terence Stamp. They go with Stamp, nicknaming him Terenzino Francobollo.* The choice is apt: they'll soon find in Stamp yet another friendly actor with a wild life, caught in the spiral of his own crises, which will eventually take him to the East (and far away from cinema) for a few years. Terenzino is also quite young, requiring work on his appearance, but the crew transforms him with ghastly makeup that has him resembling Poe himself.

The short film, thirty-seven minutes in length, is also Fellini's first with Giuseppe Rotunno, aka Peppino, who'd been contracted for *Mastorna* as well. Rotunno, born in Rome in 1923, is one of the great cinematographers of Italian cinema. He'd worked with G. R. Aldo on *Senso*, and Visconti was so pleased with his shots that, from that point on, he requested him for all of his movies, including *Rocco and His Brothers* and *Il gattopardo*. After working on *The Naked Maja*, he also became one of Ava Gardner's preferred cinematographers. Peppino will become indispensable to Federico for many years, until *E la nave va*. He's a friendly, quiet person, like Gianni Di Venanzo (though Rotunno has more experience with color), and he's not afraid of experimenting. His mantra while working with Fellini will always be: "I'm prepared for change." When shooting the night odyssey in *Toby Dammit*, Peppino and Fellini agree on an unusual visual approach, using colors somewhere between the red sunset of a Scipione† painting and dark black. In his collaboration with Rotunno, Federico discovers that the most difficult thing of all is trying to shoot in the dark. Darkness has a deepness that can determine the shape of things, the character's path. "We have to try to figure out the perspectives of darkness," the director keeps telling his cinematographer. In order to accomplish this, he needs Rotunno's expertise, for Peppino takes not only his own vision into account but also that of the audience, and knows what variables the lab can introduce as well.

Fellini's friends, the painters Fabrizio Clerici and Renzo Vespignani, help out on the set design, but in the end Piero Tosi, authoritative and lively, takes charge of the art direction. Just before they start filming, the

---

*Terenzino is a diminutive, Italianized version of Terence, while *francobollo* means postage stamp in Italian.

†Scipione (aka Gino Bonichi, 1906–1933) was a founder of the Scuola Romana.

indefatigable Dino De Laurentiis calls Fellini and floors him with the offer to direct *Waterloo*—Federico imagines himself a commanding general on the field of battle with a megaphone and trumpets, but the fantasy lasts only five minutes. He declines and returns to *Toby Dammit*, working energetically. The movie is shot in only twenty-six days, between late October and early January, partly on location and partly in studios at the Centro Sperimentale. During the edit, the director completely cuts a fifteen-minute episode of a Western-style film set that had been fun to shoot but ultimately was superfluous.

Toby Dammit, like *Il viaggio di G. Mastorna*, begins with an airplane landing. This time, instead of a deadly accident, there is the voice of the hero explaining, "It was my first time to Rome and I had the feeling that this would be an important trip in my life." The famous actor, Toby Dammit, is received by a throng of paparazzi, like Sylvia in *La dolce vita*, but there is no festive charade mood to it this time. The sunset at Fiumicino airport is spectral; the harsh flashing of the photographer's bulbs and Toby's violence in pushing the reporters away is hallucinatory. Under the influence of alcohol and drugs, the actor is fighting an enemy that only he can see: the devil in the form of a little girl, adding a pedophiliac slant to the character. Outside of a nightclub that resembles an expressionist version of the Caracalla Club from *La dolce vita*—complete with grotesque, creepy characters—Toby participates in an absurd awards ceremony. He delivers a confused speech, which opens with a monologue from *Macbeth*, and then he escapes into the night in the Ferrari he received as a gift from the producers of the movie he's come to shoot. After a wild drive, he ends up in front of a collapsed bridge; the little girl/devil reappears, taunting him into a trap that will cost him his head.

The producers are so pleased with the section that they initially consider taking it out of *Histoires extraordinaires* and filming another Fellini episode instead—he could adapt "A Predicament," the second part of "How to Write a Blackwood Article." Federico imagines setting it in Piazza del Campo in Siena, where an elderly English tourist goes up into the Torre del Mangia to watch the horse race. There's a little opening under the big clock and, when the woman sticks her head through it, the minute hand would catch her neck and slice off her head. In Poe's story, Fellini had been particularly taken with the moment in which the horrible pressure

of the minute hand pressing onto the woman's neck makes her eyes pop
out of their sockets one after the other. They could roll to the foot of
the tower and watch the rest of the scene from there. Federico goes to the
Villa Hotel in Frascati to meet with the English actress Dame Margaret
Rutherford, who plays Miss Marple in the Agatha Christie movies. Even
though it's dinnertime, the lady is wearing her swimming suit; she dives
into the pool and does several vigorous laps. Impressed, Fellini gets along
well with this athletic woman, and they make a deal. But as happens so
often in the movies, within a few days everything has changed. The producers decide that one movie about Poe is enough, and *Toby Dammit* is
back in the triptych as originally planned. *Histoires extraordinaires* opens
at Cannes on May 17, 1968, the last movie screened at the Palais. It's
May and the students of Paris are in revolt; the screening of Carlos
Saura's *Peppermint Frappé* was suspended because of public outrage.
Adding to the turmoil, there is so much noise from people disliking the
Poe movie that it's almost impossible to hear the positive reactions. The
audience doesn't like Vadim's *Metzengerstein*, based on Poe's first published
short story—Jane Fonda is miscast—and they don't like Malle's *William
Wilson*, staring Alain Delon and Brigitte Bardot, set in Bergamo. After
those, Fellini's piece is welcomed with some appreciation, to be echoed
in later reviews. When the movie opens the following season in Italy,
Fellini's episode again garners favorable reviews. Some people see it as
just an occasion to show off technical virtuosity in relation to formal perfectionism, but others detect new elements in the piece, a shift in stylistic approach. *Toby Dammit* looks like an episode extracted from *La dolce
vita*, but without either the tenderness or the exuberance. This narrative
comes out of a darker vision of life, on the heels of his frustration with
Mastorna and anxiety about his illness. In this flash of a story, Fellini expresses his emotions of the moment, the crisis of a man in middle age, as
well as his amazement at being a survivor, still standing next to a camera.
It is a wonderful dress rehearsal for a movie—for *Il viaggio di G. Mastorna*—the final performance of which is indefinitely postponed.

32

Journey into the Unknown
Fellini Satyricon

A ticket is 50,000 lire on the black market; lines in front of the Arena Theater start at three in the afternoon; extra midnight screenings are added at the Palazzo del Cinema to accommodate the throng—it's the opening of *Fellini Satyricon* on the last night of the 30th Venice Film Festival (Thursday, September 4, 1969) and, entourage and disciples in tow, Fellini is back in grand style. He's running from ten in the morning until late at night, dealing with the events and the PR with the fortitude and resigned cool of a successful artist. The press conference in the Sala Grande drew an unprecedented crowd, and Federico showed that he knew his business; he was charming, relaxed, and funny. Within a few minutes the mood shifted from slightly antagonistic to positive—as in *Julius Caesar*, people change their minds after hearing Mark Antony speak. Fellini is both clever and rather honest as he repeats that his film is a journey into the *sconosciutezza*—the unknowingness—pushing his neologism to emphasize the anomalousness of his *Satyricon*.

The audience at the opening agrees, receiving the film with somewhat stunned bewilderment. When the three hours are up, people demonstrate admiration, clap very little, and have an evident need to reflect on what they've seen. The next morning, the critics are prudent; they seem unwilling to pass judgment. Instead, they repeat the same old themes, with variations of tone from the enthusiastic to the tentative: they discuss Fellini's personal relationship with ancient culture, his oneiric vision, the masterful presentation of a filmic kaleidoscope. Many critics draw comparisons with *La dolce vita*, harking back to reviews of the earlier film which referenced Petronius's famous work. But there are no outright negative reactions this time around. The rampant moralizing of ten years ago seems to have passed out of fashion—thanks, in some respect, to Fellini himself.

Some critics venture to say that this Venice Film Festival revealed a new Fellini; the director, almost fifty now, has changed direction and burned bridges behind him in order to cross into this new territory. He has renounced his most natural abilities—to amuse and move, to win the audience over—and turned instead to more complicated questions: What were we like in the past? (Or, more to the point: Who are we? What will we be like in the future?) The goal of this movie, he says, is to "describe the life of ancient Romans the same way you might describe the natural habitat of, say, trout." Fellini had never read Petronius's work when he proposed to adapt it and signed the contract for the film. Rather it all started with an idea he'd had in 1940, while working at *Marc'Aurelio*, brainstorming with Marcello Marchesi over possible projects for Aldo Fabrizi. At the very last minute, Fellini had flirted with trying *Il viaggio di G. Mastorna* again, but Alberto Grimaldi loves *Satyricon* and prefers it. The result is a big-budget production envisioned as an austere, rationalist film.

The director aimed for total aesthetic detachment in order to distance the characters and their lives from contemporary moral judgment. He set hard limitations for himself: two unlikable protagonists, a cast of repugnant faces, dubbing so exaggerated that it looks like a technical flaw—all orchestrated to make the audience feel uncomfortable, to force people to look at history as an objective reality and from a completely alien perspective. Fellini says that *Satyricon* is a "sci-fi movie about the past"; it should be as if the audience had emerged, surprised, from a time machine to observe the ancient Romans. In this way, Fellini has made his most personal movie yet, codified in psychoanalytic terms.

It's useless to speculate on whether *Fellini Satyricon* is an authentic reflection of the decaying Roman world, or even simply Petronius's take on it. The least surprising parts of Fellini's film are those that offer historical connections, albeit embryonic, such as the emperor's murder and the consequent suicide of the two nobles in the country villa (a link to the Steiner episode in *La dolce vita*). *Satyricon* can be compared to Antonin Artaud's work *Héliogabale, ou l'anarchiste couronné* (*Heliogabalus:*

Or, The Crowned Anarchist, 1934), in that the film "help[s] the readers forget the history they learned." Fellini's fantastical inventiveness is on full display in his depiction of the grotesque wedding on Suburra (Alain Cuny plays the tyrant Lichas in the bridal veil, a part that Danny Kaye refused), as well as in the fight between Encolpio and the fake Minotaur. The atmosphere is almost always sickly and claustrophobic. Some critics compare the film to Giovanni Pastrone's 1914 silent film *Cabiria* (which featured intertitles by Gabriele d'Annunzio), suggesting that *Satyricon* is really the "nights" of Cabiria. Others correctly note the references to the world of comic strips, such as *Little Nemo* and *Flash Gordon*.

Until Fellini made *Satyricon*, people had thought of him as a *vitellone* who'd made good in the big city, someone who was just curious about the laziness of rich people, a reflective, slightly exhibitionistic director who liked to confess himself in public. The Fellini who presently interprets Petronius is now an adult who's suffered, and his desire to have fun and entertain seems to have evaporated. Seeing this latest movie, some feel nostalgia for the carefree days of *I vitelloni*, when things were only tinged with melancholy. But now Federico is more concerned with things he hasn't personally lived through: the remote past, the inexplicable, the stuff of dreams.

The director comes to Petronius's work timidly and brazenly at the same time. The timidness comes out of a past as an inattentive student who never managed after eight years of classical studies to learn enough Latin to be able to read it. The brazenness is a mark that the project will be successful. Benedetto Croce used to say that a translation can be "ugly and faithful to the original, or beautiful and unfaithful." The director makes a decision to read the book in a personal vein. It's a peculiar book, rather a mysterious fragment that some scholars claim was written during Nero's empire (some time before A.D. 69); others say it was written between the second and third century. Some say the author was Petronius Arbiter, while others assert that it was written by another, unknown Petronius. There is debate over the length, which some think represents only hefty fragments of a still longer project, while others posit that it was never actually a long book. Among this last group is the Latinist Luca Canali, Fellini's consultant, who warns him about antiquated counterfeit translations that fearfully try to mask the openly erotic content of the original. *Satyricon* itself, which might have been more explicit had it been made today, adopts a nuanced lexicon and avoids extreme situations.

The first major liberty Fellini takes is to set the action predominantly in Rome, while in Petronius's tale, everything happens in the provinces—the cities of Magna Grecia, quite different from the capital. In the original, it would seem that the story starts in Marseille, where Encolpio, sort of a hippie before his time, has offended the god Priapus, who is seeking revenge. But in the fragment that's survived, the story starts in medias res, in a city in Campania, where Encolpio has just arrived after a difficult passage on Lichas's merchant ship. The traveler is angry with his friend Ascilto for having stolen the love of young Gitone. The three attend a banquet at the house of Trimalcione, a flashy *nouveau riche* (the longest section in the fragment); Gitone leaves the party with Ascilto. Crushed, Encolpio makes friends with the old poet Eumolpo (a character not unlike Garrone-Gattone in *Moraldo in città*), but he, too, finds himself succumbing to the charms of Gitone, who, in the meantime, has come back home to roost. Having dispensed for the moment with Ascilto, Encolpio and Gitone board a ship for Taranto, but the ship, which also belongs to the merchant Lichas, is wrecked. They end up in Crotone, a city of greedy men looking for legacies. The two boys pretend that old Eumolpo is a rich businessman who has no heir. Meanwhile, a local noblewoman, Circe, has fallen in love with Encolpio, who finds himself in a conflict worthy of Stendhal when the vengeful Priapus renders him impotent. Eumolpo's lies are revealed, unfortunately, but the poet gets out of trouble by writing a will dictating that anyone who wants his money will have to eat his dead body. And the fragment ends here.

> For *Satyricon*, and then later again for *Il Casanova*, the hardest thing was to invent everything, from the big picture to the details, from the basic meaning of the movie to the faces to the smallest details of each scene. We build it all and then stand back to see it with total detachment. Your dreams belong to you but they have something foreign about them, they move you and surprise you. This is the trick of building a city and then walking through it as if by accident.

When talking about *Satyricon*, the director always notes how profoundly different it is from his previous films. Every movie before the crisis with *Il viaggio di G. Mastorna* and his illness comes out of inspiration, but with

Toby Dammit, and even more with *Satyricon*, Fellini learns he can make movies both on commission and just by choice.

In 1968, once Fellini and Grimaldi set *Mastorna* aside, they embark instead on a lush, customized film inspired by market calculations and aiming for the American audience (why not?). At least, this is what Fellini thinks he's doing. Over a relatively short period, seven months of development and preparation with only *Fellini: A Director's Notebook* as distraction, Fellini reads a number of books about the ancient Roman world and interviews historians and Latinists, such as the famous Ettore Paratore, who confuses the matter by setting Fellini off onto a highly academic track. Fellini writes the screenplay with Bernardino Zapponi and draws hundreds of faces and scenes. His goal is to achieve a portrait of the Roman world that goes beyond the false information in history books, and what remains of the Rome of emperors now, in the heart of this decrepit capital that the filmmaker has chosen to make his spiritual home. Instinctively, Fellini looks for the descendants of the ancient Romans among the workers in slaughterhouses, the Gypsies camped on the outskirts of the city, the salt-of-the-earth people in the periphery, the peasants. He doesn't want to shoot landscapes or ruins; he wants everything to be a reproduction with very little actually being shot outside of the studio—just the scenes on the sea and a few others. This is the biggest studio production in Cinecittà after *Ben-Hur*.

For the first time, the director has his own place, an apartment in cinema city. He lives like an athlete in training, waking at seven to exercise and getting massages under the direction of his trainer Ettore Bevilacqua, a former boxer. To keep the pupil fit—he should weigh 89 kilos (about 196 pounds) for his height of 1.9 meters (or six foot two)—Bevilacqua has him on a strict diet: no pasta at lunch, just grilled steak, salad, and fruit. Fellini has always been a tireless worker, and is even more so now. He labors day and night, like a condemned man, determined and hard on himself. He feels like an artisan who's discovered that the meaning of life lies in doing his job well. He insists that *Satyricon* is only partially about him; at its core, the director muses, it is "a movie I don't want to be friends with."

The idea is to round up a cast of big names: Terence Stamp (again) as Encolpio, Pierre Clémenti as Ascilto, Gert Fröbe (aka Goldfinger) as Tri-

malcione, Van Heflin as Eumolpo, and so forth. They soon realize, however, that most of those actors are not only unavailable but also very expensive. The movie must instead be sold on Fellini's name; the correct
thing to do in this case would be to let him cast as he wants, as long as he
doesn't spend too much, but with a preference for English actors since
they're planning to dub the movie in English in London. Based on head
shots, the director chooses two young, cheap actors: Hiram Keller, a veteran of the play *Hair*, as Ascilto, and Martin Potter as Encolpio. The only
actor who receives a higher salary than the Englishmen is Salvo Randone
(playing Eumolpo), who has a special relationship with Fellini and is
even allowed to avoid learning his lengthy lines by heart (they're going to
change everything while dubbing anyway). The director plans to have
him dubbed by Adolfo Geri—a great insult to the stage actors. The denouncement of Trimalcione proves a particularly complicated scene to
shoot and, due to all the camera angles, Fellini would prefer that Randone just recite numbers, but, defending his theatrical dignity, the actor
instead recites a monologue from Pirandello's *Henry IV*.

Fellini had wanted Boris Karloff, the Monster from *Frankenstein*,
to play Trimalcione, but the actor regretfully declines because of his
health—he'll die later in 1969. Mario Romagnoli, nicknamed "the Moor,"
wins the part. He has a trattoria on Vicolo delle Bollette between two
places very close to Fellini's heart, the Galleria Colonna and the Trevi
Fountain. Romagnoli is hugely honored—a big photo of him as Trimalcione still hangs in his restaurant—but has trouble getting used to the
world and pacing of the movies. He can't remember his lines and is too
embarrassed to recite numbers, so he asks to recite the menu instead.
Luigi Visconti from Bologna (stage name Fanfulla—one of Fellini's favorite variety actors) comes on to play the actor Vernacchio, but he's
scandalized by his ancestral colleague's vulgarity and wants to tone down
the part. The cast comes from everywhere—even more diverse than
usual for Fellini—for he wants strong features, matrons, lunatic homo-
sexuals, small monsters, and the elderly extracted from their rest homes.
He often selects people who already look like cartoons, but is still extremely demanding about the makeup; he counts on Piero Tosi to transform his actors.

Satyricon marks the first movie Fellini will do with Danilo Donati, who is from the first an invaluable collaborator, and one with whom Fellini will continue to work for years to come. Donati, born in 1926, is from Suzzara, near Mantova. He did costume design for Visconti's big stage productions and for variety shows. He also worked for television on *Canzonissima* and *Il Vangelo secondo Matteo* (*The Gospel According to Saint Matthew*, 1964) with Pier Paolo Pasolini, and will win an Oscar for his costumes on Franco Zeffirelli's *Romeo and Juliet* (1968). Federico is delighted to be working with such a sophisticated, cultured costume designer who also knows the art of getting a lot from a little. This new friend shares Fellini's passion for last-minute obstacles, a wicked pleasure in making rags look valuable, and the habit of staying behind the scenes and working quickly without wasting time on arguments. Donati's designs for the costumes and scenography (from drawings by Fellini) are in complete synchronicity with Fellini's taste for non-architectonic visuals that rely on framing and light.

Federico is increasingly of the opinion that, unless you are working under the strict influence of realism, in cinema you don't need to recreate things in order to represent them—you need only allude to them, as in a dream. "Image is a symbol," he said, "and reality has no symbols— you have to make them. This is precisely what painters do." Donati loves painting, and is an artist himself. His synergy with Fellini is an unspoken code that no one else can decipher. The director envies Danilo the many years he worked in television on *Canzonissima* and admires his professional efficiency—"He's a great connoisseur of art in the body of a variety-show dresser." Whatever happens, the show must go on.

When Fellini starts work on *Satyricon*, Alfredo Bini, another producer who'd registered the title in 1962, decides to push up his movie to compete. Grimaldi tries to stop him with a lawsuit and loses. And so the P.E.A. production will be called *Fellini Satyricon*, distinguishing it from the one produced by Arco Film S.r.L. The second *Satyricon*, directed by Gian Luigi Polidoro, is an undisguised attack, shot in Sperlonga for a quarter of Fellini's budget. It's a repeat of the rivalry between *Luci del varietà* and Carlo Ponti's *Vita da cani*, and again, there are many Felliniesque elements in the competing film. The screenplay was written by Riccardo Aragno, an old housemate from via Nicotera, with Rodolfo Sonego, a former candidate for production by Federiz. Ugo Tognazzi—

still enraged over the *Mastorna* ("I lost a year like a fool," he tells journalists)—is Trimalcione. Franco Fabrizi, whom Federico hasn't called since *Il bidone* (and who will remain in Fellini quarantine until *Ginger e Fred*), plays Ascilto. Mario Carotenuto, yet another former colleague who had a terrible falling-out with Fellini over *Giulietta degli spiriti*, plays Eumolpo. Some people even speculate that Bini managed to secure distribution by Angelo Rizzoli on account of another vendetta: Rizzoli still adores Fellini, but he doesn't mind irking the "dear artist" who betrayed him with not one but two Neapolitan producers—De Laurentiis and Grimaldi. Polidoro's *Satyricon*, a funny, melancholic movie, was made quickly and released in April 1969. Fellini was still working on his. The film did well at the box office—Polidoro even received a complimentary letter from Michelangelo Antonioni—but the distribution was soon halted by a court order on an obscenity charge.

Filming on *Fellini Satyricon* commences on November 9, 1968, in Studio 2 in Cinecittà, right after a party held under a wall decorated with paintings and graffiti by Antonio Scordia where Encolpio performs the opening monologue. It's finished in late May 1969. Enzo Provenzale, the general manager, ends up spending only half of the projected five billion lire budget—thanks in part to Fellini, who manages this time to stick to the script and keep on schedule. It's a cast and crew of more than 100, but at least 270 are involved on a daily basis. This is more or less the order of the scenes shot: Vernacchio; young Enotea (set in Maccarese); the villa of the suicides; old Enotea; the hermaphrodite (shot in early January); Suburra; Trimalcione (January–February); the art gallery; the labyrinth; the scene over Eumolpo's body (shot in March on the beach of Focene in Fiumicino); and the garden of delights. The final scenes on the ship are shot on the island of Ponza in the first half of May. Altogether there are eighty-nine sets built and 80,000 meters of film shot.

Ruggero Mastroianni begins to edit the film with Fellini while shooting is still in progress, and finishes his work in early June. The dubbing and the music follow. Nino Rota contributes very little to this project and collaborates heavily with Ilhan Mimaroglu, Tod Dockstader, and Andrew Rudin; it is another way in which the project differs from previous ones, as Fellini moved away from his usually suggestive musical score. There is folkloristic music from Japan, Africa, Afghanistan, Tibet, and Hungarian

Gypsies, in addition to twelve-tone classical compositions and other un-identified pieces. Professor Canali translated many of the dialogues to Latin, which the director had recorded by two German priests from the Gregorian University, and their German-accented voices play in the background of the audio track.

The first copy of the finished film comes back from Technicolor in mid-August, and, after the opening in Venice, the movie sees international success. In Italy, Gideon Bachmann releases the film *Ciao, Federico!* about the making of *Fellini Satyricon*. This is the first of a succession of movies that will accompany Fellini's new projects along with books about the work. Bachman's director's "notebook" includes a disturbing scene in which Roman Polanski and Sharon Tate visit the set; she is beautiful, smiling, her blond hair shining in the sun. On August 9, 1969, before *Ciao, Federico!* was released, the twenty-six-year-old actress would be slaughtered in her Bel Air home by fanatics.

The singularity of *Fellini Satyricon*, born of a semi-archaeological premise, is that it resonates so strongly with the realities of the day. One of the unforgettable scenes surrounding *Fellini Satyricon* was a 1:00 a.m. screening at Madison Square Garden following a rock concert. There were more than 10,000 young people in the audience: dropouts, hippies, ragamuffins. It's snowing outside, and inside there's the sense that you're floating in a cloud of hashish, finding yourself on a spaceship shooting off for distant stars. In the ship with you is the remote past (the images of the film) and the present (the audience), filled with added baggage and various unknowns. Fellini, who perhaps for the first time feels a pang of regret for his past, confesses to an irresistible nostalgia: "I'd like to be young today."

33

The Ambassadors of a Vocation
I clowns / The Clowns

At just fifty years old, Fellini has a revelation. It's March 8, 1970, and he's at the barbershop when he has the first idea that will become *Amarcord*—or so goes the legend. He won't attempt to describe this idea for a few years yet, when he announces that he is going to make a movie about Rimini—a town whose mere name he only ever begrudgingly utters—avoiding outright any geographical specificity. The papers announce the title as *L'uomo invaso* (Man Under Invasion) and explain that it will be "a science fiction, a political fiction, and a psycho-fiction about invasion. A man desperate to escape attack finds refuge in the past." More specifically, the concept isn't that different from *Giulietta degli spiriti*: the barbarians are coming—actually, they're already here—and we must face them. The only defense comes from the little mysterious voice inside that encourages, offers suggestions, and most important, remembers. But it's a long road, almost five years long. The descent to the Mothers is an existential voyage, a circumnavigation. Fellini turned the half-century mark sailing on a good wind, buoyed by faith in himself. The dark pessimism of *Toby Dammit* (a version of *Il viaggio di G. Mastorna* in miniature) is past. *Fellini Satyricon*, with its new brand of objectivity, was a detoxification; more archetypal than archaeological, it was a study in detail and the high craftsmanship of image which, by virtue of its worldwide success, placed Fellini back on the pedestal of *8½*, confirming his unchallenged mastery. For the first time, Fellini doesn't want to make a movie: rather he is inspired to interpret reality as a whole. He wants to do it on a historical and mythical level, as always, but set it on an existential plane, where time frames, dates, and individual circumstance offer a broader meaning. It will be a gradual itinerary for him, one giant thrust into the past and present through three different films: *I clowns, Roma,* and *Amarcord.*

The beginning is a false start. In January 1969, Ingmar Bergman and Liv Ullmann visit Fellini on the set of *Satyricon.* The two great directors had met the year before in a restaurant on Piazza di Spagna and are as friendly as brothers. Bergman has a sort of religious reverence for the film, and after seeing parts of it he admits to being both enthusiastic and shocked. He tells Federico that it's caused him to change his mind about many things regarding cinema. Afterward Fellini visits Bergman at his hotel in Trinità dei Monti and Bergman reciprocates with Fellini in Fregene. The meetings have a practical outcome as well, for an American producer, Martin Poll (whom Federico immediately renames Martino Pollo, for chicken), wants to recruit Bergman, Fellini, and Akira Kurosawa for a three-part movie called *Three Stories About Women.* Kurosawa declines, leaving Bergman and Fellini to make the movie, and on January 11, anxious to publicize his good fortune, the Chicken holds a press conference at the Excelsior.

Apart from being happy and honored to work together, the two directors have nothing to tell journalists about their film, except that they've renamed it *Love Duet.* During the question-and-answer section—because it's all in Italian, and because he's always more inclined to speak in absurd situations—Fellini ends up talking more than (and sometimes over) Bergman, and the director of *Winter Light* ends up feeling a little excluded. The inaugural toast to the project is similarly vexed as Ingmar, who doesn't drink alcohol, asks for mineral water. Even in private the two directors can't seem to get more specific. Bergman has an idea that will eventually become *Beröringen* (*The Touch,* 1971); meanwhile, Fellini is thinking about making a movie out of Bernardino Zapponi's screenplay *Una donna sconosciuta* (An Unknown Woman), which will eventually become *La città delle donne.* In their guarded discussions about the project, both masters make sure to cloak their thoughts; there seems to be more dividing them than keeping them together. The producer, who has already announced the collaboration, soon comes to the conclusion that the directors should work separately.

Fellini signs a contract agreeing to start shooting his episode of *Love Duet* in October or November but forgets all about it while working on *Satyricon*. Poll calls him occasionally to report that Bergman is working on his episode and wants it to run first in the diptych. Federico says no problem. Then the American producer visits Chianciano where Fellini is vacationing to report that the deal is off: Bergman's episode has become a full-length feature and is being funded by Universal. Something comes out about Fellini being angry in the press, but it doesn't affect his relationship with the Swedish director. In 1977 they will again discuss the possibility of collaborating on a project, with Luis Buñuel contributing an episode, but that movie will never be made either. Later Fellini will try to describe his peculiar relationship with Bergman to his friend Dario Zanelli: "The problem was that you can't put two babies in the same playroom together. He wanted to see my toys but didn't want to show me his."

In January 1970, after an exhilarating trip to the United States for the release of *Satyricon*, Fellini has no plans for a new project. He's been offered the job of making *Pinocchio* for TV—a book that Fellini not only likes but considers "more important than *I promessi sposi*"*—but the discussions with the producers don't lead anywhere and Luigi Comencini directs it in the end. Briefly, he returns to the possibility of making *Il viaggio di G. Mastorna* with Alberto Grimaldi, but too much has changed and Fellini doesn't feel like it's the right time. He would also like to start work on another "insta-movie" like *Fellini: A Director's Notebook*, as there are still two legitimate projects in development with producer Peter Goldfarb: a documentary about a convent in Tibet, or an interview with Mao Tse-tung. Fellini asks his friend Antonello Trombadori, a prominent Communist, to find out about Mao's availability, but then realizes that he's toying with the impossible, something that isn't really his thing anyway. He knows that he's not a very reliable reporter, better at inventing than reporting the facts. Slowly the idea of *L'uomo invaso* starts gaining ground, and he begins testing out some cinematographic ideas he'd put aside in the past, memories and fantasies. He's thinking about it in terms of a *Director's Notebook II* (the first title for the project), something quick,

---

*The Betrothed, by Alessandro Manzoni, is considered to be among the more important Italian contributions to world literature.

light, and inexpensive. He talks it over with Elio Scardamaglia at Leone Film, who gets RAI TV involved.

In the meantime there have been some marked changes in Federico's habits. He stopped smoking after his illness in 1967 and has developed an allergy to cigarette smoke, so he forces everyone, including Giulietta, who is a heavy smoker, not to light up when he's around. On the rare occasion that he accepts a dinner invitation to someone's home, he expects the host to promise that the air will remain clear. Without realizing it, Federico has become rather despotic and capricious; he's grown a little spoiled by all the constant admiration. The director is very attentive to his trainer Ettore Bevilacqua's advice concerning his health, and claims to exercise every morning, but people say that it's the former boxer who actually does the work. The last big change, which comes as a shock to those who know how dearly Federico loves cars, is that he stops driving. He'd used his car as an office for years, conducted all his important meetings in it, and then he suddenly abandons it in early 1970 on the coast of Rimini; en route to Riccione to visit the Orfei Circus, he hits a young man on a scooter, and even though the boy isn't badly hurt, Federico takes it as a sign. When a German tourist offers to buy the maestro's car, Fellini sells it on the spot and continues to Riccione in a taxi. He will never drive again.

After the uprisings of the late 1960s, which Fellini will criticize harshly in *Prova d'orchestra*, the director is inspired to avoid repetition and to express himself honestly. He suddenly takes to the idea of working for television; he's attracted to the notion that he won't have to bother with extensive preproduction and the organizational hurdles of the cinema industry. Television almost entirely eliminates the gaps between inspiration and realization; as well as greatly increasing the audience just as cinema is starting to wane. Leone Film and RAI optimistically cut a deal for three TV movies to be coproduced with France and Germany. In the meantime, Fellini and Zapponi discuss the projects at Zapponi's house in Zagarolo, deciding that the first TV movie should be about clowns, which Fellini describes as "the ambassadors of my vocation."

Preparation is hectic but entertaining, as Fellini is in constant discussion with his screenwriter over ideas. He travels around Italy a bit, visiting old friends who work in the circus and meeting new people in that world. He goes to Paris, "the city that turned the circus into a real art show," traveling with Tristan Remy, the most important historian on the subject of clowns. He is convinced that clowns belong to another time, but Fellini continues his research into the relics of what he terms the religion of laughter. He meets old and young clowns, as well as Victoria Chaplin, Charlie Chaplin's daughter. He collects tidbits about the disappearing tradition. Some of the people he meets and the conversations that he has end up in the movie—which becomes a sort of deconstructed documentary. The script is free-form and includes childhood memories, fantasies about the past, and sad stories from the present. Shooting begins on March 23 in Anzio, then moves to Ostia, Paris, and Cinecittà. The five weeks scheduled for filming turn into eleven (despite the fact that they only actually film for thirty days total), the script swells with new ideas introduced along the way, and the budget triples.

There's a break in shooting in Paris after the director hurts his hand on a broken window; in the meantime, on June 8, Fellini is named an honorary citizen of Montmartre. The budget for *I clowns* may be modest, but the reduced means force Federico to think harder—and you can't put a price tag on being able to work without any rules. Even though he shoots the film in color on 35 millimeter with a big-screen camera, Fellini turns out to be one of those filmmakers particularly sensitive to the exigencies unique to television. In fact, when screened, the picture is colloquial and intimate, far more journalistic than it is narrative. The simplicity of style and the light touch will be difficult for the director to retrieve on future movie projects: his friends who see the film have the feeling that they're talking to Federico face-to-face, listening to his unmistakable digressions, the way he blathers on in a small group.

Shakespeare wrote, "All the world's a stage, and all the men and women merely players." Fellini took that idea on, claiming that the world is a circus and the men are all clowns, of which there are two kinds: the Whiteface clown and the Auguste clown (called Tony in the Italian circus). They represent the master and the slave—the arbiter of the system and the rebel, the rich and the poor, reason and folly. Taking the circus as a global metaphor, Fellini demonstrates that he thinks all of humanity can be divided into these two categories and offers some interesting historical examples: "Hitler is a Whiteface, Mussolini is an Auguste. Pacelli

(Pope Pius XII) is a Whiteface, Roncalli (Pope John XXIII) is an Auguste. Freud is a Whiteface, Jung is an Auguste." His commentary in the film also attempts some daring historical paradigms: "The Whiteface clowns become Mothers, Fathers, the Maestro, the Artist, the Good Guy—really, they do what they're supposed to do. So the Auguste, who would fall victim to the fascination of these perfect roles if they weren't so rigorously self-satisfied, rebels and sparks an ongoing battle." So what kind of clown is Fellini? "If I were a clown myself, I think that I'd really be an Auguste. But I'm also a Whiteface. Or, perhaps, I'm the circus director." It's no accident that he depicts himself as a modern version of Monsieur Loyal at the end of 8½, megaphone in hand, directing the procession of characters.

Along with this philosophy of the world divided between Whiteface and Auguste clowns, the film displays Fellini's total distrust of factual inquiry and the documenting of reality—it's a reflowering of Fellini's old anti-Zavattini resistance to realism. The art of the great clowns in history cannot be found in the archives of cinema—just as Bomba, the mythical prostitute that Fellini had vainly searched for while researching *Le notti di Cabiria*, couldn't be found on the streets of Rome. The movie of the Fratellini Trio burns before the screening; another film about the legendary Rhum (Enrico Sprocani from Trieste) is a meaningless bit of archaeology. It's simply better to reinvent the great performers. Testimony, too, is ephemeral; it goes up in smoke the moment it's repeated. During his first trip to Paris, Fellini interviews former clown Bario Meschi, but once the camera is rolling, Meschi is too emotional to repeat his stories. Yet the director is still able to find the poetic conclusion to his film in the tape recording of that first interview: in a famous skit performed by Bario and Dario Meschi, Auguste searches desperately for Whiteface who has been declared dead . . . and then finds him in the end, playing the trumpet.

Some of the scenes written into the script will not make it into the movie, including the interview with the clowns' cobbler; the visit to the former Medrano circus, now a Bavarian beer hall; an encounter with a photographer of clowns; and a fragmented discussion with an elephant trainer. Fellini's initial hope to have Charlie Chaplin reading the manifesto of the clowns proves a pipe dream: the greatest jester of the cinema is old, sick, and basically inaccessible. There is a brief possibility of getting Fellini's friend Danny Kaye involved, but the timing doesn't work out. In the end, Fellini rounds up his usual ad hoc troupe, transforming regular actors and real-life characters into clowns, mixing them in with professionals to colorful, eclectic effect.

I clowns, at ninety-three minutes long, is premiered at the 31st Venice Film Festival, which continues after the 1968 protests without competitions or awards. On Sunday, August 30, RAI—very proud of their Fellini movie—screens it in the luxurious Palazzo Labia. Fellini is irritated that the film has become an object of contention between state-owned television and the cinema industry, and once again tries to get out of his Venetian engagement. He sends a telegram from Rome to his loyal friend Mario Longardi*: "Dear Marietto powerful winds are blowing the boat ever farther from Venice STOP I don't really want to come STOP I'll write from Pantelleria."† Longardi, desperate, calls Fellini, begging him to come, and finally Federico relents. But once in Venice he's not even cheered by the warm reception of the film. The reviews are only slightly veiled versions of the same old reservations: the movie is too reminiscent of old themes, too autobiographical, too narcissistic, some good ideas and some bad ones—a roster of opinions that will be repeated when the movie comes out at the end of the year.

There's debate over the release as well: producers and theater owners arguing about which is more important, television or movies. The theater owners think it's heresy, or at least a betrayal, to put out a new Fellini film on TV instead of on the screen. The director of programming at RAI, Angelo Romanò, is undaunted, however: "I wanted the movie and now I can broadcast it as often as I please." In the end, a compromise is reached. *I clowns* is aired for the first time on RAI 2 on Christmas Eve. TV is still only black-and-white. So, on December 27, it opens in theaters in color. The result is a double catastrophe. Since the movie is airing on a holiday, people watch it distractedly, and in fewer numbers than anticipated. The fact that the film is in theaters in full color doesn't seem to be enough of a draw, and it does miserably at the box office. Fellini watched the movie on TV in Rimini, at home with his mother, and found it too reduced, a far cry from what he'd wanted to make.

---

*Fellini's press agent.
†Pantelleria is an island on the southern coast of Sicily.

I clowns, in the years to come, will be seen in a different light, and some critics will even consider it better than other more significant Fellini movies. But for the next while, even when double-billed with *Toby Dammit* and distributed as *2 Fellini 2* (1977), it won't enjoy much success. In a peculiar move, Fellini has the actor Gigi Proietti dub him in the 1977 rerelease, a choice that could be read as an act of shyness from someone who fears he's exposed himself too much. And although Fellini never shied away from talking about himself, *I clowns* may be his most explicit, candid, and intimate public self-portrait. It also represents a critical moment, the poetic matrix of what is to come in subsequent films: *Roma*, where he again employs imaginary documentary reporting, and *Amarcord*, which takes up a deeper exploration of the author's childhood, a journey begun in the wings of *I clowns*.

34

A Second Native Land

Fellini's Roma

In October 1970, Fellini announces three forthcoming movie projects "all to be shot together." One is about Alighiero Noschese, an extraordinary Neapolitan imitator who does impressions, and whom Fellini has always admired and also feared a little for his eerie ability to assume the personalities of other people. The director also wants to return to the idea of *Una donna sconosciuta*, based on Bernardino Zapponi's screenplay—the story of a provincial factory owner during the years of fascism (the 1920s) who slowly turns into the woman who'd abandoned him. Another form of metamorphosis, the story is a compliment to Noschese's almost scientific transformations. For various reasons, neither of these projects pan out, while the third one—a film dedicated to Rome—does.

The central thrust of *Roma* is an elaboration on the idea of the present growing out of the past, and vice versa. Fellini is particularly interested in mounting a free-form production, like *I clowns*, shooting in bits and pieces, pausing at times, and not getting trapped in a conventional plot structure. Alberto Grimaldi is taken aback when Fellini presents him with a proposal for a "Sunday movie," something you shoot in your free time, a bit here and a bit there, when you can. The subject is Rome, in all of its fascinating complexity, the things about the city that catch your attention, inspire fantasy, and merit future analysis. The *ponentino* (the west wind), for example, that brings a cool breeze and relief from the summer heat every night. When does it rise? From where? And where does it go? Who and what does it encounter as it moves through the city heading eastward? Grimaldi doesn't understand the project; he doesn't

like it, and he doesn't want to do it. So Fellini approaches Elio Scardamaglia instead, and begins the project with Leone Film. Soon Ultra
Film comes on board as well. Ultra Film has state funding and is headed
up by Turi Vasile, one of the people who discovered Giulietta and launched
her at the GUF Teatro.

Federico works with Bernardino on the script; they meet in each
other's homes, at the Hotel Plaza, or in Ostia. They often roam around,
looking for ideas or testing scenes. They go down into the construction
site for the subway and the engineers take them all the way to the "mole,"
the earth-moving machine that's digging deep into the guts of the city.
They travel by boat down the Tiber, they talk to historians and experts
about Rome, they seek out curious stories in books and visit the state
archive in addition to the cemetery. Someone tells Fellini that hundreds
of cats were once brought in to exterminate the rats in the cellars of the
Palazzo di Giustizia (the courthouse) on the Lungotevere, but the rats
were so aggressive that they ate the cats, and they had to borrow leopards
from the zoo instead; it was the leopards that, in the end, managed to
devour the rats. Whether the story is true or not, the idea of these
beasts roaming freely in the bowels of the palazzo intrigues Fellini, and
he wants to include the episode in the movie. Unfortunately, the building
has just been condemned by the city zoning committee and he can't get a
permit to film there—as Orson Welles had done for *Le procès* (*The Trial*,
1962).

Gradually, deeper themes begin to emerge, engaging Fellini more than
the little curiosities. He begins keeping his notes for the screenplay in
two different categories: yesterday and today. Fellini has also considered
telling the story of Rome thirty years earlier, evidence of the autobiographical slant underlying this phase of his work. It is possible, just
barely, to see a narrative thread of personal memories in this movie: a
childhood in the provinces where everyone talks about Rome; the first arrival at Termini station, followed by a cheap hotel, San Giovanni; a fleeting love affair with a woman in a brothel, and then another one with a
German variety-show dancer. While reflecting on his past, the director
decides to approach the story of modern Rome as if it were a "documentary about the Amazon." He wants to look at everything from above,
through a new lens. In keeping with this notion, the first day of filming is

set for November 2, 1970, All Saints' Day (the Day of the Dead in Italy), and the first shots are taken from a helicopter over the cemetery of Verano (they won't actually make it into the movie). More filming is done in February and March of 1971, but these scenes will be used only as a kind of preparation for the real work, which begins in late March. Costs start to rise quickly.

One of the first scenes to be shot, at the end of March or beginning of April, is an ecclesiastical fashion show—Danilo Donati outdoes himself with ironic and burlesque costume designs. The sequence ends with Guglielmo Guasta, an old humor writer from *Marc'Aurelio*, costumed as Pope Pius XII being rolled in on a throne. Soon after, rather than adopt a traditional documentary technique, Fellini has half a kilometer of the ring road around Rome (the Raccordo Anulare) rebuilt in a Cinecittà studio: forty streetlights, fifty road signs, fifteen billboards, and a four-lane highway complete with a guardrail and two rest stops. While shooting at Villa Borghese, Lee Falk, the creator of the comic strip *Mandrake*, comes by for a visit. He's been sent by Dino De Laurentiis, who is contriving to have Fellini direct a film about this famous magician of comics. The director toys with the idea of a Mandrake project, but limits himself to a humorous photography portfolio with Marcello Mastroianni, which runs in French *Vogue*.

The end of the summer brings a surprise: the Swiss bank, Val Lugano, goes bankrupt, crumbling the empire of Ultra Film's principal stockholder, Giuseppe Pasquale. Fellini has to suspend work on *Roma*. Considering the rhapsodic quality of the film, the producer, Turi Vasile, insists they could even just stop there. Federico complains that he's only shot about half of what he wanted, three-quarters at the most. There are critical scenes yet to be shot, like the open-air feast on via Albalonga that he'd totally reconstructed (tram included) in Studio 5 at Cinecittà. The usual storm of polemics follows, but filming resumes in October with special funding from the Banca Nazionale del Lavoro. The director concedes to some cuts: a soccer match between rival teams, Rome versus Lazio; a nighttime bus ride; a chat foreshadowing the end (in the style of a variety show); and a visit to Conocchia to his father's tomb will be excised. Zapponi is opposed to this last, ominous cut. Dubbing follows, which is long and laborious despite Federico's insistence that he really needs only three actors: Alighiero Noschese, and the two Lionellos, Alberto and Oreste. The movie is finished in February 1972.

Roma (clocking in at one minute under two hours) signals a shift in the structure of Fellini's films, which from I vitelloni forward had all been broken into linked chapters. This film is even more fragmentary, unhinged, and intimate. Throughout his adventures in the city, cast here as a big metaphorical mother-whore, Fellini chatters freely, suspended between past and present. This movie comes directly out of I clowns—we might even say that it's a continuation of I clowns, just as the trail of memories about Emilia-Romagna initiated in Roma will be picked up in Amarcord. The structure of I clowns is probably stronger—the parody of documentary inquiry gives it a tightness and poetry—whereas Roma, an opera aperta,* especially in the curiously wan segues, runs the risk of redundancy or tiredness. But these are minor concerns in an otherwise alluring, distended, and robust project. Clearly Roma is another movie about death. The symbols of it appear all along the way: the first image in the movie is a scythe, the last scene has a motorcycle gang disappearing into the darkness. It is the exact opposite of what happens when the Roman frescoes in the subway tunnels disappear when exposed to light. Fellini can't not put Anna Magnani in a movie dedicated to Rome, though Anna doesn't really want to play along. She listens skeptically to all his ideas and appreciates the director's good intentions, but thinks her presence would be superfluous. In the end, she'll agree to appear in a short cameo: coming home to the Palazzo Altieri at night, she shuts the door in her friend Fellini's face, cheerfully rejecting his offer with the line "I don't trust you." These will sadly be Mamma Roma's last words on the big screen; she'll die soon after on September 26, 1973.

The guts of Rome are being devoured by the insatiable earth-moving mole; its surface is being destroyed by raucous traffic; its citizens are rough, vulgar, greedy, and dogged. The circles of the metropolis aren't all that different from the circles of Hell in Il viaggio di G. Mastorna. With stubborn artistic consistency, Fellini returns to the memories of Moraldo in città and the dilated, baroque imagery of La dolce vita. But there's a

---

*A reference to the semiologist Umberto Eco's essay "Opera aperta," wherein texts contain fields rather than strings of meaning.

difference between this film and the masterpiece shot twelve years earlier. By the 1970s, Rome is already living out a future more neurotic and frightening than what could ever have been predicted.

A structure of agglomeration suggests a rhapsodic reading, an aesthetic choice that may have well been arbitrary. When *Roma* opens in Italy on March 16, 1972, critics go on at length about the good and bad aspects of Fellini's "movies within movies." *Roma* is described as magma-like, diverse, a fantastic cornucopia, the work of an immense talent, a hundred percent Fellini; the film is compared in a flattering and juvenile way to Jean-Luc Godard and the avant-garde. The criticisms are a lack of rigor, a self-satisfied air, an obsession with monstrosity, and repetitiousness. The movie has a discreet reception in Italy and abroad, though in some cases it is acclaimed with an enthusiasm unmatched since 8½. People liked the memoiristic scenes best: meals in trattorias, roaming musicians, variety shows, brothels, and everything derelict—or *trucido*, to use the Roman slang—after twenty years of fascism, all of it a perfect transposition of memory into poetry, offered up with the shameless violence that attends such themes. It would be superfluous to add that Fellini isn't working in caricature here but rather portraying a sociological reality. As for the portrait of the present, we're given the frightening carousel of the ring road, with Fellini himself appearing to animate his film within a film. It's a shame that the ferocity of that episode doesn't carry over into the scene of the police beating up hippies in Piazza Santa Maria in Trastevere—where Fellini's fantasy is limited because it's trapped in current affairs and reality, not the most congenial subject matter. While the subway scene has a periodically sci-fi tension, the ecclesiastical fashion show is pure parody. As with other films initially misunderstood after breaking with convention, *Roma* is an extraordinary exercise, teaching spectators to be uninhibited and bold when looking at reality, to be fantastical and flamboyant, and to proudly indulge freedom.

The movie premiered internationally, out of competition, at the 26th Cannes Film Festival on May 14, 1972. It stirred up immediate controversy among feminists because of its unfortunate poster, which showed a naked woman on all fours with three breasts—a staging of the *lupa capitolina*, the she-wolf symbol of Rome. Back in Italy, the movie does well only in Rome and Milan; the rest of the country is underwhelmed.

Despite this initially diffident reception by the general public, however, *Roma* came, over time, to be the most admired of Fellini's films among intellectuals and artists. The great Belgian painter Paul Delvaux, in an interview on his eighty-ninth birthday in September 1986, aptly sums up its allure: "Fellini's *Roma*, which is pagan, papist, joyful, solar yet also mysterious under the surface, fascinated me."

35

Distant Memories
Amarcord

From 1933 to 1935 the ocean liner *Rex* was the jewel of Italian shipyards and winner of the Blue Ribbon for fastest transatlantic crossing, beating out ships like the *Ile de France, Queen Mary,* and *Europa.* In Fellini's *Amarcord* the *Rex* passes right by the city of Rimini, and hordes of local men, women, and children set out on boats of every description in order to see it up close. *Rex,* in fact, never sailed past Rimini. It came close to the Romagna coast only once, its lights spent, just after the beginning of World War II. It would have a sad fate: bombed and looted in the Gulf of Trieste, the relic eventually sank in the deep waters off Capodistria. In its heyday, however, the ship would dock in Genoa, never sailing the Adriatic route, which is to say that this scene in *Amarcord,* one of the most universally recognizable in the world of Fellini (even depicted on the poster for the Cannes Film Festival in 1982), belongs entirely to the fantasy of its author, a man who loved to remake poetry and reality according to his own ideas.

The action of *Amarcord,* dedicated to the Rimini of Federico's youth, spans from one spring to the next, from the festival of San Giuseppe with a huge bonfire in the piazza to the sunny-rainy wedding banquet of Gradisca the hairdresser. What year is the film set in? The author, characteristically reticent with details, offers contradictory clues. One character, the lawyer Titta, who also narrates the story, announces during a snowstorm, "This will be remembered as the year of the blizzard" (which actually took place in the winter of 1929). Other details indicate that we're in 1933, when the 7th Mille Miglia car race actually ran and the

Rex was christened. But then we could also be in 1935, when the song "Faccetta nera" (Little Black Face) was popular following the Ethiopia campaign, or in 1937, when the movie *Shall We Dance* with Ginger Rogers and Fred Astaire, for which we see a poster, was released. And so *Amarcord* is set in an indeterminate year sometime between 1933 and 1937, the mid-thirties. The title, derived from the expression in dialect *a m'arcord*, which means "I remember," comes from a poem by the screenwriter Tonino Guerra, who was Federico's age and also came from the vicinity.

Antonio ("Tonino") Guerra was born on March 16, 1920, in Sant'Arcangelo di Romagna, ten kilometers from Rimini. His father was a fisherman who used to fry and sell fish; his mother was illiterate. Upon returning from a German concentration camp, he became an elementary-school teacher and started writing poems in dialect that found resonance with a readership extending far beyond his region. He didn't move to Rome until after he was thirty, and unlike Fellini, kept close ties to his hometown and returned frequently for long stretches. He's introduced into the world of cinema by the painter Renzo Vespignani, a friend of Elio Petri, assistant director to Giuseppe De Santis. Marcello Mastroianni also gives Guerra a leg up in the beginning by hiring him as a consultant to help him vet scripts. After writing a few screenplays for De Santis, Tonino moves on to collaborate with Michelangelo Antonioni, Petri, Francesco Rosi, the Taviani brothers, and Theo Angelopoulos, among others. When Fellini, whom he'd known for some time, invited him to collaborate on *Amarcord*, Guerra had already become the new Cesare Zavattini; in the Italian cinema of the 1970s he was as important as the screenwriter of *Ladri di biciclette* had been during the postwar period.

When Fellini wants to rile Tonino, he merely has to note that Sant'Arcangelo was always "the periphery of Rimini"; Tonino retorts that just the sound of a fistfight was enough to send the smirking *vitelloni* of the Riviera running back up a hill. Their jibes, exchanged in dialect, were all part of a perfect mutual understanding. From Tonino's peasant roots to Fellini's urban memories, both men shared the desire to reinvent their realities. When Pier Paolo Pasolini reviewed *Amarcord*, still stinging a bit over the *Accattone* affair, he wrote that the movie should rightfully be called *Asarcurdem* (meaning "We remember") instead, as the memories of the screenwriter had blended so intricately with those of the director.

The word *amarcord* was invented by Fellini, who tested it out for the first time on a napkin in a restaurant, as if in a trance of automatic writing. It became a magic key, one of those words that enchanted him, like *"asa nisi masa"* in 8½. It was as if by just uttering the word, a whole world—slightly faded and in pieces—would come back to him: the march of the infantry, that melancholy couple, the popular mythology of *The White Sheik*, the *vitelloni*, the provincial world of *La Strada*, and the immortal prostitutes of all his films. And yet with *Amarcord* it's as if Fellini awoke one morning emancipated from the barbarians of *Giulietta degli spiriti* who'd been invading his world. He set out anew to track them down in their homes, which is to say, his childhood.

While preoccupied with this difficult interior journey, the director is unwilling to discuss what he's doing. As to the title, which they need for the press releases, he has forced his press agent, Mario Longardi, to pretend that the movie will be called *L'uomo invaso*, and to lie to the journalists, telling them that it will be a science-fiction movie. From the beginning Fellini regrets ever mentioning that the project would have something to do with Romagna and denies it subsequently. In order to allay suspicion he makes up another title, *Hammarcord*—an exotic name that could easily be the name of the Swedish scientist who figures out how to communicate with aliens. The set designer, Danilo Donati, is meanwhile constructing an entire town in Cinecittà, but the director tells visitors that it's absolutely not Rimini, even though many of them can identify features specific to the city. A small war has broken out that will rage on for the entire length of the production and even linger after: many people in Rimini are pleased, and many more are concerned that they'll be in the movie or will be able to recognize characters they know in the rare press photos that come off the set, or in the gossip that's circulating.

It must mean something that the name of the protagonist changes from Bobo in the treatment to Titta in the screenplay—the oft-mentioned friend whom Fellini referred to from his days at *Marc'Aurelio*. It's also difficult to maintain that the leader of the workers isn't entirely based on Ferruccio Benzi, Titta's own father. For that character, Fellini initially considers the hulking Nereo Rocco, a soccer coach, then contemplates having the real Titta play his own father, only to end up casting an unknown actor, Armando Brancia. The lead is played by Bruno Zanin from Veneto in his debut role—after Zanin's excellent work for Fellini, Giorgio Strehler will hire him for the part of Zorzetto in Goldoni's *Il campiello* at the Piccolo Teatro in Milan. When Titta Benzi, the lawyer, sees the movie for the first time he immediately recognizes himself in the young Zanin and is shocked by Federico's accuracy—having been a constant guest in the Benzis' home when he was young and considered a member of the family, Fellini evidently remembered the most detailed nuances of sentiments, language, habits, and tensions from forty years earlier. According to Titta, the family scenes are a precise replication of his childhood; it was as if Federico had tape-recorded those years.

Amarcord conjures up a whole school of interpreters and commentators back in Rimini who traffic in indiscretion and speculation, attempting to identify all the characters and archetypes of the film and put a historical context to the events. This is exactly the kind of intrusion on his work that Fellini hates most, and why he insists that the town in his movie belongs to a metaphysical dimension, one that could be located with only slight variations in any time or place. Characteristically, he refuses to say that the film is based on anything, let alone reality, and he never desists from the claim that he is the sole fabricator of it all. He fears the curiosity and voracity of Rimini's locals, and dreads most of all their affectionate cannibalism—which is why there isn't a single image in the film shot on the Adriatic coast.

If a sociologist were trying to study Italy between the two wars using only *Amarcord* as a source, what would he find? Tribal families, horrible schools, sexual repression, prisonlike asylums, fascism. One certainly couldn't claim that the director was magnanimous toward the society that just kept on living under fascism's thumb. *Amarcord* is a bildungsroman, Titta's sentimental education, and as such it portrays Italy's depressing provincialism with an implacable resentment—and the comedic touch doesn't diminish the intensity of the indictment. Fellini once again is rebelling against the mainstream culture and its attempts at a revisionist justification of fascism; the director will never attempt to hide the moral and cultural misery of the years of consent. And it is interesting that such a forceful condemnation of the damaging effects of fascism on Italian society comes from such a patently apolitical director. But we should also note that Fellini's disgust is directed more toward the larger context than the militant dictators themselves; for example, the scene in which Titta's father is forced to drink castor oil is not particularly fierce. Fellini is incapable of hating anyone, even the Fascists; he's left to depict them as clowns only slightly more sinister than the rest of the clowns. He's stronger when he paints history without even realizing he's doing it— when trying to re-create his teenage world, he gives the audience a much more honest picture.

The structure of the film is based on the *barzelletta*—a funny little story—of which he tells many: small local anecdotes with a beginning and end, presented in a mocking tone, and always somehow modified by the fantastical. *Amarcord* is a long conversation rife with memories, made for the director's own pleasure and with an eye to amusing its audience. Some scenes aren't much more than gags, such as the episode when a sheik appears at the Grand Hotel with his thirty concubines (the actual event had occurred more recently, while Fellini was working on *Toby Dammit*). Other chapters bear the mysterious weight of fairy tales, like the trip into the country with the crazy uncle (in a remarkable performance by Ciccio Ingrassia), who climbs up into the tree shouting, "I want a woman!" This is an example of the storyteller's strongest gifts for ambiguity and rhythm: very rarely, perhaps only in some of Eduardo De Filippo's plays, has the Italian tribal family been framed with such attention, love, and vulnerability. A perfect example is the scene of the lunchtime argument, inspired, in fact, by De Filippo's *Sabato, domenica e lunedì* (Saturday, Sunday and Monday), with a defining performance by the most Neapolitan of actresses, Pupella Maggio, clearly dubbed. The mother is the heart and center of this little old world and it's significant that she dies at the film's conclusion. *Amarcord* also ends with the marriage to a carabiniere of the sexy hairdresser Ninola, also known as Gradisca (which is how she describes herself to the prince when offering herself to him), a farewell to the proxy mother who is off to take up her new role as wife.

Like for *8½*, Gradisca was to be played by a fabulously opulent beauty that Fellini would discover traveling around Italy (with Federico not only the stories but the techniques are always the same), but then he decides that he wants Sandra Milo again. Sandrocchia is flattered and overjoyed as she prepares for the new screen test, during which Fellini puts his own hat on her head as the perfect final touch. It seems that this will be Federico's third picture with Milo, but her new husband will get in the way after a sudden burst of jealousy and some rather serious threats. It's impossible to find a compromise, so the actress must be substituted. At the last minute the producer Franco Cristaldi calls on Magali Noël. She's off on holiday in Switzerland, but remembers what a good time was had with *La dolce vita* and enthusiastically comes to the rescue, to exquisite effect. In the world of these provincial mama's boys, women can be rapt in a libidinous frenzy like Volpina, or they can display extreme aggressiveness like the matron in the smoke shop, though, at other times, the erotic fantasies of lonely women are not Fellini at his most sophisticated.

The movie opens with the premise of total subjectivity but aims for staunch objectivity: the audience's judgment on the period of the 1930s after watching the film isn't going to come out of the director's rhetoric but from the simple display of facts. *Amarcord* is remarkable in its portrayal, with just a hint of commiseration, of a rather backward community, living in the shadow of flags and still caught in Victorian emotions. This was a society that wanted to *feel*, as exemplified in that most memorable scene of the transatlantic steamer *Rex*, a pregnant symbol that would fit perfectly into a picture book by Jung. The young men, enchanted by the romantic music, dream about the exotic beauties on the terrace of the empty Grand Hotel, dancing alone as the autumn winds bluster around them. They weren't the only ones to fall for such illusions, which in that period seduced much less provincial and blander societies than that of Rimini; one need only remember the huge success that the myth of beauty and worldly possession brought the great writer F. Scott Fitzgerald.

Amarcord's 103 minutes were filmed between January and June 1973; the mood on the set was buoyant. The film came out in Italy on December 18 and was almost an unmitigated success. The critics' positive descriptors are many; the movie is affable, nice, simple, delicate, balanced, clean, elegiac, serene, mature, exuberant, civil. They call it a book of memories, a high point, a movie about magic realism, the artist at his peak. There are still detractors who complain about Fellini's exploitative poetics, repetition, harping on caricature, and vulgarity, but they are in the clear minority. On May 9, 1974, when *Amarcord* opens out of competition at the 27th Cannes

Film Festival, Federico and Giulietta are in attendance. Before the screening, Jean-Claude Brialy pays tribute to René Clair, the seventy-six-year-old director and president of the jury, whose renowned film *Entr'acte* (1924) is shown before *Amarcord*. It's a memorable evening, and the next day a newspaper calls Fellini "a descendant of Molière, Balzac, Daumier, Goya, and more recently, of Pagnol." The French audience quite likes the film and it's released immediately in theaters.

Another notable encounter occurs during this period, recorded by Paul Mazursky in his autobiography *Show Me the Magic*. Fellini writes him, "Dear Paolino, I heard that your recent movie [*Harry and Tonto*] is a big success from a young American director who came to visit me here in Rome. I don't remember his name, but I know he just made a television movie called *Duel* . . ." It was Longardi who had brought Steven Spielberg to sit across the table from Fellini at the Cesarina restaurant. Though Federico is initially peeved about having to be pleasant to yet another American tourist, he eventually warms up and encourages the young director—despite forgetting his name. Over lunch the visitor takes many pictures of his maestro-host, and years later Longardi will be moved to find enlargements of those pictures covering the walls of Spielberg's Los Angeles office.

News that *Amarcord* has won the Oscar for best foreign language film arrives in Rome early on April 9, 1975. This is Fellini's fourth Academy Award, after *La strada, La notti degli Cabiria,* and *8½.* Busy with work on *Il Casanova* and not terribly hopeful about winning, the director hadn't gone to LA, so Franco Cristaldi, the producer, accepted the prize from Jacqueline Bisset and Jack Valenti. In one of the many interviews he gave at that time, Fellini attempted to explain the international success behind the film:

> I think that if you talk about what you know and talk about your-self, and your family, your hometown, the snow and rain, about pride, stupidity, ignorance, hopes, fantasies, political and religious conditioning, when you talk honestly about the things in life, without assuming to admonish anyone and without any heavy philosophizing or trying to send messages, when you are humble and maintain above all a sense of the relativity of things—I think then

it's possible for everyone to understand what you're saying and then make it their own. It seems to me that all the characters in *Amarcord*, the people of this small city, are like that; they're enclosed in this city, a city I knew very well, and the characters, whether invented or people I knew . . . well, I invented them or I knew them very well, and they suddenly don't belong just to me, but to others too.

36

A Dispassionate Seducer
Il Casanova di Federico Fellini / Fellini's Casanova

It all starts with a signature on a contract: another offer from Dino De Laurentiis. The signature is Fellini's and the title of the film is left blank. It is 1971, and the producer has closed down Dinocittà after a decade in business—in the shadow of the decrepit set for *Il viaggio di G. Mastorna*, laid-off workers wave red banners and chant protests, and cars on their way to Circeo drive past. Dino is a savvy operator and is investing overseas; for fifteen years he will be one of the most influential producers in the United States, eventually becoming an American citizen on September 20, 1986. But for the moment he needs to build credit and, along with the letters of reference he can show to the New York finance officers, he knows that a signed contract with Fellini is worth a lot. He's bound to this old love-hate friendship (although, by now, there's more love than hate, as time has washed away the memories of arguments and legal battles). Federico is happy to sign the contract, but Dino wants a title too, and the first one Fellini thinks of is *Il Casanova*. He has never read *Histoire de ma vie* (*The Story of My Life*), by Giacomo Casanova, just as he'd never read Poe or *Satyricon*, but he's been talking about making a movie about the adventurous Venetian for almost twenty years.

Giacomo Girolamo Casanova was born in Venice on April 2, 1725 (on Calle della Commedia, no less!). He was the child of actors, studied law in Padua, avoided a life in the priesthood, and took up traveling while still very young, visiting Corfu, Constantinople, Rome, and Naples. He was a violin player, an eccentric intellectual, a writer of pamphlets, a trickster, an adventurer, a frequenter of brothels, a player, involved in the cabala and exorcisms, a Freemason, a playwright, and the self-titled Cavalier of Seingalt. He gained fame when he escaped the prison of Piombi in Venice on October 31, 1756, where he'd been jailed for heresy. More than thirty years later he wrote his *Histoire de ma vie* in French, relating the story of his adventures up through the summer of 1774, which included crossing Europe back and forth and back again, going from one royal court to the next, running into fortune and misfortune, winning prestige and suffering humiliations, publishing and being condemned, amassing sordid as well as profoundly genuine love affairs. He's finally allowed to return to Venice on November 15, 1774, but as a spy in the service of the Comitato dei Dieci (the commission of ten), and soon, after his work is banned again, he leaves his hometown forever and goes back to wandering. At the age of sixty, in September 1785, he starts working as a librarian under Count Waldstein in the Castle of Dux in Bohemia (today, Duchov), where—ignored by the nobility and mocked by the servants—he feverishly embarks on the writing of the book that will immortalize him. He died in Dux on June 4, 1798, the dawn of a new century.

Casanova's autobiography wasn't published until 1820, after Jean Laforgue had made significant edits, enhancing the libertinism (only about a sixth of the original was about seducing women) and effectively changing the spirit of the book, transforming the adventurer into a passionate liberal. Despite its adulteration, the book enjoys enormous success: De Musset and Stendhal are fans, and it's suspected that Stendhal is the true author. When historians and scholars study it, they are often surprised at how accurately it reflects the events of eighteenth-century Europe, though the amorality itself comes under frequent attack. There are divergent opinions about the protagonist: some despise him and others love him. The lovers come to be known as *casanovisti*, or casanovists. Not until 1960 will the loyal followers of the Cavalier of Seingalt have the satisfaction of seeing the publication of the original manuscript by Brockhaus publishers in Wiesbaden.

Facing a project that has actually turned concrete, Federico is forced to tackle this huge book (the Brockhaus-Plon edition is six volumes comprising more than 2,000 pages) and even thinking about it puts him into a foul mood. Some immediately claim that the director regrets his choice—

after all, the tormented story of the ambiguous and rather strange movie that will come to be called *Il Casanova di Federico Fellini* is begun with a careless signature on a carelessly drafted contract. Once again Dino and Federico reengage in the game of misunderstanding each other, and once again the collaboration ends badly. The producer's vision of Fellini's *Il Casanova* is a film that is both bold and adventurous and in line with the tastes of his American partners. The project is provisionally entitled *I sogni di Casanova* (The Dreams of Casanova) and Fellini is supposed to start work on it immediately after *Amarcord*, which he's still working on when he signs the contract. A year later De Laurentiis pulls out, despite the overwhelming success of the movie about Rimini. The official reasons are that the Americans want a celebrity to play Casanova—and after considering Marlon Brando and Al Pacino, the producers decide that they want Robert Redford—but Fellini refuses. Redford is too handsome, too un-European, too famous. The director doesn't want to make the movie in English either, which is what De Laurentiis and the studios have been counting on.

In July 1974, Cineriz buys the rights for the film, and the production moves to a small villa on via Gaeta. Andrea Rizzoli (son of Angelo, who has passed away) signs the contract on August 15 in his home on Cap Ferrat. Fellini's old friend Clemente Fracassi comes on as production manager and prepares a four-billion-lire budget. The starting date is set for October 30, and the release for October 1975. Toward the end of August, Federico returns to London to scout for his lead among British actors. The press speculates that he's going to cast Michael Caine, or the cabaret actor Tom Deal, or even a Hollywood star, maybe Jack Nicholson. But as far as Fellini is concerned, Casanova is an old *vitellone*. Alberto Sordi offers to take the part. Fellini sees *Lucky Luciano* in the interim and considers Gian Maria Volonté. In the end, he decides on the Canadian actor Donald Sutherland, whom he'd met in Parma on the set of Bernardo Bertolucci's *1900*. The deal goes forward because the actor doesn't expect a high fee (he certainly accepts less than Volonté—who doesn't really like the character—and definitely less than Redford, who asked for $1 million).

Preproduction work is proceeding in the meantime. The director wants to shoot the whole thing in the studio in Cinecittà, even the scenes set in Venice. They miss the October deadline, and then they miss the new November deadline, and, after a series of postponements, Cineriz gives up too—the business director, Fulvio Frizzi, loudly proclaims that he has no desire to go forward with the project and its excessive costs and the lack of interest already being demonstrated by the international market. On January 23, 1975, Alberto Grimaldi calls Fellini from Los Angeles; undeterred by the retreat of two such important producers, he agrees to take on the project with the following reservations: the budget mustn't exceed 5.5 billion lire and the movie should be shot in English and in London, which is cheaper. Negotiations continue for several months, and in April the news is official. Fellini and Grimaldi, after much back and forth, have come to an agreement—the producer has compromised on the demand that it be shot in London and the director has agreed to work in English. Sutherland is confirmed as the lead. Though Fellini had actually acted with Sutherland before in a cameo he did for Paul Mazursky's *Alex in Wonderland*, he doesn't remember him well and is quite tense by the time the two meet on the set in Cinecittà.

"Can you imagine being a diver who's been waiting on the diving board for three years?" complains Federico, who's grown extremely nervous while waiting to make this movie, and doesn't hesitate to admit to the press that he's lost interest in the project. He takes out his revenge on the epoch: "The 1700s—what a shitty century! All I can do with it is make an electrical wax museum!" He rails against *Histoire de ma vie*, describing it as "an intolerable, incoherent mess, a phone book." Most of all he's furious at Casanova: "The evil version of the Italian male; he's a vulgar Fascist. What is fascism after all if not a prolonged adolescence? Casanova is a super-*vitellone* but not a nice one. He's a sinister Pinocchio who refuses to turn into a well-behaved boy." On one particularly ugly day, the director vents his rage by ripping his rare Mondadori edition of *Histoire de ma vie* into shreds.

Fellini's abhorrence of the great book (which not only shocks the *casanovisti* but has them up in arms) is not exclusively motivated by circumstance. In the television documentary *E Il Casanova di Fellini?* (So What Happened to *Fellini's Casanova*?), made by his assistants Gianfranco Angelucci and Liliane Betti, Fellini delves deeply into his anthropological analysis. Beginning with a quotation from Borges, "Every writer creates his own precursors," he notes that "Italians who feel 'in the running' to be great seducers built up Casanova as their precursor. Under the daily shadow of gripping sexual frustration, it was practically destiny that the Italians gave birth to the legend of a man who conquers everyone. After years, centuries even, of the misogynistic xenophobic teachings of the Catholic Church, the Latin male has built up such a paralyzing heated longing for woman that he remains a perpetual adolescent, an individual incapable of growing up." The conclusion: "I hate Casanova."

The American producers get Gore Vidal involved in rewriting the screenplay—but Fellini won't use it; he'll be faithful to the script he wrote with Bernardino Zapponi. But Vidal asks Fellini, "What's the point of making a movie about a character you don't like?" The newspapers offer variations on the Pirandello theme*; in this version, Fellini is at war with his own character. The *casanovista* Piero Chiara declares that, in his opinion, the Cavalier of Seingalt is the most important Italian writer of the eighteenth century, and then goes on to recommend that one should reserve judgment on Fellini's film. He suspects that Fellini may actually have a good read on the character. "I think," he says, "that Fellini may even hide himself in the character. Apparent hate can be a shield hiding real love. When a director of Fellini's caliber chooses a subject like Casanova, it's because he wants to face it head-on. You can't face something head-on like this without love."

It took a while for Federico to recognize the autobiographical elements in 8½ and, in this case, the recognition that the protagonist is a kind of expressionistic self-parody will come to the director even later, long after the film is made. In the meantime, his anger gets taken out on poor "Donaldino" Sutherland, who must, according to the director, be held responsible for the fateful decision to go forward with the movie as well as all the concomitant obligations that such a decision entails, beginning with the irritation of having to shoot it in English. In the past Fellini has had difficult relationships with actors, but it was usually their fault: they weren't up to the part or committed to the movie, or they behaved poorly on the set. But Sutherland (forty at the time, with twenty years in show business behind him) is a consummate professional, and a

---

*A reference to Luigi Pirandello's *Six Characters in Search of an Author*.

talented, highly disciplined actor. He has worked with demanding directors before: Robert Aldrich, Robert Altman, and John Schlesinger, to
name but a few. He's also proud that Fellini cast him and wants to prove
that he can do it.

The protagonist has forty costume changes, ten wigs, and 126 different makeup calls. The Canadian actor never complains; he arrives three
hours before anyone else on the set to have his makeup done—a martyr,
even under the gentle ministrations of makeup artists Giannetto De
Rossi and Fabrizio Sforza. Fellini wants Sutherland's forehead to be seven
centimeters higher; his real eyebrows are plucked and fake ones drawn in
at the last minute. He tries on as many as 300 noses and chins, glued on
and then removed. Sutherland is an intellectual. He reads everything he
can about Casanova while preparing for the role and wants to discuss it
with the director. He wants to understand more, go deeper, come to a
conclusion about the character. But Fellini disappoints him by avoiding
him. He creates a dynamic with him that is the polar opposite of what he
has with Marcello Mastroianni. He never socializes with Sutherland after
work, never gives him explanations, never asks his opinion. At times, the
director's determination to impose physical deformities and humiliating
behavior on the character verges on sadism.

Many years later, Sutherland would tell the story in a documentary:
"Fellini's relationship with actors was terrible. He was a corporal, a tartar,
a dictator, a demon. He was almost hysterical. The first five or six weeks
were hell." Eventually Donaldino will come to understand that his physical appearance is simply the battleground, the field upon which the war
between Fellini and Casanova is being waged. It's an impressive battle indeed, and a privileged position from which to watch it—though a risk to
be in the middle, caught between the director and his character. The actor tries not to get angry at the provocations; he shuts up and does what's
asked of him, including learning long monologues by heart that have
been presented to him five minutes before a take. Donald is prepared for
the reporters too, who'd like to get him on record slamming the maestro
after they'd heard from the crew what was going on in the studio. Sutherland's official comment is that working with such a genius is the height of
an actor's career and he wishes that it would last forever. A diplomatic answer was never so close to reality.

For a while it seems that *Il Casanova* will never end. Filming starts on July 20, and is expected to continue for twenty-one weeks, with a vast budget that some estimates place in the realm of eight billion lire, a crew of more than one hundred, and a cast of extras and actors exceeding 200 people. The press calls the movie "the last colossus in the history of cinema." For supporting actors, the attraction is relative—in Fellini's films Fellini is the only real star. Some celebrities from the 1930s are considered for the part of Madame D'Urfé, an aging beauty, but in the end, the part is given to the American actress Cicely Browne. Another large role, the part of Sister Maddalena, goes to Margareth Clémenti from Vietnam, the wife of actor Pierre Clémenti. Photographers will take infinite pictures of the American actress Sandra Elaine Allen (Angelina the Giantess), who is seven feet five and weighs 462 pounds.

And in the middle of all of this, there's a little whodunit. On August 27, about seventy rolls of shot film stored in the warehouse at Technicolor go missing. Along with film from other projects, the first three weeks of shooting from *Il Casanova* are stolen, including the scene of Casanova's arrest on a boat during a storm. The heist is never solved— newspapers report that the thieves are demanding half a billion lire ransom, but the producer refuses to pay—and the whole ordeal drags on through May of the following year, when some of the stolen boxes reappear at Cinecittà.

By mid-December 1975, the film has missed its deadline, outspent its budget, and now some of the crew is on strike, making it difficult to finish the scene at the Piombi prison. Federico is, as usual, infuriated when outside problems affect his work and the resentment that will ultimately erupt in the movie *Prova d'orchestra* is already starting to build. On December 23, there's a big surprise under the Christmas tree: Alberto Grimaldi lays off the entire troupe. Calculating that the movie has already cost almost five billion lire and only 60 percent of it is done, the producer decided to call the whole thing off and send everyone home. Twenty-four hours later, a shocked Fellini receives an ultimatum: he must sacrifice some scenes and can only spend another billion. Fellini and Grimaldi exchange angry words in the papers but never meet in person. The director is embittered, saying, "The movie has now disintegrated and I don't believe that I can finish it." Grimaldi replies, "Fellini is worse than Attila the Hun," a statement that becomes famous across the globe. The lawyers are set loose to respond to the polemics in the press, but also to broker a negotiation.

As the battle rages, Fellini is giving rather bizarre interviews. He claims that he's received an offer from John Calley, president of Warner Brothers, to make a movie about pornography to be called *Erotikon* and that he can either make it alone or collaborate with Ingmar Bergman. Similarly improbable, though he claims it nonetheless, the Scion of Persia and the Emir of Kuwait want him to make movies about their countries. "Sing to me, oh muse, of Ciro and Serse . . . I'll remake *Anabasis of Alexander* for the glory of the sheiks." It's unclear from these comments whether Fellini is joking or really considering abandoning *Il Casanova* in pursuit of unlikely exotic adventures. His friends, of course, push him to finish the movie.

Finally, in late January 1976, Fellini and Grimaldi reach an agreement and everyone breathes a sight of relief. At Cinecittà, Alessandro von Normann handles the organization of whatever remains to be shot, like the scenes in Württenberg castle (where they resume shooting on March 23 after the three-month interruption), Casanova's days in Dux, and the complex and expensive scene at Carnivale in a reconstructed Venice with 600 extras and a gigantic figurehead of a woman that emerges from the waters of the Canal Grande, which had been commissioned to carpenters of the Carnevale in Viareggio. Between the scene in the Württenberg castle and the final shot of Casanova's dream of an iced-over Venice lagoon, there's the hallucinatory mechanical doll played by dancer Adele Angela Lojodice. Toward the end of May 1976, the newspapers announce that *Il Casanova* is at long last complete.

Soon after, during the editing phase, Fellini starts changing his tone in interviews. His antipathy for Casanova has waned; something new has cropped up between the director and his character. By the eve of the film's release in December, Fellini does an about-face, claiming "Casanova is what he is, but . . ." He admits to liking the *cavallòn* (big horse) author of that dreadful book, he likes the movie he was forced to make, and he likes Sutherland. Reliable witnesses detected a tear on the director's face when he said goodbye to the set, and when, after the last image of fake Venice had been shot, he and Donaldino embraced and affectionately, simply said farewell. They hug for a long time. As Federico breaks away from his lead actor, some onlookers have the impression that he is already missing him and feeling, perhaps, a little disturbed by the sudden recognition of the fact that he's created in Casanova a self-caricature— himself in eighteenth-century drag, flamboyantly engendering the clash between man at his worst and the world of women.

Filmed in a tempest, *Il Casanova di Federico Fellini* is a kind of descent into the abyss, a confrontation with personal demons. The ending is like *La dolce vita*: under a livid dawn sky, after an orgy, a monstrous fish appears in a fisherman's net. In *Il Casanova*, Fellini zooms in on the leviathan—there's even an allusion to it as the big head is pulled from the lagoon during Carnevale in the prologue. In the same way that the leviathan in *La dolce vita* reflected the dark soul of the hero, the big papiermâché head is a symbol of Casanova: a man with many faces—most of them already familiar. Casanova floats like Marcello on the tide of the capital's disintegration, but he's also a *vitellone* so bound to his province that he can masturbate to the joy of merely being in Paris. He's Zampanò, the Gypsy, taking down women as if they were objects he owned; he's the old con man who dies while dreaming about the big swindle; he's the director in 8½ mixing women and lies like the philanderer in *Histoires*.

In order to understand the movie, one needs perhaps to first try and forget the historical figure and the legend of Casanova. It's useless to attempt to figure out the reasons behind Fellini's choices, exclusions, and changes to the six volumes of the Brockhaus; the original manuscript is simply the occasion, the repository that inspires visual ideas, a pretext for a parade of imagery and symbols, like the storm in the lagoon or the magical escape from Piombi prison onto the moonlit rooftops; or like the sound of Enrichetta's cello after the entomological sketch performed by the hunchback Du Bois, which makes the seducer weep; or the embalmed whale in the foggy London market, a perfect blend of William Hogarth and Roland Topor, the Pre-Raphaelite tableau of the giantess and two dwarves.

Sutherland's Casanova inhabits Danilo Donati's intelligent, allusive set designs, which have the abstract precision of a cartoon. (Donati's exquisite alchemy of history and dream receives only partial credit, because Fellini puts his own name in the titles for "scenographic concept.") From his first encounter with Sister Maddalena (a name that hearkens back to *La dolce vita*), Giacomo presents himself as a sex champion in a Kama Sutra variety show. His eroticism is made of ironic hyperbole, emphasized by the flitting and chirping of his mechanical bird in the background whenever he is engaged in womanizing pursuits. We'll see him hard at work, crowned by candles as he plunges himself into the faded body of Madame d'Urfé. His pump boils over with women of every form and every age—winner of a lewd contest of endurance against his valet, he will fornicate feverishly through the comedies of Dresden, and will morbidly but vainly try to seduce the mechanical doll.

The film is another portrait of agglomeration, driven by a curiosity that seems, at times, to be Casanova's only healthy choice (such as in the scene of the interrupted suicide). In his final hours, a disgusted and reviled old man in the castle of Dux in Bohemia, the adventurer murmurs, "I had a . . ." and before he can get to the word *dream*, we see him young again in Venice, his motherland, immersed in a light that recalls the enchanted nightscapes of Paul Delvaux's paintings, dancing on the iced-over lagoon with the mechanical doll, a mechanical man himself—better yet, a mechanical bird, just like his good-luck charm. Through this antiseptic formalism, Fellini depicts an antihero bereft of faith, speared on by neuroses, stupidly clinging to the impossible dream of settling down, and consumed by the rowdy, luxurious incivility that surrounds him.

Il Casanova is not a cinematographic novel; there is no logical progression or real narrative connections. The segues between its nine or ten chapters are short and provisional, similar to captions in a comic book. Fellini's big top of a movie isn't far from the avant-garde—though American underground filmmakers have been thinking of him as such since 8½. He may have carelessly spent billions of lire to make this picture, but it isn't "industrial art" as Flaubert intended the term. *Il Casanova* is much more an example of the raw privatism of Andy Warhol.

If we were to compare *Il Casanova* and *Barry Lyndon*, released in 1975, we would find more differences than similarities. Stanley Kubrick takes his eighteenth-century costume drama seriously, working with the sociological and political aspects of the novel. He consumed entire libraries in his preparation and took a moral position on both the epoch and his character, whereas Fellini looked at Casanova's *Histoire* the way you might leaf through an old events calendar. Only impressions, resentment, and scorn are expressed. But if the 1700s of Kubrick's vision reveal deep cultural roots, the century that Fellini dreams up for his movie is rather an alarming and inscrutable prophecy. Jung might have described *Il Casanova* as a prediction about the past.

The film came out in Italy on December 7, 1976, and failed to garner the warm reception that had been expected—in part because it was released during the Christmas holidays. Critics initially have chilly praise for the movie, and then they totally reject it. Many claim (exaggerating) that Fellini's Casanova has no relationship whatsoever with the historical figure: he's construed to be a completely unhappy character, more baroque than eighteenth century, deplorable, a symbol of emptiness fated to remain empty. Other critics don't appreciate the film's visual excess and its accumulative, rather than narrative, structure. It will receive more or less the same reaction abroad. Pauline Kael, true to form, leaves the theater after an hour, irritated. It's possible that she might have come to feel differently later, however, much like Vincent Canby, who, when Fellini was given a prize in 1985 at Lincoln Center, retracted his criticism, claiming that he'd changed his mind. Kael wrote that with *Il Casanova* Fellini made "an epic poem about his own alienation," continuing, "Fellini gives big interviews. He's become the Italian Orson Welles. He talks so much about movies that maybe he doesn't even need to make them anymore—he's become the artwork himself." *Il Casanova*'s only real success is in Japan. In America it's a flop of historic proportions, despite being the first Fellini film after the popular *Amarcord*.

Federico, the critic, writes in *Fare un film*: "Now that *Il Casanova* is finished . . . it's traveling around the world securing delusion, shame, hostility, even rage wherever it goes." If Donati manages to win an Oscar in March 1977 for best costume design, the other nomination for the screenplay had little impact. Grimaldi has two explanations for the movie's failure: Sutherland's ambiguously sad performance, and the fact that Fellini refused to come to the United States to promote the picture.

The movie does have its admirers, however, despite having wounded the sensibilities of so many, and its acclaim is destined to grow over time. The weekly French magazine *L'Express* has a picture of Fellini and Georges Simenon together on the cover of a February 1977 edition.

Fellini had gone to Lausanne to be interviewed. The last time he'd seen the writer was during those heated days when Sim was presiding over the jury at Cannes and had fought to give the prize to *La dolce vita*. After seventeen years, Fellini finds Simenon in poor health, but enthusiastic about *Il Casanova*. The writer thinks it's a masterpiece, and in this dialogue full of unorthodox ideas, classifies Fellini as a "cursed poet, like Villon, Baudelaire, or van Gogh, or Poe," adding "[Casanova] echoes Goya, another cursed poet, who was also a court poet. The court used to think his work was splendid, though it was simply tragic. [Fellini has] shown the court, Venice, parties, dinners, and balls. And yet everywhere and always in [his] work, like Goya's, there's death behind the laughter." Simenon thinks of himself as something of a Casanova and he surprises Fellini by claiming that he's had sex with about 10,000 women (8,000 of which were prostitutes), and that he'd started at the age of thirteen and a half—a record that puts to shame Leporello's 1,003 Spanish women. Federico is particularly lucid in their bizarre but also revealing conversation: when Simenon asks him how he feels having finished such a stressful project, he replies, "I never manage to feel satisfied for long after I finish a movie. From the moment I begin, the only thing I want is for it to be over. It's too heavy, too stressful. But then once I'm finished, I can't relax. I have to start something new right away. Emptiness gives me the sensation of total uselessness."

The most compelling observation that Fellini makes about *Il Casanova*, however, appears in another interview in which the director admits,

What would I have liked to do with this movie? I would have liked to get once and for all at the essence of cinema and the complete movie, as I think of it. Which means transforming the film into a painting . . . If you stand in front of a painting, you have all of it, uninterrupted. You don't have that with a movie. Everything can be contained in a painting—you just look at it in order to find it, whereas a movie is an incomplete painting. The spectator doesn't watch it; the movie forces itself on the spectator, dictating a pacing and rhythm that isn't personal, that's imposed. The goal would be to make a movie that is just a single shot, one image that would be eternally fixed and constantly rich with movement.

With *Il Casanova*, I really wanted to get to that idea of a complete movie composed of fixed frames. After all, I got so close to that in *Satyricon*.

On another occasion, a few years later, the director will repeat that there is a profound relationship between his craft and the old vocation of painting he'd cultivated during his Roman bohemia. "My cinema isn't literary or narrative; it's pictorial. It's essence, style, ideology, light."

37

The Violent Years

Prova d'orchestra / Orchestra Rehearsal

In the spring of 1978, Fellini wrote in his notebook:

And what if I were to start with a convulsive, fragmented montage of sound, horribly violent excerpts from the newsreels over the last few years? A chaotic, terrifying soundtrack of gunshots, machine-gun fire, screams, and the demented drone of slogans being loudly chanted, punctuated with the wail of sirens, reverberating loud-speakers, the clash and roar of Molotov cocktails. This nightmar-ish mix, this delirious absurd universe, will be in the background. The title on the screen will read *Prova d'orchestra*.

It is one of ugliest periods in Italy's recent history. Giulio Andreotti will go to parliament for a vote of confidence for the fourth time on March 16, pinning his hopes on the notion that for the first time in thirty-one years, even the Communists will ratify his administration. The move is the fruit of negotiations led by Aldo Moro, the likely next president of the Republic to succeed Giovanni Leone. But Moro is kidnapped at 9:15 a.m. Thursday, March 16, on via Mario Fani, right in front of his house. A dispatch of the Red Brigade terrorists abduct him and kill his escort of five policemen. Fifty-five days of mounting anxiety are to follow, as the politicians, led by Bettino Craxi, advocate negotiating with the terrorist group in order to secure the Moro's release, facing stiff opposition from the ruling "party of solidity." The final act of this drama plays out on May 9, with an anonymous telephone call leading police to the body of Aldo Moro, on via Caetani near the Communist Party headquarters, stuffed inside the trunk of a car.

It is during this period that Fellini, along with Brunello Rondi, comes up with the idea for and writes *Prova d'orchestra*, the most passionate and feverish movie of his career—and also the most political. Having spent all of 1977 developing *La città delle donne*, the director decides to do "something short and cheap for TV" while waiting for the producers to make a decision on the costly project. The head of RAI 1 at the time is Mimmo Scarano, who isn't afraid of risky projects (proof of this is the famous documentary he produced about the Catanzaro trial and the bombing in Piazza Fontana*); he quickly accepts Fellini's proposal. Then, for a number of reasons, the outside producer originally hired for the project is unavailable, so RAI brings on Leonardo Pescarolo instead. Pescarolo came of age among the biggest stars of show business (his mother was Vera Vergani, a famous stage actress of the twenties and the sister of Orio Vergani, a great journalist) and is an experienced producer, yet he's still quite embarrassed to find himself in Fellini's notorious clutches.

The director doesn't want to make a straightforward documentary about an orchestra rehearsal, but he doesn't want a lighthearted fantasy like *I clowns* either. He ritualistically invites a different orchestra member to breakfast every day in his beloved Cesarina restaurant and interviews him or her. A secretary keeps notes. Fellini gradually meets the entire orchestra: violin, harp, cello, tuba, flute, piano, trumpet, bassoon, percussion instruments, trombone, oboe, and clarinet. After two weeks of breakfast interviews, the director has gathered quite a lot of information and is ready to approach the world of classical music with some sense of its everyday, professional character.

When asked about music in interviews—particularly regarding the frequent ill-fated requests to direct opera—Fellini has never hidden his distaste for the world of sound. With the remarkable exception of his

*On December 12, 1969, an explosion in Milan's Piazza Fontana killed sixteen people. An innocent anarchist brought in for questioning later fell suspiciously from a fourth floor window of the police station. Though many believe that the bomb was placed by neo-Fascists (not anarchists) with links to the Italian secret service, in the ensuing Catanzaro Trial, the right-wing administration placed blame on a Communist insurgency, creating an air of fear they hoped would allow them to consolidate power.

mysterious rapport with Nino Rota, music is mostly just noise to Fellini. He only ever apprehended a few elementary melodies (*Entrance of the Gladiators*, variety-show licks, Bach's organ music, the *Ride of the Valkyries*, and a few tunes from the jukebox). The lessons that his former editor and sophisticated musicologist, Leo Catozzo, has given him over the years fall on deaf ears.

Neither symphony nor chamber music interests Fellini, and operas make him think of funny stories—both real and invented. As a child he'd watched Riccardo Zandonai's *I Cavalieri di Ekebù* from his grandfather's lap high up in the balcony, and would be transfixed by the huge gong. He used to say that when he was young he'd been an extra in the Egyptian triumph of *Aida* at Caracalla.

Despite the fact that the idea of making a movie about an orchestra came to him as a metaphor, cinema is like an eye that registers whatever you put in front of it: the more abstract the symbol, the more concrete its screen representation must be—its gestures, words, objects. For this reason the director tries to go deeply into his subject, studying the relationship between each musician and his instrument. He listens to admissions and gossip, collects idiomatic expressions, makes note of events, and goads his breakfast dates to talk about the conductor, whom he never invites to breakfast. And yet the conductor is always a presence in the interviews, a mythical figure, scorned, idolized, despised; he's the big boss of the orchestra, the older brother, the tyrant. Sometimes he's God and sometimes the Devil, and sometimes both at once.

Fellini's imagination, stimulated by this peculiar, accelerated music course, speeds ahead of the bureaucrats at RAI. The screenplay is being typed out, the set is already built at Cinecittà—just one set, an old oratory designed by Dante Ferretti—and the contract still hasn't been drawn up. The budget is only a few hundred million lire, but Pescarolo, worried about running into difficulty with the director, is wary of advancing the money. Ultimately, however, the problems will not stem from Fellini but from slow bureaucracy and late payments. Fellini is instead to Pescarolo "an angel, a friend, and absolutely the easiest director I've worked with." He's not capricious, doesn't play the celebrity or behave stubbornly. While Leonardo is living this kind of Fellini idyll, engrossed in preparations, he makes a solemn vow: "If I get through this, I promise myself never to make another movie with Fellini." Why not? "In order to leave intact the memory of this undoubtedly unique experience."

Shooting begins on May 22 and continues for precisely four weeks. There are no delays or unexpected expenses. The editing goes on for slightly longer than planned, as Federico tries out a number of dubbing actors, makes changes to the dialogue, and is extremely particular about the dubbing in general. The producer, prepared for the worst, had fortunately included a budget for the dubbing, and resigned himself to absorbing the extra costs, though they are really quite minor in the end. Two theories exist in Cinecittà regarding the smoothness of this project, so different from the typically unpredictable Fellini affairs. The first is that Fellini, despite his reputation, is really what he claims to be: the quickest, cheapest director in Italian cinema. He knows what he wants, doesn't do many takes, and accepts all reasonable criticism. Then why do his projects cost so much? His explanation is always the same: they cost so much because of the monstrous agglomerations of landlords, vendors, freelancers, agents, mediators, and various profiteers who suck up the money. If Fellini didn't take advantage of the comforts they provided (and anyone would be subject to the temptation to accept), these people who make money off the business of cinema would earn less. And so it's the industry itself that has a stake in keeping alive the legend of Fellini, pharaoh of show business, against the director's better interests.

The second theory comes from the Fellini skeptics. The maestro's old friends suggest that Federico's method is to randomly choose someone to work with and then behave exactly the opposite of how he's expected to with that person, which would explain his choosing Pescarolo in order to demonstrate to future generations that working with Fellini can be peaceful, quick, and inexpensive. In the informal court of the newspapers, when someone accuses Fellini of megalomania and rash overspending, there will always be a few witnesses for the defense, just credible enough to embarrass the plaintiff and cast doubt on the circumstantial evidence.

Federico sees the world as an orchestra, full of funny, lovable, and horrible characters. He selects his cast, as always, focusing on the faces and ignoring whether they can play instruments or even pretend to play them. Consultants are brought on, headed up by the musician Carlo Savina, to teach his players to play. Savina uses a real baton and directs the orchestra from a position near the camera. The actor who plays the conductor is Balduin Baas from Holland, selected based on a head shot. His voice is dubbed by Oreste Lionello. The other actors aren't famous; they're extras or people scouted off the street, chosen in a hurry as always. The movie, one hour and ten minutes long, is shot in absolute secrecy; the press is not provided with any information whatsoever about the story or how it's going to be told.

The atmosphere on the set is very claustrophobic, much like *El ángel exterminador* (*Exterminating Angel*, 1962) by Luis Buñuel, a director Fellini loves. The concert hall, with its absence of historical or artistic references, is a symbol of the past, a windowless world, an interior space as opposed to the antagonistic, mysterious outside world (recalling the tug between Life and Form in Pirandello). Framed within this space, the musicians become a series of caricatures. In *I clowns* Fellini introduced the double equation of circus and existence, clowns and men, but he has grown more pessimistic since then. These clowns are more ridiculous than they are funny, and there is no longer any hope in the limbo of disingenuous people. The worst things are always on the brink of happening. There's no angelic little girl who will appear at the end, a symbol of salvation as in *La dolce vita*. Despite Fellini's previous fantasies, there are no triumphant trumpets heralding freedom. Federico identifies with the character of the Conductor (and with Voltaire's *Candide*) when he says that "you must dedicate yourself to playing your instrument well," but he's less convinced that the Jungian call to the "reality of the soul" is a solution. In fact, his other self, the Conductor, starts shouting in German on the final dissolve. Does that mean that his ultimate plea to mankind comes from a disguised superego, and that from one minute to the next, the idiot inside of us is capable of saluting the swastika? The film is a cynical, even dark meditation, and takes no consolation in hope or mercy. Fellini looks on his musicians with a repugnance that turns to violent hostility when the riot erupts.

This time, since the movie is based on the rehearsal of an orchestral piece, Rota has to compose the music before the filming so that it can be used as the playback score. His piece is composed of four movements, which the musician titles *Gemelli allo specchio* (Twins in the Mirror), *Piccolo riso melancolico* (Small Melancholic Laughter), *Piccola attesa*

(Brief Wait), and *Grande galop* (Big Dance). Each of these movements will be cut into smaller pieces, interrupted, restarted, mixed with rumbles, vibrations, and noise. After its release, some critics will register surprise that Fellini hadn't opted to go with a classical work of incontestable musical value for the program of this singular, embattled concert, in order to assert the monumental primacy of music. Others will criticize the score outright, which was sadly Rota's last, but it seems that the music's unfamiliar and cartoonish quality is integral to Fellini's mysterious intentions and lends a dash of irony to the final celebration of art as the last salvation of society.

Prova d'orchestra is shown in a preview in the screening room of the office of the president of the Republic in the Palazzo del Quirinale* on Thursday, October 19, 1978. It is well nigh a historical event; the first time that the highest officials of the state have gathered to watch a movie. Alongside President Sandro Pertini is Giulio Andreotti, president of the Consiglio, and Pietro Ingrao, president of the Camera, as well as other high-ranking officials. At the end of the screening, Pertini, a talkative politician, tells the press that the idea to have the screening there had come to him after running into the director recently. He likes the movie's message, but qualifies that the political allegory is not limited to the Italian situation. Andreotti finds a constructive ethical position in the story: everyone must start to love his instrument again and regain the joy of cooperation. Ingrao, a Communist, detects a theme of restoration and interprets the film as a call to order. His comrade Antonello Trombadori disagrees; for him, Fellini's film is a protest, an entirely justifiable response to the delirium of 1968.† Paolo Grassi, the president of RAI, is pleased that his network produced a project that attracted the interest of politicians, who are typically so uninvolved. He disagrees with the analysis, however: "I don't approve of authority, but I do approve of order." Some believe that Aldo Moro would have appreciated Fellini's indirect homage; he was the Italian politician who most liked the cinema and used to run to see movies between meetings.

Debate over *Prova d'orchestra* continues in the days to come, and

---

*The president of the Republic's official residence.
†This was the height of the youth uprising in Italy, and a period in which the student revolt became heavily involved in labor interests, provoking intense striking and violent clashes. The film is seen as a criticism of the deterioration of that movement in the years that followed.

there are more and more private screenings. Journalists in general focus their efforts on trying to decipher the alleged allegory behind the story itself. What a stroke of good luck for the tactless—at long last they've caught Fellini, the Great Individualist, struggling with social issues! They can finally try to comprehend the meaning behind his choices as well as snap a picture of him metaphorically aligning himself with a party in the voting booth; journalists flock to various ministers, party secretaries, union leaders, and writers to hear what they have to say. All of these people, and a hundred more, talk at such length about the film before its release that the space between the audience and the screen is already thick with judgment, cliché, and polemics. The public's biggest misunderstanding was to think of *Prova d'orchestra* as Fellini's first admission of political commitment, a ridiculous perception resulting from the factionalizing that had plagued the industry and distorted the understanding of Fellini's work in the 1950s. Yet Fellini had always talked about everyone when talking about himself, including society—both as it was and as it should be. Nevertheless, this film, more of a short story than a novel, constitutes one of Fellini's minor works, similar to *Fellini: A Director's Notebook* and *I clowns*, where the maestro plays at jotting down situations, archetypes, and characters without the level of commitment characteristic of his major endeavors. These films have a more joyous, expressive creativity. In fact it is in the shorter films that we see a more honest, less serious, yet boundlessly curious Fellini.

Prova d'orchestra, the allegory, is a reflection on the youth movement of 1968, with both the perspective of a decade and the evidence of a disintegrating sense of personal responsibility and political anti-professionalism that were its consequence. After his flights to the remote and recent historical and personal past—*Satyricon, I clowns, Roma, Amarcord, Il Casanova*—Fellini delivers a testament to the cult of a job well done, as well as to the terror of seeing grammar, syntax, methodology, and value systems collapse in the face of blind force, rising out of irresponsible masses (and not just out of the orchestra). His ideas can be perplexing if not read in the right way, but Fellini's unique ability is to present such notions lucidly and ironically. Another of his abilities is to show contemporary history as an unfinished chapter in the biography of humanity: when analyzing the revolution of 1968 he starts by first taking account of the losses, then disseminating the idea that there is a need to reevaluate the protagonists and challenge the mythologies. The risk, however, is to identify disorder with evil, as if the crisis of authority was a necessary symptom of imminent societal meltdown. Through his crazed orchestra the director portrays the general collapse of hope in the period following 1975—a phase of Italian history generally depicted as a kind of inward retreat—but it's not a direct consequence of disorder. It is rather a degeneration of the wrong *kind* of order. At times in the film it seems that the director's contagious bitterness—almost like Flaubert in *Bouvard et Pécuchet*—turns to anger, and it is possible that Fellini didn't take into strong enough consideration Romain Rolland's words in *Le Quatorze Juillet*: "When order is unjust, disorder is the beginning of justice." Neither, perhaps, did his public.

The battle of ideas over *Prova d'orchestra* would continue for some time among the elite, who see it in private screenings or crowd into the few special showings—like the one on December 4 at Florence's Festival dei Popoli—which attract huge numbers. The theatrical release is delayed by a set of polemics between TV and cinema distributors similar to that which plagued *I clowns*. In this instance it's the administration of RAI who has to take responsibility for the lengthy decision-making process, and the eventual limitations imposed on the distributors vying to release the film. In January 1979, the company Gaumont, owned by Roberto Rossellini's son, wins the bid for distribution when they put down a large deposit. It takes another month to make the prints for theatrical release, and by the time February 22 rolls around, the audience has lost interest. Perhaps the novelty of the event has passed; they've heard too much about the movie, or maybe they think that such a short film, produced for television, will be broadcast soon (in fact, only ten months later, on December 26, the film is shown on RAI 1). Regardless of the reason, the box-office returns in Italy are meager despite the positive reviews, which describe *Prova d'orchestra* as perfectly measured, Gogolesque, shocking, a congenial paradox, a marvelous show, a metaphysical meditation. More than one journalist will remark on the shift in Fellini's style and the absence of hope. The movie is well received when screened out of competition, as usual, at the 32nd Cannes Film Festival, and it will be positively reviewed in the United States.

38

The Bacchanalia
La città delle donne / City of Women

"Not since Méliès* has there been so much trouble over one movie"—so goes Fellini's discouraged account of *La città delle donne*, a good summation of the oddly sinister mood that plagued this film from the start. Preparations for *La città delle donne*, born out of an idea by Bernardino Zapponi for Fellini's episode in the lapsed project with Bergman, will go on for four years. The dance of the producers is slower and more confused than ever. The first partner is an American producer who disappears right away. Then Franco Rossellini (Roberto's nephew) comes on the scene, carrying his little dog who will lend his name to the production studio: Produzione Felix. The financial clout of Franco's offer comes from his partner, Bob Guccione, the multimillionaire publisher of *Penthouse*. They sign a contract around Christmas 1975, during the hiatus on *Il Casanova*. Franco Rossellini is like a divining rod in his ability to dig up producers willing to back the project—at one point there are about twenty backers on the list, each one of them funding a part of the movie—but after much discussion, another Rossellini, Renzo (Roberto's son), takes over the whole show through his studio, Gaumont. The French-Italian company was formed in 1978, in response to the belief that movie audiences in France were shrinking while the box office was still strong in Italy. The Parisian branch thinks it makes sense for the two countries to join forces against the American industry, but because of heavy bureaucracy, it will be some time before multiscreen theaters open

*Georges Méliès was a pioneer in early cinema.

on the Continent. In the meantime, Italian movies (Fellini's included) will go the way of French films, causing the company to shut down in 1985.

From the start, La città delle donne will set off alarms in the feminist movement. Without even knowing what the movie is about, scores of people begin to debate it, using the occasion to launch unrelated observations and unprovoked attacks. The film could have provided a platform for a deeper and more complex discussion of Fellini and the world of women, but such potential is spoiled by numerous misunderstandings and fed by a feminist literature that will continue to label Fellini as a champion of sexism, ignoring the fact that he is behind some of the most extraordinary female icons in modern cinema (Gelsomina, Cabiria), and that the harem dream in 8½, La Saraghina, and the repeated appearances of the megamatrons are nothing more than inventions, repetitions, and embellishments that have to be taken in a self-ironizing light. That's not even taking into account that in Giulietta degli spiriti, Fellini would be the first director to tell the story of a marriage crisis as an impetus for a woman to make a claim on independence—precisely the slogan that the feminists will later take up: I belong to myself. It's true that in Fellini's fantasies, men and women are never equal, but that's because the woman is almost always on a higher plane and shrouded in mystery. In his films, the truth-baring characters (must we return to the mythology of the "positive character"?) are always women. Only women can save men.

While developing La città delle donne, Federico has no interest in talking about it. He's suffering from an annoying and ongoing insomnia, alleviated by only rare moments of sleep ("I've slept a total of three days over five months"), which are disturbed by recurring nightmares—a condition similar to when he was working on Il viaggio di G. Mastorna. His most frequent dream requires no interpretation: he's alone on a dock in the middle of the sea surrounded by shark fins. The director tells his friends that he'd like to find a way out of the movie, but that's an exaggeration, the same thing he's said for every movie since 8½. Once the big production engine is started, it can't be stopped; the movie must go on. When journalists press him for information about the plot, Fellini is reductive: "It doesn't have anything to do with feminism. A journey into femininity? What are you talking about? It's just buffoonery, a little variety show." Perhaps he shouldn't minimize it too much, though; the budget for this "little variety show" is already five billion lire, and will increase significantly before it's over.

From the start, 1979 was an unhappy year, beginning with the death of Ettore Bevilacqua, the companionable boatswain of Fellini's fold, former boxer, masseur, and factotum. On Monday, April 9, three weeks before shooting is scheduled to begin, Federico meets up with Nino Rota at an exhibition of paintings by Fabrizio Clerici to discuss work while observing their mutual friend's art. Fellini wants music for the playback as soon as possible, so they decide to meet the next day. But at 3:00 p.m. on April 10, Fellini gets a call at Cinecittà telling him that Nino has died of a heart attack. It is as if Fellini has lost a brother; upon hearing the news, he can feel the most cheerful, childlike, Mozartean part of him slip away too. On the creative side, it's rather as if he has lost an arm. The musicians called in to fill the void will be entirely unable to replace him. For the project at hand, they turn to Luis Enríque Bacalov from Argentina, who will go on to win an Oscar for *Il postino* (*The Postman*, 1994). He's on a piano concert tour in Latin America, and is in Bogotá when he hears that Fellini wants him for a film. At first he's surprised—he didn't know about Rota's death—but later he will learn that Fellini came to him because Rota had always talked about his work with great respect. Fellini and Bacalov will have a strong relationship, often affectionately remembering the friend they had shared.

After Rota's funeral in the little church of Sant'Agostino in the center of Rome, Suso Cecchi d'Amico asks Federico to come home with her "as a witness." She has to reveal a family secret to Rota's relatives who'd come down from Milan. Nino has a daughter, conceived during a short relationship with an Italian music student during the period he spent in London right after the war. The girl was abandoned by her mother and then adopted by an English family, who paid for her and took her with them to America. Unable to handle the situation himself, Rota had always involved Suso as mediator. She kept in touch with the girl, sent her money, and arranged visits. Nina lives in Los Angeles and works in documentary film, Suso tells Fellini. She had sometimes visited her father in Italy, always very discreetly, and no one even noticed her presence in Spoleto for the premiere of *Napoli milionaria*, the opera that Rota had written with Eduardo De Filippo.

Federico is baffled and genuinely surprised to hear about his friend's emotional backstage life. Rota had never confided in him. He's impressed at how sensitively Suso has handled the situation and the same day sends her flowers with the message, "I heard you say that you don't like sending people flowers and maybe you don't like receiving them either. I send them anyway. Do what you want with them. I really like you after hearing this amazing story, and now I know that there's someone I can count on if I ever have to confess that . . . well, I'll tell you later." Perhaps Fellini is seriously contemplating sharing his complicated affairs with Suso, and it may be a real shame that he never did.

The mood is grim, but the show must go on: it's time to begin a movie that was meant to be cheerful but won't be. They start in April in Cinecittà. On May 3, Balthus visits the set with his Japanese wife, Setsuko Ideta, taking advantage of the occasion to put their daughter on the train that Marcello Mastroianni and Bernice Stegers are traveling on in the film. Fellini is happy to see the painter again; they were friends back when Balthus ran Villa Medici, but the cheerful atmosphere of the visit is ruined by news from the outside world. Armed Red Brigade terrorists have attacked the headquarters of the Christian Democrats in Piazza Nicosia. Echoes of this real-life violence will reverberate in the film, which, for the first time in Fellini's career, is set in the context of a long disturbing dream. Snàporaz (Marcello Mastroianni) follows an attractive woman off a train and ends up wandering through a series of locations and situations, a universe inhabited almost exclusively by women. They lure him in, flatter him, torment him, and finally abduct him, much like the Red Brigade.

More than two hundred women, including many militant feminists, show up for a feminist convention at the Grand Hotel Miramare. Some are there in protest, others want to engage the director in endless debate. A feminist newspaper attacks the actresses: "You women who agreed to participate in Fellini's movie, you've sold out the movement. Didn't you feel ashamed of yourself when you acted in those disgusting scenes, didn't you feel pity, or repulsion for yourself?" As the filming progresses, these ridiculous attacks occur less often, and despite the outrage, eventually disappear entirely. Federico gets some pleasure out of playing the role of a man with a harem—like Guido with his whip in 8½—but part of him wants to convince the less enraged wing of the Bacchanalia that the movie means no offense to women. Ultimately the maestro's charm is a professional tool and the unstoppable production schedule takes precedence over all else. Other famous people visit the set, including Danny Kaye, Susan Sontag, the Russian poet Yevgeni Yevtushenko, Martin Scorsese and Isabella Rossellini, Ingrid Bergman, Leonardo Sciascia, and Michel Piccoli.

The troupe heads to Fregene. In late May, they film the roller-skating scenes and start shooting scenes at Dr. Katzone's house, where a copy of a Kees van Dongen painting, forged by Antonio Scordia, hangs. Federico has cast Ettore Manni in the role of Dr. Xavier Katzone—a hateful, arrogant, authentic Casanova, who is strangely devoid of any humorous nuance. Manni had been a sex symbol in the 1950s; he'd appeared in Alberto Lattuada's *La lupa* (*She Wolf*, 1952) and Michelangelo Antonioni's *Le amiche* (*The Girlfriends*, 1955), had led a life of excess, and was a big, exuberant, passionate man. Though he's always liked people who break the rules, the director has little tolerance for unprofessional behavior on the set, and Manni, often drunk, seems frightened and subdued in a role that may well be beyond his reach. Federico tries to help the actor, even donning the red dressing gown in order to show him how to act in the scene with Marcello, but there are nevertheless daily arguments and recriminations on the set. The possibility of replacing the actor has come up, but would be problematic at this point, considering how many scenes have been shot. Federico is incredibly on edge about the situation, but Manni persists in his irresponsible behavior. One day the director is driven to such exasperation over the actor's continual bewilderment that he shouts "That's it!" and sends everyone home.

The press officer, Sonia Schoonejans, kept a fascinating journal about the production of this film, in which she repeats a story that Bacalov told about that day. After Federico's meltdown, Luis was left alone in the studio with the director, and he decided to sit at the piano and play a little Mozart. "Fellini sat down next to me, he was trembling, and also panting slightly. I was worried because I knew he had blood-pressure problems. After a bit, I stopped playing but he asked me to go on. Slowly he calmed down and when it got to the point where he could articulate himself again he started in railing against the damage caused by alcohol."

A few weeks later the situation is still the same, but then turns dramatically tragic. On July 27, in his home on via Flaminia Vecchia, Manni is handling a .38-caliber Smith & Wesson Special. The gun goes off, hitting an artery in his leg, and the actor bleeds to death. Some people say it's an accident and others think it's suicide. Schoonejans writes: "Fellini's first reaction was anger and disappointment, as if one of his characters had taken some unauthorized action upon himself, stepped out of the screenplay and become autonomous somehow. Then the anger gave way to a profound sense of discomfort."

After an investigation, the funeral is held on July 31. On August 10, right before the August 15 holiday, Gaumont suspends production and fires the crew, just as Alberto Grimaldi had done on *Il Casanova*. Manni's death has left them with the major dilemma of how to finish shooting the Katzone scenes—ideally, they would start all over again, but the set has already been dismantled and insurance won't cover the costs of rebuilding. So as not to bring financial ruin on Renzo Rossellini, Fellini determines to find a compromise solution. He'd already decided to dub Manni because of his terrible acting, and now he figures out how to eliminate him from the end, still managing to do the final scenes in the lab using Guglielmo Spoletini, Manni's double, by shooting him entirely from behind.

After a six-week hiatus, filming resumes on September 24. Fellini starts shooting the sequence of childhood dreams two days later, but they are interrupted again when a cyst in Mastroianni's eye swells—he'd had four operations for it, but it kept coming back. The cost of the movie has already ballooned to seven billion lire, and Rossellini is at his wit's end. "There wasn't a pope big enough for Michelangelo," he says, "and there isn't a producer big enough for Fellini." Finally, on October 6, something good happens: Renzo Rossellini marries princess Elisabetta (Lisa) Caracciolo di Fiorino at the bride's father's mansion in Todi and Federico is the witness. Unfortunately the newlyweds' joy will not last long. On December 8, 1984, they will be involved in a terrible automobile accident; Rossellini is left seriously handicapped and Lisa dies after four months in a coma.

On October 10, the director breaks his right arm and has to wear a cast for a month. Fortunately, the last take is on Thursday, November 29, in the open lot behind Studio 5 in Cinecittà: Snàporaz takes off in a hot-air balloon, only to be shot down again by a hooded terrorist with a machine gun. It's been more than seven months since production on the project began and the atmosphere on the set has been continuously tense. There were other distressing minor events to add to the big disruptions: Federico and his photographers and friends Pier Luigi and Tazio Secchiaroli argued, and there was a small scandal when an actress with a bit part gave an interview to a weekly magazine talking (as usual) about a purported affair with Fellini.

There's a Latin saying that Jung loved: "The dog dreams of bread and the fisherman of fish." What, then, was Snàporaz dreaming when he's on the train in the opening scene of *La città delle donne*? It's well known that "the predominant force behind dreams is wish fulfillment," and it's not terribly difficult to interpret the first and last image of the film: a train goes into a tunnel. Alfred Hitchcock ended *North by Northwest* in the same manner, leading us to understand that Cary Grant's dream of making love to his blond accomplice had finally come true. But the end of Fellini's film isn't so comforting—even though the character wakes with a half smile on his lips. *La città delle donne* is a "little dream" that refers once again to the "big dream" of *Il viaggio di G. Mastorna*: The two films have the same structure, the only difference being that *La città delle donne* is about women, while *Mastorna* was to have been about death. The director is cautious about defining this project, and, characteristically, he referred to it as "a thinglet, a joke." With Snàporaz's dream, he's not attempting to represent that "ancient piece of humanity" that Nietzsche wrote about but rather only a little residue of an embittered *Amarcord*, peculiarly devoid of a mother figure and with no gentle moments of respite, no humor. The visionary qualities here are so radically alive that the film becomes congested, and the most powerful images are those where Woman offers a perspective on reality, like the scene of the girls in the car on the brink of violence, or the moral torment of the prisoner—a very personal portrayal of Aldo Moro's plight. Snàporaz floats, abandoning himself to dream and providential irony, on the gloomy tide of the film. The contributions of Fellini's primary crew on this project are priceless: Giuseppe Rotunno is the cinematographer, Dante Ferretti designed fifty different sets, Gabriella Pescucci does the costume design, and Ruggero Mastroianni is in the editing room.

And what of the women? Radical feminists aside, the gist of *La città delle donne* is pro-woman. Insecure, perplexed, and irritated, Snàporaz doesn't even try to defend the male side, and admits to being a champion of ineptness, whereas Woman in her hundred incarnations takes over the space—she's aggressive, imposing, ever more fierce. The director seems brought to his knees (though in a slightly rebellious and sardonic way) by a superior vital force. Some critics will go so far as to interpret the image of the balloon/Madonna/whore as a parodying reference to the last lines of *Faust II*: "Eternal Womanhood Draws us on High."

La città delle donne comes out in eighty Italian theaters between the end of March and the beginning of April 1980, before the announced September release date. Federico had celebrated his sixtieth birthday on January 20, while editing the movie—there were interviews, greetings, presents even, and the predictable regretful melancholy. A few days later, January 28, Peppino De Filippo dies. He was an unforgettable "artisan of laughter" from the days when people used to laugh a lot.

Fellini's new film is received with respect rather than praise. Some comments include "typically Fellini-esque," a "catalog of the director's evolution," "a product of boundless genius," "a game with a few problems." Critics don't discuss issues of irony and humor, but rather talk about déjà vu. Many feel that although the fantasies are rich, the tone isn't always right. At the 33rd Cannes Film Festival, where the film is screened out of competition on May 19, the critics are harsher, even offering a few outright nasty reviews: *"zéro pour Fellini," "une déception lasse," "un ratage,"* and even *"une montagne de prétention et d'ennui."*

Anna Prucnal, the singer-actress who played Snàporaz's wife after Glenda Jackson turned the part down (Jackson was in a stage production at the time), gave an interview to the ineffable *Nice Matin*, conveying no enthusiasm at all over her experience. "You can't say no to Fellini; but I wouldn't do it again." Some critics wanted to see between Snàporaz and his wife a mirror image of the ongoing conflict between Federico and Giulietta, but Prucnal can only discuss her own experiences. She goes on to compare Fellini to Stalin, which is quite terrible coming from the mouth of a Pole, but then paradoxically concludes: "He's a tyrant, a monster, a madman, a genius. I love him." There are some scattered positive reviews and a spark or two of enthusiasm, but Fellini returns to Rome dejected. When he's asked how it went, he answers wanly, "Why do we continue to send our films to festivals?"

39

Ship of Fools

E la nave va / And the Ship Sails On

In the fall of 1980, in a restaurant near Piazza di Spagna, Federico is celebrating the publication of his book *Fare un film* (Making a Film) with the writer Natalia Ginzburg and other friends. The book is a collage of notes and edited excerpts from interviews, collected with the idea of explaining himself. It is the Italian edition of a book originally published in Zurich by Diogenes Verlag, a publishing house with an exclusive option on all of Fellini's literary work. The friendship between Federico and the Swiss editor Daniel Keel and his wife, Anna, a painter, blossomed quite by accident. One day the couple was walking down via Margutta, looking for the director's house in order to admire it from afar, when they ran into the man himself. The friendship soon became a strong business relationship; by arranging publications and art exhibits, Daniel helps to spread interest in Fellini's drawings, which the author had not placed great value on until then. The most important exhibit, "Fellini, ses dessins, ses photographies," is held in Paris in November 1982, eliciting quite a lot of interest.

Troubled about the reception of *La città delle donne* in Italy and abroad, the director feels a need to face his audience, which has become an unpredictable, renegade monster. At the end of the year, he and Renzo Rossellini visit eighteen movie theaters in the center and outskirts of Rome, attending first- and second-run movies. Both the producer and director are shocked to find the theaters empty almost everywhere. Cinemas in the early 1980s looked like the solemn churches in a Bergman movie. "The audience has just decamped to another planet. They're not there anymore," says Fellini. In interviews he often repeats words like *ca-*

tastrophe, apocalypse, and (warning!) *shipwreck*. On October 6 the director sums up the situation in a letter to Dino De Laurentiis, who is now living and working in Los Angeles: "Did you know that people don't go to the movies anymore here? There's no audience, and we don't know where it went. Are they all over there? If so, will you please send them back here to visit our movie theaters every once in a while too?"

What does a sixty-year-old man who's been making movies since he was twenty do in the face of such a crisis? Dino actually thinks he has a solution and doesn't lose the chance to suggest it to his old friend: Fellini should move to the United States and work in Hollywood. Dino would build bridges of gold for him—success and fame. But Federico knows he'd feel out of place in California, so far from his roots. All he can really do is keep a stiff upper lip and try to find a way to seduce the wayward fugitives back into the theaters. And so, in 1981, the director starts pretending he's optimistic and announces a number of projects. The first would be a movie about ancient Greek myths that he wants to write in English with Anthony Burgess, a writer Federico admires for his encyclopedic knowledge of culture and is ultimately intimidated by. The second project seems more feasible: a series of four thrillers for RAI TV with the title *Poliziotto* (Policeman), but the bureaucracy at the state-owned television company is so complicated that the project is soon moribund. No one takes the third project seriously, but *L'assassinio di Sarajevo* (Murder in Sarejevo) is the idea that will actually become a film.

Fellini and Tonino Guerra had written a treatment for the film a few summers earlier, and now Fellini is interested in going back to it. Franco Cristaldi thinks he might like to produce it, and RAI 1 isn't opposed. Fellini initially considers making another fake documentary, like *Prova d'orchestra*, something he can shoot quickly, maybe in black-and-white, but the producers, sitting on the idea, outdo themselves this time around. In the meantime the concept grows, becomes richer and more delineated. Months pass, and it's business as usual. Federico has to go to New York with Giulietta and Marcello Mastroianni in April for the opening of *La città delle donne* (which doesn't go over well there, either). Some people think he should make a movie called *Fellini a New York* (Fellini in New York), in the same style as *Roma*, which he contemplates before rejecting. He also has to refuse an offer from the director of the

Teatro Comunale in Bologna to do a production of *Aida*, and give a reason. A lot of time is wasted with CBS, which again wants Fellini to make Dante's *Inferno*. Urged on by Dino and others, Fellini has often been tempted by this prospect but always refuses in the end—it's an attractive notion because of the monumentality of the story to be illustrated, but it's also a risky venture. The American producers are impossible about the project from the outset; their marketing research shows that a televised Dante's *Inferno* couldn't have any nude scenes. The image of damned souls in underwear is more than enough to make discussions fall through.

There are other, ongoing invitations from an American company that wants the director to come live in the States for three months, scout around, and see if he can come up with a movie. It's more or less the same offer that Fellini had gotten twenty-five years earlier from Burt Lancaster's company. "If you sign on with another American producer," thundered De Laurentiis from Los Angeles, "I'll shoot you in the knees!" Federico is intrigued and irritated simultaneously. He's flattered by the grand deference and flexibility of the Hollywood people, at the same time that he is exasperated by lengthy bureaucracy that's dragging down his new film project. And so he accepts the Hollywood offer. The newspapers make a huge deal of the news. Fellini's unexpected decision is positioned as a parallel to Michelangelo Antonioni going to shoot *La ciurma* off the Florida coast, and there is much ink spent on the "flight of the brains" from Italy, exploring all the right and wrong reasons. Federico's trip to America won't warrant all the fuss, though, since it lasts only a week, at which point Federico's mother, who has been sick, gets sicker, and he uses that excuse to thank his hosts and return to Italy. Relieved, De Laurentiis lodges the claim that Fellini's trip to America never even happened, to which Federico responds that Dino "is a small buffoon." They have yet another argument followed by another reconciliation.

Having thus closed his brief American chapter, Fellini settles down to focus on the project that has now come to be called *E la nave va*. In April 1982 the director begins making visits to the ocean liner *Guglielmo Marconi*, which is docked, unused, in the port of Genoa, in a section owned by the company Ansaldo. Stefano Ubezio, Fellini's former assistant, now produces commercials in Milan; he puts the director in contact with Aldo Nemni, a businessman from Libya who wants to add some cinema investments to his business portfolio, which includes the import and export of reindeer hides and electronics. Maybe because Nemni has a house on Cap Ferrat, not far from Andrea Rizzoli, Fellini feels like he's found another patron—this time from North Africa. Initially, Nemni's interest was expressed more in promises than in actual money, but once he starts to kick in funds, the movie takes on life. After several months in development, the filming of *E la nave va* begins on November 15, 1982.

There's a famous Hieronymus Bosch painting in the Louvre with the title *Ship of Fools*, depicting a group of people reveling on a fragile-looking boat—clearly fated to sink into the ocean depths. But the symbol of the ferry carrying its passengers to their death is certainly more ancient than this. Remember Charon. In the *Dictionary of Subjects and Symbols in Art*, the ship of fools is described thusly:

> In the allegorical poem entitled *Das Narrenschiff* (1494) by the German intellectual and satirist Sebastian Brant, we read of a ship full of fools that sets out for the imaginary country Narragonia. In his poem, Brant presents a satirical portrait of all the flaws of contemporary society: licentiousness, all vices, drunkenness, lasciviousness, the corruption of politicians and clergy, the scourge of quackery and swindlers, etc.

The ancient theme of *stultifera navis* often appears in the movies; Stanley Kramer's *Ship of Fools* (1965), for example, starring Vivien Leigh and adapted from a beautiful novel by Katherine Anne Porter, is the story of a German luxury liner on the brink of World War II.

The big ship in the middle of the ocean—*Rex* in *Amarcord* surrounded by small boats filled with curious onlookers—is a persistent symbol in Fellini's mythology. This time, one of the small boats pulls up alongside the liner and the enchanted visitor climbs aboard, traveling back in time to when these oceangoing cities were the mausoleums of *dolce vita*. In the studios of Cinecittà, which the papers have renamed Felliniopolis, the ship is reconstructed bit by bit with extreme precision—perhaps just like it *wasn't* built originally. Wandering through the set designs, one gets the sensation of being in a hyperrealist theater created to imitate a reality that's only in fact a dream. None of this airy oceanic film is shot anywhere near the real sea, or even outside. With the help of Dante Ferretti, the set designer, the director reinvents a fabulous artwork inside the studios—Kafkaesque holds, ballrooms, austere libraries, machine rooms black with coal smoke, bountiful kitchens, and the harbor in Naples, patiently reproduced with real cobblestones. In Studio 5 a huge dining room is set onto a "balancer," a hydraulic machine invented for the express purpose of imitating the rolling sea. The walls are hung with more than thirty fancy paintings of every description and style—allegories, landscapes, Paris, London, Venice, Rome, Cairo, Paestum—all painted by Federico's old friend Rinaldo Geleng and his son Giuliano.

E la nave va was conceived of as a celebration (rare now, perhaps never to be repeated) of the extraordinary possibilities for creating illusion in cinema. There are few other movies where such an environment, depicted in its minutiae and with a playful pseudo-philological imagination, is the true substance of the film. The meaning of this movie is really in the story of the ship, with the spotlight that is like a pearl on the bridge, the flaming hell of the carbon engine, the halls for the grand events, the restaurants, the cabins, the corridors, the seagull that flies in through the window and the rhinoceros stinking up the hold.

Peppino Rotunno's photography for the cruise ship is highly original, neither black-and-white nor color. He calls it "black-and-white that can be manipulated into an endless range of sepia tones," yet he can also "make color appear or disappear." Production supervisor Pietro Notarianni oversees the building and dismantling of the set, the scheduling and general administration. He had been at Luchino Visconti's side during the ideological battles between Fellini and Visconti in the 1950s—and finds, working with Fellini, that the rivals were in fact quite similar. He admits, "Sometimes I find myself calling Federico, Luchino."

Passengers of the utmost elegance, the young ladies of 1914, the waiters, and the sailors congregate into a typical Fellini foreign legion made up of a few famous actors, many actors from Naples, and, this time around, more Brits. Freddie Jones, for one, came out of the Royal Shakespeare Company and had played under Peter Brook in *Marat/Sade*. Fellini cast him as Orlando (a name inspired by the famous television commentator Ruggero Orlando) after long debate over a roster of Italian and French actors. Marcello Mastroianni again hoped to win, but kept discreetly to the sidelines, only daring to venture, "Couldn't I be one of the guests aboard? So I can get out there on the bridge for a moment and take in the sea breeze?" Fellini replied with a chilliness that he could lay on even his best friends, "And what do *you* have to do with anything?" Some people will say that he might have done better to accept the advances of reliable old Mastroianni/Snàporaz.

Incarnating the breezy quality of Federico's own sketches, the cast forms a colorful and amusing chorus, singing verses of great Italian melodrama written by Andrea Zanzotto. Along with a return to fantasy in the arts, there's a revival of opera, which also has an influence on other filmmakers of the time—Francesco Rosi's film version of Bizet's *Carmen* is one example. Other, more famous actors among the ship's passengers include the young Sarah-Jane Varley, representing the eternal feminine as an adolescent. The great Pina Bausch from Tanztheater Wuppertal appears in the role of the blind princess, as well as others—elements creating a *La dolce vita*–esque mural.

"I like the clerical look of English actors," confesses Fellini in an interview on the set; the descriptive *clerical* has "the sense of someone putting themselves at the service of something in a more or less humble way." He picks his Brits from the catalog, based on their head shots and never having seen them act on the stage or in the movies.

They paraded them out for me at the William Morris office in London, one every ten minutes; whether they're famous or not, they're punctual, available, and pithy. The only social exchange might be a comment on the weather, something like "Nice weather today." They know that they're there only to be seen, and that we don't need to have a big debate about the movie or character. They don't try to figure out what the director thinks of them or squeeze out a promise. Nine minutes pass and they stand, nod, and leave. They are so professional that you can ask anything of them on the set, to turn cartwheels. They don't need explanations and they're not shocked by anything.

Fellini arrives on the set psychologically exhausted on November 15, 1982. For the whole four months that they shoot, he never tries to hide his tiredness.

I wrote this story with Tonino Guerra three years ago, quickly, over the summer. We were sure the movie would never be made. It was a trifle, a short script. Then there was the usual story of false starts and stultifying pauses, some enthusiasm, total loss of interest. How can you be expected to maintain for so long the scent, the truth, the inspiration of what you imagined? Three years later you've lost it. It's gone. It's rotted. So once the ship actually sailed, after all those announcements and postponements, I didn't really believe in it anymore. I was already distracted and involved in other things. The movie was like a bored guest who'd been waiting too long, so he left. But this is actually a healthy thing in cinema. Even after the original impulse is gone, the making of the movie involves so many practical issues that you forge on, not realizing that you've lost it. You shoot the movie not knowing precisely what it's about. You are passionate for the work for the sake of the work itself, a mash of paint, nails, fabric, people, outbursts, flashes of excitement, and tiredness. And so I have the fantasy that this is the way I always want it to be, never stopping. Because this is my life, or rather this *is* life. Cinema doesn't need great ideas, great loves or hates. It is a single task every day, the task of doing it. After all these years, it's the only thing that I'm sure about. It would all be meaningful to me even if the movie were never printed, edited, seen. If the camera had no film. If there weren't even a camera.

What Fellini defines as one of the "ambiguous lessons of old age" comes to him while he's making *E la nave va*:

I've decided to renounce, formally, in writing, the idea that I'm omnipotent when I'm directing. The more I'm convinced that I'm piloting the ship, the more the ship goes wherever it wants to. After the first few weeks, I'm not directing the movie anymore; the movie is directing me. It's nothing new. It happened to Geppetto too. He was still there working on his precious puppet, and then Pinocchio starts kicking him.

In terms of the movie in progress, he has a variety of things to say:

The movie crew on the ship is trying to capture a reality that is gradually losing meaning, until there's almost nothing left. The filmmakers come to realize that they have nothing to represent anymore. And maybe those of us filming them filming share their uneasiness. . . . In short, the movie is an attempt to capture a number of characters as they journey into the void, the sea. But it could be into the universe. The *Gloria N.* could also be a space-ship. This movie is meant to be cinema's last will and testament, a movie about cinema, about what it represents—the reality that wants to depict another reality but got so far away it disappeared. I want to repeat: it's been beautiful making movies, being together again, trying to re-create something, having a goal, escaping the isolation, the alienation, the indifference.

The director senses the peril but also feels extraordinarily alive as he travels on this ship that "goes wherever it wants." There are a hundred other characters tempting the director behind Orlando.

There's a fascination in the group shot, the constant temptation to let every face live the life it deserves, to go beyond the psychologies and caricatures of the faces. You would need a hundred films to tell the story of each face. I know I can't make them and I also know that I have to be constantly interesting to people. On the other hand, I'd like the movie to be very objective, a kind of cinematographic artifact found in an archive, printed, edited, and with a sound track. I've been lucky to meet some great musicians here, Verdi, Rossini, Bellini . . .

In stark contrast to the stated goal of objectivity, there is the moving run-up to the conclusion, when the director identifies with the guide, Orlando-as-journalist, and puts him behind the camera in a studio revealed as the locus and method of technical marvel. The director feels that his art has reached the end of a cycle, like the melodrama of the characters in the movie, but he reaffirms its value in challenge and magic. Those who know Fellini also recognize that the sea of his vision is a symbol of the mother's womb; it tends to reabsorb stories and characters. The ocean liner in *Amarcord* appears on the sea as an emblem of joy, change, hope, whereas here you could say that the image of the ship reverses and becomes *stultifera* in the Bosch sense—from the beginning it's clear that the *Gloria N.* will never reach its destination. The ship becomes a mirror of Western society (the society of today as much as that of 1914), grown frivolous with too much comfort, immersed in solipsistic ritual, and preoccupied by everything that stands outside this world of privilege. A simple seagull trapped in the hall can be terrifying as it flaps against the walls in its desperate flight. The image foreshadows the arrival of the Serbs, the real damned souls, incomprehensible in their pain, joy, and every spontaneous emotion. When the warship appears, it (as we read in the screenplay) "looks like a spaceship." The Slavs respond as if under siege and the movie closes on a partial apocalypse—which is the fate of the world according to some scholars of war.

"With the smoothness of a museum guide and a variety-show presenter"—as Fellini and Guerra write in the script—Freddie Jones as Orlando nervously performs an anachronism, reporting on the cruise without a microphone in front of a silent-film camera. This is another way for the director to emphasize the staged qualities of the film, however poorly. Orlando, old and dated, could be Marcello from *La dolce vita*—the stepped-on, humiliated, sensitive journalist—but the archetype for this character is actually Gattone from *Moraldo in città*. The decision to set the story in history is a tribute to the retro trends of Central Europe, fashionable in Italy in the 1980s, but also a clever parody of it. The movie walks a path of acknowledged ambiguity: the world of opera seen as a sort of picture album is ridiculous, and yet still lends some magic and affirmation to the sacred world of art. The funereal journey, bringing the ashes of the great opera singer Tetua Edmea to her final resting place, was inspired by the real event in the spring of 1979 when Maria Callas's ashes were brought to Greece and scattered in the Aegean Sea. It may look like a joke, but when the dead woman's ashes are scattered in the movie, some actors cry real tears. The plot isn't important, the characters aren't allowed any depth, and perhaps there's no moral to this story, yet this is a film with many hidden cabinets, filled with secrets and surprises. *E la nave va* is more than anything something to be looked at, suffused with activity and color. It's also an object to reflect on, though not systematically and not in the spirit of problem solving. One of Fellini's great contradictions is that although he was opposed to any kind of engagement, he can never avoid living his own moment and he can't relinquish the temptation to be a "guru." After many requests, he makes his pronouncement, offers last rites, something that people can live by. Orlando, floating on the raft with the rhinoceros, is an Ishmael who pulled Moby-Dick aboard: the Witness and the Monster, Intelligence and Nature in totality, bound together, the last thing floating on the water after the final shipwreck of all the great ships. Each is indispensable to the other, essential, inextricably bound. Raging against the dying society that rejects what is unknown (the seagull, the Serbs), Orlando embraces the beast, the primal life force, and finds nourishment in its milk. There isn't a creature more different from man than the rhino; it wanders through what Freud calls "the internal foreign country." Does its presence mean that the end of the movie is an allegory of the ego finally accepting the id? But then again, we should also be able to read *E la nave va* without any fear of super-thoughts and responsibilities. In a way, it's the fairy tale that Fellini always talked about—an illustrated edition, to leaf through image by image, forward and back, attending the inevitable miracle of revelation. Each one of us can find himself in that crowd of happy, threatening, cartoonish characters; we're all somewhere in the corners of the group portrait.

The series of anecdotes in the film makes no sense: a dream of failure and death, a slippery slope, the lead-up to a tragedy. Bombs explode, people die, survival is everyone's problem—these themes are intrinsic to our disgraceful times. We know that airplanes take off, but never know if they'll be intercepted by a missile before landing. Fellini isn't trying to represent anything specific; he makes no references to any real events past or future. He's aware of sitting on "the mouth of the volcano," as Il Granduca says in the film, but the director refuses to accept that the world will end. There will always be someone who "survives to tell it," and there will also be a rhino, his skin too tough even for bombs. So this funereal voyage harbors a mysterious vitality, even a hint of optimism. It starts in the fake silent documentary in the beginning, as well as in the surprise ending, where the movie reveals its own mystique in the remarkable scene where the director (like Prospero in Giorgio Strehler's interpretation of *The Tempest*) steps back to film the crew with his camera, unveiling the tricks and simple techniques that built the illusion.

The first screening of *E la nave va* is at the 40th Venice Film Festival, out of competition, on Saturday, September 10, 1983. The director has just returned from London where he was testing some voices with the English sound director Mike Hodges. He is formal in his participation. He stays in a hotel in the city center rather than on the Lido. He doesn't give many interviews and refuses to hold a press conference. Because of the timing, he had missed Bergman, who'd been in Venice a few days earlier to show *Fanny and Alexander*. Federico is flattered to hear that his famous colleague, after the applause from his own screening had died down, asked to see Fellini's film as a special favor, and watched it alone in one of the damp underground screening rooms—considered off limits after the 1966 flood. Fellini, however, doesn't ask to see *Fanny and Alexander*, which leads some people to wrongly think that the Swedish director has more admiration for his Italian counterpart than vice versa. The truth, though, is that Fellini loves making movies, not watching them. He has no interest in other people's films and, once he's finished, no interest in seeing his own.

Constrained to watch *E la nave va* for the last time he said, "When I'm forced to see one of my own movies, I feel the same discomfort as when I catch a glimpse of myself in a store window, a large, bumbling figure. And I also feel great fear, as if I were watching myself sitting in a chair in front of me." He adds, "I feel as if movies are ectoplasms that change according to where they are seen—like when you run into a friend in another city or situation and don't recognize him at first. It's a magic trick; movies mirror their audience. If the audience is bored, the movie looks boring to me. If the audience is restless, so am I." It's a strange comment that reveals a discomfort and uneasiness with himself, and an unwillingness to see himself from the outside, which, up to this point, he has disguised in his movies in various ways.

The movie is successful at Venice: Fellini is praised by colleagues and applauded by the public. There are a few isolated hoots at the screening in the Arena, threatening to spoil the happiness, but the next day positive reviews appear in the vast majority of papers. There's broad admiration for the stylistic attributes, as well as some small reservations about the length (two hours and five minutes), but it garners the consensus only important works receive. The reactions will be similar everywhere, especially in Paris, where it opens in January of 1984 and is declared a masterpiece. In the United States, there are some reservations; one critic calls the movie "huge and boring."

Because of the muted reception in the States, it's not one of the five films nominated for an Oscar for best foreign language film. Though it was Italy's entry, it didn't win enough votes. Some people claim that the oversight is due to a lack of screener copies; as the production group had dissolved and the Italian cinema agencies were uninvolved, no one thought to provide copies of the film to the Academy.

During the time he was developing, filming, and showing *E la nave va*, Fellini had become a charismatic figure with the media, ubiquitous in the papers and on TV, almost to the point of obsession—Federico tends to disabuse the impression of excess. The movie receives press coverage unlike many other films in the history cinema. The plot had been kept secret until the last, but still the media published news, gossip, interviews, photo spreads, television specials, and programs about the making of the film. Fellini is one of TV's preferred celebrities—all the shows want him—and he's the darling of newspaper editors. He's even cast as himself in the blockbuster *Il tassinaro*, perhaps as a favor to Alberto Sordi, whom he never used again after forcing the actor on producers when no one knew him or wanted him in their films.

Although a lightning rod of success and marketing when attracting audiences to other people's productions, Fellini's name on his own picture doesn't win a huge audience. The *Giornale dello Spettacolo* notes:

The reception to Federico Fellini's film *E la nave va* is an interesting case. The movie was praised by politicians (including the president of the Republic) when it came out, and praised by intellectuals and critics. It had a big push from television coverage. The giant promotion worked, though modestly, for the first five months only. Then, just as the movie started to play in theaters, an irreversible decline started. The fate of *E la nave va* in theaters wasn't affected by the promotion in the media. Italians evidently like to talk about culture but are actually bored of going to see it.

We could discuss at length the disconnection between the widespread interest in Fellini the character and the indifference over Fellini's art. It may be evidence that society is more interested in appearance and loves brands, but doesn't want to test them against themselves. It might be the repercussions of a new generation of remote-control spectators, who track the sensational but have lost interest in stories. Or maybe it's a symptom of the fact that Italy in the 1980s was nurturing a gap between artists and common people, between professionals and the man on the street.

Some people speculate that Fellini's later pictures didn't do well because of his reluctance to make people laugh, as if the director was a victim of Calvero syndrome—named after Chaplin's character in *Limelight*. They add that Fellini, as an old clown, is obviously aware of the tragedy inherent in the human predicament, and thus unable to laugh about it. When a reporter asks him why his funny movies never are funny, Fellini replies, "It is certainly my mission, my vocation, to make people laugh. But while you're under the spell that makes you think you're in charge of a movie, the movie starts following its own rules. The movie is autonomous; it suggests things, reveals things you hadn't seen before. It laughs or cries of its own accord."

The day that *E la nave va* is released in Italy, September 25, 1983, is declared Fellini Day in Rimini and there's a big reception with 1,500 people at the Grand Hotel, which has been all done up to look like the *Rex*. Federico and Giulietta make a television appearance that Sunday afternoon. Everyone knows that the director hates these kinds of affairs, but this time he seems almost touched when his city gives him the gift, on television, of a house on the harbor. The hope is that the prodigal son will return to his hometown. But the director, it seems, was touched prematurely: the small decrepit house is buried in liens and still belongs to the owner—the city only made a deposit on it. When the Fellinis try to actually occupy the house, they find out that, unless the city steps in to mediate, no one will pay off the money due, and after the joyful scene on TV, the gift leads to shameful court litigation that continues for years. The joke around Rimini is "Fellini may have made *Il bidone*, but Rimini conned him."

40

School for Shamans

Despite the embarrassing mess over the little house on the harbor, there will be another premiere in Rimini the following year (October 1, 1984). *Genius loci*, a short film Fellini had made advertising the aperitif Campari Bitter, is shown at Teatro Novelli for EuropaCinema. The attractive designs of the film show up on T-shirts and festival posters. The screening is one and half minutes long, which comprises two versions of the film, a sixty-second one and a thirty-second one. Unfortunately, Fellini is in Rimini for an event of other, more painful proportions; his mother has died.

In the short film Victor Poletti, the bearded actor who played Fuciletto in *E la nave va*, is sitting in a train across from a blonde, played by Silvia Dionisio. The woman picks up a remote control and starts neurotically changing the landscape outside the train window. The series of landscapes are all based on real places: Death Valley, the Middle Ages, the ruins of Petra, a moonscape. Bored, the woman tosses the remote aside. Poletti picks it up and clicks to a miniature of the Campo di Miracoli in Pisa. In the middle of the landscape stands a bottle of Campari Bitter, as tall as a bell tower.

In just one minute (although he does it in half a minute too) Fellini gives us a chapter of the story of the battle between men and women, makes a reference to the neurosis of TV, insinuates that we're disparaging the miraculous gifts of nature and history, and offers the hope that there might be a screen that will bring the joy back. The little tale is as quick as a train and has a remarkably light touch.

Federico enjoyed the experience and, after some time, will make another advertisement for a friend, Pietro Barilla, a businessman from Parma. It's a commercial for a certain pasta shape, and Fellini's idea is as witty as those he had when he was working as an assault caricaturist. There's an elegant dining room, a battalion of waiters, and an extremely gentle host, who recommends that the sophisticated lady try one of the chef's specialties. With the hint of a smile, the woman says, "Rigatoni." The commercial went well and the punch line "Rigatoni" entered common parlance.

In the fall of 1985, something bizarre happens. There's a trip to Los Angeles and then on to Mexico, all of which is kept hush-hush for a long time.

> The point of the trip: a filmmaker is fascinated by the work of a certain Latin American scholar. His books are full of the stories, characters, legends, and magic rituals of the ancient Aztecs—and the filmmaker has decided he wants to turn them into a movie. He wants to see how feasible the project is, and so plans to meet the writer and visit some of the story locations with him.

This is how the screenplay for *Viaggio a Tulun* (sometimes called "Tulum") begins. Fellini will end up publishing his version of events in a series of articles that run in the *Corriere della Sera* in May 1986. The series ends with the sentences: "The trip and the mysterious adventure really happened. I freely reconstructed it and wrote it as a movie treatment with Tullio Pinelli"—quite an unusual comment from Fellini, who'd always defended the importance of fantasy.

Let's go back to October 1984. Fellini is in development on *Ginger e Fred*. For years, he'd been passionately reading the work of Carlos Castaneda, like *The Teachings of Don Juan: A Yaqui Way of Knowledge*, and had often tried to get in touch with the Peruvian anthropologist. But he never managed to get through; there was always someone in the middle, explaining that the writer was traveling, he was impossible to reach, and so forth with evasive answers. Fellini begins to suspect that Castaneda doesn't really exist. Some claim the author is dead; others think he's in a mental institution and that his new books were written by a committee of anthropologists. Then Yogi, a young Mexican actress who shared a prickly relationship with the director on the set of *La città delle donne*, calls up out of the blue and says, "Carlos is in Rome. Do you want to meet him?"

When Federico meets Castaneda in person, he finds nothing in the author's physical appearance to suggest that he's a shaman or initiated. He's somewhere between fifty and sixty, stocky, and very gentle; he looks like a man with no mystery. Though Castaneda has seen Fellini's films and discusses them enthusiastically, the conversation never becomes intimate. The director is left with the impression that Castaneda is a difficult personality to grasp, that he keeps himself well hidden. Federico and Carlos nonetheless arrange to meet in Los Angeles and travel together "south of the border" in pursuit of mystical revelations. Fellini already has a rough idea for a story in his head and, at this point in his career, wouldn't actually mind making a movie outside of Italy. Alberto Grimaldi foots the bill for the adventure and is prepared to buy rights to all of Castaneda's books. Federico brings a small entourage along.

According to the story, all sorts of things happen on the trip except what's supposed to happen. Federico is accompanied by, among others, a skeptical journalist, Gian Maria, and by Grimaldi's son Geraldo. The director and the anthropologist meet in Los Angeles to plan their southern itinerary, but in the meantime, there are some alarming events: anonymous messages, even more mysterious phone calls. An American friend of Geraldo, Sybil, joins the group. She claims, though it's hard to believe, that she has extensive experience with the paranormal. In the end, she'll just wind up arguing with Geraldo, who gets jealous over how open she is with strangers, and the couple will abandon the group.

The disappearance of Castaneda, however, is more alarming. He's apparently been upset by the threatening messages. Then, like in an adventure story, new people unexpectedly join the expedition: Professor Tobia, an expert in pre-Columbian civilizations, and Helen, a beautiful girl with extrasensory powers. The group is caught up in a web of alarmism, foul moods, frustration, and moments of ecstasy. Traveling by airplane and car they eventually arrive at the Chichén Itzá pyramid, where human sacrifice was practiced in ancient times, but a voice on the telephone convinces them that they should go to the dead city of Tulum, in order to take a single picture of the ruins of the Temple of the Descending God, where sky and earth symbolically meet. En route, the travelers meet don Miguel, a native shaman very like the master, don Juan Matus, that Castaneda wrote about in his books. Don Miguel gets the director and company involved in a wacky ritual in which they spend an entire night either seeing or dreaming sublime and unbearable hallucinations. A hawk often flies over the group as they travel, drawing hieroglyphs in the sky. Is it just a regular bird of prey? The director and Gian Maria finally board a plane back in Los Angeles after saying goodbye to the beautiful Helen and the wise Tobia, knowing that they'd shared an experience that would be impossible to describe. All they have left from the trip is a small, insignificant, but mysterious photo of the pre-Columbian ruins. As the two Italians sit on the jumbo jet, heading home, the lights go down and a movie, *Viaggio a Tulun*, starts playing. Just like in 8½, we realize that the plot is the movie itself; it's a story about making a movie, a cinematic mandala.

Federico is constantly torn between being open and being secretive, between the desire to immerse himself in the unknown that has become so familiar to him and the need to explain things. Between flashes of childlike faith and glimpses of irony, he realizes that he's traveled thousands of miles only to find himself looking perplexed in the mirror. The screenplay is an interpretation of Castaneda's writing, a barely veiled satire, and the exotic backdrop is just a different design conveying the usual themes of the relationship between nature and culture, mystery and comedy. Fellini accepts all the rules of the game in the journey of initiation, even the strangest and most bizarre—but he can't accept the rule that forbids laughter. It might be the irresistible temptation to alleviate nervousness through laughter that blocks the miracle right before it happens, or it might be the incredible defensiveness of Fellini's psyche trying to keep the terrible collapse of his interior Great Wall of China from happening.

Through the last days of his life, Federico will continue to reflect on his Mexican jaunt, vainly trying to locate its meaning. The most likely explanation is that someone more organized and powerful wanted to control his adventure—not in order to keep him from making *Viaggio a Tulun* but because they wanted to map its direction. The last anonymous phone call (still an unknown person, but this time speaking Italian) comes to Fellini while he is at Pinelli's house soon after the first articles about his journey are published in *Corriere della Sera*. The voice just asks the director to specify in an epilogue to the articles that the events of the story really happened. And Fellini, a bit frightened, obeys.

Once a screenplay is published, as with *Viaggio a Tulun*, it generally means that the movie itself won't be made. But the Mexican adventure had so many good elements: a stimulating story, a strong character (the European intellectual trying to reconcile exotica and esoterica), the events, and the opportunity to shoot in English on location. Federico explained his decision not to make the movie:

> I got the impression that it wasn't solid enough, despite Pinelli's input, which was as usual useful for constructing the plot. But I started to have the doubts that a engineer might have: Can you build a house that has a third floor and fifth floor, but not a fourth floor? Basically I realized once again that artistic legitimacy is something quite different from having lived an event. The reality of art is actually more demanding than the reality of perception. And so *Viaggio a Tulun* ended up like *Mastorna*.

But there was a more complex explanation behind that one. Federico never did really figure out what happened on that journey to the Yucatán. He didn't know what "superior intelligence" was responsible for the phone calls and messages; he couldn't interpret their purpose. Certainly the anonymous voices achieved their goal. After the first messages, Castaneda disappeared—no one knows where he went even now. The contract for the rights to his books was ready to be signed and waiting in the Los Angeles office of Grimaldi's lawyer, but was never signed. For a dozen years, the famous anthropologist seemed to have been sucked back into the mysterious magma that had surrounded him before he appeared in Rome. He reemerged for an interview with *Corriere della Sera* in November 1997, a few months before his death, but instead of explaining what had happened he remembered how Fellini had taken him to lunch with Marcello Mastroianni to a restaurant in Rome and they were served twelve different dishes. "I was terrified. They ate everything." Castaneda then recommended that Fellini never try peyote, because "considering how much he ate, it would be disastrous." From these comments it seems clear that Castaneda didn't know Fellini very well: he was an extremely austere eater and usually only picked from other people's plates.

There's an unpublished epilogue to the story of *Viaggio a Tulun*, which

Vincenzo Mollica had been present for. He'd acted as mediator between Fellini and the comic-book artist Milo Manara when they decided to collaborate on a book in 1988. Fellini made the storyboards, constructing them as if working on a movie, and his idea was to include Castaneda as a character in the first scenes, so he sketched some rough portraits. At that point, however, the mysterious phone calls started up again. A man's voice told him to give up on the idea of drawing Carlos's image. Fellini, who'd already turned the sketches over to Mollica, immediately told him not to pass them on to Manara and to not show them to anyone. Vincenzo did as Federico asked. Castaneda was erased from the book and the phone calls stopped.

41

And Here's to You
Ginger e Fred

Production on *Ginger e Fred*, Fellini's nineteenth film, starts in Cinecittà in early 1985. No, actually, it's his eighteenth film. Really, it might be the twentieth. The maestro wreaked havoc on the numerology of his filmography, as he did with many aspects of his private life, when he put 8½ into the equation (a title that also was a likely count of his movies to that point). In the twenty-two years between 1963 and 1985, Fellini makes another eight movies, plus the episode in *Histoires extraordinaires*, and the made-for-television movies *Fellini: A Director's Notebook* and *I clowns*. The total number should be sixteen movies, three shorts, and two television movies. Adding it all up then, *Ginger e Fred* is Fellini's twenty-second movie.

The title refers to Ginger Rogers (née Virginia Katherine McMath) and Fred Astaire (really Frederic Austerlitz), born in Omaha, Nebraska. They were the most famous dancing couple in American movies, and between 1933 and 1949 made ten musicals together, including *Roberta*, *Top Hat*, and *Swing Time*. The names Ginger and Fred are the ironic monikers assumed by the two bedraggled variety-show old-timers, Amelia Bonetti and Pippo Botticella (played by Giulietta Masina and Marcello Mastroianni, respectively), who reunite after many years to dance on the television program *Ed ecco a voi* (Here's to You).

Masina had made six movies with her husband, but they hadn't worked together since *Giulietta degli spiriti* in 1965. Marcello had long been the director's alter ego as the protagonist of *La dolce vita*, 8½, and *La città delle donne*. Masina and Mastroianni have connections beyond the director, as well: like Amelia and Pippo, they first acted together back at the university theater. The two leads, typical to Fellini projects, don't know very much about what they're going to do on the set at Studio 5 in Cinecittà. Dante Ferretti has built an enormous television studio, and there is a crowd of characters assembled that seems to be predominantly made up of celebrity look-alikes—gathered in the usual impassioned flurry of mobilizing aspiring actors. Donati has prepared more than a thousand costumes. The director of photography, Ennio Guarnieri, is a new arrival to the Fellini camp and will later be replaced in the usual unpleasant way by Tonino Delli Colli. The composer, always a difficult decision since Nino Rota's death, is Nicola Piovani, who will continue to work with the director on subsequent projects.

Marcello emerges from makeup looking as old as he was supposed to and is amused to overhear someone remarking to a friend at the bar, "Have you seen how awful Mastroianni looks?" A legend arises about the hat that Marcello wears in the movie; it's said to be a magic hat that the magician Gustavo Adolfo Rol "conjured up" while in a hat shop with Federico in Milan. The director offers his usual answer: "It's not true, but I believe it," and then religiously bows to the supernatural element; he believes it's a good omen and keeps the hat on Fred's head.

As always, behind the scenes there is the familiar endless game of passing the movie from one producer to another, and the tempest of hopes raised and disappointments. The original idea was to make a series of episodes for TV, starring Masina and shot by several directors. Instead it ended up becoming a feature film by Fellini. The budget is set at nine billion lire. Alberto Grimaldi has returned from his golden Hollywood days to produce the film; the disagreements with Fellini over *Il Casanova* are now a thing of the past and their relationship has regained peaceful ground. Expectations for this film are high; Istituto Luce and RAI 1 are putting up almost all the money.

Filming begins on February 12, 1985. But the director is superstitious and Fellini's movies never start and never end; there's never an exact first day and an exact last day; it's all preceded and followed by "entrails," little bits and pieces needed here and there (or not needed, but shot nonetheless). The entrails of *Ginger e Fred* turn out to be all of the TV programming that appears on the monitors during the show, the ads, announcements of new shows, video clips, and so forth. Fellini shot many of them after his return from the Yucatán and he shows them to visitors to the set upon request. In order to represent the everyday character of television, he's had to reinvent it.

In some interviews, the director defined *Ginger e Fred* as "*La dolce vita* for the eighties," but on other occasions he tried to downplay it and called it "a little movie." Up until the very last minute, the host of the show had yet to be cast (Alberto Sordi would have been perfect, according to Fellini, except that he's too well known as Sordi), and many other decisions will be made after they've already started filming. As usual the project takes off with the best intentions: it will be a short movie, not longer than 100 minutes (the final project will run 126 minutes), and more important, this will be the eternally postponed and long-promised comedy (it will, in fact, end up rather grotesque and sentimental).

From the start, people predict that *Ginger e Fred* will be the anti-television movie, and in a sense that's true. After *Amarcord*, intended as the ultimate reconciliation between the author and the world he grew up in, Federico was suddenly inspired to become the man-against-society. *Il Casanova* takes the Mediterranean super-male to task; *Prova d'orchestra* criticizes the destructive elements of the 1968 social revolution; *La città delle donne* rails against radical feminism; *E la nave va* challenges a society ignoring signs of an imminent Apocalypse. So *Ginger e Fred*, when seen through this lens, can be thought of as the movie against mainstream television and Silvio Berlusconi. Fellini's opinion on this matter is recorded in a brusque and uncharacteristic editorial in *L'Europeo* (December 7, 1985): "Television like that doesn't deserve to survive." He's referring to privately held networks, a phenomenon that had taken off in Italy toward the end of the 1970s and proliferated wildly and without restraint. Obviously, showing hundreds of movies for free each week on thousands of local stations is driving an enormous number of viewers out of movie theaters; and it's understandable that a man of cinema like Fellini would be opposed. But what he finds most offensive—to the point of initiating legal suits to protect his copyrights—are the insane commercial interruptions inserted into the films.

> The continuous interruption of films shown on private networks are an outrage; it not only hurts the director and his work, but the spectator as well, who becomes accustomed to this hiccupping,

stuttering language, and the suspension of mental activity, to a re-peated blood clot in the flow of his attention that ends up turning the spectator into an impatient idiot, unable to concentrate, re-flect, make intelligent connections, look ahead; he loses the sense of musicality, harmony, and balance that are integral to story-telling . . . This disruption of syntax can only serve to create a race of illiterates on an epic scale.

More than television ads, the focus of *Ginger e Fred* is on the fad for new-generation variety shows (referred to as *contenitori*, or "containers," in Italian), where vestiges of old variety shows appear in a talk-show for-mat, the result being a pageant of idiocy. On several occasions while working on the film, Fellini comments that it would be difficult to really capture the loony, graceless, contradictory shamelessness that people can see on TV every day in their own homes. The idea of *Ginger e Fred* as a movie against society is particularly popular in France, where its release coincides with the debut of Cinq, a private television network originating in Italy that the Socialists granted a broadcast permit (it will have a stormy and brief life). But the true substance of this movie lies else-where.

Fellini began editing *Ginger e Fred* over the summer and was dis-tracted from his work by a series of events. On June 10, the director goes to New York to receive an award from the Lincoln Center Film Society at Avery Fisher Hall, the first non-Hollywood director to receive such a prize. They play a two-hour-long montage of excerpts from all his movies, from *Luci del varietà* to *E la nave va*, interspersed with interviews. Actors from some of his films are there and take the stage: Sordi, Anouk Aimée, Donald Sutherland, Giulietta, and Marcello. Federico is overcome by the audience's warmth. He always knew, he says, that Americans were nice, ever since he was a child and first saw Felix the Cat.

Work is interrupted again around August 15, but for reasons of a differ-ent nature. It might be the intense heat of the summer and it is certainly due to working too hard, but Federico feels sick and is hospitalized. This is an extremely unusual occurrence; he's always been healthy with the sole exception of his illness during *Mastorna*. The doctors say it's a "tem-porary blood clot" and it indeed passes within a few days, leaving him only slightly worn out. The TV audience can see this tiredness when the unforgiving cameras capture him on Friday, September 6, onstage at the Palazzo del Cinema during the closing night of the 42nd Venice Film Festival. He receives the Biennale's highest award for filmmaking, the Golden Lion, for his career achievements. It wouldn't be inappropriate for him to allow himself to feel some satisfaction at being admitted into the pantheon of great directors, but Federico is allergic to public demonstrations. "I accept and thank you," he says, "on the condition that you allow me to continue my work." In the new house on via Margutta, much smaller than the previous one, there's no "Sanctuary of Divine Love" for the awards. Where will he install this trophy that means so little?

Fellini cancels the premiere of *Ginger e Fred* at the New York Film Festival in October and decides to hold it instead at the Palazzo del Quirinale for Francesco Cossiga, president of the republic, and other politicians and intellectuals. The movie is screened late in the day on Sunday, December 15, and then followed by a dinner. The event is rather official, but there are kind words and flattery for Fellini's film and one of the guests at the dinner, the parliamentarian Giulio Andreotti, goes on to publish a review of the film two days later on the front page of *Corriere della Sera*. The paper's regular film critic justifiably allowed himself an ironic comment about the politician's contribution.

On January 13, 1986, *Ginger e Fred* opens in Paris with a gala reception in the Palais de Chaillot for Giulietta and Marcello. It's the first time that one of Fellini's films has opened abroad, and back in Italy some people take offense. The French newspapers are almost unanimous in their opinion that the old Fellini is back, and they are so enthusiastic that he is forgiven for skipping the gala (he was overcome by one of his sudden and uncontrollable urges to avoid ceremony). The Italians pay tribute to the film with a preview and gala at the Sistina in Rome on January 21, with lots of VIPs, live network coverage, and much applause. For the first time ever, the Italian press is unanimous in their praise. The reviews are also fantastic in the United States. *Time*, *Newsweek*, and *Variety* give *Ginger e Fred* major coverage and Metro-Goldwyn-Mayer will distribute the film (with disappointing results).

On February 14, there are more festivities in Berlin. The movie is the first one screened out of competition at the 36th Berlin Film Festival.

This time Federico shows up and even holds an extremely crowded press conference, the first in years. A French journalist asks if he thinks he's changed and Fellini replies, "My doctor could give you a better answer to that than I. Everyone changes, and our perspectives change too. What hasn't changed is my curiosity and the desire to see how I manage to survive something new." In the lions' den, despite having to rely on a simultaneous translator, the director wins his audience over. If he didn't take home the Oscar for best foreign language film (it would have been his fifth) on March 24, it's only because Italian producers put forth another title for Italy. Fellini is in New York promoting *Ginger e Fred*, but can't go to Hollywood for the awards ceremony (he'd been invited to present the award for best foreign language film) due to a hurt foot. The visit to New York is also disrupted by the news that Ginger Rogers has started proceedings for a lawsuit (brazen and futile in the end) against the film, inexplicably claiming that it has damaged her good name.

The box-office returns in Italy are certainly not proportionate to the excitement that the movie's launch created, or the critical praise it received. According to year-end tallies for 1985–86, the movie came in twenty-eighth. But Grimaldi will not be dismayed; he says that the final gross profit on a Fellini film has to be figured on an international level, and *Ginger e Fred* has been well received almost everywhere.

The director, just sixty-six years old, has won another battle. It's also a triumph because the movie, despite its deranged complexity, is the simple fairy tale the director has always discussed. The grandiose framework, the colossus that the protagonists participate in, doesn't take away from the story and, more important, doesn't disrupt its delicate balance either. This is in large part due to the skill of Fellini's cowriters, Tonino Guerra, whose poetic passion had been illuminating Italian cinema since the sixties, and Tullio Pinelli, another master of dramatic writing who had returned to Fellini's fold. The imagery gains enormously from Donati's costumes and Ferretti's brash set. Guarnieri, who was the director of photography for Fellini's two commercials, worked on the first half of the movie, while the second half, shot in a fake television studio in Cinecittà, was done by Tonino Delli Colli—Pier Paolo Pasolini's favorite cinematographer. Federico is enthusiastic about working with Delli Colli, a collaborator "with the ferocity of a first mate"; it's not just about Delli Colli's talent but about his way of being on the set.

As for the actors, Masina hasn't been in such amazing form as an actress and dancer since *Le notti di Cabiria*, and Mastroianni is quite simply a beautiful loser. They diligently make their way through their old dance routine, starting with "The Continental," followed by a medley of Irving Berlin songs—which is when Marcello, doing his tap-dance solo in "Cheek to Cheek," gets a cramp in his leg and falls down. In the meantime, Giulietta, who took pride in dancing well, managed to wrench a take out of Federico in which her performance and her partner's was perfect. The obvious question is: Whatever happened to this priceless scene? Will it be dug up from somewhere and added to the DVD?

All told, *Ginger e Fred* is a masterful film, one that restores the prestige of Fellini's name. But should we think of it principally as a perfect stage for two actors? Or something born out of real inspiration that offers new knowledge to what we already know about Fellini and his world? Newspapers in France are on the defensive against the invasion of Berlusconi's private television stations and almost unanimously agree that *Ginger e Fred* is a denouncement of television's cultural genocide. Others add that the film is not only against TV but a challenge to all of contemporary society—a *Prova d'orchestra II*.

The whole movie, including the title, seems elegiac and nostalgic, a contrast to the brutality of the trash, neglect, and rampant rudeness of the contemporary universe. But let's not forget that in the mid-thirties, just when Rogers and Astaire were on the silver screen, delivering their magical lessons in elegance, F. Scott Fitzgerald was raging against the vulgarity of the new world and grieving the loss of the grace and vitality of the previous decade. Nostalgia is a trap of age, and even though he surrenders to it just enough, Fellini also shows that he's keyed into it. The director's eye on Rome in the 1980s is the eye of a man who first discovered the city when it was a less rough affair, whereas the imagery of *Ginger e Fred* could perfectly illustrate Pasolini's last tracts against Rome, before he was murdered—long before he could grow old and nostalgic—on the outskirts of the metropolis. Amelia in the beginning of the film, trying to feel her way though a world that doesn't belong to her, is a self-portrait of Fellini: shy, curious, vulnerable, impatient, angry, determined. The white-haired dancer, Pippo, on the other hand, represents the director's most conciliatory qualities: lucidity, self-irony, and tolerance. Through a perfectly calibrated spectrum of emotions, the movie arrives at a fusion of Ginger and Fred—a symbiosis that we can call Federico—and then adds a woman's pragmatism and propriety, coupled with her partner's buffoonery and refusal to be a tragic character. The two dancers are utterly different, at least as different as Giulietta and Marcello were in real life, but they find common ground in a faint romanticism, full of modesty, dignity, and loyalty. They are both trying unconsciously and in a modern, secular way to keep their eyes open, even though reality can be unpleasant.

Ginger e Fred leaves us thinking of the surprise ending to the famous Italo Svevo story: Amelia and Pippo's performance on *Ed ecco a voi* can be considered "a successful prank." In Svevo's story of the same name, "Una burla riuscita," an old writer begins fantasizing about recovering lost youth and glory when he learns his novel is going to be reprinted (which is a lie), but the trick actually ends up making him a lot of money. Similarly, Ginger and Fred allow themselves to be sucked into the flattery of this performance teetering on self-mockery, but once the show's over, they have the pride of knowing that they made it and are even asked for an autograph. It would seem that Fellini thinks it's better not to miss the opportunities that life in all its singularity offers, after all. Before shutting oneself up in desperation, it's better to dance again, roll out the pranks, even if we have lived our lives like movies that we didn't understand (Ginger never realized the intensity of Fred's love) or watched them pass like a meaningless dream. The stoic message of *Ginger e Fred* is that perhaps there's nothing to understand; we just have to live. You have to learn to float the way Marcello did in *La dolce vita* . . . even though the waters are slowly flowing into the River Styx like *Mastorna*—the film that was never made.

42

Everyone Is Japanese
Intervista

Nighttime in Cinecittà. Cars exit through the gates into the street. Dogs bark and leap around as the crew starts climbing out of the cars. A camera, draped in black, arrives on a trolley. An assistant, an old-clown type, arrives and busily starts shouting orders and suggestions. Some flares go off and the first floodlight is lit. Tonino Delli Colli is with the electricians. Federico follows the activity from the steps of the main building. From around the corner, a small woman emerges into the light; she introduces herself with a bow. She's the translator for a group of Japanese journalists who want to interview Fellini. They were expected the next day but arrived early. Can they ask some questions now? The dialogue—or, rather, non-dialogue—with the sons of the land of the rising sun begins, and *Intervista* starts. Two towering cranes face each other like fabulous machines in an Ariostoesque* atmosphere. Fellini tells his interlocutors, "I'm shooting the beginning of a movie and I was thinking of starting in a dream, one of those standard flying dreams. You dream about flying in Japan, too, right?" In what the director defines as "the prisoner's dream" we see his hands groping for a way out of the darkness. It was easier to fly away in the days of 8½; it's twice as hard now and there's always the fear you won't make it. Finally the dreamer takes off; he reaches a great height and contemplates Cinecittà from above.

Started in August 1986, this film was originally called *Cinecittà*, and was conceived of in even greater secrecy than usual. Fellini invents a joke

*Ludovico Ariosto (1473–1533) was the author of *Orlando Furioso*.

to keep the journalists at bay: "How can you give an interview on a movie called *Intervista?*" which is the perfect thing to say if you want to pique the curiosity of journalists. What is Fellini up to this time?

Intervista is actually not a proper film; it's a television special, the typical Fellini show, a blending of digression and intimacy, that he began in 1968. Once again, the most apt title for the project would be *A Director's Notebook*. It's being produced by Aljosha, owned by Nastassja Kinski's husband, Ibrahim Moussa, an agent-turned-producer. RAI 1 and Cinecittà are partners too. The heads of Cinecittà see the film as a tribute project. In January 1987, the city of cinema celebrates fifty years since its inauguration by Mussolini. Federico is pleased that the coincidence leads to funding, though he didn't plan it that way. Once again, he's thinking of this television special as the first of a trilogy, with the next one dedicated to Cinema Fulgor in Rimini and the one after that to opera. It's evident almost from the start that he probably won't be able to make them all, at least not in a short time. By the middle of September, Federico is already completely immersed in his new movie and can't think of anything else.

When he first started shooting, Fellini hadn't entirely worked out the story, which is sketched out in a skimpy treatment based on conversations with the loyal Gianfranco Angelucci, who for the first time, after many contributions as a ghostwriter, will be allowed to add his name to the credits. This is a movie within a movie (really, even more than just two movies; they may contain themselves to infinity like a Russian doll), so the director decides to appear as himself and to treat the crew as if they were characters as well as crew: "When we don't know what to shoot, we'll turn the cameras around 180 degrees and film ourselves." The result is totally spontaneous, even more so than prior confession movies. There's hardly any gap between the Fellini shooting the movie and the Fellini playing the Fellini shooting the movie. Does that mean that reality and fantasy have finally merged, or does it mean that the fantasy reserve has finally dried up? Perhaps in Fellini's world reality has ceased to exist. In addition, does the fact that Fellini so courageously used the first person in 8½ allow him to be as real as he is in *Intervista?* Perhaps Fellini has become such an actor in his waking life (as people sometimes insinuate) that he can effortlessly continue his role.

The apparent ease of Fellini's intentions is in direct contradiction to the production work expected to mobilize a film: actors, extras, costumes, sets, set changes, and last-minute inventions. In the atmosphere of cheerful confusion, it's difficult to respect the rule of the secret set, not least because Federico himself is always inviting his colleagues, friends, and acquaintances who are passing by to stop in and visit. This movie is talked about as the "Cinecittà *Amarcord*"—a description the director isn't wild about. Newspapers and magazines compete for reports from witnesses and gossip about this or that scene. Any average Fellini expert is engaged in trying to put the pieces together and predict what the movie will be about.

Everyone is Japanese. This is the final meaning of the short film. When we conduct an interview or just generally want to know something about the person we're talking to, we all become the Japanese interviewers who follow Fellini from the beginning to the end: speaking another language, we express ourselves poorly, and barely understand each other. We are curious, clumsy, and even funny. We discover that we're outsiders in the same moment that we're struggling to be insiders. We're babies pretending to be grown-ups. We are all shooting for absurd goals, unattainable aspirations. We're alone even as we work at a gratifying, entertaining job, surrounded by friends, like Federico himself as he's shooting *Intervista*. We are always somehow unhappy, even when we're at the height of happiness, and vice versa. *Intervista* is a new self-portrait of the director at work—like 8½, but instead of Marcello Mastroianni, we have Fellini himself. The idea, too, is real: the movie that the director pretends he's making, Kafka's *Amerika*, is one that he really did think about making more than once. It's a fake chronicle of the moment, a virtual work diary, where the characters, names, and facts are often true.

Federico asked for Mastroianni's help convincing Anita Ekberg to do a screen test for the character of Brunelda in *Amerika*. We see the two friends approaching Villa Pandora in Grottaferrata where Anitona lives. Federico cheerfully announces himself through the door intercom but Ekberg is suspicious ("Which Federico?") and takes some time to open the door. But then she's happy to see her old friends, and at last lets the camera inside amid the ferocious guard dogs. The Swedish woman hugs Marcello and soon the whole point of the visit is forgotten and they throw an impromptu party instead. Summoning up the superpowers of Mandrake, Mastroianni utters the magic formula, "Mandrake's magic wand / my order is immediate / I want back / the glorious old days!" And a white sheet appears and Nino Rota's music plays in the background and images from the movie about via Veneto appear. Marcello and Silvia dance at Caracalla, the scene at the Trevi Fountain. The two actors watch their own legend, repeating the famous lines along with the characters. The scene is like a version of *Ginger e Fred* in cinema verité, and yet it's obvious that Marcello, at least, is playing it down—as usual. The dogs outside listen as if enchanted by the sound track. The deeper meaning, the organic roots of Fellini's vision have survived and it's stronger than the regret for time past, stronger than the conviction that craftsmanship is the only therapy for the dissolution of everything. His vision consists in accepting the world according to the simple philosophy: I joke, therefore I am.

There are two onscreen interviews in *Intervista*. One is in the present between the Japanese journalists and Fellini as he is today. The second is in the past, Fellini as a young man (played by Sergio Rubini) interviews a celebrity at Cinecittà. Both interviews, though they occur fifty years apart, are failures. The Japanese interviewers will learn nothing about Fellini; and the celebrity, seen through the eyes of the young journalist, is like a creature from another planet. Yet both of the interviewers, despite not having managed to communicate with their subject, return home with memories, characters, scenes, images, and laughter. They find life and its passions—despite the fact that there may not be any hard truth in passion, or any formulaic path to truth. Of all the intimate cinematic Fellini projects (from *A Director's Notebook* to *I clowns*), *Intervista* reveals a spontaneous Fellini, one who makes friends with the audience and is prepared to be seen in his everyday shape. This time the director reveals what a spectacle his movie productions are—it doesn't even matter that *Amerika* is an imaginary movie. The real movie is the one we see, and it's airy and warm, amusing and alarming, with a tremendous emotional charge as it looks to the past.

Near the end, *Intervista* turns into something like a captain's log of a journey into the void—just like *E la nave va* is a befuddled elegy of a "last stand"—and it's not incidental that it suddenly comes to resemble the scene of Lieutenant Colonel George Armstrong Custer being crushed by the Sioux at Little Big Horn. At dawn the production manager announces, "I think they will attack," and around the Cinecittà set, the skewed television antennas turn into spears wielded by Indians on horse-back who are charging the last cinema command post. An infernal spaghetti-Western carousel starts up; in the middle, the filmmakers hud-dle together, surrounded by a circus of television Indians, a replaying of the apocalyptic prophecy of *Ginger e Fred*. Fellini's apocalypse doesn't end in total catastrophe, however. The author finds something to smile about, a way to diminish the tragedy and postpone it. He keeps alive the absurd hope that, after the big shipwreck, there will always be a rowboat ready to sail him into the horizon of a new film. We're back again in Stu-dio 5 in Cinecittà. It's dark and empty. Fellini's voice is heard, saying, "So the movie should end here. Actually it's finished." The escape dream ends in the studio, now bright with light. In the olden days, producers would always ask for "a ray of sunlight"—here they are given an artificial ray of floodlight. All is set to start on the first take of the next movie: "Lights, camera, action."

Filming on *Intervista* drags on through the end of 1986 and beyond, with many interruptions, mostly because of funding. The director takes advantage of the breaks to edit what he's already shot with Nino Baragli, so by mid-January, the film is more or less ready for dubbing and final ed-its. At this point, it runs one hour and 45 minutes, too long for a televi-sion special. The idea has already been put forth to run the film in theaters before issuing it on video—inevitable given the five-billion-lire price tag. Federico is unsure about this tactic, considering that there are elements of the film—such as the lack of a real story or the presence of such an intimate tone—that don't lend themselves to the mainstream cir-cuit. Beyond a certain point, however, the director has no more say in the matter. The decision will be left to the producers.

Fellini works for many months, driven by his characteristic enthusiasm. He's extremely attentive to each detail of a framework that has rapidly spun out more broadly and become more complicated than he had in-tended. As he toils on in his life and his job, the director ends up falling in love with the work itself, happily confirming his revelation of recent years that there is "dignity in doing." It's clear that the process is more important to him than the results. More than finishing, he takes pleasure in the ritual of going to Cinecittà each morning, immersing himself in the fantasy and precision that will keep him occupied late into the night.

Doing battle with the usual spectrum of doubts, Federico agrees to show *Intervista* out of competition in the 40th Cannes Film Festival—mostly because the time has come to make a rough cut of the film, making the deadline a practical necessity. The screening is set for Monday, May 18, the day before the festival ends. Federico arrives on the Croisette in the rain as the festival is winding down. He has time to chat with some Italian journalists and then climb the stairs of the Palais to the cheers of the public. Marcello isn't there because he's in Budapest working on a film. But he's already received his special praise at the opening of *Oci ciornie* by Nikita Mikhalkov, and will be celebrated again at the closing ceremonies, where he'll be awarded the prize for best actor. The screening of *Intervista* is one of the triumphs of Fellini's career: the ovation that erupts at the final frame seems like it will never end. The French press is wholly positive about the film—a consensus that the director hasn't had since *Amarcord*. The jury, headed up by Yves Montand, shares the enthusiasm and invents a special award for Fellini even though the film is out of competition: the Fortieth Anniversary Prize. Nobody thought to tell Federico, though, who learns of the honor only after he is back in Rome. On Tuesday, May 19, Moussa will accept the award on his behalf. In Italy, *Intervista* will be distributed by Academy, an avant-garde company owned by Manfredi and Vania Traxler that specializes in independent film. But it doesn't do well when it's released in theaters in October. The reviews are fantastic but no one goes to see it—especially not in nonurban areas. Such a bad performance in the theaters is totally unexpected, as the movie is appearing at all the international festivals, even taking the grand prize at the 15th Moscow Film Festival. Fellini accepts the award from Robert De Niro, president of the jury, in July, a repeat of his success in bringing 8½ to Moscow. In 1963, Federico vows that from this moment on he will never enter another festival competition—but he soon changes his mind. At the end of July, the movie opens to enthusiastic audiences in Rimini and the piazza of Locarno is packed with people waiting to see the film in August. *Intervista* gets standing ovations at the festival in Montreal, capping off a summer of success.

As Cinecittà is buzzing with preparations for the fiftieth anniversary celebration, Fellini has come to be considered the absolute master of his special brand of big Italian cinema. Rumors have been circulating for some time that he will be nominated *senatore a vita,** which, rather than pleasing him, makes him embarrassed. Perhaps the director's furious constant activity grows out of a fear of stopping. He has so many projects and so many ideas left. He returns to the idea of making a movie about Dante's *Divine Comedy*—more precisely, about the *Inferno*—and the idea of doing something with Greek myths is also still on the table, but how much would such monuments cost? Occasionally a producer will put forth the idea of making *Mastorna* at last—or why not finally tell the mysterious story of the *Viaggio a Tulun?*

Senatore a vita, lifetime senator, is the most important honorific a person can be awarded in Italy.

43

The Nostalgia of Silence
La voce della luna / The Voice of the Moon

In August of 1988, RAI TV proudly announces two new Fellini projects: a TV special about acting, *Attore*, with Marcello Mastroianni and Giulietta, and a feature-film project, called *Venezia*, to be modeled after *Roma*—an "invented documentary" made up of short scenes, notes, and unlinked chapters. Some of it will be shot on location in the Laguna and the rest in the Cinecittà studios. Unfortunately, after the triumphant announcement, *Venezia* never gets made; negotiations drag on and after a few months the director realizes that he's already moved on to something else.

He'd jotted the idea down somewhere, after reading in a dispatch from the Frankfurt Book Fair about a novel that had come out in November 1987 called *Il poema dei lunatici* by Ermanno Cavazzoni. The author is a forty-something professor at the University of Bologna, from Reggio Emilia. Other than Poe, Petronius, Casanova, and that bit of Kafka for *Intervista*, Fellini has never taken inspiration from a book, but he's never claimed that he wouldn't, either. Over the last few years, as a consequence of insomnia, he's become an omnivorous, extremely well-informed reader of contemporary literature, especially Italian. Sometimes, after devouring a novel during the night, he'd call the writer early in the morning, waking him with congratulations and lucid analysis. This is what happened to a shocked Cavazzoni. Fellini calls to tell him that he admires the anthropological rhapsody that reflects the everyday folly of a rural environment. The filmmaker immediately recognizes the potential of the book to return him to his confused, old project of depicting the natural world—the soil, the seasons, sun and rain, day and night. He likes the notion that at night the water in the well is awakened by the moon and starts uttering faint messages that only madmen and vagabonds can vaguely perceive. The fantastical elements of La strada seem reflected here, but with a new, picaresque energy that is at moments organically comical, but mostly just unsettling. Federico decides to follow the wanderings of Cavazzoni's most peculiar couple—two offbeat characters, a little like Don Quixote and Sancho Panza—in order to rediscover rural culture with all of its Catholic and pagan influences, fascism and consumerism, utopia and degeneration. It is a kaleidoscope of atmospheres, landscapes, rivers, meadows, and small towns, inhabited by figures unbound by any logical behavior.

Fellini briefly flirts with a return to neorealism and his first idea is to improvise everything on location—like they did with Paisà. Later, he collaborates with Tullio Pinelli and they write a short script in two weeks. In September, the director travels extensively up and down the Po, stopping near Reggiolo where the film, going at this point under the title Il poemetto della luna (Little Poem of the Moon), is supposed to be shot: first on a farm in Brugneto and then between Novellara and the river. Local reporters claim that "the movie people" had 600 haystacks put aside for the threshing scene.

Torn between contradictory impulses, the director feeds his own illusion that this will be a speedy undertaking, like Intervista. He tells everyone that he wants to make a "movie out of nothing, a film that will self-produce"—he fancies that pronouncement brings a skeptical smile to the lips of Mario Cecchi Gori and his son Vittorio. The producers have in fact signed on to a project that will cost fifteen billion lire. And when the move is complete, Federico will say of his partners, "They were perfect. I never saw them, but they made sure I had everything I needed."

Still not entirely sure about what he is doing, the director taps into the big-chief determination in himself and starts constructing a town. He chooses building plans and material, bricks, colors, signs. This time the town, with its piazza, church, and stores, will rise up not in Cinecittà but on the former site of Dinocittà on via Pontina—where until only recently the ghost city of Il viaggio di G. Mastorna had still been standing. Usually wary of bad omens, Federico now seems unconcerned about returning to the scene of the crime. Agreeing with the Cecchi Goris, he'd rather shoot in the Empire Studios (as they're now known, having passed through several owners) because, while Cinecittà is besieged with big buildings (as we can see in *Intervista*) the Empire Studios are in the countryside and give Fellini the chance to reconstruct a Padania only a hop, skip, and a jump from the main offices.

Pietro Notarianni runs the production again, but has some difficulty at the start, which leads to a changing of the guards: Danilo Donati, the set designer, storms off the set and Dante Ferretti steps in to take his place. Fellini oversees the construction of the houses, the laying of the streets, and the set decoration: something clicks inside of him when he sees the village come alive—a window opening, a kiosk in the piazza, someone sitting in a café. "If I ended up making this movie," he will later say, "it's because I built the town and it took on a life. I didn't try to make Reggiolo or any other real Italian place. I'd actually be quite pleased if someone mistook it for an Indian village, or a Brazilian one, or another planet." This is clearly no *Amarcord*: no childhood memories, no nostalgia.

The most curious innovation is the casting of two famous comedians for the leads: the Tuscan Roberto Benigni, who had directed and starred in the hugely successful *Il piccolo diavolo* (*The Little Devil*, 1988), and Paolo Villaggio from Genoa, who'd recently starred in *Fantozzi va in pensione* (Fantozzi Retires, 1988), the latest in a successful series of movies. From the first photos that come off the set, it's clear that Roberto and Paolo have been physically altered. Benigni in little spectacles assumes the spirited role of the "so-called Mr. Salvini," a fake inspector of wells, while Villaggio, in a gray beard and long hair, plays the former prefect, Gonnella. Throughout the long weeks of work, actors and director exchange extravagant compliments in the media, a triangle of communications whereby the three men each reflect and become essential to the rest. Benigni, overcome with joy about being involved, makes up affectionate nicknames and issues lightning-speed wisecracks; he dedicates notes and poems to Fellini and the rest of the crew. Villaggio is more reserved; he thinks of himself as a natural comedian but worries that he's not a natural actor, and locked into a serious character, he's afraid that the director will be unhappy with his performance. These anxieties—which soon prove to be unfounded—aside, the mood on the set is peaceful, flush with mutual admiration and real affinity, everyone endeavoring to reassure the maestro, who is quite forthcoming about his own psychodrama over the project. As usual, in fact, even more than usual, he claims not to have the slightest idea what he's doing; he even grows angry when people don't believe him when he says that this fairy tale he's made up doesn't make sense to him and that he doesn't know how to end it.

Behind the scenes there's a minor crisis with Pinelli, as the screenwriter will confess a few years later:

The total understanding that Fellini and I always shared wasn't there when we were working on *La voce della luna*. From the moment we started, I could tell that we were on different wavelengths; he understood the movie in one way and I understood in another way. More significantly, he'd changed the way he worked. At a certain point he said, "I can't work the way I used to, with a screenplay and dialogues. Now I just want an outline, and then I improvise while I'm shooting." So after some lengthy discussion we wrote a short treatment, which I thought was going to be developed and then *it* [would be] turned into the screenplay. But he typed up the sketch as if it were complete and started work, improvising as he went, and I think that hurt the movie.

To those who worked on it, however, *La voce della luna* will be remembered as one of the most serenely uninhibited of Fellini's sets. In fact, when the filming, which started on February 22 (after the usual phase of secret preliminary work), approached its end, everyone found themselves fearing, rather than longing for, the last day. At the final dinner in mid-June, the last time that the troupe will convene, Benigni outdoes himself and recites a wonderful poem in *ottava rima*,* recounting everything that had happened and been felt over the last months.

Is this a film that reveals mysteries, draws us into the ineffable? It certainly poses questions with the brash innocence of a child. There are attempts to communicate with the dead, for instance—"Is it possible that we don't know anything about you? Where are you?"—as well as attempts to communicate with the living (who are living, but not entirely

*With the rhyme on the eighth beat.

normal). Examples include the character of Ivo, half Pinocchio and half Giacomo Leopardi (though Fellini will insist that he's based on Mestolino, a forgotten Yambo character), and Gonnella, the paranoid ex-prefect. Each emerges from the crowd, with his own personal, conflicted makeup.

Now that he's nearing his twilight years, the director walks back over the same road that brought him to Gelsomina: the magic scenes of his childhood in Gambettola. But the outer rings of the consumer world have turned into a grotesque carnival of superfluous structures. The *dolce vita* has moved to the suburbs, exacerbating the vulgarity of events like the *gnoccate* (potato-dumpling festivals for gorging oneself), the beauty pageants, the political-religious sponsored events. People hoot and holler, play loud music, even shoot guns on occasion, and all this ruckus risks drowning out the voice of the moon forever. But maybe that's just an imaginary, fragmented murmur that only madmen and worshippers can hear. After all, capturing the moon, as the Micheluzzi brothers do, only results in another meeting with loathsome politicians who want to turn it into an official event. And the moral that the madman Salvini takes away from this contemporary malaise is worthy of reflection: "If we all quieted down a little, maybe we'd understand something."

As Benigni wraps up the film with this message, we are all bitterly aware that the world of silence, poetry, and ecstasy is behind us, and that our destiny will be to embark upon our little path toward the hereafter in the midst of an infernal uproar. The rhapsodic quality of this picture is similar to *La città delle donne*; it also goes against the current like *Satyricon* and *Il Casanova* did. The film is the fantasy of an unhappy philosopher who has projected his ideas onto Cavazzoni's novel. As for the first-person point of view in the movie, it's shared by two different figures: the eternally hypercreative, moody adolescent, and the old man who stoically suffers life's inevitable checkmate. You have to wonder from what dark frustrated recesses of buffoonery* Paolo Villaggio managed to extract Broderick Crawford's desperate stare from *Il bidone*. And as we watch Benigni, hunched over and bowlegged as he races under the stage of the beauty pageant, we realize that Federico has found his super-

---

*The character that Villaggio has played in other films, Fantozzi, is the quintessential buffoon, and requires quite a different kind of performance than the one he delivers for *La voce della luna*.

puppet, the ultimate imp. The newspapers report that they are planning to make *Pinocchio* together, but Benigni will end up making it alone in 2002, with set and costumes by Donati.

As the century enters its last decade, Fellini quotes himself and revisits past work; he commemorates it, repeats it, reinvents it, and contradicts it. Nicola Piovani's delicate musical mosaic echoes Nino Rota, sending an unequivocal signal, a familiar motif, an antidote for depression. The old ideas are back. It might well be true what the oboe player says—"Music promises, but doesn't keep the promises"—and yet, each time one of those anthems of optimism bursts through the pessimistic atmosphere of *La voce della luna*, there's a moment of playfulness. Fellini's fans can find solace in the notion that even though the maestro is weary and disconsolate, he's still there, immersed in the task of finding an answer to the amorphous chaos of existence. The answer might be cryptic, hostile, derisive, even disdainful, but it will also be stylistically impeccable, highly artistic, and professionally unassailable.

The media celebrated the occasion of Federico's seventieth birthday on January 20, 1990, just a few days before *La voce della luna* was released on February 1. The response to the picture is warm; it garners admiring or at very least respectful reviews, with a few moments of genuine enthusiasm and a few outright pans. Considering the slump in the cinema industry, the movie even does pretty well at the box office. Federico is surprised that young people, who now constitute the mainstream audience, are drawn to his film. Some of them stand by his front door; having memorized lines from the film, they want to ask questions. But as usual, Federico is ready to turn the page and start working on his next project. Unfortunately, however, his proposals for the television programs have gotten tangled up somewhere in the corridors of RAI's business offices, and other tentative ideas, with the Japanese or the Russians, never materialize.

The director is forced into a long sabbatical, and for the first and last time, he takes up a political battle—challenging the commercial interruptions of films that are being broadcast on television. After a provisional success in the Senate, where the law abolishing ads during films unexpectedly passes, the House adds some amendments that effectively legally reinstate the commercials and postpone a further decision about restrictions. It's worth citing some extracts from the eloquent and severe admonishment that Fellini published in *Videolettera* (a publication of Associazione Nazionale Autori Cinematografici, the national association of filmmakers) in June of 1990.

> And so we're still here debating this matter. That's incredible to me. I mean, you cannot agree that there is any lawfulness at all to be discussed in this assault—the violence of which would be *criminal* if inflicted on a person—a work of art has its own life and is a person with a character and a personality. To interrupt a film, to mutilate and mortify it, change its structure, rhythm, sense, and meaning for *commercials* should be a matter for the courts!

His intolerance for such stupidity had already filtered into *Ginger e Fred*, and the pessimism of *La voce della luna* results from a complete understanding of the difficult period that Italy was passing through. The assault of commercials on what the director held dearest alarmed him as a sure sign of irreversible decline.

When *La voce della luna* shows out of competition at the 43rd Cannes Film Festival, the director, for the first time, isn't there. In keeping with the message of the movie, he claims that certain rituals have tired him and that he no longer wants to contribute to a society of perpetual confusion. It's only out of friendship that he goes to the Palazzo del Cinema on the Lido in Venice to present Mastroianni with the Golden Lion for lifetime achievement. Onstage at the awards ceremony, the two old friends are entirely endearing, but Federico reveals his churlish mood the instant he comes offstage. The event is too disorderly and he leaves as soon as he can.

The national prizes aren't forthcoming with *La voce della luna*, and once again the Italians send another movie to the Oscars. But the Japanese come through with a fabulous surprise, the Praemium Imperiale, which comes with a check for a hundred million lire. In order to accept the prize, however, Federico has to go to Tokyo. As allergic to travel as ever, he proposes to a shocked jury, "If I give you a discount, say, of fifty million, will you deliver the check to me here at Caffe Canova?" Eventually the director agrees to go with Giulietta, and they spend an extraordinary week at the Hotel Okura in Tokyo. They then visit Kyoto, attending a showing of *La voce della luna* at Miyukiza cinema. The Praemium Imperiale, backed by the generous businessman Shikanai Nobutaka (who will, unfortunately, die a few days later), is a sort of Nobel for mastery in the visual arts, and a tuxedo-clad Fellini will accept it in a solemn ceremony on October 23. The director is also invited to the palace of soon-to-be-emperor Akihito, whom Fellini meets along with his gracious wife, Michiko; as the son of a traveling salesman from Gambettola, he can't complain about how far he's come. But his dinner with Akira Kurosawa is intimate and pleasant. In keeping with Japanese custom, the two men, both shoeless, sit on the floor of the famous Ten Masa restaurant in the Kanda quarter and enjoy delicious fried fish. Federico likes everything about this trip, as intense and short as a dream, but he particularly appreciates the courtesy, discretion, and quietness of the Japanese, who don't, however, fail to recognize him in the street and greet him with deep bows and smiles. The smiles are plentiful for Giulietta, who is much more popular and venerated in Japan than in Italy. Something else manages to impress the director on this trip: all of *La strada* fits onto a small, palm-sized disk—as of yet not available on the market—and the sound and images are perfect. He is deeply moved: "The Japanese enabled to me to hear Nino's music exactly as it sounded almost forty years ago when we recorded it at Fono Roma."

Fellini suffers a big blow the following spring when, after a long paralysis, his brother, Riccardo, dies on March 26. For decades, the relationship between the two had been not broken, but nonexistent. Maddalena was quite devastated by the rift and would always mention both of her brothers in the same breath. After his dreams of becoming a professional singer and actor had faded, Riccardo tried to follow in Federico's footsteps by making a quiet, fragile, episodic film, *Storie sulla sabbia* (Stories in the Sand, 1963). He also had some success in television. While working on a documentary in the Rome zoo, a chimpanzee bit off his thumb; afterward, when people asked how he was, Riccardo would answer, "I'm not the one with problems, the monkey is; ever since it ate my thumb it's lost its appetite for anything else." This typically Fellini-esque quip demonstrates the sense of humor and attitude the brothers shared. Some friends thought that had the two not been brothers they would have been best friends, but that wasn't the case. Federico had made the mistake of not getting involved in his brother's life and career, and when Riccardo was asked what he thought of *Amarcord*, he'd reply, "I haven't seen it." Tormented by regret over the mistakes he'd made in the relationship, Federico will visit a number of clinics in early 1991, desperately trying to find a place for his invalid brother. The sight of so much sadness on those rounds depressed him. In the end, Riccardo won't need hospitalization; he will die before it comes to that. *Trespassing* on March 26, Federico's "little brother" is buried at Bosa in Sardinia.

Fellini's diversion in this period comes from working on a few books about cinema. Although he's not involved in any active creative project, his life continues as always. He spends his days on the phone, in meetings, talking business aimlessly over breakfast, dining with a close friend in a favorite restaurant, reading papers during the day and books at night; surprises and discoveries are seldom really new in the sleepy Roman microcosm. He takes it all in as he always has, in exactly the same manner as he did in the years after the war—he's open and focused, thoughtful and available.

There are those who complain that Fellini is too focused on the past: he repeats things he's already said, ideas already articulated. He's wasting time. Other people look to him as they would a guru, waiting to hear him predict the fate of the world, or what one should think and do next. Some consider him yesterday's news, and still others expect that old age will bring an even higher vision and more useful prophecies. That theory seems almost confirmed by the suddenly quite serious and thoughtful interview that Fellini will give the Canadian director Damien Pettigrew in April 1992, the maestro's last long intimate discussion. Someone who's there for it comes up with a motto summarizing Fellini's entire career, tracing the trajectory from comic to stoic: "From *Marc'Aurelio* to Marcus Aurelius"—from gags to philosophy.

44

The Autumn of the Patriarch

Three Commercials for Banca di Roma

Fellini's last work runs just under seven minutes—actually, to be precise, the sum length of all three commercials he made for Banca di Roma (1:51, 2:10, 2:90) is just six minutes and ten seconds, from which you'd have to subtract the codas (where the logo appears) for all three ads. Obviously length is no predictor of value; otherwise, how does one value Mozart's Viennese Sonatina, or a Picasso sketch, or a high note from Pavarotti that lasts only a few seconds? Could we say they are without value, that they don't represent Mozart, Picasso, or Pavarotti? That anyone else at all could have made them? Obviously not. These six minutes of commercial aren't important only for Fellini's name but because the director leaves his last will and testament in these three short stories, a year before his death. *Testimonial* was, after all, a noun that he used quite frequently, and, paradoxically, he never did write a will for his estate. It's not that Federico had some gloomy foreboding when he made the ads—quite the opposite. The bright cheerful photos from the set of the commercials are the last images of the director in full throttle. He's the demiurge: happy, smiling, affectionate, the perfect tour guide, just as he was for all twenty-four films he made throughout his forty-year career. He was a ringleader, spirited, communicative, everyone's friend. These ads are the miracle that, for a few weeks, restores to our hero the joy of life; the possibility of working in a certain way; being on the set; giving orders; building and dismantling; improvising scenes and lines; forming with the people around him—and the visitors, the journalists, the boy at the bar—a multiplicity of relationships based on give-and-take.

In Federico's life, these three commercial spots are a kind of Indian summer, the golden autumn of a patriarch of cinema who, for a moment, holds again the reins of creation. It all comes as a surprise, an unexpected gift that follows a long and exasperating period of inactivity that descended upon him in February 1990 after *La voce della luna*. For the first time in his life, after he'd finished edits, Federico didn't launch immediately into a new movie. Both public entities and private companies fear him: he spends too much and the movies don't earn back. He'd be happy just doing something for television, and revisits the idea of a special called *Attore*. It would be a way of calling back into his service all the old and new traveling companions—Giulietta and Marcello Mastroianni, Paolo Villaggio and Roberto Benigni—coaxing them into confessions and reflections about their craft, a quiet, inexpensive project. But public television stations have their pace, obstacles and distractions, bureaucracy and political timing. The committee doesn't meet, the network executive doesn't sign, and the foreign backers appear and disappear, while the great puppeteer fades into inactivity for two long years—years during which his health is still good and he's chomping at the bit. In an effort to compromise, he makes the project less ambitious and even less expensive, offering to make a movie about actors that's just a dialogue between him and Villaggio: "He's the ideal mask, the last transformation of the clown. I'm thinking of an indiscreet, brash face-to-face, a chat about life and work." It seems incredible that even this simple project never develops. Federico is so discouraged that he can't talk about it. His worst moment comes when he realizes that he himself is resigned and finds himself trying to comfort others—"No, look, it's fine . . ."

It's not fine at all. In *Corriere della Sera* on January 19, 1992, the day before his birthday, an article runs under the headline FELLINI, OUT OF WORK ON HIS BIRTHDAY, and the subtitle is, "It's the director's seventy-second birthday and he hasn't worked in two years. What's happening to Italian cinema?" A year later, on January 21, 1993, the year of Fellini's death, *Corriere della Sera* revisits the situation:

Last year our paper noted somewhat bitterly the occasion of Federico Fellini's seventy-second birthday with a front-page article criticizing RAI, state-owned companies, and the Italian film sector at large for allowing our most popular and talented director to languish without work. There was an immediate response, an uproar of protests, a storm of letters, telephone calls, and reassurances. People objected, "No! What are you saying? We're here, we're ready for him . . ." But once the party ended, nothing ever came of it.

After congratulating Fellini on his forthcoming Oscar for lifetime achievement, the article recommends that President Scalfaro at long last nominate Fellini senator for life. But the director dies nine months later, without ever having heard from Palazzo del Quirinale. Only after he's dead will he be recognized by the administration—with a public funeral.

It's under these circumstances that Fellini is commissioned in 1992 to make three commercials for Banca di Roma. There are several versions of how the project came about. Some claim that when Paolo Villaggio was hired to appear in the ads, he suggested that Fellini direct them. Others say that the roles were reversed, and that Fellini called on Villaggio after Cesare Geronzi from the bank personally contacted him. Either way, the director accepted the bank's offer with a long letter dated February 18, 1992. The letter says that he's cordially and gratefully available and also that he's very clear on the problem of making the "abstract ideas of the banking world comprehensible and sympathetic to the audience." Fellini adds,

> Banks, with their marble, their austere monetary dimensions, the complex of cashiers and accountants, are perceived with fear rather than respect, and thus, also with an inevitable sense of alienation. For this reason the content of the message must communicate the exact opposite. The ad should make banks appear friendly, available, and eager to help.

This "Letter to the President [of the bank]," tackling the subject of the ad, is a tiny masterpiece that could be studied by marketing professionals. Fellini's cautious and deep, intelligent and stimulating approach is confirmation of the absolute seriousness with which he approached any communication challenge. For him, there was no job that should be done sloppily. He took to heart, for himself above all, the message at the beginning of *Prova d'orchestra*: "The secret to survival is to be able to play one's instrument well." The letter continues with scores of ideas for the plot of the commercial itself—although none of these ideas will be used in the end. The wealth of Fellini's imagination is admirable as always, and his openness to the project is the same as when he used to fill the pages of *Marc'Aurelio* with his words. (It's regrettable that Fellini didn't exploit more fully his ability for continuous invention in the cinema, adopting the principles of *caméra-stylo*.) There are stories as well as dreams included among the many ideas Fellini sent to Geronzi, but the three commercials will ultimately be based on dreams alone. Seen together, the ads are like a trial run of *Il viaggio di G. Mastorna*, the movie made of fantasy and reverie that Fellini had been thinking about for twenty-five years.

In the first dream, Paolo Villaggio drives into a tunnel; the soothing strains of a piece by Rossini play in the background. The lovely moment is suddenly disrupted by a thunderous cracking sound. Boulders and water start to fall, fault lines fill the tunnel, and then a block of cement caves in. The hero has obviously been dreaming and the dream has turned into a nightmare. He leaps from his bed and finds himself face-to-face with his psychoanalyst, Fernando Rey (who'd acted in Buñuel's films). The psychoanalyst comforts his patient: "You will have good dreams now, thanks to the security that Banca di Roma provides." The doors of the bank open wide and Villaggio finds himself in bed, in his pajamas, in the middle of a big bank. A note: Fellini was offered a huge sum to play the analyst himself—and though the director wasn't so wealthy that he could be reckless about the expenses of impending old age, he refused.

In the second dream, Villaggio is dressed as a schoolboy in a sailor's outfit, following an exotic beauty down into a basement. A lion with flaming eyes suddenly appears before him, but strangely the beast is crying. The boy can't keep himself from crying either. The psychoanalyst's diagnosis: "Why must you keep a lion in the basement, humiliating and degrading it? You need security if you want to live well. At Banca di Roma . . ."

The third and last dream (which also appears in Fellini's Dream Book on October 30, 1974) has Villaggio at breakfast in the countryside with the beautiful Anna Falchi. He realizes that his chair is stuck on a train track and the girl, who is now up in a tree, warns that the train is coming closer. Fortunately, at that point the psychoanalyst appears and explains: "You can't let situations get the better of you. Make sure that you have security." And again, the Banca di Roma ending.

The significant thing here is that Federico, when asked to invent little stories for these commercials, was right to turn to his own dreams, recorded so many years earlier. In fact, toward the end of his life, the shadow of the great film he never made, *Il viaggio di G. Mastorna*, weighs heavier on him, and he perhaps regrets not having done it. The writer Ermanno Cavazzoni has said that during the filming of *La voce della luna*, he realized that Fellini wasn't adapting his novel so much as he was culling variations for atmospheres and themes from his own *Mastorna*. The same could be said about the bank commercials. Fellini was horribly aware of the fact that he would never get to make the movie he'd continually postponed, and so he made some ads about it. The critics should have been able to pick up on this, but almost no one actually noticed. The showing of the commercials at the Venice Film Festival on September 9, 1992, garnered little attention and only about twenty spectators. Had the great magician lost his appeal?

45

The Start of a Great Future

What should I do? I don't like to travel. I don't go to museums, or the cinema or theater. There's always Rome, that's true, and there's my Piazza del Popolo, but I don't have any friends, and I don't have a talent for great passion and I don't have any work. Everyone treats me like a monument, but they won't let me make movies. My work was like a diving suit that allowed me to plunge into the ocean of existence. Now I have to go without a diving suit—but I'm no fish. Or, maybe I am.

The disarming confession, unmistakably truthful, appears at the end of one of the many roman à clefs written by one of Fellini's lovers. *L'ultima donna* (The Last Woman) is by Rosita Steenbeek, a pretty girl from Holland who (using thinly veiled aliases) tells the story of her affair with the maestro, Marcello Leoni, and casts him as a rival for her affections with a very identifiable Alberto Moravia. Fantasy or reality?

In complete contrast to the stagnation of his life, good news arrives at the beginning of 1993, the year of Federico and Giulietta's golden anniversary. On January 20, Fellini's seventy-third birthday, Federico is told that the Hollywood Academy wants to present him with a lifetime achievement award. When the journalists descend, pressing him for comments, the director simply answers, "I only hope that this will lead to some work!" He receives congratulations from everywhere and is particularly moved by the burst of spontaneous applause that erupts from the taxi drivers, Gypsies, and waiters at Caffè Canova in Piazza del Popolo.

But making the trip to Los Angeles seems unlikely, because of his delicate health. The previous fall, Federico had suffered an aortic aneurysm, which gave him arthritis in his neck, causing vertigo, and he has circulation problems in one leg. When walking in Milan one day, according to Vincenzo Mollica, who was with him, Fellini suddenly swerved and started shouting, "A dog! A dog!" It took him a few minutes before he realized that the shooting pain in his shin *wasn't* an animal biting him.

After the incident, Federico has difficulty standing and is consumed by a fear of falling. Concerned about these symptoms, he decides not to go to California and asks Mollica to help him record a video to send in his stead, thanking the academy. Federico spends an entire afternoon in the news studio of Saxa Rubra trying to work out his speech in English and, as always, being attentive to details—characteristically, he wants to do the editing himself too. Giulietta will change his mind in the end, convincing him to face the exertion and risks of the trip. Once in Hollywood, he checks into the Beverly Hilton Hotel, and immediately calls an Italian doctor because he doesn't feel well. The doctor recommends that he have an operation as soon as possible.

On March 29, Federico walks a little delicately onto the stage of the Dorothy Chandler Pavilion to accept his award from Sophia Loren and Marcello Mastroianni. He's not allowed to improvise his speech, as he would have liked, because it has to last exactly thirty seconds and must be read from a teleprompter. Yet the old showman manages to amuse and move the audience with a short speech delivered in his sketchy English: "I want to thank all of you to make me feel in this way. In these circumstances it's easy to be generous and thank everybody. I would like, naturally, to thank all the people that had worked with me. I cannot nominate everyone. Let me make only one name of an actress who is also my wife. Thank you, dear Giulietta, and please stop crying! Grazie." In a radio interview he adds some more ironic comments: "I can't even die now. I've had so many gratifications, there's no good reason that I *should* die. Maybe that's it, I have secured immortality because dying doesn't make sense anymore, because all good things are possible, and all the displays of affection and respect have come my way now."

Back in Rome after the festivities, life goes back to how it was. The movie projects are as elusive as ever and Fellini's health starts to deteriorate. After many second thoughts, Fellini checks into the Cantonal Hospital in Zurich on June 16 for an angioplasty on his femoral artery. The difficult operation starts at 7:30 a.m. and is over by noon, but an hour later he has to undergo another surgery because of internal bleeding. The operations, and three anesthesia treatments, last fourteen hours altogether, during which time they also perform heart bypass surgery. He leaves the hospital on June 28, and stays on in Zurich for a few weeks with Giulietta. Then he moves to Rimini. On August 3, he has breakfast with his sister, Maddalena, and her husband, Giorgio Fabbri, at the Grand Hotel, and then goes back to his room, suite 315, where at 3:30 p.m. he has a stroke. He's hospitalized at Ospedale Infermi and the doctors diagnose him as having a cerebral ischemia with paralysis on the left side of his body, and reduced motor abilities. The doctors' conclusions are extremely cautious but not catastrophic; still, the news hits the summer newspapers like a bomb.

Among the journalists, friends, well-wishers, and passersby who descend on the hospital, Gianfranco Angelucci meets an attractive middle-aged woman who stands patiently in the hall and periodically asks for news on the patient's condition. In his book, *Federico F.*, a highly detailed and discreet novelization of the long road of the director's life, Angelucci recounts the woman's unusual story. Eleonora Diodati, a former actress, met Federico during the period of *Il bidone* and then again decades later on *La voce della luna*. We can imagine that this second encounter was particularly warm, and may have been the last burst of passion in the maestro's secret life, based on the series of twenty-nine pictures he drew during that time. The drawings were done in pens, markers, heavy pencil, and watercolor. Diodati kept them, and they could be compared to Picasso's exuberant last works. Angelucci talks of an "erotic exaltation tinged with love and abandonment," but in fact, the drawings are a surprise beyond every description: grotesque, frantic sex scenes, crudely ironic and only occasionally comical. Not only evidence of yet another secret element in Fellini's parallel life, the drawings are also proof of the talented artist's evolution; among the caricatures, sketches for set designs and costumes, and other miscellaneous sketches he left behind, he shows a growing sense of unique figurative interpretations that he casts in aggressive expressionism. On the threshold of old age, Fellini seems to have become the painter that he wanted to be when he was young.

His recovery is slow and there seems to be no chance that he will regain full functionality. On August 30, he moves to the Ospedale San Giorgio in Ferrara, which he finds even more depressing, and where, with great effort, he begins to teach his body how to move again. His progress is modest, but when troubling news arrives about Giulietta's health—she'd fallen extremely ill in the interim—Federico asks to be moved to Rome to see her. The trip, conducted without the doctor's approval and with great difficulty, ends up in the headlines. Giulietta visits her husband on October 1, wearing a turban that fails to conceal the loss of hair from chemotherapy. Fellini is skeptical about his rehabilitation and wants to go home. On October 9, they transfer him to the Policlinico Umberto I in Rome where, by unhappy coincidence, he's put into the same first-floor room where his brother, Riccardo, died. Restless, Federico is having difficulty sleeping and suffers night panics. He asks his old friend Rinaldo Geleng to stay with him for a few nights; between the anxiety attacks and sudden bouts of difficult breathing, Geleng doesn't get any sleep.

During this tragic period, there are characteristic flashes of Fellini's good cheer. One example is the little scene that Vincenzo Mollica describes in *Federico Fellini autore di testi*:

> I saw Federico for the last time the day before he went into a coma. At a certain point, Rinaldo Geleng arrived with a magazine that had Valeria Marini on the cover. In the picture, she was facing away from the camera and wearing such a thin piece of fabric that she was basically naked. Federico asked Geleng for the magazine, and right on her ass he drew a little figure saying "I want to stay here"; the balloon and the figure with the tiny head were identical to the figures in the comic strips he drew for *420*.

The patient's condition is stable and doesn't seem cause for any particular concern, so on Sunday, October 17, the doctors let Federico out for lunch with Giulietta and some friends at a restaurant on Porta Pia. Afterward they take him to visit his new office at via Capo le Case 18, the same building where Geleng lives. He likes it and thinks he'll be able to work well there. From the way he's talking it seems clear that he's resigned to the idea that he'll no longer make movies, but he is planning to start painting seriously. In fact, he asks them to get him an easel, brushes, and paints, and is looking forward to being able to use them in his peaceful new studio.

But this lovely plan, which he'd thought of as a kind of compromise to the irreparable damage of his illness, was never to be realized. He returned to the Policlinico and, while eating dinner in bed, suffered a sudden sense of suffocation, followed by unconsciousness. For days he'll be in an irreversible coma, as the press frantically covers his condition, worrying furiously as the days pass about the presumed excessive use of the life support system. The maestro never comes out of the coma, and dies in the middle of the day on October 31, the day after the celebration that never took place for his fiftieth wedding anniversary. We might say that Federico handled the last act of his life as if it were one of his films—never sealed with the words "The End," because he believed that "the end arrives through many little details, day by day, and there is no precise moment that is the ending of a movie."

The grief over his death is indescribable. The director is dressed in the tuxedo he wore for his Oscar acceptance; the coffin is set for viewing on November 2 in Studio 5 at Cinecittà—his favorite studio—in front of the light-blue landscape of *Intervista*. The workers at the studio mount it for free. There is a silent and endless procession; some people estimate the huge crowd at about 70,000 people. The official funeral is held at Basilica di Santa Maria degli Angeli in Piazza Esedra. Giulietta is there, visibly sicker—she will die five months later, on March 23, 1994. Federico's corpse is transferred to Rimini for the final farewell and he is buried in the family tomb. There isn't a newspaper in the world that describes the event as anything other than a loss for humanity. In this burst of affection, one headline stands out, bearing a hopeful message that we can take to be a certainty: FOR FELLINI, THIS IS THE START OF A GREAT FUTURE.

Time Line

1856

April 15: Luigi Fellini, Federico's paternal grandfather, is born. He's a farmer and a shop-keeper.

1860

July 12: Francesca Lombardini, Fellini's paternal grandmother, is born in Sant'Angelo di Gatteo.

1866

Riccardo Barbiani, Fellini's maternal grandfather, is born in Rimini. He moves to Rome July 18, 1885, and starts a wholesale egg business.

1870

April 14: Maddalena Leali, Fellini's maternal grandmother, is born in Rome. She dies in 1909.

1883

Early in the year, probably in the parish of Balignano, Luigi Fellini marries Francesca Lombardini. Five children are born to the couple: Agostina Elvira (August 16, 1884, the only one who will live her whole life in Gambettola), Leo (August 29, 1887; he dies January 4, 1947), Ida (April 11, 1889; she dies December 2, 1945), Urbano (February 27, 1894; Fellini's father), and Domenico (called Federico; born July 5, 1896; died on the battlefield October 27, 1918). The Fellini family has a dairy farm and a small general market on via Sopra Rigossa.

1896

November 4: Ida Barbiani, Fellini's mother, is born in Rome.

1915

Urbano moves to Rome and works as an apprentice baker at the pastificio Pantanella. He falls in love with his neighbor on via Manin, Ida Barbiani.

1917

The match between Ida and Urbano is vehemently opposed by the Barbiani family, and the couple flees Rome for Urbano's parents' home in Gambettola.

1918

August 19: Civil marriage between Urbano and Ida (the religious ceremony will be held on January 22, 1919, at Santa Maria Maggiore in Rome).

1919

At the end of the year, the Fellinis move to Rimini, where Urbano begins working as a traveling salesman and wholesale vendor.

1920

January 20, 9:30 p.m.: In Rimini, in the Fellini home on viale Dardanelli 10, Federico is born. The Fellinis move temporarily to Rome but return shortly thereafter to Rimini, where they move three times, from corso d'Augusto to via Gambalunga to via Clementini.

1921

February 22, 8:15 a.m.: In San Giorgio di Piano, Bologna, on via Umberto I number 24, Giulia (later Giulietta) Anna Masina is born to Anna Flavia Pasqualin, a schoolteacher, and Gaetano Masina, a violinist. She is the oldest of four children: Eugenia (b. 1922), and the twins Mario and Maria (b. 1928).

March 1: Fellini's brother, Riccardo, is born in Rimini.

Summer: Fellini spends his first vacation in Gambettola (he will return every year until either 1925 or 1929, when his paternal grandparents sell their house and move to Rimini).

1923

January 23: Grandfather Riccardo Barbiani dies in Tolentino without having reconciled with his daughter Ida.

1924

Autumn: Fellini attends elementary school with the Sisters of Vincenzo.

1926

September: Fellini starts at Carlo Tonni public school on via Gambalunga; he will stay at this school.

Young Giulietta is a frequent guest at her uncle Eugenio Pasqualin and aunt Giulia Sardi's home in Rome, via Lutezia 11. After her husband's death, Aunt Giulia invites Giulietta to come live with her in Rome and keep her company.

1927

Summer: The first escape: Fellini allegedly runs away with the circus clown Pierino (the event never actually occurred).

1929

February: The Fellini family moves to via Clementini 9.

June: Fellini graduates from elementary school.

October 7: Fellini's sister, Maria Maddalena, is born in Rimini.

1930

September: Fellini enrolls at the Ginnasio-Liceo Giosuè Carducci, on via Gambalunga (the school's name will change to Giulio Cesare, Palazzo Bunadrata, corso d'Augusto). He will stay at this school for eight years, until graduation.

1931

April 21: The Fellinis move to via Dante.

1933

The year of the VII Mille Miglia car race and the maiden voyage of the transatlantic ocean liner *Rex*, later referenced in *Amarcord*.

Fellini visits Rome with his parents. The family will repeat the trip the following year.

1934

April 23: A drawing by Achille Beltrame of an enormous fish washed up on the beach in Rimini is published in *Domenica del Corriere*. (This is the monster that appears at the end of *La dolce vita*.)

1936

August: Fellini goes camping in Verrucchio with the scouts, GIL (Gioventù Italiana del Littorio).

October: the 1936–37 school year begins—the period evoked in Fellini's column "Secondo liceo," which appears first in *Marc'Aurelio* and then in *Travaso delle Idee*.

1937

Summer: Fellini and the painter Demos Bonini open a portrait shop and name it Febo (Fellini-Bonini) in Palazzo Malatesta, at the corner of via Tempio Malatestiano.

1938

February 6: Fellini's first publication appears in *Domenica del Corriere* in the "Postcards from Our Readers" section.

February 27: Fellini publishes his first cartoon in the Florentine weekly *420*, where he will go on to contribute drawings and short articles for two years.

July: Fellini sits for his final state exams at the Liceo Monti in Cesena and at the Morgagni in Forlì. He has to retake his military culture exam and passes on the second round, obtaining his diploma.

Autumn: Fellini enrolls in law school at the Università di Roma and plans his move to the capital.

November 11: A group photo is taken of the Rimini gang at Caffè Ausonia. Fellini is wearing a black shirt and brandishing a uniformed friend's fist in jest.

1939

January 4: Fellini is accompanied by friends as far as Bologna, and then continues on to Rome. Upon arrival, he presents himself at the newspaper *Marc'Aurelio* at via Regina Elena 68 (now via Barberini), where he is received by the production manager Stefano Vanzina (aka Steno, 1915–88), future fellow director. On the same occasion, he meets Ruggero Maccari (1919–89), future fellow screenwriter, with whom he begins to collaborate.

March 7: Fellini publishes his first article in *Marc'Aurelio*, entitled "È permesso?" (May I Come In?).

March 14: Ida, Federico, and Maddalena officially move to Rome, via Albalonga 13, first floor, apartment 8, near Piazza Re di Roma (the neighborhood later evoked in *Roma*).

June 17: Fellini publishes the first of many regular columns, entitled "Il raccontino pubblicitario" (The Little Advertisement Tale).

June 18: Fellini's interview with Aldo Fabrizi (1905–90) comes out in *CineMagazzino*, giving birth to a friendship and eventual professional collaboration.

1940

Early in the year: Fellini begins writing for radio.

June 10: Italy enters the war against France and England.

Autumn: Giulietta begins performing with the company Teatro GUF.

October 23: The film *Il pirata sono io* (*I'm the Pirate*) by Mario Mattoli (1898–1980) and starring Erminio Macario (1902–80) comes out. This is Fellini's first job working as a gag writer.

Fellini collaborates (uncredited) with a group of young writers assisting Cesare Zavattini (1902–89). There, he meets Piero Tellini (1917–85), with whom he will team up for a while.

December 12: Fellini and Ruggero Maccari's radio script "Il cerino" (The Match) is broadcast during the intermission on the program *Caleidoscopio*.

1941

February: Fellini is applauded by the audience at Cinemateatro Quattro Fontane; he is there as the guest of honor of the satirical magazine *Baffi '41*.

May 6: Zavattini, Fabrizi, and Fellini finish the story for the film *Avanti c'è posto* (*Before the Postman*).

Fellini moves to the boardinghouse at via Nicotera 26, room 9, when Ida and little Maddalena leave Rome to return to Rimini.

1942

April: The film *Documento Z-3* comes out. Fellini contributes to the screenplay, uncredited.

June: *Avanti c'è posto*, starring Aldo Fabrizi, goes into production. Fellini is credited among the writers as "Federico."

August 30: *Avanti c'è posto* is released and is a great success.

September 3: First episode of the radio program *Terziglio* is broadcast; the theme is "Una lettera d'amore" (A Love Letter).

Autumn: Fellini first meets the actress Giulietta Masina in the office of EIAR.
November: Fellini makes a lucky escape from Libya, where he was working on the movie *I cavalieri del deserto* (Knights of the Desert); production was suspended because of the war.
December 17: The film *Quarta pagina* (¾ *of a Page*) comes out. Fellini works on the screenplay.

1943
January 23: Allied forces conquer Tripoli.
January: Fellini and Giulietta are engaged.
June 24: The film *Campo de' Fiori* comes out. Fellini works on the story.
September 8: Italian Armistice is declared.
October 30: Fellini and Giulietta are married. The newlyweds will live in Giulietta's aunt Giulia Pasqualina's house at via Lutezia 11, first floor, apartment 6.
November 1: American planes bomb Rimini, the first of 396 bombardments, which will persist through September 1944.
December 16: The film *L'ultima carrozzella* (*The Last Wagon*) comes out. Fellini worked on the screenplay.

1944
June 4: Rome is liberated.
June 12: Riccardo marries his singing teacher Alessandra, Giulio Moreschi's daughter. Their daughter, Rita, is born in 1945.
Summer: Fellini sets up the Funny-Face Shop, drawing caricatures of Allied soldiers for money.
September 22: Rimini is liberated.

1945
January 17: Roberto Rossellini (1906–77) begins shooting *Romà, città aperta*. Fellini secures Aldo Fabrizi for the film and collaborates on the screenplay.
March 22: Pierfederico (called Federichino) is born to Fellini and Giulietta. The baby will live only until April 24.
September 24: Opening of *Romà, città aperta* at the Festival del Teatro Quirino.

1946
January 15: Rossellini begins work on *Paisà*, filming the Sicilian section in Maiori. In the same region they shoot the segment in the monastery, before moving on in March to Naples and then Florence. Fellini is cowriter on the screenplay and assistant director.
April: The last episode of the partisan sequence of *Paisà* is filmed at the mouth of the Po River.
September 17: *Paisà* shows at the Venice Film Festival.
Winter: Fellini begins collaborating with Tullio Pinelli (b. 1908) on the screenplay for *Il passatore* (*A Bullet for Stefano*).

1947

March 13: Sergio Amidei (1904–81) and Fellini receive Oscar nominations for the screenplay for *Roma, città aperta*.

1948

February: Fellini meets Marcello Mastroianni (1924–96), who is appearing with Giulietta in *Angelica* by Leo Ferrero at the Teatro delle Arti.

August 29: Alberto Lattuada's (1913–2005) film *Senza pietà* (*Without Pity*) shows at the 9th Venice Film Festival. Fellini is cowriter on the screenplay and assistant director. Giulietta wins a huge round of applause for her performance.

October 30: Rossellini's *L'amore* is released. Fellini appears in the film with Anna Magnani (1908–73) in the section *Il miracolo*.

November 21: After a screening of *Ladri di biciclette* (*The Bicycle Thief*) at the Circolo Romano del Cinema, Fellini enthusiastically telephones Cesare Zavattini to congratulate him.

1949

August 22: Fellini attends the 10th Venice Film Festival with Lattuada for the screening (out of competition) of *Il mulino del Po* (*The Mill on the Po*).

1950

Early in the year: Fellini, Lattuada, and their wives, Giulietta and Carla Del Poggio, form a production collective to make the independent film *Luci del varietà* (*Variety Lights*).

February: Fellini, Amidei, Alfred Hayes, Marcello Pagliero, and Rossellini receive an Oscar nomination for the screenplay for *Paisà*.

Summer: *Luci del varietà* is in production in Rome and Capranica.

August 27: The writer Cesare Pavese (1908–50) commits suicide in a hotel in Turin. Pinelli, his former schoolmate, will evoke his story in the character of Steiner for *La dolce vita*.

December 6: *Luci del varietà* comes out; the production company goes bankrupt.

1951

Summer: Fellini makes his first trip to Paris in the company of Pinelli in order to discuss *Europa '51* with Rossellini.

September: Production begins on *Lo sceicco bianco* (*The White Sheik*) in Fiumicino. The scene is reshot the next day on the beach by the restaurant Mastino di Fregene.

1952

February 10: Filming wraps on *Lo sceicco bianco* in Saint Peter's Square.

April 23: Initially selected to run in competition at Cannes, *Lo sceicco bianco* is then dropped from the selection.

April 24: The U.S. Supreme Court makes a decision on the Joseph Burstyn case (U.S. distributor for *Il miracolo*), determining that any censure of a religious nature is illegitimate.

September 6: *Lo sceicco bianco* debuts at the 13th Venice Film Festival.

September 20: *Lo sceicco bianco* is released.
December: Production begins on *I vitelloni*.

1953
June 28: Maria Maddalena Fellini marries Giorgio Fabbri in Rimini. Their daughter, Francesca, is born May 14, 1965.
August 26: *I vitelloni* shows at the 14th Venice Film Festival. On September 4 the film wins a Silver Lion.
September 17: *I vitelloni* is released.
Late October: Production begins on *La strada*.
November 26: The omnibus film *L'amore in città* (*Love in the City*) is released. Fellini directs the episode entitled *Un'agenzia matrimoniale* (*A Marriage Agency*).

1954
Spring: Production wraps on *La strada*. Fellini falls into a deep depression and briefly enters psychoanalysis with Emilio Servadio. He meets Lea Giacomini and they begin an affair that lasts several years.
September 6: *La strada* is shown at the 15th Venice Film Festival. On September 7, the film wins a Silver Lion.
September 22: *La strada* is released.

1955
March: Producer Dino De Laurentiis holds a gala at the Salle Pleyel in Paris to celebrate the French release of *La strada*.
Late April: Production begins on *Il bidone* (*The Swindle*) in Marino. Giulietta's aunt, Giulia Sardi, dies.
June 10–17: The New Year's Eve party scene from *Il bidone* is shot at the Titanus studios.
July 16: Filming wraps on *Il bidone* in the Titanus studios. *La strada* receives Silver Ribbons for best producers (Carlo Ponti and De Laurentiis) and best director.
September 5: Editing wraps on *Il bidone* at 3:00 a.m. at the studio on via Margutta after nineteen straight hours of work.
September 9: *Il bidone* receives harsh criticism at the 16th Venice Film Festival.
October 7: A heavily recut version of *Il bidone* is released.
Fellini visits the doctor-writer Mario Tobino (1910–91) in the women's asylum in Maggiano, Lucca, to discuss adapting his novel, *Le libere donne di Magliano* (The Free Women of Magliano), for the screen.

1956
January 12: Official registration at city hall of the Fellinis' move from via Lutezia to via Archimede 141A, fourth floor, apartment 12.
March: The treatment is completed on *Le libere donne di Magliano*, but the film will never be made.
Spring: While developing *Le notti di Cabiria*, (*The Nights of Cabiria*), Fellini explores the outskirts of Rome with Pier Paolo Pasolini (1922–75).

May 1: A statue of Jesus is delivered by helicopter to Saint Peter's Square—the inspiration for the beginning of *La dolce vita*.

May 31: Fellini's father, Urbano, dies in Rimini.

July 9: Filming begins on *Le notti di Cabiria*.

October 1: Production wraps on *Le notti di Cabiria*.

1957

March 9: In the wake of several attempts to censor *Le notti di Cabiria*, Fellini, in consultation with Father Angelo Arpa (b. 1909), decides to screen the film for the Archbishop of Genoa, Giuseppe Siri (1906–89).

March 27: *La strada* receives an Oscar nomination for best screenplay (Fellini, Pinelli, Flaiano, Brunello Rondi) and wins the Oscar for best foreign language film.

May 10: *Le notti di Cabiria* shows at the 10th Cannes Film Festival.

May 14: Fellini meets Anna Giovannini (b. 1916) in the Ruschena bakery and they begin an affair that will continue for the rest of Fellini's life.

May 16: Giulietta "et son personage" unanimously wins the prize for best actress for *Le notti di Cabiria* "avec homage à Fellini."

July: Fellini finishes the treatment for *Viaggio con Anita* (or *Viaggio d'amore*), with Sophia Loren as the star. The film will not be made.

October 9: *Le notti di Cabiria* is released.

October: Fellini accepts a prize from the Screen Directors Guild in Hollywood for *La strada* while in the United States for the release of *Le notti di Cabiria*.

1958

March 26: Oscar nomination for the screenplay of *I vitelloni* (Fellini, Tullio Pinelli, Ennio Flaiano). *Le notti di Cabiria* wins the Oscar for the best foreign language film. Giulietta accepts the award at the RKO Pantages Theater.

Spring: Unable to make *Viaggio con Anita* because Loren is unavailable, Fellini returns to his idea for *Moraldo in città* (Moraldo in the City).

August 15: Tazio Secchiaroli (1925–98) and other society photojournalists (who will be dubbed paparazzi in *La dolce vita*) open hunting season on celebrities on via Veneto, stealing shots of the ex-king Farouk at the Café de Paris, of Ava Gardner with Anthony Franciosa at Brick's Top, and of Anthony Steel and Anita Ekberg in the entrance of Vecchia Roma.

August: Pierluigi Praturlon (1924–99) takes pictures of Anita Ekberg, fully dressed, in the Trevi Fountain; the photos will be published in *Tempo Illustrato* in September.

October 9: Pope Pius XII dies.

December 5: The Turkish dancer Haish Nana undresses for a spontaneous striptease during a party in the Rugantino nightclub. The police come.

1959

January: De Laurentiis disagrees with Fellini about *La dolce vita* and sells the project to Peppino Amato, who secures backing from Angelo Rizzoli (1889–70).

February 22: Fellini goes to Milan to see Elio Vittorini (1908–66) at the writer's house in Porta Ticinese and offers him the part of Steiner.

March 16, 11:35 a.m.: Production begins on *La dolce vita* in Studio 14 of Cinecittà: Anita climbing the stairs to the cupola in Saint Peter's.

April 1–3: The scene with Anita in the Trevi Fountain is filmed.

April 21: The scene with Anouk Aimée at the Tivoli baths is filmed.

May 11: The scene of the aristocrats at Bassano di Sutri is filmed.

June 6: The sidewalk in front of Café de Paris on via Veneto is rebuilt in Studio 5 at Cinecittà.

June 20–24: The scene of the fake miracle near Bagni di Tivoli is filmed.

Late June: The scene at the Steiner house is shot in Cinecittà.

August 15: Nadia Gray's striptease is shot in Cinecittà.

August 27: Filming wraps on *La dolce vita* at Passo Oscuro.

1960

February 3: The gala opening for *La dolce vita* is held at the Cinema Fiamma in Rome.

February 5: There is a stormy screening of *La dolce vita* at the Cinema Capitol in Milan.

February 17: In parliament, undersecretary Domenico Magrì responds to the ministers who have requested that *La dolce vita* be banned.

Spring: Construction on Fellini's first house in Fregene on via Portovenere begins.

May: The jury of the 13th Cannes Film Festival, presided over by Georges Simenon (1903–89), unanimously awards the Palme d'Or to *La dolce vita*.

September: Fellini rents and decorates the new office of Federiz, via della Croce 70.

October: Federiz cancels *Accattone*, permanently compromising Fellini and Pasolini's friendship.

End of the year: After many years, Fellini visits his relatives in Gambettola.

1961

April 19: *La dolce vita* is released in New York at the Henry Miller Theater.

Summer: Filming begins in the Eur neighborhood of Rome and elsewhere for *Le tentazioni del dottor Antonio* (*The Temptations of Doctor Antonio*), a section of the omnibus *Boccaccio '70*.

1962

January 15: Ground is broken for the ultra-modern studio lot of Dinocittà, founded by De Laurentiis on via Pontina.

February 22: *Boccaccio '70* opens in Milan.

April 9: *La dolce vita* receives Oscar nominations for best director, screenplay (Fellini, Pinelli, Flaiano, Brunello Rondi), best art and set direction, and best costumes in a black-and-white film (Piero Gherardi, who wins the Oscar in this category).

In issue 27 of *L'Europeo* a ghostwritten article about via Veneto is published under Fellini's name.

May 7: *Boccaccio '70* opens the 15th Cannes Film Festival (out of competition).

May 9: Shooting starts on *8½*.

October 14: Shooting wraps on *8½*.

Rizzoli publishes *Storia di Federico Fellini*, written by Angelo Solmi, the first biography of the director.

1963

February 14: 8½ is released.

May: 8½ shows out of competition at the 16th Cannes Film Festival.

June: Fellini is in New York with Mastroianni.

July 7: 8½ receives the Grolla d'Oro at Saint Vincent Film Festival for best director.

July 18: 8½ is shown at the Moscow Film Festival. On July 21 it wins first prize in the competition.

1964

February 13: Fellini signs a secret contract with De Laurentiis to do *Giulietta degli spiriti* (*Juliet of the Spirits*), if Rizzoli pulls out.

April: On the flight to New York, organized by Rizzoli, Flaiano gets angry about being seated in coach.

April 13: Fellini, Giulietta, and Rizzoli et al. attend the Academy Awards at the Santa Monica Civic Auditorium. 8½ has been nominated in four categories. Gherardi wins for best costume design in black-and-white, and the film wins the best foreign language film. The next day, Fellini tours Disneyland with Walt Disney.

April 22: 8½ wins seven Silver Ribbons.

June 2: Fellini is named a Grande Ufficiale and Giulietta is named Commendatore.

June 25: 8½ is released in the United States.

Summer: Fellini experiments with LSD under the care of Emilio Servadio.

July 27: Filming starts on *Giulietta degli spiriti* in San Pellegrino.

December 5: Sergio Zavoli's television special *Un'ora (e ½) con Federico Fellini* (An Hour [and a Half] with Federico Fellini) is broadcast—the first of numerous programs on the director.

1965

January 31: Shooting wraps on *Giulietta degli spiriti* in Fregene.

Spring: Fellini goes to Milan to meet Dino Buzzati (1906–72) and propose a collaboration on the story for *Il viaggio di G. Mastorna*.

June 29: Ernst Bernhard (1896–1965), the Jungian psychologist who has been treating Fellini for four years, dies.

July 21: Fellini meets Almerina and Dino Buzzati in Turin for a séance with Fellini's friend Gustavo Adolfo Rol (1903–94) at his apartment on via Silvio Pellico 31.

August 11: Fellini writes a letter to De Laurentiis, planning to start production on *Il viaggio di G. Mastorna* in February or March.

Summer: The Fellinis change houses in Fregene, moving to via Volosca. Fellini works with Buzzati on *Il viaggio di G. Mastorna*. Fellini has an argument with Luigi Chiarini (1900–75) over the fact that *Giulietta degli spiriti* will not appear at the Venice Film Festival.

October 22: *Giulietta degli spiriti* is released.

November: There is a party in Fellini and Giulietta's honor at Jacqueline Kennedy's house in New York for the U.S. launch of *Giulietta degli spiriti*.

1966

January 4: *Giulietta degli spiriti* is released in the United States.

January 29: Neil Simon's musical *Sweet Charity*, based on *Le notti di Cabiria*, opens at the Palace Theatre in New York (lyrics by Dorothy Fields, music by Cy Coleman). The lead is played by Gwen Verdon (608 shows). Bob Fosse makes a film based on the musical starring Shirley MacLaine in 1969. Fellini's name does not appear on any of these projects.

February 3: Gianni Di Venzanzo (b. 1920) dies in Rome.

Giulietta debuts a radio program called *Lettere aperte a Giulietta Masina* (Open Letters to Giulietta Masina), which will stay on the air until 1969. A column in the daily newspaper *La Stampa* is born out of the radio show.

The Fellinis abandon their apartment in Rome to move to the new, bigger villa in Fregene, with the idea that they'll stay there year-round.

February 10: Fellini writes to De Laurentiis confirming Mastroianni for the lead in *Mastorna*, to start production July 13.

May 2: The Fellinis and the Buzzatis attend the opening night of the play by Salvato Cappelli (1911–83), *Duecentomila e uno* (Two hundred thousand and one), directed by Giorgio Strehler (1921–97) at the Piccolo Teatro in Milan.

Carla Fracci performs in the ballet *La strada* with music by Nino Rota at La Scala in Milan.

May 21: Fellini writes De Laurentiis asking him to hold the contract with Mastroianni for *Mastorna*—he's not sure Mastroianni's right for the part.

May 25: Fellini writes to Buzzati about his thoughts for the story of *Mastorna*.

July: Buzzati delivers a rewrite of the dialogues.

Summer: Construction of the set for *Mastorna* at Dinocittà begins.

September 14: De Laurentiis announces a delay in production on *Mastorna*. His notice crosses with Fellini's letter of the same day, saying that he doesn't want to do the film.

September 24: De Laurentiis has the Fellinis' valuables seized from the villa on via Volosca in partial payment for damages incurred on the canceled film.

September 26: De Laurentiis has a lien put on Fellini's assets and monies owed him by Cineriz Distribuzione and Rizzoli Film.

1967

January 19: Fellini and De Laurentiis make a settlement.

March 18: Ugo Tognazzi (1922–90) signs the contract to play *Mastorna*.

April 10: Fellini is rushed to the Salvator Mundi clinic on via Gianicolo, following an attack of acute pleurisy exacerbated by an injection.

May 3: Fellini recovers, leaves the clinic, and goes to convalesce in Manziana, then in Campocatino near Fiuggi. He writes "Il mio paese" ("My Town") for an anthology *La mia Rimini* (My Rimini) that comes out with Cappelli of Bologna. He stops smoking.

July: Fellini begins a collaboration with Bernadino Zapponi (1927–2000).

August 21: Fellini signs a contract with De Laurentiis to make three films instead of *Mastorna*, none of which will be made.

September: Mario Longardi becomes Fellini's personal press secretary.

September 25: Producer Alberto Grimaldi (b. 1925) buys out Fellini's *Mastorna* contract from De Laurentiis.

October: Fellini begins work on *Toby Dammit* for the omnibus *Histoires extraordinaires*.

1968

January 23: Grimaldi announces that *Mastorna* will start production in March. Fellini travels to Bulgaria and Romania to scout locations.

March 16: The book *La mia Rimini* is presented at the Grand Hotel in Rimini.

May 17: *Histoires extraordinaires* is the last film screened at the 21st Cannes Film Festival before the festival is called off in the wake of the uprisings in France.

September–October: Fellini films *Fellini: A Director's Notebook* while in development on *Satyricon*.

November 5: The Fellinis move definitively back to Rome, to via Margutta 110A, apartment 5, former home of the widow of comedy writer Aldo De Benedetti.

November 9: Filming begins on *Satyricon* at Cinecittà.

December 14: The program *Canzonissima* visits the set of *Satyricon* and films the director's shooting of the earthquake scene in Suburra.

1969

January 11: Press conference with Ingmar Bergman to announce *Love Duet*, which will not be made.

May 23: Filming wraps on *Satyricon* on the island of Ponza.

September 4: *Satyricon* screens out of competition at the 30th Venice Film Festival.

September 18: *Satyricon* is released in Italy.

The Fellinis sell their villa in Fregene to pay off their taxes to Fellini's former schoolmate Ercole Sega—who had correctly diagnosed Fellini's illness in April 1967.

November 30: Fellini, Giulietta, Mastroianni, et al. appear in the broadcast *L'invité du dimanche* on Antenne 2 for the French release of *Satyricon*.

1970

January: There is a U.S. press tour with Giulietta, Grimaldi, and Longardi for *Satyricon*. In Los Angeles Fellini meets Paul Mazursky and is interviewed by Dick Cavett and David Frost.

Following a minor traffic accident in Rimini, Fellini sells his car and never drives again.

February: Fellini is in Paris to scout locations for *I clowns*.

March 8: Fellini has the seed of the idea that will become *Amarcord*.

March 11: *Satyricon* is released in the United States.

March 23: Filming starts on *I clowns*.

July 9: Performing as himself, Fellini works with Donald Sutherland at Cinecittà in Mazursky's *Alex in Wonderland*.

August 30: *I clowns* is screened at the 31st Venice Film Festival.

November 2: First takes (unused) for *Roma* at the cemetery of Verano are shot from a helicopter.

December 25: Television broadcast premiere in black-and-white of *I clowns*. It comes out in color in the movie theaters on December 27.

1971
Late March: Filming starts on *Roma*.
Late summer: Production is suspended on *Roma*.
October: Production resumes on *Roma*.

1972
February: Production wraps on *Roma*.
March 16: *Roma* is released.
May 14: *Roma* screens out of competition at the 26th Cannes Film Festival.
November 20: Ennio Flaiano (b. 1910) dies in Rome.
Christmas: A special edition of *Vogue* comes out, entitled *Vogue Fellini*, featuring Mastroianni as Mandrake.

1973
January–June: *Amarcord* is filmed.
Summer: An agreement is made with De Laurentiis to make *Casanova*. After a year he will pull out of the project.
July: Filming of the *Rex* at Cinecittà.
December 18: *Amarcord* is released.

1974
Publication of the collection *Quattro film* (Four Films) by Einaudi is protested by Fellini's screenwriters, whose names do not appear prominently on the book.
May 9: *Amarcord* opens the 27th Cannes Film Festival out of competition.
Fellini dines with the young director Steven Spielberg during his first European trip.
September 27: Fellini grants Diogenes Verlag the exclusive rights to his writings and drawings.
December 21: Ettore Scola's *C'eravamo tanto amati* (*We All Loved Each Other So Much*) comes out. Fellini appears as himself alongside Mastroianni, reprising the scene at the Trevi Fountain from *La dolce vita*.

1975
March: Giulietta's book *Il diario degli altri* (*The Diary of Others*) is published, a collection of her letters to readers that appeared in her column in *La Stampa*.
April 8: Fellini is not at the Dorothy Chandler Pavilion to accept the Oscar for *Amarcord* for best foreign language film. The following year, after the film has been released in the United States, it garners nominations for best director and best screenplay.
May: Fellini has his first meeting at Cinecittà with Donald Sutherland, who is cast as the lead in *Il Casanova*.
July 20: Production begins on *Il Casanova*.

August: Fellini goes to New York with Giulietta and Tonino Guerra for the American opening of *Amarcord*.

September 24: First television broadcast of *La dolce vita*.

December 23: Grimaldi suspends production on *Il Casanova*.

1976

March 23: Production resumes on *Il Casanova* after negotiations with Grimaldi.

May 21: Production wraps on *Il Casanova*.

November: Fellini shows outtakes from *Il Casanova* to Akira Kurosawa (1910–98), who is passing through Rome.

December 7: *Il Casanova* is released.

1977

January: Fellini visits Georges Simenon (1930–89) in Lausanne, at his house on Avenue des Figuiers 12, for an interview that appears in *L'Express* (February 21–27) entitled "Fellini-Simenon: Casanova notre frère."

Fellini works on *La città delle donne* (*City of Women*).

March 28: Danilo Donati (1926–2001) wins the Oscar for best costume design for *Il Casanova*.

September 21: The *Literaturnaya Gazeta* publishes an interview with Fellini by Arkadi Vaksberg in which Fellini claims to make movies "only for the paycheck." Fellini tries to clarify that the journalist didn't understand that he was kidding.

December 25: Fellini delivers an emotional tribute on television to Charlie Chaplin on the occasion of his death.

1978

March 16: Aldo Moro is kidnapped by the Red Brigades, who kill the prime minister fifty-five days later.

May 22: Filming starts on *Prova d'orchestra* (*Orchestra Rehearsal*) at Cinecittà and wraps in four weeks.

August: After discovering a mutual passion for comic books, Fellini strikes up an enduring friendship with the television journalist Vincenzo Mollica when he comes to Chianciano to interview Fellini.

October 19: There is a preview screening of *Prova d'orchestra* for President Sandro Pertini at the Palazzo del Quirinale.

1979

February 22: *Prova d'orchestra* is released.

February: Fellini's personal trainer, former boxer Ettore Bevilacqua, dies.

April 10: Nino Rota (b. 1911) dies in Rome.

April 17: Production begins on *La città delle donne* (*City of Women*) at Cinecittà.

May 10: *Prova d'orchestra* screens out of competition at the 32nd Cannes Film Festival.

July 27: Ettore Manni (b. 1927), an actor in *La città delle donne*, shoots himself in the leg and bleeds to death.

August 10: Gaumont suspends production on *La città delle donne* until a solution can be found for the character that Manni was playing.

September 24: Production on *La città delle donne* resumes.

October 6: Fellini attends the wedding of Renzo Rossellini, producer of *La città delle donne*, to princess Elisabetta Caracciolo di Fiorino in Todi.

October 10: Fellini falls on the set; he breaks his arm and has to wear a cast.

November 29: Production wraps on *La città delle donne*.

1980

March 28: *La città delle donne* is released.

May 19: *La città delle donne* screens out of competition at the 33rd Cannes Film Festival.

June: Fellini publishes his book *Fare un film* (Making a Movie) with Einaudi.

1982

April: Researching *E la nave va* (*And the Ship Sails On*), Fellini visits the out-of-commission superliner *Guglielmo Marconi* at the Ansaldo harbor in Genoa.

May: Reprising the theme of Rex from *Amarcord*, Fellini paints the poster for the 35th Cannes Film Festival.

May 9: Arthur Kopit's interpretation of 8½, the musical *Nine*, opens on Broadway (without Fellini's name attached). Music and lyrics are by Maury Yeston, and the lead actor is Raul Julia (1940–94), with his harem of women.

September: There is a delayed opening of *Amarcord*, with big cuts, in the USSR at Fakel cinema: inspires polemics, and has popular success.

November 15: Production begins on *E la nave va* at Cinecittà.

November: Daniel Keel of Diogenes Verlag organizes the first major exhibition of Fellini's drawings in Paris, "Fellini, ses dessins, ses photographies."

1983

March 17: Production wraps on *E la nave va*.

May 31: Fellini writes to Stanley Kubrick (1928–99) asking advice about the English-language dubbing on *E la nave va*.

July: Fellini convinces Simenon to change his Italian publishers, encouraging him to switch to Adelphi.

September 10: *E la nave va* screens out of competition at the 40th Venice Film Festival.

September 25: During a celebration of Fellini's Day in Rimini, on a live TV broadcast of *Domenica in*, Fellini is given a house by the people of Rimini. The Fellinis will, however, be unable to actually take possession of the property at via Sinistra del Porto 146.

October 7: *E la nave va* is released.

October: Giovanni Grazzini's (1925–2001) book *Intervista sul cinema*—interviews with Fellini—comes out after six long years marked by retractions and conflict between the two men.

December 21: *Il tassinaro* (*The Taxi Driver*) with Alberto Sordi is released. Fellini appears in the movie as himself.

1984

June 13: Fellini is an honorary guard at the funeral of Enrico Berlinguer, secretary of the Communist Party.

June: Fellini makes the ad *Oh, che bel paesaggio* (Oh, What a Lovely Landscape) for Bitter Campari.

September 27: After a long illness, Ida Fellini dies in Rimini; she was eighty-eight years old.

1985

February 12: Production begins on *Ginger e Fred*.

August: Fellini falls ill. The sickness, diagnosed as transitory ischemia, has no lasting negative effects.

September 6: Fellini receives the Golden Lion for lifetime achievement on the closing night of the 42nd Venice Film Festival.

Fellini makes a one-minute ad for Barilla pasta entitled *Alta società—Rigatoni* (High Society—Rigatoni).

October: Fellini makes a journey to Tulum in the Yucatán with the Peruvian anthropologist Carlos Castaneda (1925–98).

December 15: preview screening of *Ginger e Fred* at the Palazzo del Quirinale for president Francesco Cossiga. Giulio Andreotti will review the film on the front page of *Corriere della Sera*.

1986

January 13: *Ginger e Fred* is screened in a gala event at the Palais de Chaillot in Paris.

January 22: *Ginger e Fred* is released in Italy.

February 14: Fellini goes to the 36th Berlin Film Festival, where *Ginger e Fred* opens the festival.

March 12: Sporting a yarmulke, Fellini attends the marriage of Raffaele Nemni, son of Aldo (producer of *E la nave va*), at the Jewish Temple in Milan.

March 28: In New York with Giulietta for the premiere of *Ginger e Fred*, Fellini accepts a medal for lifetime achievement from Elia Kazan.

May 18: The first of the installments of the serial story *Viaggio a Tulun*, written with Pinelli, appears in *Corriere della Sera*.

June: Milan Kundera writes an article entitled "Fellini, the Vision of Kafka" for the first issue of the Parisian magazine *Le Messager européen*.

August: Work begins on *Intervista*.

1987

Mid-January: Work wraps on *Intervista*.

May 1: Editor Raffaele Crovi presents Fellini with the first copy of the biography *Fellini*, by Tullio Kezich at the Bar Canova.

May 19: Although *Intervista* was screened out of competition, the Cannes Film Festival jury, presided over by Yves Montand (1921–91), unanimously decides to present it with the special Fortieth Anniversary Prize.

July: *Intervista* wins the grand prize at the 15th Moscow Film Festival from a unanimous jury presided over by Robert De Niro.

September 27: Fellini visits the Museo del Cinema in Turin.

September 28: *Intervista* is released.

1988

November: Fellini's book *Un regista a Cinecittà* (A Director in Cinecittà) comes out.

1989

February 13: Fellini participates in the demonstration against commercials during the televised broadcast of movies, which is hosted by a collective of left-wing parties at the Teatro Eliseo.

February 22: Production begins on *La voce della luna* (*The Voice of the Moon*) at Empire Studios (formerly Dinocittà).

April 2: Fellini films the scene of the Festa della Gnocca (a dumpling feast).

Mid-June: Filming wraps on *La voce della luna*.

Viaggio a Tulun comes out as a comic book with drawings by Milo Manara.

1990

January 31: Preview screening of *La voce della luna* at the Cinema Etoile in Rome.

March 21: The Senate approves the referendum that limits advertising interruptions during televised broadcasts of films. Fellini fought hard over this issue.

May: Fellini is not at the out-of-competition screening of *La voce della luna* at the 43rd Cannes Film Festival.

June 2: *La voce della luna* wins three David di Donatella Awards for Paolo Villaggio (best actor), Dante Ferretti (production design), and Nino Baragli (editing).

June: Fellini records a polemical treatise on behalf of Italian artists for *Videolettera* against ads during films broadcast on TV.

September 6: At the Venice Film Festival, Fellini presents the Golden Lion for career achievement to Mastroianni.

October: Fellini and Giulietta go to Japan to accept the Praemium Imperiale. The couple is received by the emperor and invited out to dinner by Kurosawa.

1991

March 26: Fellini's brother, Riccardo, dies. He's buried in Sardegna, the home of Lina, his last companion.

October 28: There is a tribute to Giulietta at the Festival di Salsomaggiore.

1992

Fellini and Leo Pescarolo conceive of a television project entitled *Attore* or *Storie di attori*, and Fellini is meanwhile also thinking of other programs he could work on after that: *Napoli*, *L'Inferno*, *L'America*, and *L'opera lirica*.

April: Canadian director Damien Pettigrew films a long interview with Fellini for a documentary that will be called *Fellini: I'm a Big Liar* (2002).

June 8: Fellini starts working on three commercials for Banca di Roma.

July–August: The monthly magazine *Il Grifo* publishes the Milo Manara comic-book collaboration *Il viaggio di G. Mastorna detto Fernet* in installments.

September: Fellini delivers his story for the *Venezia* special.

September 29: Fellini receives the Premio Nuovo Antologia a Campione.

October: Fellini meets Charles Schulz, creator of *Peanuts*, who gives him an autographed drawing of Snoopy.

1993

February 8: Fellini writes to the provost of the University of Bologna, declining the offer of an honorary degree.

March 29: Fellini receives the Lifetime Achievement Award at the Oscar ceremony in the Dorothy Chandler Pavilion in Los Angeles.

June 16: Fellini has heart bypass surgery at the Cantonal Hospital in Zurich.

June 28: After being released from the hospital, he lingers in Zurich.

August 3: He has a stroke while at the Grand Hotel in Rimini and is brought to the Ospedale Infermi. The stroke leaves the left side of his body paralyzed.

August 30: He's transferred to the Ospedale San Giorgio in Ferrara for rehabilitation.

September 18: Worried about Giulietta, who is also in the hospital, Fellini has himself moved to Rome to be near her at least briefly.

October 9: He's transferred to the Policlinico Umberto I in Rome.

October 17: Allowed to leave the hospital for the day, Fellini brunches at the restaurant Il Bersagliere with Giulietta, but upon returning to the clinic he falls into an irreversible coma.

October 26: Martin Scorsese inaugurates the eight-week tribute *Tutto Fellini* at Film Forum in New York.

October 30: It is Federico and Giulietta's fiftieth wedding anniversary.

October 31: Federico Fellini passes away at noon.

November 2: In Studio 5 of Cinecittà there is a memorial service and viewing attended by tens of thousands of Romans.

1994

March 23: Giulietta Masina dies in Rome.

2002

May 21: Maddalena Fabbri, sister of Federico, dies in Rimini after a long illness.

The historical material on the Fellini family is taken in part from various publications about Rimini; among those are *Federico Fellini, mio cugino—Dai ricordi di Fernanda Bellagamba* (Federico Fellini, My Cousin—Memories of Fernanda Bellagamba) by Ezio Lorenzini and *Storia in briciole d'una casalinga straripata* (Crumbs of a Story by an Overwhelmed Housewife) by Maddalena Fellini.

Acknowledgments

This biography is an updated and broad revision of my previous one, *Fellini* (published by Camunia, May 1987, and Rizzoli, September 1988). My reconstruction of the life and work of the director is based in large part on memories from a friendship that endured for more than forty years and was the source of numerous articles and books written by me both before and after the director's death. Among those, I'll note *Su La dolce vita con Federico Fellini* (On *La dolce vita* with Federico Fellini, 1960, expanded edition, 1996); *L'intervista lunga in Giulietta degli spiriti* (The Long Interview in *Giulietta degli spiriti*, 1965); *Giulietta Masina* (1991); *Fellini del giorno dopo* (Fellini, the Day After, 1996), *Primavera a Cinecittà—Il cinema italiano alla svolta della "Dolce vita"* (Springtime in Cinecittà: Italian Cinema in the Wake of *Dolce Vita*, 1990). Contrary to his habits and claims otherwise, Federico closely monitored the manuscript for the first version of the biography, and he confirmed its validity. Though he would purport to be forgetful, he had an extraordinary memory and never relied on documents. In fact, he kept nothing, not letters, contracts, reviews, photographs. He tore everything up, driven by what he called "the murderer's complex."

This book is also based on numerous conversations carried out over more than half a century with an endless array of people with any variety of connections to the director—not infrequently, I had those conversations for the pure pleasure of talking about a friend. It's impossible for me to remember all of the interlocutors with whom I've discussed the events and themes of this biography, but among those who are no longer with us, I'd like to recognize with great affection Giulietta, Liliana Betti, Salvato Cappelli, Alain Cuny, Luigi De Laurentiis, Gianni Di Venanzo, Riccardo Fellini, Clemente Fracassi, Piero Gherardi, Luigi Giacosi, Ruggero Maccari, Otello Martelli, Marcello Mastroianni, Alessandro von Normann,

Anthony Quinn, Pier Paolo Pasolini, François Périer, Enzo Provenzale, Massimo Mida Puccini, Nino Rota, Luigi Rovere, Stefano Vanzina (Steno) . . . And I'll stop there, despite the fact that the list could go on. I should thank many others who are, happily, still alive, as well as the archives, institutes, film libraries, and museums that have allowed me to carry out my research, to watch films, and then to watch them again— but that list would be too long and I'm sure I'd leave someone out.

I think I've read, reread, annotated, and occasionally contested almost everything that's ever been printed (article, essay, or book) about the director, which is why I've avoided bibliographical citations that are already readily available and published elsewhere. Two ample resources, both compiled in 1978, are Barbara Anne Price and Theodore Price, *Federico Fellini: An Annotated International Bibliography* (Metuchen, N.J. and London: Scarecrow), and John C. Stubbs, *Federico Fellini: A Guide to References and Resources* (London/Boston: G. K. Hall & Co.). Marco Bertozzi's painstakingly accurate three-volume *BiblioFellini* is in the process of being completed (with the assistance of Giuseppe Ricci and Simone Casevecchia). The first volume came out in 2002, and was published by the Scuola Nazionale di Cinema and the Fondazione Federico Fellini. Peter Bondanella's *Federico Fellini's Cinema* is rigorous, very well footnoted, and makes good use of the important manuscripts and documents acquired by the Lilly Library of Rare Books at Indiana University. If you are looking for more reading material, do note that certain books that I've referenced in the pages of this biography should be approached with extreme caution—especially those authored by women with whom Fellini was romantically involved.

I can't sign off on this new—and as far as I'm concerned, definitive— biography without thanking those closest to me: Gianfranco Angelucci, Alessandra Levantesi, and Vincenzo Mollica, who pored exhaustively over the manuscript and offered often helpful suggestions. I should also send a very special thanks to my incomparable friend, the late Leopoldo Trieste, who more than half a century ago eased my entry into the Fellini circle.

On the editorial side, I must again express my appreciation to Farrar, Straus and Giroux for their staunch professionalism, and to the careful editing of Denise Oswald.

—Tullio Kezich

Index